Communications
in Computer and Information Science **1916**

Rationale

The CCIS series is devoted to the publication of proceedings of computer science conferences. Its aim is to efficiently disseminate original research results in informatics in printed and electronic form. While the focus is on publication of peer-reviewed full papers presenting mature work, inclusion of reviewed short papers reporting on work in progress is welcome, too. Besides globally relevant meetings with internationally representative program committees guaranteeing a strict peer-reviewing and paper selection process, conferences run by societies or of high regional or national relevance are also considered for publication.

Topics

The topical scope of CCIS spans the entire spectrum of informatics ranging from foundational topics in the theory of computing to information and communications science and technology and a broad variety of interdisciplinary application fields.

Information for Volume Editors and Authors

Publication in CCIS is free of charge. No royalties are paid, however, we offer registered conference participants temporary free access to the online version of the conference proceedings on SpringerLink (http://link.springer.com) by means of an http referrer from the conference website and/or a number of complimentary printed copies, as specified in the official acceptance email of the event.

CCIS proceedings can be published in time for distribution at conferences or as post-proceedings, and delivered in the form of printed books and/or electronically as USBs and/or e-content licenses for accessing proceedings at SpringerLink. Furthermore, CCIS proceedings are included in the CCIS electronic book series hosted in the SpringerLink digital library at http://link.springer.com/bookseries/7899. Conferences publishing in CCIS are allowed to use Online Conference Service (OCS) for managing the whole proceedings lifecycle (from submission and reviewing to preparing for publication) free of charge.

Publication process

The language of publication is exclusively English. Authors publishing in CCIS have to sign the Springer CCIS copyright transfer form, however, they are free to use their material published in CCIS for substantially changed, more elaborate subsequent publications elsewhere. For the preparation of the camera-ready papers/files, authors have to strictly adhere to the Springer CCIS Authors' Instructions and are strongly encouraged to use the CCIS LaTeX style files or templates.

Abstracting/Indexing

CCIS is abstracted/indexed in DBLP, Google Scholar, EI-Compendex, Mathematical Reviews, SCImago, Scopus. CCIS volumes are also submitted for the inclusion in ISI Proceedings.

How to start

To start the evaluation of your proposal for inclusion in the CCIS series, please send an e-mail to ccis@springer.com.

Łukasz Tomczyk

Editor

New Media Pedagogy: Research Trends, Methodological Challenges and Successful Implementations

First International Conference, NMP 2022
Kraków, Poland, October 10–12, 2022
Revised Selected Papers

 Springer

Editor
Łukasz Tomczyk 🔟
Jagiellonian University
Kraków, Poland

ISSN 1865-0929 ISSN 1865-0937 (electronic)
Communications in Computer and Information Science
ISBN 978-3-031-44580-4 ISBN 978-3-031-44581-1 (eBook)
https://doi.org/10.1007/978-3-031-44581-1

This Springer imprint is published by the registered company Springer Nature Switzerland AG
The registered company address is: Gewerbestrasse 11, 6330 Cham, Switzerland

Paper in this product is recyclable.

Preface

Introduction to New Media Pedagogy - Research Trends, Methodological Challenges and Successful Implementations

This publication results from the international conference New Media Pedagogy - research trends, methodological challenges and successful implementations (NMP 2022). The event was organised on 10–12 October 2022 by the Institute of Pedagogy at the Jagiellonian University and the Department of Education, Cultural Heritage and Tourism at the University of Macerata (Italy). The conference received the scientific patronage of the Polish Academy of Sciences - Rome Division and was implemented with the support of the National Agency for Academic Exchange NAWA under the M. Bekker project (PPN/BEK/2020/1/00176).

The aim of the conference was to contribute to the global discussion on the development directions of media pedagogy. This goal stems from the intense transformation associated with the implementation of ICT in education, which necessitates attempts to seek answers related to current research directions in the use of new media in schooling. The conference therefore aimed to provide researchers from all over the world with an insight into the ways in which new media can be used effectively by stakeholders focused on K12 education and university education (with a particular focus on the training of future pedagogical staff).

The NMP 2022 conference prepared the following panels - thematic areas: 1. Teacher education in the information society: a) teacher education curricula in the era of widespread digitalisation; b) digital competences of future and current teachers; c) the role of universities in educating staff for the digital school. 2. Digitally-enhanced didactics: a) pedagogical innovations using ICT; b) e-learning, blended learning, crisis e-learning; c) digital didactic means, methods and forms. 3. Digital inclusion and exclusion: a) minimising the digital divide; b) enhancing digital competence across age and social groups; c) sustainability of the information society. 4. Identity of media pedagogy: a) theoretical foundations of media pedagogy; b) research methodology on the use of ICT in education; c) research programmes focused on the digitalisation of education.

Substantive support in the organisation of the conference was offered by 41 experts - recognised and respected scholars dealing with the processes of digitalisation of education. Among those invited were: Isabella Crespi - University of Macerata, Italy; Linda Daniela - University of Latvia, Latvia; Laura Fedeli - University of Macerata, Italy; Francisco David Guillen-Gamez - University of Cordoba, Spain; Ludvik Eger - University of West Bohemia, Czech Republic; Viktorija Florjančič - University of Primorska - Slovenia; Paul Flynn - University of Galway, Ireland; Raffaele Di Fuccio - University of Foggia, Italy; Anna Gaweł - Jagiellonian University, Poland; Akhmad Habibi - University of Jambi, Indonesia; Leen d'Haenens - KU Leuven, Belgium; Therese Keane - Swinburne University, Australia; Janina Kostkiewicz - Jagiellonian University, Poland; Pierpaolo Limone - University of Foggia, Italy; Ana Loureiro -

Politécnico de Santarém/Escola Superior de Educação, Portugal; Maria Lidia Mascia - University of Cagliari, Italy; Ford Lumban Gaol - BINUS University, Indonesia; Anders D. Olofsson - Umeå University, Sweden; Julio Ruiz Palmer - University of Malaga, Spain; Valentina Pennazio - University of Genoa, Italy; Maria Pietronilla Penna - University of Cagliari, Italy; Piotr Plichta - University of Wrocław, Poland; Katarzyna Potyrała - Pedagogical University, Poland; Jacek Pyżalski - Adam Mickiewicz University, Poland; Roberta Renati - University of Cagliari, Italy; Bethany Rice - Towson University, USA; Natale Salvatore Bonfiglio - University of Cagliari, Italy; Fazilat Siddiq - University of South-Eastern Norway, Norway; Francisco Simões - Centro de Investigação e de Intervenção Social, Portugal; Harco Leslie Hendric Spits Warnars - BINUS University, Indonesia; Solomon Sunday Oyelere - Luleå University of Technology, Sweden; Agnieszka Stefaniak-Hrycko - Scientific Station of the Polish Academy of Sciences (PAN) in Rome, Italy; Lazar Stošić - University MB, Serbia; Zofia Szarota - WSB University, Poland; Michał Szyszka - WSB University, Poland; Arthur Tatnall - Victoria University, Australia; Łukasz Tomczyk - Jagiellonian University, Poland; Giusi Toto - University of Foggia, Italy; Hüseyin Uzunboylu - Near East University, North Cyprus; Natalia Walter - Adam Mickiewicz University, Poland; Ewa Ziemba - University of Economics in Katowice, Poland.

This book arising from the NMP 2022 conference stems from a natural need to share research findings among the global community of media educators. Finally, after a review process, 55 papers, prepared by 100 media educators, were selected for presentation at the event. The conference attracted researchers from: North America, South America, Africa, Asia, Oceania and Europe. Speakers attending the NMP conference came from 26 countries: Albania, Canada, China, Croatia, Czech Republic, Dominican Republic, Ecuador, Greece, India, Italy, Lithuania, Macedonia, Malaysia, Morocco, Norway, Poland, Portugal, Romania, Serbia, Slovenia, Spain, Sweden, Turkey, Uganda, the UK and the USA. Finally, after the review process, 20 articles were selected for publication, so the success rate was 36.36%.

At this point, sincere thanks must be given to the reviewers who contributed significantly to the quality of the papers submitted to NMP22. A special word of appreciation therefore goes to the fewer than sixty reviewers, representing scholars from dozens of countries: Abdelmajid el Hajaji, Akhmad Habibi, Alessia Scarinci, Amra Kozo, Aneta Kochanowicz, Arberore Bicaj, Armand Faganel, Boris Kožuh, Celestino Rodríguez, Christine Liao, Christine Silva, Claudia Blanca, Gonzales, Emmanouil Fokides, Dominika Jagielska, Filipe Moreira, Francesco Sulla, Francisco Alcantud Marin, Francisco David Guillen Gamez, Hana Zelená, Hasan Saliu, Hubert Przybycień, Issam Elfilali, Jan Beseda, Katarzyna Smoter, Lazar Stosic, Ljiljan Veselinović, Lucie Rohlíková, Ludvik Eger, Maria José Loureiro, Maria Mpakatsaki, Mario Grande de Prado, Mary Elizabeth Meier, Mauricio González Arias, Michaela Šmídová, Michał Klichowski, Michał Szyszka, Mohammad Nor Afandi Ibrahim, Natalia Walter, Nektarios Moumoutzis, Paul Flyyn, Polixeni Arapi, Rachid Boudri, Raffaele Di Fuccio, Robert Sweeny, Roberta Renati, Rofiza Bt. Aboo Bakar, Salvatore Iuso, Salvo Bonfiglio, Selma Smajlovic, Siri Sollied Madsen, Sławomir Trusz, Solomon Sunday, Sylwia Opozda Suder, Urszula Szuścik, Vasil Zagorov, Verónica Martínez, Veselin Chantov, Zuzanna Sury.

The articles selected for publication address the range of challenges posed by the widespread and irreversible digitalisation of the space of everyday life. The papers included in this publication are the result of a cumulative research effort that demonstrates what a dynamic and multifaceted discipline media pedagogy is becoming. The NMP volume can be divided into several areas. The first series of papers is related to digital competence. This section opens with a study by researchers from Bosnia and Herzegovina, Amina Ðipa and Lejla Turulja, who draw attention to issues of digital competence and higher education. The second in this group of papers, written by Sheila García-Martín and Judit García-Martín, attempts to highlight digital competences in teacher education in the post-COVID era using the Spanish experience as an example. The third paper, authored by young Italian researchers from the University of Fogia, namely Piergiorgio Guarini, Marco di Furia and Benedetta Ragni, is an attempt to structure the theoretical framework related to the formation of teacher digital competence. The fourth article in this section, produced by Slovenian researchers Aleksander Janeš and Andreja Klančar, is a research communication highlighting the importance of attitudes towards new technologies among teachers representing the first educational threshold. The series of papers of relevance to contemporary media pedagogy, which relate directly to the functioning of modern teachers in the information society, closes with a paper by Serbian researchers Nedeljko M. Milanović, Jelena Maksimović and Jelena Osmanović Zajić. The section devoted to digital competence of contemporary teachers is currently one of the most dynamically developing research areas in media pedagogy [1]. Such a state of affairs is probably due to the experiences accumulated during the COVID-19 pandemic, which had a significant impact on the style of new media use in the school environment and, at the same time, gave impetus to research on the level of digitalisation of contemporary education [2].

Another section that can be distinguished from the submitted papers dealt with issues on the intersection of media pedagogy and special pedagogy. The papers in this division show explicitly that new media are as effective a means of bridging developmental deficits as traditional analogue solutions [3]. The assumption of increasing the effectiveness of activities assigned to special pedagogy through the use of ICT was presented in the context of correcting pronunciation defects by Polish authors Anna Michniuk and Maria Faściszewska. They show in their paper an original solution that can be used in speech therapy activities. The second study in this section presents the experience of Spanish researchers Aitor Larraceleta, Luis Castejón and José Carlos Núñez, who characterise the training of pedagogical staff focused on working with autistic children.

The third block of articles deals with the possibilities of implementing ICT in specific didactics. This section presents new and innovative solutions that support the teaching and learning process. The third section is also an example of activities that represent the opportunities paradigm of media pedagogy within NMP22 [4]. This group of studies opens with an article by Polish researcher Monika Frania, who describes the possibility of transforming solutions known and popular in the offline sphere into cyberspace. In her article, Frania focuses on the digital escape room. Another article, by Portuguese researchers Sara Martins and Carlos Santos, deals with the identification of plants using educational software. An interesting perspective on the use of new media in history education can be found in a paper by Croatian PhD student Miljenko Hajdarovic. In the following text, by Malaysian researcher Saima Khan, a data set on the use of digital storytelling in the teaching and learning of English can be found. In turn, a research report by Emmanouela V. Seiradakis of the Technical University of Crete shows the possibilities of using tablets in pre-school education. The next article, written by Greek researchers Sofia-Maria Poulimenou, Polyxeni Kaimara and Ioannis Deliyannis, characterises the possibilities of discovering the history of the city through the ludic use of edtech. In a similar trend to the previous ones, there is also an article prepared by Joanna Sikorska which shows the possibility of using ICT in museum education. The last paper in this group, authored by Richard Kabiito and Karen Keifer-Boyd, an international team from Uganda and the United States, provides an opportunity to understand what bioethics is and how it can be exhibited through ICT. The collection of articles presented in this section is the largest group of papers within NMP 2022 and exposes the importance and multifaceted possibilities of contemporary edtech. The articles presented also emphasise the role of pedagogical and andragogical innovations using the multimediality, speed and multifaceted application of ICT.

The fourth group of articles presented under NMP 2022 is related to e-learning. In the era of the COVID and now post-COVID epidemic, teaching and learning at a distance using ICT has undergone a dynamic change due to technical reasons, the number of solutions supporting the process, as well as improvements in the methodology of this form of education [5]. In this group of studies, several important research results for media pedagogy can be highlighted. One of them is an article by Czech researcher Michal Cerny, who draws attention to the possibilities of analysing behaviour on university e-learning platforms. In turn, a team of Malaysian researchers, Sedigheh Moghavvemi, Phoong Seuk Wai and Phoong Seuk Yen, highlight the importance of solutions based on the increasingly popular blended learning methodology to support student development. On the other hand, a Moroccan team comprising Abdelmounim Bouziane, Wadi Tahri and Karima Bouziane presents in their chapter the results of a study on satisfaction with remote education during a pandemic. All of the articles related to e-learning follow the research work of recent months, which has emerged from the transposition of learning from the traditional analogue space to virtual environments.

The NMP 2022 conference volume closes with two papers on the digital divide. The first one, prepared by Plamena Zlatkova and Marchela Borisova, presents the issues of digital competence and the digital divide through the prism of Bulgarian experts specialising in the development of the information society. The last study, prepared by a team of Polish researchers Łukasz Tomczyk, Joanna Wnęk-Gozdek and Katarzyna Potyrała, draws attention to the issues of digital exclusion of seniors and the development of geragogy.

The NMP 2022 conference undoubtedly proved to be a platform for the exchange of research experiences, a place to discuss methodological aspects of research related to media pedagogy, and also provided an opportunity to internationalise researchers from dozens of countries. This conference publication is the first in a series of conferences in this area. At the same time, in giving the study to the readers, I cordially invite them to participate in the next editions of NMP (more information on the conference website: http://www.ict-education.pl/).

Łukasz Tomczyk

References

1. Tomczyk, Ł., & Fedeli, L. (Eds.): Digital Literacy for Teachers. Lecture Notes in Educational Technology. Singapore: Springer (2022). https://doi.org/10.1007/978-981-19-1738-7
2. Svihus, C. L.: Online teaching in higher education during the COVID-19 pandemic. Education and Information Technologies (2023). https://doi.org/10.1007/s10639-023-11971-7
3. Plichta, P.: The use of information and communication technologies by young people with intellectual disabilities in the context of digital inequalities and digital exclusion. E-methodology, 5(5), 10–23 (2018)
4. Pyżalski, J.: Jasna strona-partycypacja i zaangażowanie dzieci i młodzieży w korzystne rozwojowo i prospołeczne działania. Dziecko krzywdzone. Teoria, badania, praktyka, 16(1), 288–303 (2017).
5. Siddiq, F., Olofsson, A. D., Lindberg, J. O., & Tomczyk, L.: Special issue: What will be the new normal? Digital competence and 21st-century skills: critical and emergent issues in education. Education and Information Technologies (2023). https://doi.org/10.1007/s10639-023-12067-y

Organization

Chair of the Conference Board

Łukasz Tomczyk   Jagiellonian University, Poland

Scientific Conference Board

Ernesto Colomo Magana   University of Malaga, Spain
Isabella Crespi   University of Macerata, Italy
Linda Daniela   University of Latvia, Latvia
Laura Fedeli   University of Macerata, Italy
Francisco David Guillen-Gamez   University of Cordoba, Spain
Ludvik Eger   University of West Bohemia, Czech Republic
Maria Amelia Eliseo   Universidade Presbiteriana Mackenzie, Brazil
Viktorija Florjančič   University of Primorska, Slovenia
Paul Flynn   University of Galway, Ireland
Raffaele Di Fuccio   University of Foggia, Italy
Anna Gaweł   Jagiellonian University, Poland
Akhmad Habibi   University of Jambi, Indonesia
Leen d'Haenens   KU Leuven, Belgium
Therese Keane   Swinburne University, Australia
Janina Kostkiewicz   Jagiellonian University, Poland
Pierpaolo Limone   University of Foggia, Italy
Ana Loureiro   Politécnico de Santarém/Escola Superior de
                                  Educação, Portugal
Maria Lidia Mascia   University of Cagliari, Italy
Ford Lumban Gaol   BINUS University, Indonesia
Anders D. Olofsson   Umeå University, Sweden
Julio Ruiz Palmer   University of Malaga, Spain
Valentina Pennazio   University of Genoa, Italy
Maria Pietronilla Penna   University of Cagliari, Italy
Piotr Plichta   University of Wrocław, Poland
Katarzyna Potyrała   Pedagogical University, Poland
Jacek Pyżalski   Adam Mickiewicz University, Poland
Roberta Renati   University of Cagliari, Italy
Bethany Rice   Towson University, USA
Natale Salvatore Bonfiglio   University of Cagliari, Italy

Fazilat Siddiq	University of South-Eastern Norway, Norway
Francisco Simões	Centro de Investigação e de Intervenção Social, Portugal
Harco Leslie Hendric Spits Warnars	BINUS University, Indonesia
Solomon Sunday Oyelere	Luleå University of Technology, Sweden
Agnieszka Stefaniak-Hrycko	Scientific Station of the Polish Academy of Sciences (PAN) in Rome, Italy
Lazar Stošić	University MB, Serbia
Zofia Szarota	WSB University, Poland
Michał Szyszka	WSB University, Poland
Arthur Tatnall	Victoria University, Australia
Giusi Toto	University of Foggia, Italy
Hüseyin Uzunboylu	Near East University, North Cyprus
Natalia Walter	Adam Mickiewicz University, Poland
Ewa Ziemba	University of Economics in Katowice, Poland

The Technical Program Committee

| Łukasz Tomczyk (TPC Chair) | Jagiellonian University, Poland |

TPC Members

Laura Fedeli	University of Macerata, Italy
Piergiorgio Guarini	Foggia University, Italy
Maria Lidia Mascia	University of Cagliari, Italy
Natalia Demeshkant	Pedagogical University, Poland
Katarzyna Potyrała	Cracow University of Technology, Poland

Contents

The Role of Higher Education Curriculum Quality in Fostering Digital Skills of University Students

Amina Đipa[1]([✉]) [ID] and Lejla Turulja[2] [ID]

[1] Faculty of Educational Sciences, University of Sarajevo, Skenderija 72, 7100 Sarajevo, Bosnia and Herzegovina
aminadz@pf.unsa.ba
[2] School of Economics and Business, University of Sarajevo, Trg oslobođenja 1, 7100 Sarajevo, Bosnia and Herzegovina
lejla.turulja@efsa.unsa.ba

Abstract. This study aims to investigate the relationship between program curriculum quality and students' digital skills, as well as the impact of six dimensions of digital skills on social studies students individually. A total of 148 students comprised the research sample. Technological or instrumental skills, communication skills, information skills, critical skills, personal safety skills, and device safety skills were the six dimensions of digital skills evaluated in the study. SmartPLS 4 was used to analyze data using partial least squares structural equation modeling (PLS-SEM). The results demonstrated that the quality of the curriculum had a significant impact on the technological or instrumental skills, communication skills, information skills, and critical skills of the students. It was determined, however, that the quality of the curriculum has no significant effect on students' personal safety skills. In addition, our findings demonstrated that the curriculum's quality had a positive impact on device security skills. The results suggest that the quality of the curriculum plays an important role in shaping students' digital competences, and that educational programs aimed at enhancing the development of digital skills should consider the multidimensional nature of digital skills and the role of the curriculum in promoting digital competences.

Keywords: curriculum quality · digital skills · technological skills · communication skills · information skills · critical skills · personal safety skills · digital devices skills

1 Introduction

It is well known fact that digital technologies are integral part of everyday professional and personal lives [1]. Given that developed digital literacy skills enables students to take advantage of digital technologies [2], it is becoming increasingly important to act in order to ensure the development of various aspects of students' digital literacy skills during the study process. Intensive technological growth significantly affects all aspect of society,

Ł. Tomczyk (Ed.): NMP 2022, CCIS 1916, pp. 1–21, 2023.
https://doi.org/10.1007/978-3-031-44581-1_1

including educational systems at all levels [3]. Higher education is not an exception, therefore, universities have a responsibility to ensure that graduates have the skills to make use of new technologies [4]. Digital skills are becoming increasingly important for students to succeed academically and professionally in today's digital age [5]. Students must develop various competencies such as technological, communicational, critical, and security skills in order to thrive in this digital era [6]. These competencies can be obtained through the curricula of their educational institutions. However, the quality of the curriculum is critical in determining the level of digital skill development of students.

The literature on the relationship between curriculum quality and digital skills of students remains scant. Previous research has focused on analyzing the impact of individual curriculum components on students' digital competencies. For instance, [7], investigated how different pedagogical aspects can support the development of students' digital competence in school, whereas [8], examined the design approach to developing digital competence by integrating knowledge, skills, and attitudes across disciplines. The authors [9], conducted a study that evaluated the basic ICT competencies of new business school students in order to identify pedagogical aspects that could be enhanced to improve students' digital skills. While these studies provide valuable insights into the development of digital skills in educational settings, a deeper comprehension of the factors that contribute to the development of digital skills among students is required. Although some studies have been conducted to investigate the relationship between curriculum quality and students' overall academic performance. However, few studies have specifically examined the impact of program curriculum quality on individual dimensions of students' digital skills. Digital skills are multidimensional constructs that include technological or instrumental skills, communication skills, information skills, critical skills, personal security skills, and device security skills. Hence, this study aims to fill a gap in the literature by investigating the impact of curriculum quality on the development of each of these six dimensions of students' digital skills.

To achieve this goal, data were collected from 148 students enrolled in social studies programs at a School Economics and Business and a Faculty of Pedagogy of University of Sarajevo. The data was analyzed using the Partial Least Squares Structural Equation Modeling (PLS-SEM) technique in SmartPLS 4. The PLS-SEM technique is a powerful tool for testing multiple hypotheses at the same time and investigating both direct and indirect effects of the independent variable on the dependent variable.

This study proposes two conceptual models, baseline and extended model. The baseline model focuses on the overall relationship between the program's curriculum quality and students' digital skills. The baseline model assumes that the quality of the program's curriculum has an overall impact on students' digital skills, without distinguishing the impact on each specific dimension of digital skills. The extended model investigates the relationship between the program's curriculum quality and each of the six dimensions of students' digital skills. The extended model adds six separate latent variables to the baseline model: technological or instrumental skills, communication skills, information skills, critical skills, personal security skills, and device security skills. The model assumes that the curriculum quality of the program has a direct impact on each of these six dimensions of digital skills.

The study's findings can provide valuable insights into how higher education institutions can improve the quality of their curricula and help students develop digital skills. Educational institutions can create more effective programs that prepare students for success in the digital age by better understanding the relationship between curriculum quality and the various dimensions of digital skills.

2 Literature Review

Increasing technological progress forces dramatic reassessment and conversation about the necessary skills that will, above all, enable individuals to compete on the labor market [10]. Recent reports [11–13] indicate on digital skills as those that contribute to better employability. Despite the emphasis on the importance of digital skills, until now, no consensus has been reached on the definition of digital skills. Part of the reason for this is that even the term itself varies in different contexts, from "digital skills" to "digital literacy", "competence", ability, knowledge, "understanding". The variety of terms reflects the fact that digital skills can refer not only to specific knowledge, but also to a combination or different behaviours, habits, aptitudes and critical understanding [14] For the purposes of this study, we single out the following definition, which we consider suitable for the context of this work. According to [6] digital skills are multidimensional construct consisting of 6 dimensions:

– Technological or instrumental skills refer to the ability to use digital technologies such as computers, smartphones, and other electronic devices, as well as the various software applications and tools that are available.
– Communications skills include the capacity to communicate effectively using digital technologies, such as social media platforms, email, and instant messaging.
– Information skills include the capacity to locate, evaluate, and utilize online information.
– Critical skills include the ability to analyze and evaluate information presented online, including the ability to recognize bias and when information is incomplete or deceptive.
– Personal safety skills pertain to the capacity to manage privacy and ensure personal safety when utilizing digital technologies.
– Device security skills include the ability to protect digital devices from potential threats like viruses and malware.

The fourth industrial revolution has a dramatic impact on labor market. Although a significant reversal is already evident, it is expected that the changes in labor market demands will continue or even develop rapidly in the next few decades [15]. In that respect, the labor market today demands „transversal or „resilience skills", namely those skills that are resilient and applicable in various work contexts. In light of this, nowadays employers want their workforce to be ready to work with latest and newest technologies [16]. Higher education institutions must be aware of the above-mentioned requirements regarding the required skills in the labor market, as well as the needs of employers, however, there are often statements that the initial education of students (future experts in a certain field) does not correspond to the development of skills required on the labor market, and the question of reconceptualizing the university curriculum is often raised [17]. Because of that, it is important, through educational process, to act on the development of skills that are current actual on the labor market, among others, and on digital skills that are considered crucial for university students [18].

The constant expansion of digital technologies causes changes in the labor market, which are reflected in the increased demand for workers with digital skills. This is supported by the data presented in Table 1, which indicate that workers with advanced digital skills are in high demand in today's labor market [13].

Table 1. Job roles in increasing and decreasing demand across industries.

Increasing demand		Decreasing demand	
1	Data Analysts and Scientists	1	Data Entry Clerks
2	AI and Machine Learning	2	Administrative and Executive Secretaries
3	Big Data Specialists	3	Accounting, Bookkeeping and Payroll Clerks
4	Process Automation Specialists	4	Accountants and Auditors
5	Business Development Professionals	5	Assembly and Factory Workers
6	Digital Transformation Specialists	6	Business Services and Administration Managers
7	Information Security Analysts	7	Client Information and Customer Service Workers
8	Software and Application Developers	8	General and Operations Managers

Note: Adopted from World Economic forum (2020)

It is apparent from the Table 1 that digital skills are vital for the future of employment [19]. The increasing demand for digital skills in the labor market intensifies the importance of developing students' digital skills during university education. Identifying digital skills as those that contribute to better employability of students [20], obliges higher education systems to act adequately in the area of developing students' digital skills, otherwise, he becomes a waste if produces unemployable graduates [21].

In every area, including the education, to make certain progress, it is necessary to constantly take care and invest efforts in order to ensure the quality of education. That becomes even more important, if we take into account the fact that the quality of education contributes to and affects labor productivity and the overall economic growth of country [22]. Besides that, the importance of quality education is emphasized in Agenda 2030 for Sustainable Development, where one of the goals of sustainable development (precisely SDG 4) refers to quality of education. This underlines the importance of improving the quality of education in order to achieve the goals of sustainable development.

Reflections on education quality issues are always necessary for all levels of education, including higher education. Because of the importance of these issues, various directions for the improvement of quality education can be found in the literature. An example of such a document is Standards and Guidlines for Quality Assurance in the European Higher Education Area.

In context of higher education, quality can refers to diverse functions of the university [23]. In the framework of this paper, the focus is on considering the aspect of quality which is related to the aspects of the teaching process. In this regard, there are many factors that determine and depend on the quality of education. The two most frequently emphasized factors refer to the quality of the teaching staff and the quality of the curriculum. The curriculum is precisely one of the key factors with the greatest effect on the quality of education [24]. What is important to emphasize is that quality education comprises effective and purposeful educational curriculum [25].

The increasing demands for digital skills in the labor market represent challenges for the field of higher education, which are impossible to overcome without a quality curriculum for the technological era. According to [26], the starting point when considering a 'quality curriculum' cannot begin without understanding the term curriculum. Due to its complexity, there is no unequivocal and generally accepted definition of the term curriculum [27], Although, literature contains many definition about curriculum of various authors. One author defined curriculum in terms of catalog of elaborated contents, which are transferred to teaching through the processes of programming and planning as an organized and active acquisition of knowledge, abilities and skills [28]. Others authors viewed it as a phenomenon which includes many dimensions of learning, including rationale, aims, content, methods, resources, time, assessment, etc.; which refers to various levels of planning and decision-making on learning (for example, at the supra-, macro-, meso-, micro- and nano-levels); or, international, national, local, classroom and individual levels; and which relates to multiple representations of learning [29]. The above mentioned definitions indicate that curriculum is a complex, multidimensional and contextual term that can be viewed in terms of body of contents or a learing process. What is missing from the aforementioned definitions is the consideration of the curriculum in the context of contemporary conditions, which implies the inclusion of digital technology as a potential resource for enriching the curriculum. So, for the purposes of this study, we single out the following definition, which we consider suitable for the context of this work. According to [30], curriculum is a form of organising learning by focusing on present-day contexts, which can be enriched by the use of information and communication digital technology. This definition, unlike the others, emphasizes that regardless of whether curriculum is viewed as a body of contents or a learning process, it may be supported by technologies [30], That type of curriculum envisages tasks such as digital storytelling or electronic portfolio within which students can develop and strengthen digital skills. Such curriucum has power to foster digital skills of students, only if it is created and contains quality in itself. Quality curriculum must contain in itself planning and forecasting ways to encourage digital skills, considering their importance in today's labor market. More precisely, it is important that the constituent elements of the curriculum (teaching methods, ways of evaluating and monitoring student achievements, learning outcomes) reflect the inclusion of fostering digital skills through curriculum. Unafortunately, according to [31], digital skills have little integration in the university curricula, despite the emphasized importance of these skills as those that contribute to better employability. The previous theoretical analysis shows the establishment of the curriculum as one of the factors on which the quality of education depends, as well as the increasing emphasis on digital skills in today's labor market. Starting from the fact that students are the future workforce who are expected to demonstrate digital skills in the workplace, this research aims to reveal and illuminate the role of the higher education curriculum in fostering the development of students' digital skills.

3 Hypotheses Development

This research proposed the baseline and the extended model. The explanations of both models and their constituent hypotheses are provided below.

3.1 Baseline Model

The baseline model suggests that the quality of a program's curriculum has an effect on its students' digital skills. In practice, this means that students are more likely to develop strong digital skills in programs with high-quality curricula than in programs with lower-quality curricula. This model intends to contribute to theory and practice by emphasizing the significance of the overall curriculum's quality in shaping students' digital skills. Fostering digital skills of students depends of quality of curriculum. Quality curriculum is one that, among other things, ensures and supports the acquisition of digital skills necessary for success in the digital era. The goal of this study was to examine student perceptions about the role of curriculum in fostering their digital skills from their experiences. Hence, based on the discussion, the following hypothesis is proposed:

H. The quality of the program's curriculum influences the digital skills of the students.

3.2 Extended Model

The extended model expands the original hypothesis by examining the relationship between curriculum quality and multiple dimensions of digital skills, in a way that deconstructs the hypothesis so that, rather than observing curriculum quality as a multi-dimensional construct, it observes the impact of its individual dimensions on students' digital skills. By incorporating new hypotheses focusing on technology skills, communication skills, information skills, critical thinking skills, personal safety skills, and device safety skills, the proposed model provides a more complete understanding of how curriculum quality can influence student outcomes in a digital environment.

In the time of COVID-19 we have witnessed the importance of developing all dimensions of digital skills, including, technological skills. These are the skills that students need to use software or operate a digital device [32]. Various authors conducted research about technological skills of students. For example, one study was conducted to explore technological skills from various aspects, including question about what technological skills students develop throughout their academic career. According to [33], students believed that some areas of technological skills developed more during higher education, some less. As an example of those who developed more, they stated the use and selection of appropriate digital technologies for interaction, while on the other hand, as examples of those who developed less, they stated solving problem situations in the digital environment. The lack of technological skills can have a profound effect on people's overall life opportunities and employability [33], so it is crucial that higher education curriculum ensure adequate support in fostering this dimension of digital skills. Communication is a multifaceted phenomenon. Communication digital skills involve expressiveness, which refers to ability to express feelings and reactions clearly and openly in a digital environment. Besides that, these skills involve building and maintaining contacts, which are preconditions for using network contacts who possess the resources necessary to facilitate resource mobilization. And one more important component of these skills, include networking which refers to individuals' ability to make online connections and contacts for instrumental or expressive returns.

According to [34], information skills present set of abilities that enable university students to recognize specific information need or goals; to search, evaluate, read, analyze, synthesize, and use the gathered information to accomplish the goals; as well as to communicate the information processes and goals. Nowadays students have the possibility to access numerous sources on any subject. However, it depends on the level of information digital skills whether the student will be able to assess the reliability of information, as well as its value of use. That is why it is important that informational digital skills take their position within the curriculum. In the digital age critical digital thinking skills seem to be very important, because of the fact that people in an online environment have possibilities to participate and create resources with various intentions and competencies [32], Precisely because of this, it is important to teach students to critically judge the content. There is data indicating that these skills contribute to better academic achievement, improved employability, higher financial status and better decision-making [35]. Considering the above, it is important that higher education curricula foresee ways of building students' critical digital skills. Following the logic and rationale of the basic hypothesis of the base model and considering the discussion, the following hypotheses were proposed:

H1. The quality of the program's curriculum influences the technological skills of the students.
H2. The quality of the program's curriculum influences the communication skills of the students.
H3. The quality of the program's curriculum influences the information skills of the students.
H4. The quality of the program's curriculum influences the critical thinking skills of the students.
H5. The quality of the program's curriculum influences the students' personal security skills.
H6. Students' device security skills are influenced by the quality of the program's curriculum.

4   Methodology

This study used a quantitative research approach and a cross-sectional design, which means that data was collected from a single point in time. A survey was used to collect data from students enrolled at a School Economics and Business and a Faculty of

Pedagogy of University of Sarajevo. The data were collected through an online survey administered with LimeSurvey, a web-based survey application. An email containing a formal invitation to participate in the study and a link to the survey was sent to participants in order to solicit their participation in the study. Participants were assured of confidentiality and made aware that participation is voluntary. The survey was conducted anonymously, and no identifying information was collected. The online survey was available for four weeks, allowing respondents to complete it at their convenience.

The questionnaire was divided into two sections. The first section collected demographic data such as gender, age, and studying program. The second section included questions about students' digital skills and the program's curriculum quality. The questions were adapted from previous validated empirical research studies on digital skills and curriculum quality. The measures used in this study were adopted from prior empirical research studies that had been validated. A multidimensional scale adapted from [36], was utilized to assess the quality of the program's curriculum. The scale measured students' perceptions of the curriculum's quality with regard to its provision, content, instructional methods, and evaluation. A multidimensional scale adapted from [6], was utilized to evaluate the digital skills of students. The scale measured six facets of digital competence: technological or instrumental skills, communication skills, information skills, critical skills, personal security skills, and device security skills. For both constructs, a 5-point Likert scale ranging from 1 (strongly disagree) to 5 (strongly agree) was adopted.

The survey data were analyzed using Partial Least Squares Structural Equation Modeling (PLS-SEM) using SmartPLS 4. PLS-SEM is an effective statistical method for analyzing complex data sets and evaluating complex models. PLS-SEM is especially useful for small sample sizes because it permits estimation of latent variables even when the sample size is small. This study made use of PLS-SEM to examine direct effects of the independent variable (quality of the program's curriculum) on the dependent variable (dimensions of digital skills).

5   Results

The first step of the PLS-SEM analysis is to evaluate the measurement model's reliability and validity. The measurement model consists of latent variables and their corresponding indicators. The two-step methodology for evaluating the reliability and validity of the measurement model includes evaluating the following:

- Internal Consistency (Reliability): Internal consistency measures the correlation between the items that measure each latent variable. In this step, we evaluate the measurement model's reliability by calculating the Composite Reliability (CR) coefficient for each latent variable. Results in the Table 1 indicates CR values exceed the criterion of 0.70, ranging between 0.788 and 0.882 (Table 2).
- Validity refers to the degree to which the measurement model measures the latent variables it is intended to measure accurately. In this step, we examine the convergent and discriminant validity of the measurement model to determine its validity.

Table 2. Internal consistency, convergent validity, composite reliability, and AVE

Construct	Items	Loadings	CR	AVE
Curriculum Provision (PRV)	STR1	0.844	0.851	0.656
	STR2	0.829		
	STR3	0.753		
Instructional Content (CNT)	SAD2	0.656	0.788	0.555
	SAD3	0.820		
	SAD4	0.750		
Instructional Methods (MTH)	MET1	0.815	0.869	0.625
	MET2	0.802		
	MET3	0.794		
	MET4	0.749		
Course Evaluation (EVL)	EVA1	0.829	0.869	0.690
	EVA2	0.896		
	EVA3	0.762		
Technological Skill (TS)	TEC1	0.705	0.864	0.516
	TEC2	0.679		
	TEC3	0.836		
	TEC4	0.661		
	TEC5	0.744		
	TEC7	0.667		
Personal Security Skill (PSS)	SIG1	0.860	0.858	0.604
	SIG2	0.681		
	SIG3	0.732		
	SIG4	0.822		
Critical Skill (CS)	KRIT1	0.781	0.882	0.603
	KRIT2	0.835		
	KRIT3	0.840		
	KRIT4	0.810		
	KRIT5	0.586		
Devices Security Skill (DSS)	ZAS1	0.712	0.843	0.574
	ZAS2	0.822		
	ZAS3	0.763		
	ZAS4	0.730		

(continued)

Table 2. (*continued*)

Construct	Items	Loadings	CR	AVE
Informational Skill (IS)	INT1	0.753	0.856	0.546
	INT2	0.716		
	INT3	0.818		
	INT4	0.774		
	INT5	0.617		
Communication Skill (COM)	COM1	0.681	0.865	0.620
	COM2	0.905		
	COM3	0.848		
	COM4	0.690		

Convergent validity measures the degree to which the items used to measure each latent variable are interrelated. By examining the factor loadings and the average variance extracted (AVE) values, convergence validity is evaluated. Factor loadings represent the strength of the association between each item and the latent variable, whereas AVE values represent the proportion of item variance that is explained by the latent variable. A common rule of thumb is that standardized external loadings should be 0.708 or higher, but researchers often obtain weaker external loadings (<0.70) in social science studies, so indicators with loadings greater than 0.4 can be retained (Hair et al., 2017). AVE values greater than 0.5 indicate sufficient convergent validity. Given that all factor loadings are greater than 0.6 and all AVEs are greater than 0.5, convergent validity of the measurement model can be asserted.

Discriminant validity measures the degree to which items that measure one latent variable are distinct from those that measure other latent variables. Using the cross-loadings and the Fornell-Larcker criterion, the discriminant validity is determined (Hair et al., 2017). According to the Fornell-Larcker criterion, the square root of the AVE of each construct should be greater than its highest correlation with any other construct to confirm discriminant validity (Table 3).

Additionally, discriminant validity was confirmed by checking the HTMT criterion, which is the ratio of the between-trait correlations to the within-trait correlations. HTMT value above 0.90 suggests a lack of discriminant validity. Both Fornell-Larcker criterion and HTMT ratio confirmed discriminant validity of the model (Table 4).

After confirming the measurement model's internal consistency, convergent validity, and discriminant validity, we can test the structural model. The purpose of the structural model is to examine the relationships proposed by structural models. Hence, the second step of the PLS-SEM analysis involves evaluating the structural model. In this step, we assess the significance of the path coefficients and the relationships between the variables. Path coefficients reveal the strength and direction of the associations between

Table 3. Discriminant validity - the Fornell-Larcker criterion (Fornell & Larcker, 1981)

	CNT	COM	CS	DSS	EVL	IS	MTH	PRV	PSS	TS
CNT	**0.745**									
COM	0.206	**0.787**								
CS	0.146	0.442	**0.776**							
DSS	0.131	0.346	0.556	**0.758**						
EVL	0.371	0.138	0.248	0.255	**0.831**					
IS	0.261	0.531	0.693	0.683	0.288	**0.739**				
MTH	0.448	0.134	0.151	0.163	0.606	0.205	**0.790**			
PRV	0.520	0.069	0.066	0.193	0.536	0.182	0.445	**0.810**		
PSS	0.086	0.563	0.427	0.503	0.108	0.496	0.101	−0.011	**0.777**	
TS	0.262	0.587	0.494	0.518	0.255	0.564	0.216	0.195	0.575	**0.718**

Note: The square root of the AVE is on diagonal

Table 4. Heterotrait-monotrait ratio (HTMT)

	CNT	COM	CS	DSS	EVL	IS	MTH	PRV	PSS	TS
CNT										
COM	0.307									
CS	0.206	0.549								
DSS	0.246	0.448	0.705							
EVL	0.541	0.185	0.310	0.336						
IS	0.361	0.663	0.845	0.878	0.375					
MTH	0.615	0.171	0.187	0.215	0.764	0.256				
PRV	0.777	0.160	0.141	0.254	0.708	0.235	0.561			
PSS	0.139	0.694	0.522	0.638	0.174	0.601	0.152	0.141		
TS	0.382	0.727	0.604	0.653	0.323	0.686	0.278	0.250	0.690	

variables. Using t-tests, the significance of the relationships is determined. A significant relationship indicates that it is unlikely that the relationship between the variables occurred by chance.

The structural model assessment procedure consisted of following steps was utilized to evaluate the proposed models:

- Collinearity Issues: Using the variance inflation factor (VIF), collinearity issues in the structural model were evaluated. Each predictor's tolerance value was greater than 0.20 and less than 5 (VIF ranger from 1.000 to 3.113), indicating that there were no collinearity issues.

- Importance and Significance: Using bootstrapping to determine the significance of path coefficients, the importance and relevance of structural model relationships were evaluated. The minimum number of bootstrap samples was set to 5,000 (bias-corrected and accelerated bootstrap - BCa).
- R^2: The R^2 level of each endogenous construct was evaluated. R^2 values of 0.75, 0.50, and 0.25, respectively, were characterized as substantial, moderate, and weak.
- Size of the f^2 Effect: The size of the f^2 effect was evaluated for each exogenous construct. Effects with f^2 values of 0.02, 0.15, and 0.35 were categorized as small, medium, and large, respectively.
- Predictive Relevance Q^2: The predictive relevance Q^2 of each endogenous construct was evaluated. Q^2 values greater than 0 indicated that the exogenous constructs had predictive relevance for the under consideration endogenous construct (Hair et al., 2017).

5.1 Baseline Model Estimation

The primary hypothesis of the study was that the quality of a program's curriculum influences the level of digital skills possessed by students and this hypothesis construct the baseline model of this research (H. The quality of the program's curriculum influences the digital skills of the students). The analysis revealed a statistically significant and positive relation between the curriculum quality of the program and students' digital skills ($\beta = 0.273$, t = 3.082, p = 0.002). This finding lends support to the study's main hypothesis, which proposes that the quality of the program's curriculum plays a significant role in enhancing students' digital skills (Table 5).

Table 5. Hypothesis testing results – baseline model

Hypothesis		Original sample	Standard deviation	T statistics	P values	f^2	Q^2
H	QUAL - > DIG	0.273	0.089	3.082	0.002	0.079	0.030
C	SEX - > DIG	0.045	0.311	0.143	0.886	0.000	0.030
C	PROG - > DIG	0.066	0.084	0.786	0.432	0.004	0.030
R^2 (DIG) = 0.067							

In addition, the analysis included two control variables: gender (SEX) and program (PROG). The results revealed a non-significant relationship between gender and digital skills among students ($\beta = 0.045$, t = 0.143, p = 0.886), indicating that gender does not significantly influence students' digital skills. Similarly, a program had a non-significant relationship with students' digital skills ($\beta = 0.066$, t = 0.786, p = 0.432), indicating that the program of study does not influence students' digital skills significantly. Hence, these results indicate that the quality of the program's curriculum is a significant factor in shaping students' digital skills, whereas gender and program of study play no significant roles. These findings have significant implications for the design of educational programs aimed at enhancing students' digital skills.

The R2 value for this relationship was 0.067, indicating that the quality of the program's curriculum explains only a small portion of the variation in students' digital skills. However, it is important to note that many scholars point out that it is difficult to give basic rules for acceptable R2 values because it depends on the complexity of the model and the research discipline. So, for example, R2 values of 0.20 are considered high in disciplines such as consumer behavior and other social science disciplines (Hair et al., 2017). The relationship between curriculum quality and student's digital skills had a f^2 value of 0.079, indicating a moderate effect size. In contrast, the f^2 values for the relationships between gender (SEX) and students' digital skills and between program of study (PROG) and students' digital skills were 0.000 and 0.004, indicating very small or negligible effect sizes, respectively. The predictive significance of the exogenous constructs (QUAL, SEX, and PROG) for the endogenous construct (DIG) was evaluated using the Q^2 value, which estimates the amount of variance in the endogenous construct that is predicted by the exogenous constructs. The Q^2 value for students' DIG was 0.030, indicating that exogenous constructs explain a small portion of the variance in students' digital skills (Fig. 1).

5.2 Extended Model Estimation

The extended model is an expansion of the research's main hypothesis, which states that the quality of the program's curriculum influences the level of digital skills among students. The extended model proposes that digital skills are a six-dimensional construct consisting of technological or instrumental skills, communication skills, information skills, critical skills, personal security skills, and device security skills. Each of the six additional hypotheses in the extended model examines the relationship between the quality of the program's curriculum and one of the six dimensions of digital skills.

The model's six additional hypotheses are as follows:

- H1. The quality of the program's curriculum influences the technological skills of the students.
- H2. The quality of the program's curriculum influences the communication skills of the students.
- H3. The quality of the program's curriculum influences the information skills of the students.
- H4. The quality of the program's curriculum influences the critical thinking skills of the students.
- H5. The quality of the program's curriculum influences the students' personal security skills.
- H6. Students' device security skills are influenced by the quality of the program's curriculum.

By adding these six additional hypotheses to the research model, the extended model provides a more complete understanding of the relationship between the program's curriculum quality and students' digital skills. It enables examination of the influence

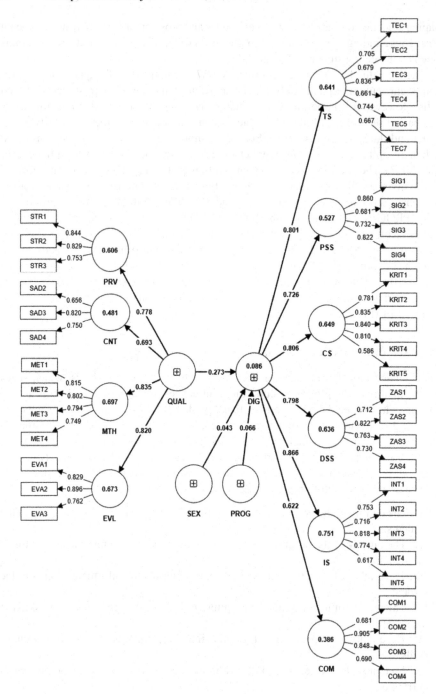

Fig. 1. PLS-SEM baseline model

of the program's curriculum on specific dimensions of digital skills, which can inform the development of more effective educational programs that target the specific digital competencies that are most crucial to students' academic and professional endeavors (Table 6).

Table 6. Hypothesis testing results – extended model

Hypothesis		Original sample	Standard deviation	T statistics	P values	f^2	Q^2
H1	QUAL -> TS	0.317	0.069	4.564	0.000	0.112	0.042
H2	QUAL -> COM	0.177	0.081	2.194	0.028	0.032	0.013
H3	QUAL -> IS	0.306	0.071	4.329	0.000	0.103	0.044
H4	QUAL -> CS	0.229	0.097	2.375	0.018	0.056	0.022
H5	*QUAL -> PSS*	*0.142*	*0.147*	*0.966*	*0.334*	*0.021*	*-0.002*
H6	QUAL -> DSS	0.266	0.085	3.135	0.002	0.076	0.029
R^2 (TS) =	0.094						
R^2 (COM) =	0.025						
R^2 (IS) =	0.088						
R^2 (CS) =	0.046						
R^2 (PSS) =	0.014						
R^2 (DSS) =	0.064						

The analysis revealed that five out of the six hypotheses were supported. The first hypothesis (H1) stated that the quality of the program's curriculum influences the technological or instrumental skills (TS) of the students. The results demonstrated a statistically significant and positive correlation between the quality of the program's curriculum and students' technological or instrumental skills ($\beta = 0.317$, t = 4.564, p = 0.000), thereby providing support for hypothesis 1. The quality of the program's curriculum influences the students' communication skills (COM), according to the second hypothesis (H2). The results demonstrated a statistically significant and positive correlation between the quality of the program's curriculum and the students' communication skills ($\beta = 0.177$, t = 2.194, p = 0.028), providing support for hypothesis 2. Students' information skills (IS) are influenced by the quality of the program's curriculum, according to hypothesis 3 (H3). The results demonstrated a statistically significant and positive correlation between the quality of the program's curriculum and the students' information skills (β

= 0.306, t = 4.329, p = 0.000), providing support for hypothesis 3. The quality of the program's curriculum influences the students' critical thinking abilities (CT). The results demonstrated a statistically significant and positive correlation between the quality of the program's curriculum and the students' critical thinking skills ($\beta = 0.229$, t = 2.375, p = 0.018), providing support for hypothesis 4. The quality of the program's curriculum influences the students' personal security skills (PSS), according to hypothesis 5. The results indicated a non-significant correlation between the quality of the program's curriculum and students' personal security skills ($\beta = 0.142$, t = 0.966, p = 0.334), indicating that the quality of the program's curriculum does not significantly affect students' personal security skills. Students' device security skills (DSS) are influenced by the curriculum quality of a program, according to Hypothesis 6 (H6). The results demonstrated a statistically significant and positive correlation between the quality of the program's curriculum and students' device security skills ($\beta = 0.266$, t = 3.135, p = 0.002), lending support to hypothesis 6 (Fig. 2).

In this study, the R^2 values are generally low, with the highest value being 9.4% for technological or instrumental skills and the lowest value being 1.6% for personal security skills. While the quality of the program's curriculum is a significant predictor of some dimensions of digital skills, other factors contribute to the development of students' digital skills in addition to the quality of the program's curriculum. This result is consistent with prior research that has emphasized the multifaceted nature of digital skills and the significance of considering multiple factors that influence their development. Despite the fact that the R^2 values in this study are relatively low, it is important to note that they represent a statistically significant proportion of the variance in the endogenous constructs. The f^2 values in this study range from 0.021 for personal security skills to 0.112 for technological or instrumental skills. In this study, the f^2 values for all six endogenous constructs fall within the range of small to medium effect sizes. This indicates that the quality of the program's curriculum has a moderate effect on the digital skills development of students. The highest f^2 value is for technological or instrumental skills (0.112), indicating that the quality of the program's curriculum has a moderate effect on this dimension of digital skills. In this study, the Q^2 values for personal security skills range from -0.002 to 0.04 for information skills. A Q^2 value of 0 indicates that the exogenous construct does not have predictive relevance for the endogenous construct, whereas a Q^2 value greater than 0 indicates that the exogenous construct does have predictive relevance. All six endogenous constructs have positive Q^2 values in this study, indicating that the quality of the program's curriculum has some predictive significance for the growth of students' digital skills.

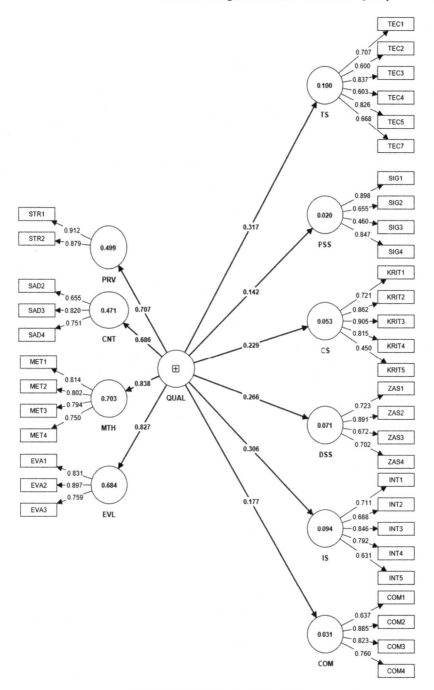

Fig. 2. PLS-SEM extended model

6 Conclusion

This study examined the six-dimensional relationship between the quality of the program's curriculum and students' digital skills. Our findings indicate that the quality of a program's curriculum is a significant predictor of some dimensions of digital skills; however, factors other than the curriculum also contribute to the development of these skills. As indicated by low-to-moderate R^2, f^2, and Q^2 values, we discovered that the quality of the program's curriculum has a moderate effect on the development of students' digital skills.

In this study, we evaluated both a basic and an extended model. In the first, the effect of the program's curriculum quality on the digital skills of students was examined. In the extended model, the impact of curriculum quality on six dimensions of students' digital skills was investigated. The results indicate that curriculum quality significantly influences five of the six dimensions of digital skills. First, we discovered that curriculum quality has a significant and positive effect on technological or instrumental skills (H1), suggesting that students who receive a curriculum of high quality are more likely to develop effective digital technology skills. Second, the results indicate that curriculum quality has a significant and positive effect on communication skills (H2), indicating that a high-quality curriculum can assist students in communicating effectively via digital technologies. Thirdly, the research discovered that curriculum quality has a significant and positive effect on information skills (H3), suggesting that students who receive a high-quality curriculum are better able to locate, acquire, and evaluate information in a digital environment. The results indicate that curriculum quality has a significant and positive effect on critical skills (H4), indicating that a high-quality curriculum can assist students in developing critical thinking and analysis skills in a digital context. The results indicated that the quality of the curriculum did not have a significant effect on personal safety skills (H5), indicating that factors other than the curriculum, such as individual characteristics and contextual factors, may play a larger role in shaping students' ability to manage online privacy and ensure personal safety in the digital environment. The results indicate that curriculum quality has a significant and positive effect on device security skills (H6), suggesting that a quality curriculum can assist students in taking precautions to protect digital devices and avoid potential threats.

This study makes a number of theoretical contributions to the literature on the development of digital skills in education. First, our research contributes to the existing literature by examining the relationship between program curriculum quality and six dimensions of digital skills, namely technological or instrumental skills, communication skills, information skills, critical skills, personal safety skills, and device safety skills. This allows for a deeper understanding of the factors that contribute to the development of digital competencies in students. Second, our research emphasizes the significance of taking a multidimensional approach to the development of digital skills, one that takes individual characteristics, contextual factors, and educational programs into account. This suggests that effective digital skill development necessitates a holistic and comprehensive approach that takes multiple factors into account, as opposed to focusing solely on curriculum or individual characteristics. Thirdly, our study contributes to the larger body of research on digital skills and their significance in the digital age. Our findings indicate that digital skills are crucial for success in a variety of academic and professional domains, and they highlight the need for educational programs that encourage the development of these skills among students.

This study's findings have significant implications for educational programs designed to improve students' digital skills. The results indicate that the quality of the program's curriculum is an important consideration in the development of digital skills, but it is not sufficient on its own. Other individual and contextual factors, such as individual characteristics, the learning environment, and broader socioeconomic factors, also significantly influence the development of digital competencies.

In light of these findings, we recommend that educational programs take a multifaceted, comprehensive approach to the development of digital skills. This may involve the incorporation of relevant curricula, the provision of opportunities for hands-on practice with digital tools and technologies, and the consideration of individual and contextual factors that shape digital learning and work environments. Such an approach can aid in equipping students with the digital skills necessary to thrive in an increasingly digital world.

A limitation of this study is that it was conducted on a relatively small sample of 148 students from only two academic disciplines, economics and education. This may limit our findings' applicability to other student populations or disciplines. To increase the generalizability of our findings, future research may replicate our study with larger and more diverse samples. Students' digital skills were evaluated based on self-reported measures, which may be subject to bias and inaccuracy. Future research could include additional measures, such as performance-based assessments or objective measures of digital skills, to provide a more thorough and dependable evaluation of students' digital competencies. Other individual and contextual factors, such as prior experience with digital technologies, access to digital resources, and social and cultural factors may also play a significant role in influencing the growth of digital skills. Future research could examine the relative contribution of these variables to the digital competencies of students.

References

1. Grosseck, Gabriela, Malița, Laura, Bunoiu, M.ădălin: Higher education institutions towards digital transformation—the WUT case. In: Curaj, Adrian, Deca, Ligia, Pricopie, Remus (eds.) European Higher Education Area: Challenges for a New Decade, pp. 565–581. Springer, Cham (2020). https://doi.org/10.1007/978-3-030-56316-5_35
2. Arslantas, K.T., Gul, A.: Digital literacy skills of university students: a mixed method analysis. Educ. Inf. Technol. **27**, 5605–5625 (2022)
3. Bećirović, S., Dervić, M.: Students perspectives of digital transformation of higher education in Bosnia and Herzegovina. Electron. J. Inf. Syst. Dev. Countr. **89**(2), 1–22 (2022)
4. Jorgensen, T.: Digital skills- Where universities matter. EUA (2019). https://eua.eu/resour ces/publications/851:digital-skills-%C3%A2%E2%82%AC%E2%80%9C-where-universit ies-matter.html
5. Tzafilkou, K., Perifanou, M., Economides, A.A.: Development and validation of students' digital competence scale (SDiCoS). Int. J. Educ. Technol. High. Educ. **19**(30), 1–20 (2022)

6. Rodríguez-de-Dios, I., van Oosten, J.M.F., Igartua, J.J.: A study of the relationship between parental mediation and adolescents' digital skills, online risks and online opportunities. Comput. Hum. Behav. **82**, 186–198 (2018)
7. Pöntinen, S., Räty-Záborszky, S.: Pedagogical aspects to support students' evolving digital competence at school. Eur. Early Child. Educ. Res. J. **28**(2), 182–196 (2020)
8. Tudor, S.L.: A teaching approach of the digital competence into the school curriculum. In: 2016 8th International Conference on Electronics, Computers and Artificial Intelligence (ECAI), pp. 1–4 (2016)
9. Araiza-Vázquez, M.J., Pedraza-Sánchez, E.Y.: Discernment of Digital Competences in Students of a Business School. In: EDULEARN19 Proceedings, pp. 4737–4747 (2019)
10. Akour, M., Alenezi, M.: Higher education future in the era of digital transformation. Educ. Sci. **12**(11), 1–14 (2022)
11. Morgan, J. P.: Improving digital skills for employability. Good Things Foundation (2019). https://www.goodthingsfoundation.org/insights/improving-digital-skills-for-employability/
12. World Economic Forum. : The future of jobs: Employment, skills and workforce strategy for the fourth industrial revolution. Global Challenge Insight Report (2016). https://www3.wef orum.org/docs/WEF_Future_of_Jobs.pdf
13. World Eonomic Forum.:The future of jobs (2020). https://www.weforum.org/reports/the-fut ure-of-jobs-report-2020/
14. International Labour Organization: Changing demands for skills in digital economies and societies (2021). https://www.ilo.org/wcmsp5/groups/public/---ed_emp/---ifp_skills/docume nts/publication/wcms_831372.pdf
15. Organisation for Economic Co-operation and Development: Skills for jobs (2018). https:// www.oecd.org/els/emp/Skills-for-jobs-brochure-2018.pdf
16. Abrosimova, G.A.: Digital literacy and digital skills in university study. Int. J. High. Educ. **9**(8), 52–58 (2020)
17. Camović, Dž., Isanović-Hadžiomerović, A.: Razvoj funkcionalnih znanja i vještina studenata: primjena Kolbovog modela u inicijalnom obrazovanju nastavnika. In: Branković, J. (ed.) Zbornik radova: Značaj nauke/znanosti u razvoju funkcionalnihznanja i vještina učenika i studenata, pp. 287–303. Federalno ministarstvo obrazovanja i nauke, Sarajevo (2021)
18. Silva-Quiroz, J., Morales-Morgado, E.M.: Assessing digital competence and its relationship with the socioeconomic level of Chilean university students. Int. J. Educ. Technol. High. Educ. **19**(1), 1–18 (2022)
19. Torbaghan, M.E., Sasidhran, M., Jefferson, I., Watkins, J.: Preparing students for a digitized future. IEEE Trans. Educ. **66**(1), 1–10 (2023)
20. Vrana, R.: Digital literacy as a boost factor in employability of students. Commun. Comput. Inf. Sci. **676**, 169–178 (2016)
21. Netshifhefhe, L., Nobongoza, V., Maphosa, C.: Quality assuring and learning processes in higher education: a critical appraisal. J. Commun. **7**(1), 65–78 (2016)
22. Bocean, C., Poposecu, D.V., Logofatu, M.: Quality in education- approaches and frameworks. Econ. Sci. Ser. **18**(2), 199–204 (2018)
23. McCowan, T.: Quality of higher education in Kenya: addressing the curriculum. Int. J. Educ. Dev. **60**, 128–137 (2018)
24. Shafi, M.M., Neyestani, M.R., Jafari, S.E., Taghvaei, V.: The quality improvement indicators of the curriculum at the technical and vocational higher education. Int. J. Instr. **14**(1), 65–84 (2021)
25. Nkulu-Ily, S.Y.: Implementation of e-learning curriculum in higher education. Eur. J. Open Dist. E-Learn. **25**(1), 62–73 (2023)
26. Twining, P., et al.: Developing a quality curriculum in a technological era. Educ. Tech. Res. Dev. **69**, 2285–2308 (2021)

27. Domović, V.: Kurikulum – osnovni pojmovi. In: Vizek Vidović, V. (ed.) Planiranje kurikuluma usmjerenoga na kompetencije u obrazovanju učitelja i nastavnika, pp. 19–32 (2009)

28. Marsh, C.: Kurikulum:temeljni pojmovi. Educa (1994)

29. Stabback, P.: What makes a quality curriculum? In-Progress reflection no. 2 on "current and critical issues in curriculum and learning". UNESCO International Bureau of Education (2016)

30. Viana, J., Peralta, H.: Online learning: from the curriculum for all to the curriculum for each individual. J. New Approaches Educ. Res. **10**(1), 2254–7339 (2021)

31. Mousseli, S., Hassan, M.: Integrating digital skills into higher education curricula: a Syrian public universities analaysis. J. Serv. Innov. Sustain. Dev. **3**(1), 83–94 (2022)

32. Laar, E., Deursen, A., Dijk, J., Hann, J.: Determinants of 21st-century skills and 21st-century digital skills for workers: a systematic literature review. Sage Open 1–14 (2020)

33. Rodrigues, A.L., Cerdeira, L., Machado-Taylor, M.D., Alves, H.: Technological skills in higher education - different needs and different uses. Educ. Sci. **11**(1), 1–12 (2021)

34. Karim, A.A., Din, R., Razak, N.A.: Investigating students' ways of learning information skills in Malaysian higher education. Procedia Soc. Behav. Sci. **15**, 3849–3854 (2011)

35. Tan, A.J.Y., Davies, J.L., Nicolson, R.I., Karaminis, T.: Learning critical thinking skills online: can precision teaching help. Educ. Technol. Res. Dev. 1–22 (2023)

36. Zhang, J., Wang, J., Min, S.D., Chen, K.K., Huang, H.: Influence of curriculum quality and educational service quality on student experiences: a case study in sport management programs. J. Hosp. Leis. Sport Tour. Educ. **18**, 81–91 (2016)

Digital Literacy in Teacher Education: Transforming Pedagogy for the Modern Era

Sheila García-Martín[1] and Judit García-Martín[2](✉)

[1] Universidad de León, León, Castilla y León, Spain
sgarcm@unileon.es
[2] Universidad de Salamanca, Salamanca, Castilla y León, Spain
jgarm@usal.es

Abstract. This chapter describes research developed in the Spanish educational framework in 2020, during the period of home confinement, which was carried out with the purpose of reducing the spread of the COVID-19 disease. The aim of this research is to find out about the use of Information and Communication Technologies (ICT) and two groups of digital technologies and the effects of this use. The tools analyzed were: i) six digital tools for communication and ii) nine digital tools for instructional design, in a group of 108 practicing teachers, aged between 23 and 65 years. They participated in this study by answering an online questionnaire called EDU-COVID [1]. Most of the teachers worked in public schools (69.4%), in several autonomous communities in Spain. The largest representation was from Castile and Leon (39.8%). These analyses revealed statistically significant differences in perceptions of the use of digital tools according to variables such as gender and type of school. Based on these findings, the study discusses and evaluates the educational suggestions of the new educational reforms aimed at digitizing teaching. The research provides information on the impact of digital technologies on teaching, assessing ongoing efforts to improve the quality of teachers' ICT instruction.

Keywords: Teachers · digital literacy · ICT · digital technology

1 Introduction

Current knowledge society and the evolution of Information and Communication Technologies (ICTs) have led to great advances in different spheres of action: social, cultural, and academic areas [2, 3].

On the one hand, previous studies have demonstrated that attitudes are an important predictor of the use of the digital tools [2–4]. On the other hand, other recent studies have signaled that the attitudes and beliefs of teaching faculty on the use of digital tools are a barrier to the integration of the same tools, due to the fear of change, the lack of training and personal use are presented as traditional obstacles to their integration in the teaching-learning process [1, 5–9].

Self-efficacy, which refers to the belief that a person has about their ability to perform a behavior successfully [10], is presented as an important determinant of the behavioral

Ł. Tomczyk (Ed.): NMP 2022, CCIS 1916, pp. 22–29, 2023.
https://doi.org/10.1007/978-3-031-44581-1_2

intention of use, that is, there is reliable evidence that having a positive judgment about one's ability influences the acceptance of digital tools in teaching [11]. In fact, a recent study reveals that pre-service teachers with higher levels of internet self-efficacy and lower levels of anxiety are more likely to have higher levels of digital citizenship [12].

At the same time, the digital competence of teachers seems to be another of the predictors affecting the use of digital tools in the educational process.

In line with this, in the Spanish educational framework, a common reference framework for the diagnosis and optimization of teachers' digital competence was defined in 2017 through a detailed report prepared by the National Institute of Technology and Teacher Training [13] linked to the Ministry of Education, Culture and Sport (MECD) of the Spanish Government.

Furthermore, teachers are considered to have a high level of digital competence when they are not only able to use technologies to enrich their teaching strategies, but also to propose and develop innovative practices based on the possibilities offered by digital tools [14].

In recent years and in view of the exponential increase in the use of technologies in educational processes, there is a greater demand for digitally competent teachers and the need for new approaches when it comes to integrating technologies in education [15]. Thus, being able to integrate and use digital tools in the educational process implies having a set of generic skills and skills specific to the teaching profession itself [16].

In the spring of 2020, teaching faculty were obligated to use their digital skills and technological capabilities to comply with the educational, social and health requirements during the COVID- 19 pandemic, suddenly becoming teachers 3.0 [2, 6].

For this reason, it is considered essential to examine the use of two groups of tools by active teachers in compulsory education in Spain: i) those that facilitate communication and ii) those that promote instructional design. Within the first group, we examine videoconferencing tools such as FaceTime, Skype, Microsfot Teams, Google Meet..., video viewing tools such as YouTube or Vimeo, synchronous communication applications (WhatsApp, Telegram...), social networks (Facebook, Linkedin...), image sharing tools (Instagram, Flickr, Picassa...) and microblogging tools such as Twitter, Tumblr... And, within the second category, tools for editing content collaboratively (Google Tools, Microsoft 360...), survey tools (Google Forms...), recording tools (Camstudio...), tools for creating interactive content such as Canva, Genially..., tools for gamification (Google Tools, Microsoft 360...), tools for creating interactive content such as Canva, Genially... Those aimed at gamification such as Educaplay, Socrative..., those that facilitate video editing (Imovie, FinalCut...), those for blogging, wiki and those focused on programming such as Jommla, Scratch...

2   Method

2.1   Research Objective

The aim of this study is to examine the use of digital tools by active teachers of compulsory education in Spain, during the ninety-nine days of home confinement, as well as to know their assessments regarding said tools and their own use.

2.2 Participants

The participants of this study are 108 active teachers of compulsory education in Spain, between 23 and 65 years old (see Fig. 1). Of which, the majority carry out their teaching work in public educational centers (69.4%), not being career civil servants in most cases (66.7%).

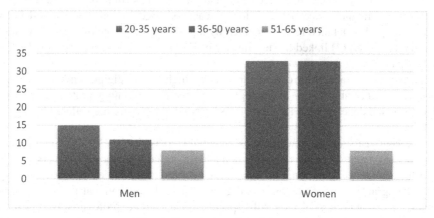

Fig. 1. Description of participants

In the spring of 2020, data is collected from teachers in a total of several autonomous communities from Spain. Most of the teachers surveyed carry out their academic work in Castilla y León (39.8%). According to García-Martín and García-Sánchez, 2013 [5], the largest autonomous community in Spain and the third largest territory in the European Union. Also, this is the most typically Spanish, applicable, and representative region in Spain, and historically has a greater linguistic heritage (Castilian Spanish) and cultural tradition.

2.3 Design and Instrument

This study is based on a quantitative research design, supported by an exploratory descriptive and correlation approach in which the survey method is used through the design and application of an online questionnaire, the EDU-COVID [1] through the Google Forms web tool. The reliability of the instrument is acceptable ($\alpha = .61$). This score may be due to the number of items, the number of response alternatives and the proportion of variance in the test.

3 Results

3.1 Teachers' Perceptions About the Use of Digital Tools

For Communication
According to the use of six digital tools *for communication*, as can be seen in Fig. 2, the teachers use social networks daily (58,3%) and the video conferences tools such as FaceTime, Skype, Microsoft Teams, Google Meet (36,1%). However, only 12% of the participants use microblogging (Twitter, Tumblr…).

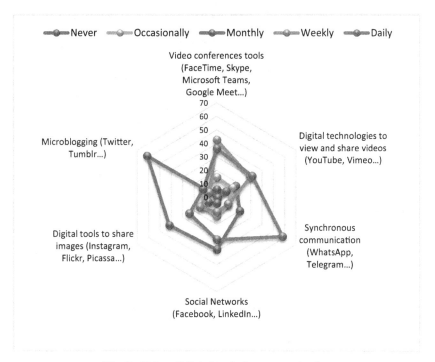

Fig. 2. Using of digital tools for communication

For Instructional Design
In relation to the use of nine digital tools for instructional design, as can be seen in Fig. 3, collaborative content editing tools such as documents, spreadsheets, Google, or Prezi presentations are the most used by teachers that have participated. However, less than 1% of participants use programming technologies like Jommla, Scratch…

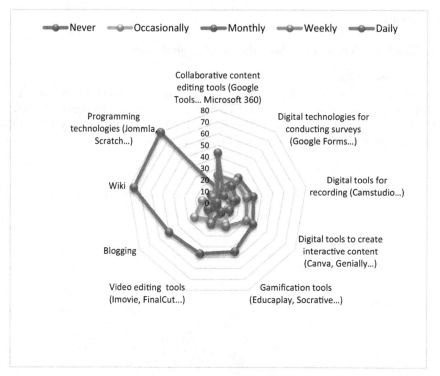

Fig. 3. Using of digital tools for instructional design

3.2 Patterns of Digital Tools Use Among Spanish Teachers

Sex

A pattern of differential use is obtained between male and female teachers in relation to virtual teaching platforms: Moodle, E-dixgal and Escholarium. Being significantly higher, in the case of male teachers [eg. $M_{MoodleFemale} = 2.76$ vs. $M_{MoodleFemale} = 2.15$; $p = .009$]. At the same time, men use digital tools to a greater extent for collaborative content creation, while women use more gamification tools [eg. $M_{GamificationFemale} = 2.36$ vs. $M_{GamificationMale} = 2.12$; $p = .026$].

In reference to the assessment of the tools and their own use during confinement, it is the women teachers who feel more satisfied. However, it is the men who claim to have made a deeper use. As well as the male teachers consider that the teaching developed during the exceptional state has guaranteed the achievement of objectives and the obtaining of learning results, to a greater extent, than the women.

Type of Center

In relation to the type of center (public or concerted), statistically significant differences are observed, with medium and large effect sizes, in the variables related to the use of Google Classroom [$p = .019$, $\eta^2 = .073$], of Escholarium [$p = .028$, $\eta^2 = .066$]; of digital tools or applications for the design of online surveys such as Google Forms,

Mentimeter and SurveyMonkey [$p = .010$, $\eta^2 = .085$] and of digital tools or applications for programming such as Joomla and Scratch [$p = .009$, $\eta^2 = .086$].

There is evidence of a pattern of differential use between teachers of public and concerted schools, to the benefit of teachers of concerted education, in various variables such as the use of Escholarium as a virtual teaching platform [$M_{Public} = 1$ vs. $M_{Concerted} = 1.08$; $p = .030$]; the use of digital tools or applications for conducting online surveys such as Google Forms, Mentimeter and SurveyMonkey [$M_{Public} = 2.48$ vs. $M_{Concerted} = 3.38$; $p = .016$] and the use of digital tools or programming applications such as Joomla and Scratch [$M_{Public} = 1.27$ vs. $M_{Concerted} = 1.92$; $p = .015$].

3.3 Teachers' Perceptions About the Teaching Given During the Confinement

According to the evaluation of the teaching given by teachers during confinement, as can be seen in Fig. 4, the teachers consider that the most of them affirm that didn't guaranteed the achievement of the objectives, the obtaining learning outcomes, the acquisition of skills and the assimilation of content.

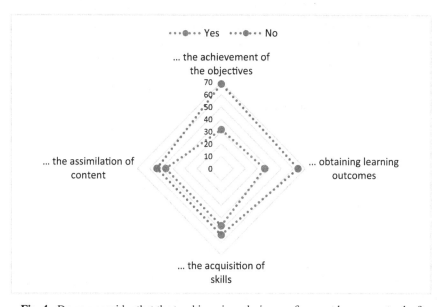

Fig. 4. Do you consider that the teaching given during confinement has guaranteed…?

4 Conclusions

Based on the stated objective and the results obtained, it is observed that the most used tools during the pandemic were the educational platforms, Moodle and Google Classroom, which may be due to the fact that part of the teachers surveyed exercised their professional work at higher education levels in which Moodle is the most used learning management system [17, 18]. Followed by the use of collaborative content editing tools between teachers, online surveys and audio and video recording.

All this can be understood by the need to evaluate or take exams online, as well as to develop masterful teaching sessions synchronously or asynchronously through audio and video recording [19]. In relation to the assessment of the use of digital tools, eight out of ten teachers are satisfied with their use, and more than 90% considered that it was relevant, necessary, and functional.

Finally, it is necessary to conclude that, in recent years, in educational contexts, improvements in teaching have been related to the use of technology in the classroom, so that teachers, to a greater or lesser extent, have had develop a certain digital competence to respond to the demand for the integration of these tools in the teaching and learning processes. However, the COVID-19 pandemic and the consequent confinement have produced a substantial change in the teaching and learning process, giving rise to a reality that has surpassed any prediction; The much-mentioned educational digitization is, today, a reality that is here to stay.

So, training and research on integrating digital tools into classrooms must be addressed from multivariate approaches, understanding that educational digitization is the result of several personal, formative, and contextual factors whose relationships can be very complex [20]. In this sense, España Digital 2026 is the agenda for the digital transformation of schools in Spain, whose objectives include developing digital competences for education, from the digitization of schools to universities, including vocational training, providing technological resources for the development of digital skills in education and increasing the number of graduates in digital areas, both in university education and vocational training. To this end, various programs are currently being implemented in collaboration with the Autonomous Communities with a twofold objective. On the one hand, to develop digital skills for compulsory education and, on the other hand, to support the digital transformation of the education system by equipping schools and students with devices.

Finally, it should be noted that one of the key elements to ensure the success of educational digitization is teachers that are in active of compulsory education in Spain, as they are responsible for adapting and applying digital tools in the teaching and learning process [1, 6–9, 11, 12, 20]. In this respect, the European Framework of Digital Competence Framework for Citizens (DigComp) has become a widely accepted tool for measuring and certifying digital competence and has been used as a basis for teacher training and professional development in Europe and beyond. As citizens, educators need to be qualified with these competences to participate in society, both personally and professionally. At the same time, we must emphasize that not only an optimal level of digital competence must be achieved, but we must also consider if teachers see and believe in the advantages and possibilities provided by technology, and receive the necessary training and support, digital tools can be effectively integrated into the educational process [6–8].

References

1. García-Martín, J., García-Martín, S.: Uso de herramientas digitales para la docencia en España durante la pandemia por COVID-19. Rev. Española Educ. Comparada **38**, 151–173 (2021)
2. García-Martín, J., García-Sánchez, J.N.: The digital divide of know-how and use of digital technologies in higher education: the case of a college in Latin America in the COVID-19 era. Int. J. Environ. Res. Public Health **19**(6), 3358 (2022)

3. Oliveira, G., Teixeira, J.G., Torres, A., Morais, C.: An exploratory study on the emergency remote education experience of higher education students and teachers during the COVID-19 pandemic. Br. J. Educ. Technol. **52**, 1357–1376 (2021)

4. García-Martín, S., Cantón-Mayo, I.: Use of technologies and academic performance in adolescent students. Comunicar Media Educ. Res. J. **59**, 73–81 (2019)

5. García-Martín, J., García-Sánchez, J.N.: Patterns of Web 2.0 tool use among young Spanish people. Comput. Educ. **67**, 105–120 (2013)

6. Mañanes-Manrique, J., García-Martín, J.: La competencia digital del profesorado de Educación Primaria durante la pandemia (COVID-19). Profesorado Rev. Curríc. Formación Prof. **26**(2), 125–140 (2022)

7. García-Martín, J., García-Sánchez, J.N.: Pre-service teachers' perceptions of the competence dimensions of digital literacy and of psychological and educational measures. Comput. Educ. **107**, 54–67 (2017)

8. García-Martin, J., Rico, R., García-Martín, S.: The perceived self-efficacy of teachers in the use of digital tools during the COVID-19 pandemic: a comparative study between Spain and the United States. Behav. Sci. **13**(3), 1–13 (2023)

9. Tondeur, J., Aesaert, K., Prestridge, S., Consuegra, E.: A multilevel analysis of what matters in the training of pre-service teacher's ICT competencies. Comput. Educ. **122**, 32–42 (2018)

10. Bandura, A.: Social Foundations of Thought and Action. Prentice Hall, Hoboken (1986)

11. Adukaite, A., van Zyl, I., Er, Ş., Cantoni, L.: Teacher perceptions on the use of digital gamified learning in tourism education: the case of South African secondary schools. Comput. Educ. **111**, 172–190 (2017)

12. Choi, M., Cristol, D., Gimbert, B.: Teachers as digital citizens: the influence of individual backgrounds, internet use and psychological characteristics on teachers' levels of digital citizenship. Comput. Educ. **121**, 143–161 (2018)

13. Instituto Nacional de Tecnologías Educativas y de Formación del Profesorado (2017). Marco común de competencia digital docente. INTEF. https://aprende.intef.es/sites/default/files/2018-05/2017_1020_Marco-Com%C3%BAn-de-Competencia-Digital-Docente.pdf

14. Esteve, F., Castañeda, L., Adell, J.: Un modelo holístico de competencia docente para el mundo digital. Rev. Interuniversitaria Formación Prof. **91**(32.1), 105–116 (2018)

15. Instefjord, E.J., Munthe, E.: Educating digitally competent teachers: a study of integration of professional digital competence in teacher education. Teach. Teach. Educ. **67**, 37–45 (2017). https://doi.org/10.1016/j.tate.2017.05.016

16. Lund, A., Furberg, A., Bakken, J., Engelien, K.L.: What does professional digital competence mean in teacher education? Nordic J. Digit. Lit. **9**(4), 281–299 (2014)

17. Del Prete, A., Cabero, J.: EL uso del Ambiente Virtual de Aprendizaje entre el profesorado de educación superior: un análisis de género. RED. Rev. Educ. Dist. **62**(4), 1–20 (2020)

18. Martínez-Sarmiento, L., Gaeta, M.: Utilización de la plataforma virtual Moodle para el desarrollo del aprendizaje autorregulado en estudiantes universitarios. Educar **55**(2), 479–498 (2019)

19. García-Peñalvo, F.J., Corell, A., Abella-García, V., Grande, M.: La evaluación online en la educación superior en tiempos de la COVID-19. Educ. Knowl. Soc. (EKS) 21–26 (2020)

20. Almerich, G., Suárez, J.M., Jornet, J.M., Orellana, M.N.: Las competencias y el uso de las tecnologías de información y comunicación (TIC) por el profesorado: estructura dimensional. Rev. Electrón. Invest. Educ **13**, 28–42 (2011)

Digital Competences and Didactic Technologies Training for Teachers in Service: From DigCompEdu to a National Framework

Piergiorgio Guarini$^{(\boxtimes)}$ ⓘ, Marco di Furia ⓘ, and Benedetta Ragni ⓘ

Learning Science Hub, Università di Foggia, Via Arpi 176, 71121 Foggia, Italy
`piergiorgio.guarini@unifg.it`

Abstract. In the Italian school systems, teachers are not obliged to attend training courses about digital competences, innovative didactic methodologies or didactic technologies.

As a matter of fact, there are some previsions about providing to teachers the possibility to train on the topics above mentioned (and many mores); the training, in a *longlife learning* perspective [1] is also highly recommended, but there are no statutory provisions [2].

This contribution proposes a framework in order to provide a structured training for teachers in services, linking the training to the possibility to develop a career in the Italian school systems, possibility that has always been theorized, but never implemented.

The framework should be introduced and structured by the Italian Higher Education Institutions, modeling it on the multilevel organization of the DigCompEdu, starting from the earliest levels (A1 and A2), giving teachers the possibility to become leaders and innovators [3] in the training topic they choose to train in.

Keywords: Teachers' Training · Teachers' Career · Longlife Learning

1 Evolution of Teacher Education in Italy

Nowadays, in Italy, there is no provision for teachers to pursue a career as it is commonly understood in the working world.

The teachers do not change positions and cannot obtain promotions within the school system: they maintain the same "status" from the moment they are placed on the tenure track until reaching retirement age.

On the other hand, teachers' salary does not stand still but grows (as it should) as the years go by, thanks to the so-called "seniority steps" that teachers can accumulate throughout their service.

To understand the current situation, it may be useful to (briefly) review the history of in-service teachers' training and the evaluation of the skills they have acquired.

In the 1970s, with the delegated decrees ("decreti delegati") of 1974, the principles of egalitarianism and the uniqueness of the teacher's function were affirmed, subject to

Ł. Tomczyk (Ed.): NMP 2022, CCIS 1916, pp. 30–41, 2023.
https://doi.org/10.1007/978-3-031-44581-1_3

the principle of non-assessment of teachers themselves, whose economic remuneration continues to depend only on years of seniority [1].

In 1999, Education Minister Berlinguer proposed a form of salary differentiation, aimed at virtuous and deserving teachers, subject to participation in a competition based on qualifications and examinations, reserved for teachers with at least 10 years of service behind them. The proposal, however, was never implemented [4].

It would have to wait another ten years, until 2009, for the evaluation of school teaching staff topic to return to the political debate. This was the topic of the "Brunetta reform" (named after the Education Minister Brunetta) which sought to bring the system of performance measurement and evaluation proper to the managerial philosophy found in private companies into the public administration, in order to create some kind of ranking of Italian teachers, which could act as a guide toward structuring a career for teachers [5].

A small step toward further salary differentiation is taken in 2015 with Law 107/2015 so-called "Good School" ("Buona Scuola") through the introduction of an ancillary annual bonus. The school principal will decide which teachers will deserve such bonus, based on criteria established by the evaluation committee [6], regarding training paths defined as mandatory, permanent and structural by the law itself, despite the fact that there was no provision for minimum or maximum hours of training to be attended.

Nevertheless, an Italian teacher has no possibility of developing or embarking on a "career" that entails different tasks from the organization of curricular activity, practical teaching during classroom hours and the organization of afternoon workshops, however related to the educational offerings of the Italian school system.

Teachers evaluation, from the perspective of professional development that this paper addresses, is an aspect analyzed and investigated by the OECD already in the three-year period 2009–2013. As revealed by the Eurydice report in the 2016 [7], the most widespread form of teachers' skills and preparation evaluation among European countries is periodic and conducted within the school itself.

2   Current Framework of In-Service Teachers' Training

Currently, we are in a period of introducing and structuring compulsory training courses for Italian teaching staff.

There are various experiences and best practices regarding the training of future teachers, both in Bachelor's and Master's degrees programs in Italian universities, but it is not the intention of this contribution to present a review of these practices.

Rather, the writers' intention is to point out how much attention is (rightly) given to the theoretical training of future teachers before they become in-service, as well as to internship and practical training during the years of theoretical training, thanks to the experiences of organizing teacher training that have followed in Italy over the past decade.

On the other hand, the reality of in-service teachers training is different: after the aforementioned "Good School" law, a mandatory training and refresher courses for Italian teachers has never been triggered nor has it come into force: the repeated invitations, on the part of the legislature, to use the training tools made available for teachers, have not been followed by any means of monitoring the use of these tools and training opportunities, let alone periodic evaluation of teachers' skills and methodological knowledge [2].

In the very last few years, new attempts have been made to reorganize in-service teachers training. The most recent, with Law 79/2022 converting Decree Law (DL) 36 of April 30, 2022 [8], confirms the establishment of the School of Higher Education (Scuola di alta formazione), which will be supervised by the Ministry of Education itself.

The School of Higher Education will be promoter and coordinator of training initiatives for in-service teachers, which will have to take place outside working hours (despite the ruling of the European Court of Justice, issued on October 28, 2021 in Case C-909/19, specific that compulsory training is always part of workers' working hours); participation in training activities outside working hours will be paid and compulsory for tenured teachers, but only voluntary for in-service teachers [9].

The training must include the teaching of knowledges useful for developing teachers' digital skills, as well as critical and responsible use of digital tools themselves, providing a framework for in-service teachers' permanent training and updating.

DL 36/2022 appears, therefore, to establish so-called "middle management," which means allow teachers to become professional figures supporting school autonomy, its organizational system and the teaching and collegial work, through training paths centered on the development of skills and competencies in the areas of planning, mentoring and tutoring, as well as true guidance of the development of individual students' individual skills.

Financial incentives are provided for tenured teachers who wish to participate in these trainings, which will not, for reasons of theme and space, be described in detail.

In order to increase the performance of pupils and to promote the inclusion of out-of-school experiences, there are annual mid-term verifications as well as a final verification, during which the teacher, after the aforementioned training courses, will have to demonstrate that he or she has achieved the level of training deemed necessary by referring to the objectives set. Those verifications, both intermediate and final, will be supported by the teachers' evaluation committee, with the integration of a technical or school manager, who is external to the institution to which the teacher being evaluated belongs.

There are 15 yearly hours of training for kindergarten and elementary teachers, and 30 yearly hours for junior high school and high school teachers.

3   A Proposal to Structure a Career Pathway for In-Service Teachers

Despite the latest attempt to organize DL 36/2022 attempts to give an increasingly solid structure to training for tenured and in-service teachers, the framework outlined so far still has flaws.

The distinction perpetrated between tenured and in-service teachers, with obligation and economic incentive for the former and not for the latter, already produces an inequality of treatment at the outset; moreover, the choice to allow the participation of some teachers and not others, could exclude, from the training paths, good teachers who could bring enormous added value to the whole school community.

For these reasons, in this section will outline a structured proposal for teachers' education that could integrate a (so far) nonexistent possibility of professional career development among Italian teachers. This proposal is in no way intended to be (nor does it present itself as) the solution for teachers' education needs and teacher career development, nor even as a definitive solution to these questions.

The basic idea would be to merge the teachers' education pathway with the career development perspective.

Using, as a reference, the European framework of digital competencies for teachers (DigCompEdu) [3], the training and career structure for teachers should be organized in 6 different "steps" of training on the topics of, to name a few, innovative teaching methodologies and innovative digital teaching methodologies, design of teaching activities in teaching and learning processes, with a look on personalized teaching according to the needs of each student [10], about the possibility of using digital technologies to use ubiquitous and hybrid learning not only in conditions of extreme necessity, but as a concrete and daily possibility to enable access to education for all pupils and all students, according to their needs [11].

The various "steps," will be shaped following the different levels of competence in which the DigCompEdu framework is articulated:

1. A1 (awareness): gaining a basic knowledge and use of the topics and subjects covered by the training, such as innovative teaching methodologies and the use of technology with regard to preparing classroom training interventions, communicating with pupils and students, their families, and their colleagues;
2. A2 (exploration): begin to explore the possibilities of using the skills acquired to improve as educators in all aspects and phases of the teaching experience;
3. B1 (integration): becoming capable of integrating the skills and knowledge acquired in one's professional activity contexts, being able to use them in creative and innovative ways as well;
4. B2 (expertise): at this stage, the focus is on developing critical use of acquired knowledge and tools;
5. C1 (leadership): the trainee educator acquires such competence of the topics learned that he or she can become a leader in multiplying knowledge of them, becoming a trainer himself or herself, both within his or her own educational institution (peer educator to colleagues) and in other contexts;
6. C2 (innovation): the trained teacher, in addition to being a leader and having acquired the skills to be able to pass on the skills learned to others, has now incorporated these skills into his or her daily work practice, himself or herself becoming a creator and experimenter (pioneer) in the various disciplines he or she has been trained in [12].

The proposed structure cannot be separated from the coordination of an institution body in charge of organizing this training as well as training the experts who will be the trainers/tutors of training teachers.

The role can easily be filled by the aforementioned School of Higher Education in collaboration and coordination with Italian universities as well as the Conference of Rectors of Italian Universities (CRUI).

Participation in this training should be provided on a totally voluntary basis, with no compulsory requirement to complete all the steps at the beginning of this path. Any teacher must feel and be free to participate in the training up to the desired point, with the only "rule" for which there can be no "skips": the training path must be chronological and orderly, with no possibility of skipping any "step" or being able to start the training from a point other than A1.

This is necessary, both for a homogeneity of training of the faculty and because, as already mentioned, the framework will develop a real career: having successfully passed a "step" and verified the knowledge acquired with in progress and final evaluations, a new position is acquired, which will clearly provide an economic adjustment for the duly trained teacher. This is due to the time devoted to training, as well as the commitment that implementing the acquired knowledge will entail.

The training course for each "step" will be of one year's duration and must include no less than 1,500 h of lectures and practice (i.e., 60 CFUs). A shorter time frame would not allow serious and structured acquisition of knowledge.

This already tends to go in response to a major and obvious criticism that can be made of the proposed model: how to disincentivize the participation of teachers who would only want to take advantage of the increase in economic remuneration.

As just laid out, a pathway with a minimum duration of one year for each higher career level is not such a comfortable choice. The commitment required will obviously be serious and constant.

Moreover, in progress and final evaluation of acquired skills will not be automatic and will rather be organized and managed by the School of Higher Education. Teachers' competencies as well as their career prospects are at stake. Without going further into the economic discourse, these two features, with the repercussions they may have on pupils and students and the whole school system, are enough to not only propose but indeed demand a serious and non-fallacious evaluation of the skills that teachers will go on to acquire.

4 Practical Examples of Teacher Training: Digital Game Based Learning and Enquiry Based Learning

To best exemplify the proposed model, we will illustrate the step-by-step organization of the training course concerning two innovative teaching methodologies: Digital Game Based Learning (DGBL) and Enquiry Based Learning (EBL).

We choose two methodologies that are very familiar to our research group in the Learning Science hub in University of Foggia, in order to present a detailed proposal of a well-known topic, that can be precise and not superficial nor incomplete.

DGBL is a methodology based on the use of a fundamental characteristic during learning processes: motivation. The most illustrative place where the transformation of participation motivation into competence learning and subsequent acquisition of these competences takes place is, without a shadow of a doubt, the world of video games [13].

Video game designers have a great deal of competence and ability in keeping the video game player's concentration and motivation high. As the latter is confronted with enigmas, puzzles and challenges of all sorts, organized by increasing levels of difficulty, in which, usually, in order to solve a level it is necessary to have acquired skills and competences in the previous levels, the gamer therefore learns by following the model of Learning By Doing, mediated, however, by the video game experience, which succeeds in 'hiding' the learning process behind a design, gameplay, graphics and storytelling specially conceived to immerse the gamer in a different virtual reality, an alternative to our life and everyday life, in which he or she can engage in exploits and challenges that would not normally be within our reach (or would not exist at all).

A very important feature of video games, which does not exist in reality and which allows us to experience all possible experiences, dangers and mistakes, is the possibility of trying and trying again the same challenge or overcoming the same obstacle or solving the same problem an infinite number of times.

With a simple save of the progress made (many video games provide for an automatic save), it is even possible to cause the death of one's digital avatar in an attempt to solve the problem or overcome the obstacle: if the gamer is unsuccessful because he chose the wrong key combination or applied a sub-optimal strategy, he can simply and trivially try again a few seconds later, reloading from the point of the last save.

Negative and unsuccessful experiences are not failures and do not generate frustration, as the video game is designed to be solved and completed: it does not have to be so difficult that it generates frustration such as to lead the video player to abandon the venture. Negative experiences, therefore, become the moments of greatest learning, during and after which the gamer is aware of what actions led to the failure, giving him/her the possibility to remedy or change certain decisions and/or actions, so that he/she can aim at solving the problem and/or overcoming the level, causing an involuntary but effective acquisition of skills and knowledge, boosted by the satisfaction of having completed the task [14, 15].

A different insight would merit the possibility of online video gaming, sharing information and skills with other video gamers from all over the world, but it is not the aim of this section to provide a comprehensive examination of DGBL.

EBL, on the other hand, is a pedagogical approach already recommended by the European Commission.

The method is based on the conception of the scientific method and on doing research (as the word Enquiry implies).

During the enquiry, students are asked to ask questions, search for evidence and scientific proofs that support the demonstration of the hypotheses that the students have to formulate in order to solve the questions posed. The formulation of the hypotheses, the interpretation of the evidence gathered, the exposition and justification of the explanation, of the solution chosen, are the fundamental parts of this approach.

For the use of EBL, the lecturer must be duly trained, conducting training on the method itself, the application possibilities and actual practical experience. Students, in order to be able to conduct such exploration activities in search of the solution or explanation to their problem, must be duly motivated.

The EBL provides for four types of investigation:

1. Confirmatory investigation of known topics and phenomena, with the possibility of predicting the results. Students can act and move very autonomously;

2. Structured enquiry, where the teacher is more present, as he provides both the hypothesis and the research method, leaving the students to engage in the search for the solution;
3. Guided enquiry, similar to structured enquiry but with a more lateral role of the teacher. The latter merely provides the problem, leaving the students free to choose which procedure to follow and how to present the results;
4. Open investigation, which however requires a high degree of cognitive and investigative skills on the part of the students, who choose both the hypothesis to be investigated and the procedure to be followed.

The logic behind EBL is a circular diagram involving the various stages of investigate, create, discuss, reflect, ask and investigate again, without investigation necessarily being the starting point.

We offer a table summary of the main features of the two models so far (Table 1):

Table 1. DGBL and EBL characteristics [16].

Digital Game-Based Learning	- Flow experience
	- Reperire informazioni velocemente
	- Decision seeking
	- Comportamento esplorativo
	- Percezione di controllo
	- Problem solving
	- Collaborazione in rete
Enquiry Based Learning	- Research based
	- Formulare domande di ricerca
	- Ricercare evidenze scientifiche
	- Developing explanatory hypotheses
	- Falsifying hypotheses
	- Communicate and justify the pre-chosen explanation
	- Confirmatory enquiry
	- Structured enquiry
	- Guided investigation
	- Open enquiry

How, then, to translate the possibilities of acquiring the knowledge necessary for learning these models, within the organization proposed in the previous paragraph?

Training will have to be organized, almost following the principles of Digital Game-Based Learning, by increasing degrees of difficulty, commitment and learning. It is by no means expected that teachers will immediately and completely acquire all the skills and notions necessary to suddenly become great experts on the subject on which they are going to train, nor that they will become pioneers and innovators of (for example) new learning methodologies after a few months or a few years of training.

Each 'step' in the proposed structure will provide a certain package of knowledge, which will enable the trainers to become more and more skilled and experienced in their chosen training topic.

Speaking of the specific case of Digital Game-Based Learning, we must remember that research in the area of learning technologies has always been criticized for lacking solid theoretical ground [17]. In this proposal, on the contrary, the theoretical framework is definitely taken into consideration, as nothing can be left to chance when we talk about teacher training, given the repercussions that the organization of such training will have, in cascade, on Italian students.

Moreover, the choice of giving, as an example, a structure to the DGBL's 'step' training is due to the absolutely positive value that digital technologies assume in educational contexts: in addition to the now well-known ability of digital natives with digital technologies and tools, the promotion of a learning environment with positive human-computer interaction is capable of promoting the understanding and acquisition of socially desirable behaviours, as well as a healthy lifestyle [18].

A proposal for organizing training in the six 'steps' based on the DigCompEdu model for the methodologies just outlined can be as follows (Table 2):

Table 2. Proposal for structuring training for Digital Game-Based Learning based on the DigCompEdu framework

Level A1	Level A2	Level B1
Theoretical framework of methodology, history of practical applications of video games in educational environments and in teaching and learning processes. Practical use of video games as learners and verification of knowledge learning through their use	Theoretical overview of Serious Games, the possibilities of their use and practical applications in educational environments and teaching and learning processes. Practical use as learners of Serious Games and verification of the further specificity of the tool for learning knowledge	Theoretical framework on Game Design and the design of educational content to be learnt through Serious Games. Understanding of the mechanisms behind the organization of the storytelling within the video game and of the concatenation necessary, between the various levels of the game, for testing the acquisition of skills by proposing levels of increasing difficulty
Level B2	Level C1	Level C2
Design and Game Design experiences by the trainee teachers, who will have the opportunity to design, write and see realized (with trained technical experts) a Serious Game of their own design. During all phases of the process, trainee teachers will be able to self-assess their skills and knowledge acquired during the previous levels	Leader-ship training and knowledge multiplication. Trainee teachers will acquire the necessary skills to plan, organize and realize training courses for their fellow teachers, both in their own school and in other schools Practical experience in the organization and realization of individual training modules to be offered to evaluators	Advanced training in programming and coding for the practical realization of Serious Games. Trainee teachers will be trained in the skills needed to make Serious Games themselves, so that they can practically realize their ideas. Trainee teachers will try their hand at realizing a Serious Game as the final product of the training course

Designing and using digital learning environments, among which Serious Games, as shown in the example, takes inspiration from experiential learning and reflective observation (learning circle), which is the result of research by Piaget, Lewin, Dewey and Kold [19].

It is evident that this proposed model must provide for a serious and structured system of teacher evaluation and self-assessment. Given the difficulty in standardizing teacher evaluations already noted in the 2016 Eurydice report, it is not the intention to propose a structured evaluation model on this occasion. In the further reflection on how to structure a career perspective for teachers, however, it seems unquestionable that such a system will have to be envisaged, structured and implemented, referring to scientific studies already present in the literature [20].

As an aside, it is worth mentioning, however, that the way in which this training model is to be administered, as well as the way in which it is to be structured and the possibility of career advancement, cannot disregard the implementation of hybrid, ubiquitous and blended teaching models, both in order to allow the widest and most continuous participation possible of the teachers who will access the training, and to show, in concrete terms, the practical implementation of a training course organized through the use of innovative teaching technologies [21].

5 Discussions

Every proposal, as it should be, especially if presented as already fundamentally structured, cannot be welcomed with open arms and without any criticism from the academic scientific community.

For this reason, as already stated in the course of this work, it is by no means the intention of the authors to presume to be able to resolve the long-standing issue of career prospects for lecturers in a few thousand words.

Nevertheless, every proposal should start from somewhere, and in the authors' opinion the best place to start is with a critical analysis of the knowledge, expertise and experience already possessed by the academic community, relying and building on the work of the luminaries of the organization of training, teaching and learning experiences such as Misha and Koehler and all the other authors mentioned in this work.

The discussion regarding this proposal can clearly be wide-ranging, as organizational aspects (e.g. the organization of and participation in the training itself, the ways and means of access and participation of teachers who want to train), logistical aspects (the physical and hybrid locations in which the training is to take place), and logistical aspects (the physical and hybrid locations in which the training is to take place) must be clarified, the organization and provision of the aforementioned venues), responsibilities (who bears the various organizational burdens, the administration of the training intervention, the mid-term and final evaluation), economics (which and how much funding to dedicate to this type of organization, the necessary authorizations) and many others.

Despite the fact that there are so many aspects and facets that need future clarification, and that they would all deserve, without exception, an equally long work expressly dedicated to them, the idea of basing the training and structuring of a possible career for teachers on the DigCompEdu framework, also has, as a reference, the possibility of bringing the skills of Italian teachers to be increasingly homologated to the European standard, which, especially with regard to digital skills, is unfortunately far from being achieved [22].

6 Conclusions

Although the authors are aware that they do not pretend to present a work that would change the training of in-service teachers and the related prospects for the realization of a career path designed specifically for them, it is not the authors' intention to perform a mere writing exercise.

As stated in the introduction and in the course of this contribution, in-service teacher training does not have a defined structure, nor is it compulsory or propaedeutic in relation to the performance of the teacher's daily and curricular functions.

As much as training and self-training should (must) be a personal propensity, aimed at continuous updating for the purpose of improving one's skills (and, therefore, improving the offer one can propose to one's students), it is no longer conceivable, nowadays, to complete one's career path, from the first day of entering the classroom until retirement, based on the skills acquired exclusively during the training prior to taking up one's duties.

All this can be summarized in the concept of lifelong learning [23], i.e. constant and continuous learning throughout one's life. This concept, when referred to vocational training, has long since been standardized, as far as its key competences are concerned, by the European Union [24] and, in cascade, the national systems have adapted to it.

Without going into technical regulatory detail, which is not the subject of this contribution, the structure of training and career possibilities outlined above is part of the new training offers made available in recent years (such as, for example, Massive Online Open Courses, MOOCs), thanks to the questioning of the Humboldtian organization of the school and university system [25]. The 'novelty' of the proposal, if it can be called in this way, is the structuring of an offer designed for a specific professional category, i.e. school teachers, usable yes at any time during their career, but not open to everyone.

In conclusion, this contribution hopes to add arguments to the current debate on the structuring of a career prospect for teachers, starting from pre-existing references, good practices and expertise already usable throughout the Italian "school system", integrating all this with European Union indications and adding an innovative structure that provides a serious, structured and continuously monitored pathway for the organization and provision of teacher training.

References

1. Guerrini, V.: Valutazione e autovalutazione degli insegnanti. Riflessioni per promuovere processi di professionalizzazione in un'ottica life long learning. Lifelong Lifewide Learn. **14**(31), 1–16 (2018)
2. Trinchero, R., Calvani, A., Marzano, A., Vivanet, G.: Qualità degli insegnanti: formazione, reclutamento, avanzamento di carriera. Quale scenario? Giornale italiano della ricerca educativa **25**, 22–34 (2020)

3. Guarini, P.: Improve ICT teaching in Italian teachers' education. A proposal, in teleXbe 2021 (Technology Enhanced Learning Environments for Blended Education), paper n. 36. CEUR-WS, Aachen (2021)
4. Fondazione Agnelli: La valutazione della scuola. Roma-Bari: Laterza (2014)
5. Magni, F.: Formazione iniziale e reclutamento degli insegnanti in Italia: percorso storico e prospettive pedagogiche. Edizioni Studium Srl (2020)
6. Legge 13 luglio 2015 n. 107 "Riforma del sistema nazionale di istruzione e formazione e delega per il riordino delle disposizioni legislative vigenti", GU Serie Generale n. 162 del 15 luglio 2015
7. Eurydice: La professione docente in Europa: pratiche, percezioni e politiche. Bruxelles: Eurydice (2016)
8. Decreto-Legge 30 aprile 2022, n. 36 Ulteriori misure urgenti per l'attuazione del Piano nazionale di ripresa e resilienza (PNRR). (22G00049) (GU Serie Generale n.100 del 30-04-2022)
9. Corte di Giustizia UE, Sez. 10, 28 ottobre 2021, n. 909 - C-909/19 - Il tempo speso per la formazione obbligatoria rientra nell'orario di lavoro e va retribuito
10. Limone, P.: Ambienti di apprendimento e progettazione didattica proposte per un sistema educativo transmediale. 2nd edn. Carocci, Roma (2021)
11. Limone, P., Toto, G.A.: Ambienti di apprendimento digitale e ubiquitous learning: prospettive applicative e di didattica nella scuola post-Covid-19 Dirigenti Scuola 39, 10–19 (2020)
12. https://joint-research-centre.ec.europa.eu/digcompedu/digcompedu-framewok/digcompedu-proficiency-levels_en. Accessed 30 Apr 2023
13. Prensky, M.: Digital Game-Based Learning. McGraw Hill, New York (2003)
14. Pellas, N., Fotaris, P., Kazanidis, I., Wells, D.: Augmenting the learning experience in primary and secondary school education: a systematic review of recent trends in augmented reality game-based learning. Virtual Reality 23(4), 329–346 (2019)
15. Emerson, A., Cloude, E.B., Azevedo, R., Lester, J.: Multimodal learning analytics for game-based learning. Br. J. Edu. Technol. 51(5), 1505–1526 (2020)
16. Toto, G.A.: Expertise docente: teorie, modelli didattici e strumenti innovativi, p. 148. FrancoAngeli, Milano (2019)
17. Mishra, P., Koelher, M.: Technological pedagogical content knowledge: a framework for teacher knowledge. Teach. Coll. Rec. 108(6), 1017–1054 (2006)
18. Toto, G.A.: Effects and consequences of media technology on learning and innovative educational strategies. Online J. Commu. Media Technol. 9(1), e201902 (2018)
19. Traetta, L., Toto, G.A., Lombardi, D.: Modelli di insegnamento/apprendimento innovativi nella didattica e nella formazione professionale dei docenti. Lifelong Lifewide Learn. 17(39), 141–156 (2021)
20. Bušelić, V., Pažur Aničić, K.: Developing ICT students' generic skills in higher education: towards a model for competence assessment and evaluation. In: Proceedings of the Central European Conference on Information and Intelligent Systems (CECIIS) (2019)
21. Guarini P., Rossi M., Peconio G., di Furia M., Lombardi D., Finestrone F.,: Capabilities approach e didattica digitale. In: Di Fuccio, R. (ed.) I sensi nel digitale. Le Tangible User Interfaces innovano la pratica pedagogica. Progedit, Bari (2022)
22. OECD Teaching and Learning International Survey (2018)
23. Smith, M.K., Ferrier, F.: Lifelong learning. The encyclopedia of informal education (2001)

24. Key competences for lifelong learning, European reference framework, annex of a Recommendation of the European Parliament and of the Council of 18 December 2006 on key competences for lifelong learning in Official Journal of the European Union, 30 December 2006/L394 (2008). https://op.europa.eu/en/publication-detail/-/publication/5719a044-b659-46de-b58b-606bc5b084c1

25. Brandser, G.C.: Humboldt revisited: the institutional drama of academic identity. Berghahn Books, New York (2022)

Attitudes of Preservice Teachers About the Use of Digital Technologies and the Use of Digital Technologies in Primary Education

Aleksander Janeš[1]([⊠]) [iD] and Andreja Klančar[2] [iD]

[1] Faculty of Management, University of Primorska, Koper, Slovenia
aleksander.janes@fm-kp.si
[2] Faculty of Education, University of Primorska, Koper, Slovenia
andreja.klancar@pef.upr.si

Abstract. This study investigates preservice teachers' knowledge and skills, use of digital technology and attitudes towards technology in the educational setting. Therefore, the survey goal was to identify the most influential factors for the future use of digital tools in preservice teachers' pedagogical work. The sample included 85 answers out of 150 sent surveys, which were analyzed descriptively and using statistical methods. Analysis findings pointed to variables of computer use and application of tools in the future use of digital tools. The most influential factors in this context seem to be knowledge and skills about digital tools and attitude towards digital tools.

The main findings show that the sample of preservice teachers is a relatively young generation that, uses computer and digital tools frequently and will use digital tools when working with pupils in primary education.

The paper's main contribution is in the identification of influential factors that outline the necessity of implementing digital tools in pedagogical work. The limitations of the research are mainly that only one measurement was performed on the population of all years of undergraduate study of preservice teachers at the Faculty of Education, University of Primorska, Slovenia. In future research, it is necessary to perform further measurements and comparisons between years of study, as well as measurements and comparisons between study programs.

Keywords: Attitude · Digital tools · Knowledge and skills

1   Introduction

Digital competences, as confirmed by many authors, are "integrated and functional use of digital knowledge, skills and attitudes" [1, 15, 19, 21, 22, 24, 25, 39, 46, 53, 56]. In explaining the use of 'digital competency' rather than 'digital literacy' authors argue that digital literacy is more often used in European policy and initiatives relating to e-inclusion whereas competence is employed more in an educational context [25, 39].

In England, Norway, Finland, Sweden and the Dutch-speaking part of Belgium, the analysis of educational technology curricula at the primary school level, showed

© The Author(s), under exclusive license to Springer Nature Switzerland AG 2023
Ł. Tomczyk (Ed.): NMP 2022, CCIS 1916, pp. 42–58, 2023.
https://doi.org/10.1007/978-3-031-44581-1_4

that national governments define digital literacy in their curricula in diverging ways. Different terms refer to the concept of digital literacy, such as digitally skilled, competent, and literate, Information and Communication Technology (ICT) competent and ICT capable. Different terms are used, and each of their definitions contains different semantic meanings, ranging from the use of basic ICT skills to complex problem-solving abilities. This permissive use of concepts in national educational technology curricula supports [37] the view that the notion of digital literacy is poorly understood in formal education and many terms are used to describe various sets of technology-related capabilities.

This differentiation of the terms is echoed in a European Commission report which argued that digital literacy is needed to achieve digital competence suggesting that digital competence is more broad ranging than digital literacy: "Digital competence involves the confident and critical use of Information Society Technology (IST) for work, leisure and communication. It is underpinned by basic skills in ICT: the use of computers to retrieve, assess, store, produce, present and exchange information, and to communicate and participate in collaborative networks via the Internet" [15], pp. 15–16.

The importance of interpersonal and (meta)cognitive skills is further stressed by the European Recommendations on Key Competences for Lifelong Learning which views a series of core transversal aspects as embedded throughout the eight Key Competences: critical thinking, problem-solving, teamwork, communication and negotiation skills, analytical skills, creativity, and intercultural skills [15, 16] as cited in [8].

Other authors argue that digital competence can be regarded, as conceptualized in the work of the Key Competences working group, [17]-Council Recommendation of 22 May 2018 on key competences for lifelong learning. 2018/C, 189/01, as an underpinning element in digital literacy. Digital literacy involves the successful usage of digital competence within life situations [36], p. 256. It follows from the literature that digital literacy defines a broader concept and includes digital competences.

This study investigates preservice teachers' knowledge and skills, use of digital technology and attitudes towards technology in educational settings.

According to [65] digital tools equal digital technology (DT). In this paper, the term digital tools are used in context with individual tools (e.g., video, animation, communication programs, word, excel, etc.), which are listed in the questionnaire and used in pedagogical processes. The term digital technology is used as the broadest concept in the digitization of pedagogical processes.

Research Question: How will the future use of digital technology in the educational environment be related to the knowledge, skills, and attitudes of preservice students?

2 Literature Review

2.1 Digital Competence

Digital Competence is the set of knowledge, skills, and attitudes (thus including abilities, strategies, values and awareness) that are required when using ICT and digital media to perform tasks; solve problems; communicate; manage information; collaborate; create and share content; and build knowledge effectively, efficiently, appropriately, critically, creatively, autonomously, flexibly, ethically, reflectively for work, leisure, participation, learning, socializing, consuming, and empowerment [19], p. 3; as cited in [39].

In 2017, the term "digital competence" is explicitly context-defined for teachers, as professional digital competence (PDC) is introduced through the Professional Digital Competence Framework for Teachers. This framework defined an extensive and complex understanding of teachers' PDC. The technological, pedagogical, and content knowledge (TPACK) [27] appears to represent a recurrent framework when Norwegian researchers are conceptualizing and defining digital technology, even though theory development by Norwegian researchers seems to increasingly take the place of this and other international frameworks. In different ways, they aim for concepts and definitions that are broad and include the multitude of challenges and possibilities created by digital technology development [61].

The studies that have most explicitly developed items for measuring preservice teachers overall PDC are [21, 24, 46], and [56]. Descriptions of the methods and questionnaires used, point to measurement which is mostly performed through the self-reporting of elements like skills, usage, and attitudes. Further, wordings such as "use of digital tools" and "use of ICT" are repeated in combination with phrases such as "pedagogical, didactical, for learning, and for teaching", as cited in [61].

[56], p. 5285 does not propose some definition or model but, rather, refers to the definitions of [57] and [31], and from these, they derive three defined aspects of PDC understanding: pedagogic and didactic, subject-specific, and technological.

[25] Janssen et al. (2013) identified twelve different areas that encompass digital competence composed of knowledge, skills, and attitudes, i.e., digital competence building blocks. The DigiComp 2.0, a revision of the original 2013 framework, offers a similar set of dimensions. While the dimensions have undergone refinement and updating, the framework maintains the overall structure of 5 competence areas: information, communication, content creation, safety and problem-solving [65].

Furthermore, no clear descriptions are given about the interpretation of curriculum objectives such as skills, competences, knowledge, or attitudes. Therefore, several Nordic researchers have selected the term 'digital competence' instead of other similar terms [1], p. 143; [18, 39].

In general, PDC encompasses a double challenge for teachers because they need to be skilled in using digital technologies for certain professional tasks and their main challenge is to foster productive and relevant use of digital technology among preservice teachers at all levels of education [32].

2.2 Attitudes in Addition to Knowledge and Skills

Attitudes are an important component of competences. Professional attitude (ATT) towards digital tools is a factor that influences preservice teachers' use of digital technologies in their classrooms [3, 6, 50, 68].

[4] examined the effects of the attitudes of the preservice teachers towards Web general (WEB-G), Web-Communication (WEB-C), Web pedagogical knowledge (WEBPK), Web pedagogical self-efficacy (WEB-PCK) and Web-based instruction (WBI). They collected research data among 416 preservice teachers attending the education faculty and analyzed the attitude scale applied to determine the participants' attitudes towards WEB-PCK. It was found that gender differences still existed for university students or for adult users in terms of evaluation of access to the internet and its

use, attitudes towards the internet, internet use frequency and internet efficacy [13, 26, 30, 43, 66] as cited in [4]. The findings obtained in the study show that if students have learning management system (LMS) usage skills and knowledge, perception of distance education is a useful and easy way of learning. Consequently, students will be more likely to enjoy distance education courses [4].

Also, teachers' Internet experiences influence their intention to use digital technology. Their attitudes toward ICT have been found to be affected by their knowledge and experience and skills of ICT as well [67]. Teachers who feel confident in their computer ability also tend to have positive views on the use of ICT in the classroom and vice-versa [10, 14, 23]. Based on these studies, we can summarize that there is a probable correlation between teachers' ICT experiences and their beliefs about the integration of digital technology [40].

Developing student skills and knowledge about ICT requires trained teachers, in skills, knowledge and methods of teaching. In this sense, it is necessary that the teachers develop their pedagogical content knowledge that includes an appropriate level of what we call digital competence. Teaching digital competence is the result of combining the knowledge and technological skills, knowledge of the methodological possibilities offered by technological resources and the attitude one has towards the exploitation of ICT to transform and improve education [44] as cited in [53]. Several authors concluded that measures for the development and implementation of ICT in education can be effective only if the teacher has a positive attitude towards the ICT's benefits and potential [39, 44, 45] as cited in [53, 58]. Based on the literature review, we assume that very few studies have examined in-service or preservice teachers' ideas-attitudes about incorporating digital technology into their teaching practice [40].

3   Methodology

Descriptive, Pearson correlation and linear regression (method Enter) statistical methods were used in the research analysis. The sample consists of 85 full-time and part-time preservice teachers of the Faculty of Education-higher Professional program of the University of Primorska, Slovenia. The lower response rate is due to the involvement of very young regular students who are not keen on answering online questionnaires. Data were collected in the spring semester of 2021–22 and processed using IBM SPSS Statistics 28.

For the research, an online questionnaire was used, which contained open-ended questions, optional questions and five-point Likert-type scales (from 1: Strongly disagree, to 5: Strongly agree). The questionnaire was developed and tested by [34, 35] at UiT the Arctic University of Norway.

We used closed-ended questions to obtain demographic and computer use frequency data, the question of past digital tools use was an open-ended question, and the remaining questions were answered using a five-point Likert-type scale of views. These issues were thematically divided into three constructs: application of digital tools in future (AT), professional digital competencies (PDC), and professional attitude towards digital technology (ATT). Cronbach's Alpha was used as a measure of internal consistency or validity (Table 3). [11], p.102 stated that if the number of construct's items is greater than

10 Cronbach's Alpha greater or equal to 0.7 is preferred. If the number of construct's items is smaller than 10 Cronbach's Alpha greater than 0.5 is preferred.

Normality tests were performed and most data on variables and constructs are acceptably normally distributed. Furthermore, the variance inflation factor (VIF) was calculated and is 1.845 for both independent variables ATT and PDC. The normality of the distribution of residuals has been tested and represents some slight deviation but residuals follow the line. We have a normal distribution in this case. The Breusch-Pagan statistic was used and indicated that the error term is the same across all values of the independent variables. Cook's distance was calculated which is less than 1 (0.000 for Minimum, 0.168 for Maximum, and 0.012 for Mean).

4   Empirical Findings and Discussion

The data that are presented in this paper are part of an international survey DigiCross involving Norway, Slovenia, Portugal, Turkey, Ukraine, and Jordan. In this paper, only Slovenian data and findings are presented. The data can be accessed on dedicated platforms.

4.1   Professional Digital Competence Construct

A range of outcomes from the measurement of the PDC construct pointed to difficulties in this area (Table 1). The nation-average scores for "Familiarity with digital tools that can help diversify teaching" (4.037) and "Self-confidence in the use of digital tools" (4.012) for Slovenian preservice teachers were both rather neutral. Slovenia deviates the most in the first two variables, which may be a sign of the continuous process of incorporating digital capabilities into Slovenian curricula.

The majority of responses indicated neutrality toward the following variables: "I find it easy to become familiar with new digital tools" (nations average = 3.839), "I can use digital tools which are appropriate for the subjects I am teaching" (nations average = 3.925), "It is difficult to use digital tools as an educational resource within my subject" (nations average = 3.791), "When I am using digital tools it is difficult to adjust the content to the individual student's needs" (nations average = 3.319), "I have no clear idea of learning outcome when using digital tools in my teaching" (nations average = 3.749) and "I use digital tools when giving feedback to students" (nations average = 3.396).

The construct's statements were accepted or rejected by a portion of the preservice teachers while being entirely accepted or rejected by a portion of them. Therefore, given that digital competencies are acknowledged as a common element in literature, that may be generated by imposed national education policy. Preservice teachers don't seem to be certain that using DT results in improved learning and more enthusiasm from students in primary schools [7].

The various teacher preparation programs in Slovenia are designed to get pre-service students ready to work within the rules. Between these programs, there are differences in how digital competency is approached and where it fits into curricula and educational policy. Slovenia is currently in the process of integrating digital capabilities into the

Table 1. Averages of the Construct PDC.

Construct variables	Average (SD)
I am familiar with digital tools that can help diversify teaching	3.48 (0.811)
I am, in general, confident when using digital tools	3.48 (0.921)
I find it easy to become familiar with new digital tools	3.62 (0.886)
I can use digital tools which are appropriate for the subjects I am teaching	3.56 (0.698)
It is difficult to use digital tools as an educational resource within my subject	3.56 (0.763)
When I am using digital tools, it is difficult to adjust the content to the individual students needs	3.04 (0.879)
I have no clear idea of learning outcome when using digital tools in my teaching	3.35 (0.960)
I use digital tools when giving feedback to students	3.48 (0.781)

Note: PDC–Professional digital competence; SD-Standard Deviation.

curricula at all levels of education (from kindergartens to universities), where digital competence is becoming vital and important across all programs and all subjects.

The survey's findings are consistent with those of several authors, who have found that teacher education still shows a general lack of knowledge and abilities among preservation teachers and teacher educators regarding how to use digital technology in a pedagogical and didactic manner [46], p. 253, [63]. According to the findings, future teachers exhibit a somewhat average degree of digital competence and struggle to align DT and content [20]. Numerous authors have noted that pre-service teachers frequently believe they lack the necessary skills to teach and learn in classrooms using DT [41, 47, 59], as mentioned in [62]. Preservice teachers and teacher educators should get the skills necessary to select and use the proper digital tools in the classroom, as well as the chance to do so while pursuing their education and receiving on-the-job training, according to [51]. According to research, using digital technology does not necessarily result in the development or improvement of advanced digital competence. As opposed to skills (i.e., quality of use) or competence (i.e., attitudes and use strategies), European assessments currently place a greater emphasis on measuring access and use [2].

DigCompEdu is compatible with the TPACK theory, according to authors [69], and it must be properly incorporated if teachers want to advance their digital professional development. Therefore, combining these two study methodologies is necessary in order to create a legitimate and trustworthy tool for assessing academic teachers' digital competency. The evaluation of students' use of technology in schools and higher education institutions, however, cannot be done instantly, directly, or generally since TPACK is focused on teacher understanding [71].

How to comprehend and relate to students' various levels of digital experiences and skills under various conditions (such as internal and external variables) is a basic concern for educators. How to encourage students to take the initiative in creating their own digital competencies for life. Whether enrolling in higher education for undergraduate study or continuing education, students are technologically literate. Since many intricate demographics and other factors play a part in determining when students master fundamental digital competencies, current discussions in this field cannot provide a convincing resolution. It is generally acknowledged that higher education has not completely embraced digital capabilities as a fundamental, core literacy [38].

4.2 Professional Attitude Construct

According to the results of the measurement of the ATT construct, there were both advantages and disadvantages to using DT in the future (Table 2).

A majority of respondents agreed with the claim that "when I use digital tools in my teaching, I find it adds value" and their responses were below the national average (4.023).

Responses to the statement "The use of digital tools is essential for good teaching" are indifferent (national average = 3.415). This implies that even if preservice teachers have experience in the design of technology-enhanced classes, they still lack experience in putting those teachings into practice. This may provide credence to the notion that preservice instructors would gain knowledge through their own experiences actively participating in these procedures [58, 72]. Here, the teacher's reflection is a crucial component.

The claim that "Society's expectations of the impact of digital tools are exag-gerated" found that Slovenian respondents are above the nation's average (2.965) and are neutral regarding society's expectations of the impact of digital technologies. This may indicate that they have a favourable attitude toward the educational application of DT and are aware of the value of knowledge and skill development for employment and daily living in a digital society.

The responses to the claim that "Expectations related to the use of digital tools in education frustrates me" are generally neutral. This generally favourable assessment of the statement by student teachers demonstrates a favourable attitude toward the pedagogical use of digital technology (national average = 3.496).

"At my university, expectations of the impact of digital tools are exaggerated in professional debates": Perception is neutral, according to respondents, with a national average of 3.255.

The nation's average score for this statement, "The use of digital tools is disruptive for the relationship between student and teacher", was 3.646.

Digital tools have the potential to increase students' interest in the subject I am teaching. Most respondents (country average = 4.082) agreed with the statement. Preservice teachers expressed their attitude toward the pedagogical use of DT in agreement with the statement "I like testing new digital tools in my teaching", as Slovenian respondents are neutral to the statement and under the national average (3.941). Results for the final five variables show that most respondents had a favourable attitude toward DT's pedagogical use. This implies that a portion of the preservice teachers entirely agreed with the claims, while a portion of the preservice teachers disagreed completely.

This may imply that these digital pedagogies enhance student engagement in learning more so than teacher-centred strategies [45, 58].

Table 2. Averages of the Construct Professional Attitude (ATT) towards DT in education.

Construct variables	Average (SD)
When I use digital tools in my teaching, I find it adds value	4.07 (0.651)
The use of digital tools is essential for good teaching	3.34 (0.867)
Society's expectations of the impact of digital tools are exaggerated	3.08 (0.759)
Expectations related to the use of digital tools in education frustrate me	3.32 (0.966)
In professional debates at my university, the expectations of the impact of digital tools are exaggerated	3.47 (0.749)
The use of digital tools is disruptive to the relationship between student and teacher	3.53 (0.983)
Digital tools can make the students more interested in the subject I am teaching	4.14 (0.693)
I like testing new digital tools in my teaching	3.65 (0.869)

Note: ATT–Professional attitude (attitude towards digital technology in education. SD-Standard Deviation.

Professional attitude (ATT) towards using DT in education is a factor that influences preservice teachers' use of DT in their classrooms. According to research, preservice teachers' attitudes about technology play a significant role in determining how successfully they will integrate technology in the future [6, 50], and [68].

The findings are consistent with a number of studies that claim that attitudes toward teaching and digital literacy are two key elements impacting both in-service and preservice teachers' digital practices [28, 60], as referenced in [33]. There is a likelihood that there is a causal relationship between teachers' views and their level of digital competence. More precisely, as noted in [33], favourable attitudes support increases in teachers' digital competence [48–50], and [60]. The authors also make note of the fact that teachers' openness and favourable views regarding the use of DT in the classroom seem to be significant aspects of their digital competence [9, 12, 20, 34, 35, 52]. Teachers' beliefs, attitudes, and efficacy, according to Palak and Walls [42], are crucial for the effective integration of DT in education [29]. As a result, studies have generally found that preservice teachers have favourable attitudes toward the use of DT in the classroom [39].

We may sum up by saying that, regardless of age, exhibiting a better approach toward DT will put preservice and in-service teachers in a position to establish professional digital competence more firmly [9] as cited in [20].

4.3 Other Constructs and Factors

Although the PDC, ATT, and AT constructs or factors are explored in the literature there are several other constructs and factors researched by many authors: beliefs, self-efficacy; commitment to the profession; commitment to career choice scale; work commitment index; single item teaching scenario; single item commitment question; in-service teacher education; self-perception and self-confidence, collaboration with expert

ICT staff or the perceived pressure in the school context, attitudes (i.e., confidence, beliefs and self-efficacy), and school culture [50, 58, 73].

For example, commitment is a complex, multifaceted construct. The most utilized predictor of commitment is self-efficacy [73].

Cuhadar [74] asserts that setting an example for future teachers is essential for the success of teacher education. This takes into account classes that receive DT help at every stage of the teaching and learning processes. Although preservice teachers may gain some theoretical understanding of the use of DT in a classroom setting, it will be challenging for preservice teachers to put their theoretical understanding into practice and develop it into a skill if teacher educators do not support their classes with successful DT applications.

Finding discrepancies between what is evaluated and what ought to be examined could lead to insightful recommendations about the subject matter of the next studies on educational technology and the procedures for conducting evaluations [71]. The researchers and experts generally agreed that the eight dimensions—learning outcomes, affective elements, behaviour, design, technology, teaching/pedagogy, presence, and the institutional environment—identified from the earlier review of what had been evaluated [70] were valuable.

4.4   Cronbach's Alpha and Correlations Coefficients

Cronbach's Alpha (Table 3) was used as a measure of the internal consistency of the questionnaire. The results were found to be sufficient to conduct further statistical analyses. This is viewed as the most appropriate measure of reliability when applying Likert-scale statements [54].

Table 3. Cronbach Alpha.

Construct	Items	Slovenia
USE	16	0.857
PDC	8	0.731
ATT	8	0.743

Note: USE–Use of digital tools in the pedagogical work of preservice teachers; PDC–Professional digital competence; ATT–Professional attitude (attitude towards digital technology in education).

The correlation analysis show (Table 4), that the professional application of digital tools in future (AT) correlates relatively low with PDC, and slightly more with professional attitude (ATT). All correlations are relatively low, positive, and significant. Correlations majorities are statistically significant at the level of 0.01. In terms of the implementation of DT, a generally low correlation is linked to a very invasive top-down national governance of education. This results in a situation where external factors are governing educators' application of tools. And when use is driven by both external and internal forces, correlation is lower as there are other factors explaining some of the practitioners' use of technology. Bergum Johanson et al. [5] reported that several researchers in Norway have highlighted a lack of connection between what is stated about digital knowledge and skills in international and national plans for teacher education, what is happening in school practice, and the preservice teachers' experiences of their learning of digital knowledge and skills in their teacher education.

Table 4. Preservice teachers' professional application of digital tools correlated with PDC and ATT.

Pearson corr.	PDC	ATT
AT	0.340**	0.363**

Note: ** Significant at the 0.01 level (2-tailed).
AT – application of tools in future.
PDC – Professional digital competence.
ATT – Professional attitude (attitude towards digital technology in education).

Table 5 presents the correlation between PDC and ATT which is significant, positive, above 0.5 and moderately positive (0.677). That shows the importance of both constructs for the future use of digital technology. Results can be tied to several research which suggest that teachers' attitudes and digital competence are two crucial factors influencing both in-service and preservice teachers' digital practices [28, 60] as cited in [33].

Table 5. Preservice teachers' PDC and ATT correlation.

Pearson corr.	ATT
PDC	0.677**

Note: **. Significant at the 0.01 level (2-tailed).
PDC – Professional digital competence.
ATT – Professional attitude (attitude towards digital technology in education).

Experiential learning for preservice teachers must be implemented, but it relies on how educational institutions think about it and how higher education teachers feel about DT. Furthermore, relatively few researchers have looked at preservice teachers' beliefs or attitudes regarding integrating DT into their classroom practices. [5, 40].

4.5 Linear Regression Results

Analysis with method Enter (Table 6) showed that the regression model explains 12.7% of the future use of digital tools in pedagogical work-AT construct, with predictors of PDC and ATT toward the use of digital tools. But there is still 87.3% of unexplained variance, which depends on other factors that are not included in the model. Regarding the explanatory power of the regression coefficients, we can summarize that in the case of Slovenia, the ATT regression coefficient is higher than PDC's regression coefficient.

The results also showed that Standardized Coefficients Beta are not significant. This could point to the relatively small sample and the fact that most data on variables and constructs are acceptably normally distributed.

Table 6. The explanatory power of the predictors.

Nation	R	Adjusted R^2	Sig.	Stand. Coeff. Beta	Stand. Coeff. Beta	Sig.
Slovenia	0.385	0.127	<0.001	0.244 (ATT)	0.175 (PDC)	>0.05

Note: Dependent Variable: AT – application of tools in future.
Independent variables: PDC – Professional digital competence; ATT – Professional attitude (attitude towards digital technology in education). Method Enter.

A second linear regression was performed using the method Stepwise (Table 7). The regression model explains 12.1% of the future use of digital tools in pedagogical work-AT construct, with predictors of PDC and ATT toward the use of digital tools. A Durbin–Watson test for autocorrelation in the residuals from a regression analysis is in the range of 1.5 to 2.5, which is a relatively normal and acceptable range without autocorrelation [75].

Table 7. The explanatory power of the predictors-Model1.

Nation	R	Adjusted R^2	Stand. Coeff. Beta	Stand. Coeff. Beta	Sig.	Durbin-Watson
Slovenia	0.363	0.121	0.363 (ATT)	- (Constant)	< 0,001	2.383

Note: Dependent Variable: AT – application of tools in future.
Independent variables: PDC – Professional digital competence; ATT – Professional attitude (attitude towards digital technology in education). Variance inflation factor (VIF) was calculated and is 1.845 for both independent variables ATT and PDC. Method Stepwise.

Survey results can be tied to the findings of many authors who found that preservice teachers' beliefs regarding the usefulness of technology and their computer self-efficacy had a direct impact on their intention to utilize technology in the classroom. In general, although preservice teachers at present are familiar with DT, they seem to have rather limited experience in taking advantage of DT in teaching and learning compared with in-service teachers [55, 64] as cited in [40]. Also, teachers' Internet experiences influence their intention to use digital technology. Their attitudes toward DT have been found to be affected by their knowledge and experience and skills of DT as well [67]. Teachers who feel confident in their computer ability also tend to have positive views on the use of DT in the classroom and vice-versa [10, 14], and [23]. Based on these studies, we can summarize that there is a probable correlation and even causality between teachers' DT experiences and their beliefs about the integration of digital technology [40, 50] which should be further investigated.

5 Conclusion

This study investigates preservice teachers' knowledge and skills, use of digital technology and attitudes towards technology in the educational setting.

To answer the research question: "How will the future use of digital technology in the educational environment be related to the knowledge, skills, and attitudes of preservice students?" The correlation analysis showed significant and relatively weak to moderate correlations between AT, PDC and ATT constructs of the Slovenian sample. Regression analysis showed that the regression model explains 12.7% (method Enter) and 12.1% (method Stepwise) of the future use of digital tools in pedagogical work-AT construct, with predictors of PDC and ATT toward the use of digital tools. But there is still more than 80% of the unexplained variance, which depends on other factors that are not included in the model. Finding and including the remaining associated factors in the regression model makes sense. The importance of PDC and ATT constructs is demonstrated by the current study as well as studies from other authors. The indicated purpose to employ digital technology in the future also demonstrates the readiness of preservice teachers to integrate technology into their pedagogical activity. For effective use of digital technology in pedagogical processes with primary school students, preservice teachers also require their own experience in addition to integrating it into study processes.

The research is constrained using a single measurement, a small sample size, and the involvement of just one Slovenian faculty of education. The use of focus groups after polling preservice teachers, regular measurements, and the inclusion of other significant components in the model all present opportunities for future research.

References

1. Aesaert, K., Vanderlinde, R., Tondeur, J., van Braak, J.: The content of educational technology curricula: a cross-curricular state of the art. Educ. Tech. Res. Dev. **61**(1), 131–151 (2013)
2. Ala-Mutka, K.: Mapping digital competence: towards a conceptual understanding. Publications Office of the European Union, Luxembourg (2011). https://doi.org/10.13140/RG.2.2.18046.00322
3. Allport, G.W.: Attitudes. In: Murchinson, C. (ed.) A Handbook of Social Psychology, pp. 789–844. Clark University Press, Worcester (1935)
4. Basaran, B., Yalman, M.: Examining preservice teachers' levels of self-efficacy perceptions regarding Web. Int. J. Inf. Learn. Technol. **37**(4), 153–178 (2020). https://doi.org/10.1108/IJILT-11-2019-0105
5. Bergum Johanson, L., Leming, T., Johannessen, B.-H., Solhaug, T.: Competence in digital interaction and communication—a study of first-year preservice teachers' competence in digital interaction and communication at the start of their teacher education. Teach. Educator (2022). https://doi.org/10.1080/08878730.2022.2122095
6. Blackwell, C.K., Lauricella, A.R., Wartella, E.: Factors influencing digital technology use in early childhood education. Comput. Educ. **77**, 82–90 (2014). https://doi.org/10.1016/j.compedu.2014.04.013

7. Brito, R., Silva, J., Patricia Dias, P.: From perception to action: the adoption and use of digital technologies by pre-school and primary school. Int. J. Innov. Res. Educ. Sci. **10**(2), 2349–5219 (2023)

8. Caena, F., Redecker, C.: Aligning teacher competence frameworks to 21st century challenges: the case for the European digital competence framework for educators (Digcompedu). Eur. J. Educ. **54**, 356–369 (2019). https://doi.org/10.1111/ejed.12345

9. Casillas, S., Cabezas, M., García, F.J.: Digital competence of early childhood education teachers: Attitude, knowledge and use of ICT. Eur. J. Teach. Educ. **43**(2), 210–223 (2020)

10. Celik, V., Yesilyurt, E.: Attitudes to technology, perceived computer self-efficacy and computer anxiety as predictors of computer supported education. Comput. Educ. **60**(1), 148–158 (2013)

11. Cortina, J.M.: What is coefficient alpha? An examination of theory and applications. J. Appl. Psychol. **78**(1), 98–104 (1993). https://doi.org/10.1037/0021-9010.78.1.98

12. Dumford, A.D., Miller, A.L.: Online learning in higher education: exploring advantages and disadvantages for engagement. J. Comput. High. Educ. **30**, 452–465 (2018). https://doi.org/10.1007/s12528-018-9179-z

13. Durndell, A., Haag, Z.: Computer self-efficacy, computer anxiety, attitudes towards the internet and reported experience with the internet, by gender, in an East European sample. Comput. Hum. Behav. **18**(5), 521–535 (2002)

14. Efe, H.A.: The relation between science student teachers' educational use of web 2.0 technologies and their computer self-efficacy. J. Baltic Sci. Educ. **14**(1), 142–154 (2015)

15. European Commission. Recommendation on key competences for lifelong learning. Council of 18 December 2006 on key competences for lifelong learning (2006). 2006/962/EC, L. 394/15. http://eur-lex.europa.eu/legal-content/en/TXT/?uri=CELEX:32006H0962&qid=1496720114366. Accessed 15 Nov 2021

16. European Council. Council Recommendation of 22 May 2018 on Key Competences for LifeLong Learning, 2018/C189/01. European Council, Brussels, Belgium (2018)

17. European Commission, Directorate-General for Education, Youth, Sport and Culture. Key competences for lifelong learning. Publications Office (2019). https://data.europa.eu/doi/10.2766/569540. Accessed 05 Apr 2021

18. Erstad, O., Kjällander, S., Järvelä, S.: Facing the challenges of 'digital competence' a Nordic agenda for curriculum development for the 21st century. Nordic J. Digit. Lit. **16**(2), 77–87 (2021). https://doi.org/10.18261/issn.1891-943x-2021-02-02

19. Joint Research Centre, Institute for Prospective Technological Studies, Ferrari, A.: Digital competence in practice: an analysis of frameworks. Publications Office, Seville (2012). https://data.europa.eu/doi/10.2791/82116

20. Galindo-Domínguez, H., José Bezanilla, M.: Digital competence in the training of pre-service teachers: perceptions of students in the degrees of early childhood education and primary education. J. Digit. Learn. Teach. Educ. **37**(4), 262–278 (2021). https://doi.org/10.1080/21532974.2021.1934757

21. Gudmundsdottir, G.B., Hatlevik, O.E.: Newly qualified teachers' professional digitalcompetence: implications for teacher education. Eur. J. Teach. Educ. **41**(2), 214–231 (2018). https://doi.org/10.1080/02619768.2017.1416085

22. Hämäläinen, R., Nissinen, K., Mannonen, J., Lämsä, J., Leino, K., Taajamo, M.: Understanding teaching professionals' digital competence: what do PIAAC and TALIS reveal about technology-related skills, attitudes, and knowledge? Comput. Hum. Behav. **117**, 106672 (2021). https://doi.org/10.1016/j.chb.2020.106672

23. Inan, F.A., Lowther, D.L., Ross, S.M., Strahl, D.: Pattern of classroom activities during students' use of computers: relations between instructional strategies and computer applications. Teach. Teach. Educ. **26**(3), 540–546 (2010)

24. Instefjord, E.J., Munthe, E.: Educating digitally competent teachers: a study of integration of professional digital competence in teacher education. Teach. Teach. Educ. **67**, 37–45 (2017). https://doi.org/10.1016/j.tate.2017.05.016

25. Janssen, J., Stoyanov, S., Ferrari, A., Punie, Y., Pannekeet, K., Sloep, P.: Experts' views on digital competence: commonalities and differences. Comput. Educ. **68**, 473–481 (2013). https://doi.org/10.1016/j.compedu.2013.06.008

26. Joiner, R., Gavin, J., Duffield, J., Brosnan, M., Crook, C., Durndell, A., et al.: Gender, internet identification, and internet anxiety: correlates of internet use. Cyberpsychol. Behav. **8**(4), 371–378 (2005)

27. Koehler, M., Mishra, P.: What is technological pedagogical content knowledge (TPACK)? Contemp. Issues Technol. Teach. Educ. **9**(1), 60–70 (2009)

28. Kucirkova, N., Rowsell, J., Falloon, G. (eds.): The Routledge International Handbook of Learning with Technology in Early Childhood. Routledge, London-New York (2019)

29. Kundu, A., Bej, T., Dey, K.N.: An empirical study on the correlation between teacher efficacy and ICT infrastructure. Int. J. Inf. Learn. Technol. **37**(4), 213–238 (2020). https://doi.org/10.1108/IJILT-04-2020-0050

30. Li, N., Kirkup, G.: Gender and cultural differences in Internet use: a study of China and the UK. Comput. Educ. **48**(2), 301–317 (2007)

31. Lund, A., Furberg, A., Bakken, J., Engelien, K.L.: What does professional digital competence mean in teacher education? Nordic J. Digit. Lit. **9**(4), 280–298 (2014). https://doi.org/10.18261/ISSN1891-943X-2014-04-04

32. Lund, A., Erikson, T., Teacher education as transformation: some lessons learned from a center for excellence in education. Acta Didactica Norge **10**(2), 53–72 (2016). https://www.journals.uio.no/index.php/adno/article/view/2483/2458

33. Luo, W., Berson, I.R., Berson, M.J., Li, H.: Are early childhood teachers ready for digital transformation of instruction in Mainland China? Child Youth Serv. Rev. **120**, 105718 (2021). https://doi.org/10.1016/j.childyouth.2020.105718

34. Madsen, S.S., Thorvaldsen, S., Sollied, S.: Are teacher students' deep learning and critical thinking at risk of being limited in digital learning environments? In: Hernandez-Serrano, M.J. (ed.) Teacher Education in the 21st Century – Emerging Skills for a Changing World. IntechOpen (2021)

35. Madsen, S., Thorvaldsen, S.: Implications of the imposed and extensive use of online education in an early childhood education program. Nordisk barnehageforskning **19**(1), 1–20 (2022). https://doi.org/10.23865/nbf.v19.258

36. Martin, A., Grudziecki, J.: DigEuLit: concepts and tools for digital literacy development. Innov. Teach. Learn. Inf. Comput. Sci. **5**(4), 249–267 (2006). https://doi.org/10.11120/ital.2006.05040249

37. Markauskaite, L.: Exploring the structure of trainee teachers' ICT literacy: the main components of, and relationships between, general cognitive and technical capabilities. Educ. Tech. Res. Dev. **55**(6), 547–572 (2007)

38. Martzoukou, K., Fulton, C., Kostagiolas, P., Lavranos, C.: A study of higher education students' self-perceived digital competences for learning and everyday life online participation. J. Doc. **76**(6), 1413–1458 (2020). https://doi.org/10.1108/JD-03-2020-0041

39. McGarr, O., McDonagh, A.: Digital competence in teacher education. Output 1 of the erasmus+ funded developing student teachers' digital competence (DICTE) project (2019). https://dicte.oslomet.no/. Accessed 19 May 2022

40. Mou, T.-Y., Kao, C.-P.: Online academic learning beliefs and strategies: a comparison of preservice and in-service early childhood teachers. Online Inf. Rev. **45**(1), 65–83 (2021). https://doi.org/10.1108/OIR-08-2019-0274

41. Ottenbreit-Leftwich, A.T., Glazewski, K.D., Newby, T.J., Ertmer, P.A.: Teacher value beliefs associated with using technology: addressing professional and student needs. Comput. Educ. **55**(3), 1321–1335 (2010). https://doi.org/10.1016/j.compedu.2010.06.002

42. Palak, D., Walls, R.T.: Teachers' beliefs and technology practices: a mixed-methods approach. J. Res. Technol. Educ. **41**, 417–441 (2009). https://doi.org/10.1080/15391523.2009.10782537

43. Peng, H.Y., Tsai, C.C., Wu, Y.T.: University students' self-efficacy and their attitudes toward the internet: the role of students' perceptions of the internet. Educ. Stud. **32**(1), 73–86 (2006)

44. Petko, D.: Teachers' pedagogical beliefs and their use of digital media in classrooms: Sharpening the focus of the 'will, skill, tool' model and integrating teachers' constructivist orientations. Comput. Educ. **58**(4), 1351–1359 (2012). https://doi.org/10.1016/j.compedu.2011.12.01

45. Prestridge, S.: The beliefs behind the teacher that influences their ICT practices. Comput. Educ. **58**(1), 449e458 (2012)

46. Røkenes, F.M., Krumsvik, R.J.: Prepared to teach ESL with ICT? A study of digitalcompetence in Norwegian teacher education. Comput. Educ. **97**, 1–20 (2016). https://doi.org/10.1016/j.compedu.2016.02.014

47. Sang, G., Valcke, M., Van Braak, J., Tondeur, J.: Student teachers' thinking processes and ICT integration: predictors of prospective teaching behaviours with educational technology. Comput. Educ. **54**(1), 103–112 (2010). https://doi.org/10.1016/j.compedu.2009.07.010

48. Scherer, R., Tondeur, J., Siddiq, F., Baran, E.: The importance of attitudes toward technology for preservice teachers' technological, pedagogical, and content knowledge: comparing structural equation modeling approaches. Comput. Hum. Behav. **80**, 67–80 (2018). https://doi.org/10.1016/j.chb.2017.11.003

49. Siddiq, F., Scherer, R., Tondeur, J.: Teachers' emphasis on developing students' digital information and communication skills (TEDDICS): a new construct in 21stcentury education. Comput. Educ. **92**, 1–14 (2016)

50. Sosa Díaz, M.J., Valverde Berrocoso, J.: Perfiles docentes en el contexto de la transformación digital de la escuela. Bordón. Rev. Pedag. **72**(1), 151–173 (2020). https://doi.org/10.13042/Bordon.2020.72965

51. Spante, M., Sofkova, H.S., Lundin, M., Algers, A.: Digital competence and digital literacy in higher education research: systematic review of concept use. Cogent Educ. **5**(1), 1519143 (2018). https://doi.org/10.1080/2331186X.2018.1519143

52. Štemberger, T., Čotar Konrad, S.: Attitudes towards using digital technologies in education as an important factor in developing digital competence: the case of Slovenian student teachers. Int. J. Emerg. Technol. Learn. **16**(14), 83–98 (2021). https://doi.org/10.3991/ijet.v16i14.22649

53. Svensson, M., Baelo, R.: Teacher students' perceptions of their digital competence. Procedia Soc. Behav. Sci. **180**, 1527–1534 (2015). https://doi.org/10.1016/j.sbspro.2015.02.302

54. Taherdoost, H.: Validity and reliability of the research instrument: how to test the validation of a questionnaire/survey in a research. Int. J. Acad. Res. Manage. **5**(3), 28–36 (2016). https://doi.org/10.2139/ssrn.3205040

55. Teo, T.: Examining the intention to use technology among pre-service teachers: an integration of the technology acceptance model and theory of planned behavior. Interact. Learn. Environ. **20**(1), 3–18 (2012)

56. Thorvaldsen, S., Madsen, S.S.: Perspectives on the tensions in teaching with technology in Norwegian teacher education analysed using Argyris and Schön's theory of action. Educ. Inf. Technol. **25**(6), 5281–5299 (2020). https://doi.org/10.1007/s10639-020-10221-4

57. Tømte, C., Olsen, D.S.: IKT og læring i høyere utdanning: kvalitativ undersøkelse om hvordan IKT påvirker læring i høyere utdanning [ICT and learning in higher education: Qualitative research on how ICT affects learning in higher education.]. NIFU (2013). http://hdl.handle.net/11250/280479

58. Tømte, C., Enochsson, A.-B., Buskqvist, U., Kårstein, A.: Educating online student teachers to master professional digital competence: the TPACK-framework goes online. Comput. Educ. **84**, 26–35 (2015). https://doi.org/10.1016/j.compedu.2015.01.005

59. Tondeur, J., Van Braak, J., Guoyuan, S., Voogt, J., Fisser, P., Ottenbreit-Leftwich, A.S.: Preparing student teachers to integrate ICT in classroom practice: a synthesis of qualitative evidence. Comput. Educ. **59**(1), 134–144 (2012). https://doi.org/10.1016/j.compedu.2011.10.009

60. Tondeur, J., Scherer, R., Siddiq, F., Baran, E.: Enhancing preservice teachers' technological pedagogical content knowledge (TPACK): a mixed-method study. Educ. Tech. Res. Dev. **68**(1), 319–343 (2020). https://doi.org/10.1007/s11423-019-09692-1

61. Tveiterås, N.C., Madsen, S.S.: From tools to complexity?—a systematic literature analysis of digital competence among preservice teachers in Norway. In: Tomczyk, Ł., Fedeli, L. (eds.) Digital Literacy for Teachers. Lecture Notes in Educational Technology, pp. 345-389. Springer, Singapore (2022). https://doi.org/10.1007/978-981-19-1738-7_18

62. Uerz, D., Volman, M., Kral, M.: Teacher educators' competences in fostering student teachers' proficiency in teaching and learning with technology: an overview of relevant research literature. Teach. Teach. Educ. **70**, 12–23 (2018). https://doi.org/10.1016/j.tate.2017.11.005

63. Urrea-Solano, M., Hernández-Amorós, M.J., Merma-Molina, G., Baena-Morales, S.: The learning of E- sustainability competences: a comparative study between future early childhood and primary school teachers. Educ. Sci. **11**, 644 (2021). https://doi.org/10.3390/educsci11 100644

64. Vartiainen, H., Liljeström, A., Enkenberg, J.: Design-oriented pedagogy for technology enhanced learning to cross over the borders between formal and informal environments. J. Univ. Comput. Sci. **18**(15), 2097–2119 (2012)

65. Vuorikari, R., Punie, Y., Carretero Gomez S., Van den Brande, G.: DigComp 2.0: the digital competence framework for citizens. Update phase 1: the conceptual reference model. Publication Office of the European Union, Luxembourg EUR 27948 EN (2016). doi:https://doi.org/10.2791/11517

66. Wu, Y.T., Tsai, C.C.: Developing an information commitment survey for assessing students' web information searching strategies and evaluative standards for web materials. Educ. Technol. Soc. **10**(2), 120–132 (2006)

67. Yukselturk, E., Altiok, S.: An investigation of the effects of programming with Scratch on the preservice IT teachers' self-efficacy perceptions and attitudes towards computer programming. Br. J. Edu. Technol. **48**(3), 789–801 (2017)

68. Yusop, F.D.: A dataset of factors that influence preservice teachers' intentions to use web 2.0 technologies in future teaching practices. Br. J. Educ. Technol. **46**(5), 1075–1080 (2015). https://doi.org/10.1111/bjet.12330

69. Demeshkant, N., Trusz, S., Potyrała, K.: Interrelationship between levels of digital competences and technological, pedagogical and content knowledge (TPACK): a preliminary study with Polish academic teachers. Technol. Pedag. Educ. (2022). https://doi.org/10.1080/147 5939X.2022.2092547

70. Lai, J.W., Bower, M.: How is the use of technology in education evaluated? A systematic review. Comput. Educ. **133**, 27–42 (2019). https://doi.org/10.1016/j.compedu.2019.01.010

71. Lai, J.W.M., Bower, M., De Nobile, J., Breyer, Y.: What should we evaluate when we use technology in education? J. Comput. Assist. Learn. **38**(3), 743–757 (2022). https://doi.org/10.1111/jcal.12645

72. Voogt, J., Fisser, P., Pareja Roblin, N., Tondeur, J., van Braak, J.: Technological pedagogical content knowledge: a review of the literature. J. Comput. Assist. Learn. **29**(2), 109–121 (2013)

73. Chesnut, S.R.: On the measurement of preservice teacher commitment: examining the relationship between four operational definitions and self-efficacy beliefs. Teach. Teach. Educ. **68**, 170–180 (2017). https://doi.org/10.1016/j.tate.2017.09.003

74. Cuhadar, C.: Investigation of pre-service teachers' levels of readiness to technology integration in education. Contemp. Educ. Technol. **9**(1), 61–75 (2018). https://doi.org/10.30935/cedtech/6211.www.scopus.com
75. Gujarati, D.N.: Basic Econometrics. McGraw-Hill, New York (1995)

Teacher's Skills for Application of Modern Technology in Educational Work

Nedeljko M. Milanović[1] , Jelena Maksimović[2]([✉]) ,
and Jelena Osmanović Zajić[1,2]

[1] Faculty of Education in Jagodina, University of Kragujevac, Milana Mijalkovića 14,
35000 Jagodina, Serbia
[2] Faculty of Philosophy, University of Niš, Ćirila i Metodija 2, 18101 Niš, Serbia
`jelena.maksimovic@filfak.ni.ac.rs`

Abstract. This topic is dealt with by numerous relevant researches, so we tried to contribute empirical research to the ICT aspect in teaching. The aim of this research is to determine and analyze teachers' views on their own skills for the application of modern technology in educational work. A descriptive method with surveying and scaling techniques was used, and a questionnaire instrument with an assessment scale was created based on numerous papers dealing with this topic. 157 respondents participated in this empirical research. The analyzed data show the following: teachers know the specifics and pedagogical importance of applying modern technology in educational work; teachers have acquired skills for using modern technology during education, professional development, private courses and through independent studies and research; teachers believe that institutions that prepare teachers and teaching staff should continue to pay attention to teaching subjects that concern modern technology in teaching; a significant number of teachers believe that they have developed ICT skills and have a desire for more frequent training in this area, where they stated what they would like to learn and apply in practice. This research opens up questions for practical answers in which all ways could be adequately answered to the teachers' proposals, whereby an interesting idea could be directed towards cooperation with the local community and the realization of these proposals.

Keywords: Teacher · Modern Technology · ICT · Skills · Competences

1 Introduction

Frequent and current topics and discussions in the sphere of modernization of formal education, for the most part, emphasize the importance of modern technology in educational work. Therefore, information and communication technologies have had a strong impact on education as well [24]. "Digitalization in education is a process that supports more successful learning, teaching and better organization of students' leisure time" [7]. In order to realize modern concepts of teaching and extracurricular activities, as well as the application of information and communication technologies in working with

© The Author(s), under exclusive license to Springer Nature Switzerland AG 2023
Ł. Tomczyk (Ed.): NMP 2022, CCIS 1916, pp. 59–68, 2023.
https://doi.org/10.1007/978-3-031-44581-1_5

students, the functions of teachers must include the aspect of digital competence. The role of teachers is to encourage an information and communication literate society, where they need to have developed competencies in this area [27]. Digital competences of teachers are one of the relevant factors that influence the quality of the teaching process today. Therefore, we can agree that "digital competencies enable teachers to work modern information and communication technologies, computers, databases, in order to achieve their goals in the context of their work" [4]. Research findings [23] show that teachers and educators do not have sufficiently developed information and communication competences, but that there is motivation to acquire knowledge in this sphere. The results of the following research show that as many as 58% of teachers have professional competencies in the field of information and communication technologies [26]. Research findings show that teacher competencies influence the introduction and application of information and communication technologies [2]. The obtained research results show that the ICT competence of teachers is significantly influenced by participation in seminars and trainings related to ICT [3]. The findings show that teachers apply ICT on a daily basis, but state that there are certain obstacles to adequate application [21]. "The most important complementary, interconnected, aspects of the process of knowledge construction in collaborative professional development of teachers through ICT are: conducting professional development of teachers, providing support and feedback, and formal recognition and applicability of what has been learned" [18]. Continuous training of teachers in the field of ICT is very important, because there are various possibilities for creating lessons [25]. Also, the research results show that teachers have a desire to improve further in the application of ICT in teaching [8]. As technology advances very quickly, it is necessary for teachers, as much as possible, to follow technological innovations, familiarize themselves with them and strive to improve educational work.

With our work, we will try to analyze the views of teachers about their own skills for the application of modern technology in educational work.

2 Methodological Framework of the Research

There are a number of dilemmas and divided opinions about whether the use of modern technology is overemphasized in the life of children and young people, we must admit that it is very difficult to imagine life today without the use of technology. Certainly, excessive use of modern technology among students, as well as ignorance about the use and management of technology and adequate behavior in the Internet world, are problems that the school, as a key institution, must pay attention to and, through various programs, educate students on how to use technology correctly and with quality. Therefore, the application of modern technology requires and implies good training and preparation of teachers in this sphere, while the focus of our research is based on the following problem: *how teachers evaluate their own skills regarding the application of modern technology in educational work?*

Therefore, the aim of the work is to determine and analyze the views of teachers about their own skills for the application of modern technology in educational work.

The research tasks are:

1. To examine whether teachers are familiar with the characteristics, specifics, and pedagogical importance of information and communication technologies in education;
2. To examine where teachers acquired skills for using modern technology in educational work;
3. To determine whether faculties that prepare teachers and teaching staff should pay attention to teaching subjects that concern the application of modern technology in educational work;
4. To examine the teachers' reasons why it is or is not necessary to pay attention to teaching subjects that concern the application of modern technology in teaching;
5. Whether, according to the teacher's opinion, the modern teacher as a reflective practitioner must possess ICT skills;
6. To examine whether teachers consider themselves to have well-developed ICT skills;
7. To examine whether teachers would like to have the possibility to expand their knowledge and skills more often in the sphere of application of modern technology;
8. To examine teachers what they would like to learn by improving in this area.

The sample consists of 157 teachers from the Republic of Serbia. From the sociodemographic variables, we took into account the teacher's gender and their level of education (Table 1).

Table 1. Sociodemographic characteristics of teachers

Variables	Frequencies (f)	Percentages (%)
Gender		
Female	93	59.2
Male	64	40.8
Level of education		
College	48	30.6
Master's degree	109	69.4

The descriptive method was used in the research, while the surveying and scaling techniques were used. Based on numerous papers dealing with this topic, an instrument (TSMT-2021) for this research was created. The questions in the instrument were of closed and open type. The research was conducted in 2021 electronically using a Google questionnaire. In addition to the basic information provided in the introductory part of the instrument, each question contained a clear explanation intended for the respondents. The collected data were processed in the program SPSS (Statistical Program for Social Science).

3   Research Results

Today, a lot is written and often spoken about the use of modern technology in educational work when it comes to ways of modernizing and innovating formal education. Based on the theoretical presentation and the set methodological framework, in this part we will present the results of the conducted empirical research.

In line with the much-discussed importance of using modern technology, the first research task was to examine whether teachers are familiar with the characteristics, specifics, and pedagogical importance of information and communication technologies in education. With this introductory question, we obtain the information needed for further consideration and consideration of this topic. 98.1% of teachers are familiar with the characteristics, specifics and pedagogical importance of modern technology in educational work, while only 1.9% of teachers answered that they are partially familiar. We can see that there were no negative answers to this question.

The modern era has enabled modern teachers to acquire and improve their skills in various ways, both through formal and informal education. Accordingly, as part of teachers' familiarity with the characteristics and importance of the application of modern technology in the process of upbringing and education, we wanted to examine where teachers acquired skills for the application of technology in educational work (Table 2).

Table 2. Answers of teachers where they acquired skills for the application of modern technology

	Frequencies (f)	Percentages (%)	Valid percentages
At education/study	89	56.7	56.7
During professional empowerment within the work	30	19.1	19.1
As part of a private course that I financed myself	20	12.7	12.7
I researched and studied on my own	18	11.5	11.5
In total:	157	100	100

The largest number of teachers acquired skills for using modern technology during their education at college. Accordingly, the next task was to determine whether teaching, pedagogic and other faculties that prepare teaching staff should pay attention to subjects related to the application of modern technology in educational work.

The largest number of teachers fully agree with the statement that faculties that prepare teachers should pay attention to teaching subjects about modern technology in educational work. Based on the contingency coefficient, which was calculated from the distribution shown in Table 3, the value of which is -0.59, at the level of statistical significance of $p = 0.00$, the results showed that there is a connection between professional education and teachers' opinions, whether they think that teacher, pedagogic and other faculties that prepare teachers or teaching staff should pay attention to subjects related to the application of information and communication technologies in teaching.

The research indicates that the correlation coefficient is statistically significant and negative ($C = -0.59$; $p = 0.00$). Therefore, the analyzed results show that teachers with a master's degree more often stated that they completely agree with the statement that teaching, pedagogic and other faculties that prepare teachers or teaching staff should pay attention to teaching subjects that concern the application of modern technologies in educational work.

Table 3. Correlation between level of education and teachers' opinions about paying attention to subjects during studies that concern modern technology in educational work

		Do you think that teaching, pedagogic and other faculties that prepare teaching staff should pay special attention to teaching subjects that concern modern technologies in educational work?				
		I totally agree	I agree	I'm undecided	I don't agree	in total
Level of education	College	17	24	6	1	48
	Master's degree	99	9	1	0	109
	in total	116	33	7	1	157

If the teachers answered positively (I completely agree and agree) that teaching, pedagogic and other faculties that prepare teachers and teaching staff should pay attention to subjects related to the application of information and communication technologies in teaching, they were required to state the reasons (Table 4).

Table 4. Teachers' reasons why attention should be paid to teaching subjects related to modern technology in educational work

	Frequencies (f)	Percentages (%)	Valid percentages
Educational work should follow the development of technology in order to modernize this dynamic process	53	33.8	33.8
We should work on training staff for the application of modern technology and enable them to improve their current knowledge and skills	96	61.1	61.1
They answered in the negative	8	5.1	5.1
In total:	157	100	100

The teachers who answered negatively (I'm undecided, I don't agree and I don't agree at all) stated that more attention should be paid to pedagogical, psychological and didactic-methodical subjects and content and stated that the application of modern technology burdens teachers in their daily work. Therefore, this group of respondents (5.1%) states that it is necessary to pay less attention to subjects related to the application of modern technology in educational work. Certainly, in addition to teaching subjects that concern the acquisition of knowledge and skills in the field of psychology, pedagogy, methodology and other relevant sciences and scientific disciplines that the respondents mentioned, future teachers and teachers of this higher education institution must also be prepared for the application of modern technology, because the time in which we live requires the use of this technology in the process of upbringing and education, good knowledge of information and communication technologies and well-developed digital competence of educators, teachers and teachers. The application of information and communication technologies has a unique pedagogical value that teachers and other practitioners should know and adequately use, apply, develop and initiate in educational work. Teachers list some of the practical proposals aimed at the dedication of the aspect of information and communication technologies in the school environment:

- Established forms of professional development that would be specifically directed towards the application of basic programs in teaching, as well as giving ideas to apply modern technologies in a more modern and interesting way for students. Some teachers argue that, for example, they have skills and knowledge in the PowerPoint program, but that they do not know how to make presentations and slides more interesting and interactive. They believe that it is not enough to just give instructions for making a presentation, but that it is also necessary to include practice in order to master other techniques in order to make the presentation more effective and of better quality for work;
- Formation of professional groups at the school level that would carry out internal training of teachers;
- ICT competent teachers can give lectures and trainings as well as accredited seminars that other practitioners could attend;
- Day of digital competences within the school, in which both students and teachers would participate and mutually exchange knowledge and skills in the field of using modern technology. One group of teachers states that younger and/or teachers with better digital and ICT skills and competences work and demonstrate to those teachers who are not sufficiently developed these skills.

These are just some of the teachers' suggestions on how it is possible to direct attention to technology and its application in the process of upbringing and education.

Whether, according to the teacher's opinion, the modern teacher as a reflective practitioner must possess ICT skills. Only 5.73% of teachers answer that they are determined to be responsible with the offered item, while all other teachers answer very positively, choosing the highest answer modality that reflects a positive attitude. Many authors believe that teachers' information and communication skills are an important condition for quality educational work, so the next task was to examine whether teachers consider themselves to have well-developed ICT skills. 91.1% of teachers believe that they have developed ICT skills, while 8.9% of teachers state that more training and seminars are needed to improve their ICT skills, while none of the surveyed teachers answered that they do not have developed these skills. This question is very broad and opens up opportunities for discussion from different perspectives. In accordance with that, the concept of a reflective practitioner teacher also implies constant improvement in various spheres [17] and the strengthening of skills and competences [16] so our task was to examine whether teachers would like to have the opportunity to expand their knowledge and skills more often in the field of applying modern technology in education and what they would like to learn. 83.4% of teachers state that they would like to have the opportunity to expand and improve their knowledge and skills in the field of information and communication technologies more often. A high percentage of teachers interested in further professional empowerment in the field of digitization show that it is necessary to provide teachers with different opportunities to see, learn and apply different techniques and create diverse content using modern technology. We asked the teachers (with an open-ended question in the instrument) to answer what they would like to learn additionally regarding the use of modern technology. They mostly stated that they have a desire to learn how to create interactive games for students to refresh or learn new material, to create their own website, a portal where they would post materials both for their students and for all those who want something new and interesting to learn, as well as creating an educational blog. Teachers point out that they would use their own websites, portals and blogs to post interesting materials that they cannot often devote enough time to during classes. Precisely, teaching approaches based on educational computer games or blended learning which use Moodle system have proven to be very effective approaches that encourage student engagement during the teaching process [5, 19]. A smaller number of teachers answered that creating educational games on computers would also help students who need additional help and support. The teachers' answers are very interesting and directed towards serious topics that would certainly improve their competences and improve the quality of teaching and learning.

4 Discussion

A special group of competencies for functioning in various aspects of life are represented by digital skills, which are extremely necessary for a modern individual [14]. Many researchers [9, 11, 12, 15, 22, 28] are interested in numerous topics concerning modern technology and aspects of educational work, looking at the skills and competencies of teachers in this sphere and generally considering this current topic from different perspectives. Therefore, guided by the received answers, we observe that the teachers' self-assessment of familiarity with the characteristics, specifics and pedagogical importance of modern technology within the process of upbringing and education is very positive, where mostly all respondents answered that they are familiar. There is a high percentage of teachers who choose the highest response modalities. Skills in this sphere were very much needed by teachers even during the pandemic, with the results [10] of the survey showing that 52.2% of teachers self-assessed that they partially possess digital competencies. The teachers answer that during schooling/faculty, during formal education, they most often acquired knowledge and skills in the ICT field, but there are also other ways in which they developed these skills. These results show a very positive practice of institutions. As technology is very close to students, it is necessary for teachers to directly and indirectly involve students, while providing them with pedagogical guidelines. Therefore, positive examples may include the involvement of students in the creation of teaching units with a focus on the application of information and communication technologies, whereby students would be actively engaged to search for materials and immediately acquire knowledge. So, teachers' awareness of various ways of working and their digital competence open the possibility for innovation in working with students. Certainly, the role of teachers is very important, because the magic wand is in their hands and they are leaders and practitioners who need to introduce innovations [13]. Also, "key research results indicate that teaching faculties at universities pay more attention to the use of digital technologies in teaching compared to non-teaching faculties that have teacher profiles" [20]. Teachers believe that higher education institutions that prepare teaching staff should pay more attention to the aspect of modern technology, while a small percentage of teachers who expressed negative agreement with this item believe that these higher education institutions should focus more attention on other contents.In everyday life, among certain people we can hear and see resistance to modern technology, but when we look at this topic through educational work, technology has many positive sides, whereby teachers should use it in the process of upbringing and education and guide children how to use it. Therefore, we are witnessing that we live in digitalized social circumstances, but as many authors point out, this group of skills is very relevant and a large percentage of teachers believe that they have well-developed these skills and have the desire to improve further, while they believe that the modern teacher as a reflective the practitioner should possess this group of skills. Research results show that the courses and trainings were very useful and help teachers in developing ICT skills, but certain difficulties were also observed [1]. The obtained results of the research show that the impact of the training had positive outcomes in terms of the development of teachers' digital competences [6]. The research results show a high readiness of teachers for training through various forms in the sphere of modern technology [12]. The findings of our research also show that the teachers presented and gave suggestions in the practical domain very widely and comprehensively. The teachers clearly stated what they would like to learn and in which segments they would like to develop their own skills, which is certainly an important factor in the further development of their skills. Therefore, the practical suggestions that the teachers mentioned can serve as a basis for creating programs aimed at professional development and strengthening of the pedagogical staff.

5   Conclusion

This topic is dealt with by numerous relevant researches, so we tried to contribute empirical research to the ICT aspect in teaching. With this article, we tried to present the results of empirical research that focused on teachers' assessment of their own skills for using modern technology in working with students. The obtained results indicate a positive attitude of teachers towards ICT skills, the improvement of skills in this area with clear proposals concerning the practical domain, which is one of the characteristics of a teacher who is a reflective practitioner. In this context, their proposals are numerous and concern better practice, the learning of typical students and students who need support, as well as promoting the work of teachers in various creative ways. Ideas for further consideration of this topic can be in the implementation of the mentioned suggestions of teachers through a partnership between teachers/schools and the local community. Parents of students who are involved in this field and/or have well-developed ICT skills themselves can be involved and transfer knowledge and skills to students and teachers, learning and collaborating with each other through ICT topics. Many authors agree that in order to modernize the teaching activity of the school, it is necessary to empower and enable teachers to improve and advance their previous knowledge and skills, because this is one of the conditions for the development of digital competence among students. Further research can focus on looking at sociodemographic characteristics and teachers' self-assessment of skills for applying modern technology in educational work.

References

1. Abuhmaid, A.: ICT training courses for teacher professional development in Jordan. Turkish Online J. Educ. Technol. TOJET **10**(4), 195–210 (2011). https://files.eric.ed.gov/fulltext/EJ9 46628.pdf
2. Bariu, T., Chun, X., Boudouaia, A.: Influence of teachers' competencies on ICT implementation in Kenyan universities. Educ. Res. Int. (2022). https://doi.org/10.1155/2022/137 0052
3. Dela Fuente, J.A.D., Biñas, L.C.: Teachers' competence in information and communications technology (ICT) as an educational tool in teaching: an empirical analysis for program intervention. J. Res. Educ. Sci. Technol. **5**(2), 61–76 (2020). https://www.academia.edu/456 34787/Teachers_Competence_in_Information_and_Communications_Technology_ICT_ as_an_Educational_Tool_in_Teaching_An_Empirical_Analysis_for_Program_Intervention
4. Dobrić, T., Đurić, I.: Uloga i značaj nastavnika u sistemu učenja na daljinu. Zbornik radova Filozofskog fakulteta u Prištini **51**(4), 387–406 (2021). https://doi.org/10.5937/ZRFFP51-31212
5. Dorocki, M., Radulović, B., Stojanović, M., Gajić, O.: Impact of blended learning approach on students' achievement and mental effort. Can. J. Phys. **100**(3), 193–199 (2022). https://doi.org/10.1139/cjp-2019-0602
6. ElSayary, A.: The impact of a professional upskilling training programme on developing teachers' digital competence. J. Comput. Assist. Learn. (2023). https://doi.org/10.1111/jcal.12788
7. Joksimović, B.: Položaj učenika u nastavi podržanoj savremenim tehnologijama. In: Editor, Vukotić, P. (eds). CONFERENCE 2015, *Sistem obrazovanja i digitalna kultura*, vol. 48, pp. 107–122. Podgoroca, Crnogorska Akademija nauka i umjetnosti (2015)
8. Kalogiannakis, M.: Training with ICT for ICT from the trainee's perspective. A local ICT teacher training experience. Educ. Inf. Technol, **15**(1), 3–17 (2010). https://doi.org/10.1007/s10639-008-9079-3
9. König, J., Heine, S., Jäger-Biela, D., Rothland, M.: ICT integration in teachers' lesson plans: a scoping review of empirical studies. Eur. J. Teacher Educ. 1–29 (2022). https://doi.org/10.1080/02619768.2022.2138323
10. Maksimović, J., Milanović, N., Osmanović Zajić, J.: (Samo)procena nastavnikao o kvalitetu onlajn nastave tokom pandemije kovid-19. In: Marinković, S. (prir. i ur.), Nauka, nastava, učenje u izmenjenom društvenom kontekstu, pp. 231–244. Užice: Pedagoški fakultet (2021)
11. Maksimović, J., Osmanović Zajić, J., Banđur, V.: Samoprocena osposobljenosti nastavnika za primenu obrazovno-računarskog softvera u vaspitno-obrazovnoj praksi. Inovacije u nastavi-časopis za savremenu nastavu **34**(2), 130–145 (2021). https://doi.org/10.5937/inovacije210 2130M

12. Maksimović, J., Osmanović, J., Mamutović, A.: Kompetencije nastavnika za medijsko obrazovanje. In medias res: časopis filozofije medija **9**(17), 2685–2707 (2020). https://doi.org/10.46640/imr.9.17.7

13. Milanović, N., Maksimović, J.: Primena radionica u prvom ciklusu obaveznog obrazovanja. Pedagoška stvarnost **67**(1), 41–51 (2021). https://doi.org/10.19090/ps.2021.1.41-51

14. Niyazova, A.Y., Chistyakov, A.A., Volosova, N.Y., Krokhina, J.A., Sokolova, N.L., Chirkina, S.E.: Evaluation of pre-service teachers' digital skills and ICT competencies in context of the demands of the 21st century. Online J. Commun. Media Technol. **13**(3), e202337 (2023). https://doi.org/10.30935/ojcmt/13355

15. Omar, M.K., Mohmad, I.R.: Pedagogy, ICT skills, and online teaching readiness as factors on digital competency practices among secondary school teachers in Malaysia. Asian J. Vocat. Educ. Humanit. **4**(1), 1–9 (2023). https://doi.org/10.53797/ajvah.v4i1.1.2023

16. Osmanović, J., Maksimović, J.: Kompetencije nastavnika istraživača refleksivne prakse. *Godišnjak za pedagogiju* **2**(1), 79–88 (2017). https://doi.org/10.46630/gped.1.2017.07

17. Osmanović Zajić, J., Maksimović, J., Milanović, N.: Personal and professional empowerment of reflective practitioner teachers during the COVID-19 pandemic. Prob. Educ. 21st Century **80**(2), 371–385 (2022). https://doi.org/10.33225/pec/22.80.371

18. Ovesni, K., Stanojević, J.J., Radović, V.: Informaciono-komunikacione tehnologije u usavršavanju nastavnika srednjih stručnih škola. *Inovacije u nastavi* **32**(3), 61–73 (2019). https://doi.org/10.5937/inovacije1903061O

19. Radulović, B.: Educational efficiency and students' involvement of teaching approach based on game-based student response system. J. Baltic Sci. Educ. **20**(3), 495–506 (2021). https://doi.org/10.33225/jbse/21.20.495

20. Ristić, M.: *Digitalne kompetencije nastavnika i saradnika*. Trendovi razvoja: Digitalizacija visokog obrazovanja. In: Katić, V. (eds). CONFERENCE 2018, Digitalizacija visokog obrazovanja, vol. 48, pp. 1–14. Fakultet tehničkih nauka, Univerzitet u Novom Sadu (2018)

21. Rogošić, S., Baranović, B., Šabić, J.: Primjena IKT-a u procesu učenja, poučavanja i vrednovanja u srednjim strukovnim školama: kvalitativna analiza. Metodički ogledi: časopis za filozofiju odgoja **28**(1), 63–88 (2021). https://doi.org/10.21464/mo.28.1.6

22. Rubach, C., Lazarides, R.: A systematic review of research examining teachers' competence-related beliefs about ICT use: frameworks and related measures. Bildung für eine digitale Zukunft, 189–230 (2023). https://doi.org/10.1007/978-3-658-37895-0_8

23. Soleša, D., Soleša-Grijak. Đ: Ict kompetencije učitelja i odgojitelja. Croatian J. Educ. **13**(2), 8–37 (2011). https://hrcak.srce.hr/76347

24. Sušić, M.: Informacijsko-komunikacijske kompetencije nastavnika kao zahtjev savremene nastave i koncepta cjeloživotnog učenja. Društvene i humanističke studije: časopis Filozofskog fakulteta u Tuzli **15**(15), 273–298 (2021). https://doi.org/10.51558/2490-3647.2021.6.2.273

25. Tedla, B.A.: Understanding the importance, impacts and barriers of ICT on teaching and learning in East African countries. Int. J. e-Learning Secur. (IJeLS) **2**(3/4), 199–207 (2012)

26. Vitanova, V., Atanasova-Pachemska, T., Iliev, D., Pachemska, S.: Factors affecting the development of ICT competencies of teachers in primary schools. Procedia-Soc. Behav. Sci. **191**, 1087–1094 (2015). https://doi.org/10.1016/j.sbspro.2015.04.344

27. Yieng, W.A., Daud, K.: ICT competencies among school teachers: a review of literature. J. Educ. Learn. (EduLearn) **12**(3), 376–381 (2018). https://doi.org/10.11591/edulearn.v12i3.5579

28. Džinović, M., Milanović, K., Mandić, D., Živković, L., Janković, N.: The use of ICT in social, environmental and scientific education in Serbian primary schools. In: Vasilj, M. (ed.) Pedagogy, Education and Instruction, Conference Proceedings, 3rd International Scientific Conference, pp. 852–862. Mostar (2016)

Using Digital Media in Speech Therapy

Anna Michniuk[1]([⊠]) [iD] and Maria Faściszewska[2] [iD]

[1] Adam Mickiewicz University, Międzychodzka st. 5, 61-712 Poznań, Poland
anna.michniuk@amu.edu.pl
[2] University of Gdańsk, Wita Stwosza st. 51, 80-308 Gdańsk, Poland
maria.fasciszewska@ug.edu.pl

Abstract. The COVID-19 pandemic has spread remote work, education, bureaucracy, and treatment. Also, it is observed that during the pandemic, speech therapy became more popular. This article reviews the possibilities of using digital media in speech therapy. It presents some research from different countries about the awareness of online speech therapy and its opportunities. The authors briefly describe three programs (*Kokolingo, mTalent Logopedia, Afast. Powiedz to!*), which could be helpful in logopedic practice. This is an introduction to their study about how Polish speech therapists use digital media during prevention, diagnosis, therapy, and consultations with patients' caregivers and other specialists. The results of this study will be published in 2024.

Keywords: Digital Media · Speech Therapy · Teletherapy

1   Introduction: Digital Media and Media Competencies

Media is a medium that lets information be transmitted. It could be divided into traditional media, like newspapers, and new or even new media, like the Internet [1–3]. Digital media are the effect of revolutionary progress in human information transmission and storage [4]. Digital media needs special tools and machines to be read, watched, listened to, created, or edited. Examples are computer games, mobile applications, online information services, podcasts, e-books, and augmented reality (AR). The last one is "an improved form of the actual physical world that is accomplished over the practice of digital visual sound, elements, and other sensual stimuli carried via engineering" [5].

To use digital media as effectively and safely as it is possible, users must have digital competencies. One of the most popular concepts describing the set of digital competencies desired by contemporary citizens is the idea of DigComp. It is a combination of knowledge, skills, and attitudes, which we should have to "… the confident, critical and responsible use of, and engagement with, digital technologies for learning, at work, and for participation in society" [6]. The first version of DigComp was published in 2013. Now (from March 2022), we have the fourth iteration of the framework. Updating this idea results from the changes and development of the digital environment. It provides more than 250 new examples of knowledge, skills, and attitudes that help citizens engage

Ł. Tomczyk (Ed.): NMP 2022, CCIS 1916, pp. 69–82, 2023.
https://doi.org/10.1007/978-3-031-44581-1_6

confidently, critically, and safely with digital technologies and new and emerging ones, such as systems driven by artificial intelligence (AI).

Digital competencies are a part of the Key Competence Framework for Lifelong Learning and are interlinked with other competencies like 1) science, technology, engineering, and mathematical; 2) languages, 3) literacy, cultural awareness, and expression; 4) entrepreneurship; 5) civic competence, 6) personal, social, and learning to learn. These competencies are essential for citizens' fulfillment, a healthy and sustainable lifestyle, employability, active citizenship, and social inclusion [7]. They could make our lives more effective because of their multidimensionality and rapidly changing. All generations should be able to experience using media in different ways, also in education and therapy. Having digital competencies let people learn new things, find solutions for their various problems, cure for the disease they face, and also consult with specialists from around the world. It is meaningful in every field. Moreover, as adults, we can be good models for young generations and show them how to use new technology smartly.

2   Online Speech Therapy vs. The COVID-19 Pandemic

In the literature, we can find many terms connected with telemedicine and online therapy, like, for example, *digital practice* [8], *teletherapy* [9], *online speech therapy* [10], *online counseling* [11], and *telepractice* [12]. The thing that connects all of these terms is that they are carried out remotely, via more simple media, such as the telephone, or more advanced, such as the Internet. The article will use the terms teletherapy, online speech therapy, and remote speech therapy interchangeably. All of these terms we understand as remote work with the patient using the Internet and devices that allow people to use it (i.e., a computer, tablet, smartphone).

Teletherapy can be carried out in three forms: 1) synchronous, 2) asynchronous, and 3) hybrid. The first is conducted in real-time with audio and video. Examples could be group meetings and consultations between a patient/caregiver and a therapist. The second one carries on at different times. A therapist and a patient participate in the exchange of information at a time convenient for them. Some examples are transmitting voice clips, audiological testing results, and sending educational materials (photos, graphics, records, movies, and messages). The last one, hybrid, combines synchronous and asynchronous working with patients. It could include in-person meetings with the patient [13].

Online practice is a relatively new thing in the world of speech therapy. In the 2020 systematic review conducted by K. Weidner K. and J. Lowman in Perspectives, ASHA examined the literature on adult telepractice services from 2014 to 2019, concluding that there is evidence to support the continued use of adult speech therapy telepractice. Still, more research is needed on its effectiveness [14].

The literature suggests that the use and implementation of telepractice in speech therapy in different countries varies widely. In the USA in 2002, a study developed by ASHA reported that only 11% of respondents (audiologists and speech therapists) delivered telepractice services, and 43% expressed interest in using it in the future [15]. Initially, telepractice was carried on by audio sessions via telephone calls, but videoconferencing became increasingly used with the development of technology. In 2016, a study by ASHA showed that 64% of the 476 respondents were already using telepractice to deliver services [16].

The use of digital media by speech therapists became increasingly popular during the COVID-19 pandemic because of the lockdown when the opportunities to meet with specialists were limited. The SLT profession responded with innovation and used telepractice to maintain the delivery of their services to ensure continuity and effective care for the patient.

Only 3% of healthcare professionals in Ireland used video consultations with patients before the COVID-19 pandemic. Moreover, the online survey of speech-language therapists (SLTs) in Ireland by E. Farren, D. Quigley, and Y. Lynch in 2021[17] carried out to investigate their perceptions of telepractice found that more than half of participants (173) declared teleworking (51%, N = 89) while 49% did not (N = 84). The results of the research conducted by Anna Karowicz in July 2020 (computer-assisted web interview) show that 85,5% of respondents - Polish speech therapists (N = 340) working online during lockdown.14,5% of them stop working on those days, and 1,7% (only six respondents) still work in the office. Before the COVID-19 pandemic, 326 surveyed speech therapists (95.9%) had not previously tried to use distance therapy techniques [18].

The introduction of using digital technology during the COVID-19 pandemic lockdown took work and effort. People needed to prepare for this. The study (N = 16) conducted by E. Y. L. Kwok, J. Chiu, P. Rosenbaum, B. J. Cunningham in Canada with sixteen frontline speech-language pathologists and assistants from one publicly funded program in Ontario showed six stages of using digital technology in therapy during the COVID-19 pandemic: shocking abrupt lockdown; weeks of uncertainty; telepractice (treatment using a video calling app) emerged as an option; preparation for telepractice; telepractice trials; and finally, full implementation of telepractice. Moreover, focus group discussions (N = 8) show that the specialists felt their transition to online therapy was a success, but it needs time to consider telepractice a sustainable practice [19].

This scheme was observed in many countries and fields. For example, the Polish education system described three stages of online education. The first one, from March to June 2020, was full of confusion, uncertainty, attempts to wait out, teaching in different ways, and using other media. The second stage started in September 2020 and, in the beginning, was focused on testing students and teaching as many topics as possible offline. At the end of this stage (December 2020), schools understood that they must be prepared for online learning in the coming months. In the last stage, it was the time of the "new normal". Everything was the same, like in real school, but it was online [20]. Because in Poland, speech therapy is strongly connected with schools (speech therapists work primarily in schools and psychological and pedagogical counseling centers), it could be said that the problem with having online therapy has similar stages.

The COVID-19 pandemic gave the opportunity of increasing interest in online speech therapy. But many studies still need to be conducted to check the effectiveness and determine the principles of using digital media in therapy and logopedic practice with different, specific disorders.

3   Issues and Concerns About Using Digital Media During Speech Therapy

Digital media can be used in speech therapy for different disorders. The study, conducted among 173 SLTs in Ireland using an online survey to explore the use of telepractice, showed that the most common groups of telepractice patients were children with speech disorders (14%, n = 33), children with developmental language disorders (DLD) (14%, n = 33), autism spectrum disorder (10%, n = 23) and adults with dysphagia (11%, n = 27) [17]. In the research conducted by M. Szurek in Poland before COVID-19 [21] (84%, 32 responders) believed that using media in speech therapy is helpful. However, respondents used media on average once every three meetings (84%, 32 people) and for 5–10 min during a 45–60-min therapy session.

However, there are certain limitations to online speech therapy. Some disorders, such as Orofacial Myofunctional Disorders, are challenging to conduct online. This is because, in the treatment, SLT uses massages, spatulas, vibrators, etc., to help normalize facial and lip structures. This may soon change, as products such as Smart Palate Speech Therapy are being developed, where a custom-made SmartPalate and a computer interface allow lip and tongue movements to be monitored in real-time [22]. On the other hand, patients will need specialized equipment or software to benefit from such therapy. This may increase the overall cost of treatment and thus may only be available to some patients.

Moreover, in Poland, researchers at the Silesian University of Technology (Department of Informatics and Medical Devices Faculty of Biomedical Engineering) and the University of Silesia in Katowice (Faculty of Humanities, Institute of Linguistics) are working on something different. They would like to produce a tool to analyze the work of facial and head muscles. It could help diagnose how patients breathe, swallow, and speak [23].

One of the opportunities for using digital media during speech therapy is working in a hybrid form. In this case, the important thing is that the therapist should prepare a plan and the rules of the procedure to achieve the goal [13]. This form of therapy will be good, especially for people with severe communication difficulties and complex physical or cognitive disabilities who cannot consistently participate in stationary therapy on their own or find it more exhausting. The results of the pilot study prepared by T. Chaudhary, A. Kanodia, H. Verma, H.A. Sigh, A.K. Mishra, and K. Sikka in India compare online teletherapy with face-to-face therapy for speech-language disorders (N = 20, five patients in each category, like disorders of fluency, voice, adult neurogenic, and swallowing) show a positive correlation between face-to-face therapy and teletherapy for progress made by the participant and overall satisfaction parameters. Moreover, all participants felt that teletherapy was a more convenient, cheaper, and comfortable method (rated 4 or 5) of delivering services, and most of them agreed that they would use or recommend having online speech therapy (except one, who had terrible Internet connection during therapy sessions) [24]. But on the other hand, too much emphasis on digital media or only using digital media in therapy may reduce the opportunities for personal interaction between therapist and patient.

The next issue connected with using digital media by speech therapists is the effort to provide the apps, special electronic devices, Internet access to the office, and personal competencies/personalities of the therapists. The lack of knowledge about the possibilities of using digital media during therapy, technology failures, problems with the Internet connection, and loss of vision and sound can lead to session interruptions or altogether terminate a session. It can affect therapy progress and cause frustration for the patient and therapist [8, 9, 24]. Also, various personality traits of therapists could have great relevance for using digital resources in speech and language therapy. But in B. Szabó, S. Dirks, and A.L. Scherger's research [25], the number of interviews was deficient (N = 5), so it should be done again with a bigger group. In a study conducted by R. Patel, E. Loraine, and M. Gréaux, with a broader study group, UK pediatric SLTs (N = 424) reported similar factors such as specialized training (27%), funding for workplace devices (22%), and supportive leadership (19%) were most likely to have facilitated sustained digital practice – helping respondents to use technology during a pandemic. The results also indicate a significant increase in frequency, convenience, and confidence associated with SLTs' use of digital practice during COVID-19 compared to before the pandemic [8].

Conducting speech therapy online is also hindered by the many distractions and interruptions at the patient's therapy location, such as home or daycare. These distractions and interruptions can disorganize or even stop the therapy session and reduce the effectiveness of the therapy. It is also a significant challenge for therapists to ensure the therapy process's safety and protect sensitive patient information. These things are presented in more than just studies connected with online speech therapy. It also could be found in different areas, like using digital technology by teachers in the teaching-learning process [26]. So it is more like a general concern, not only linked to speech therapy with digital media.

Another issue with using digital media during speech therapy is that electronic media primarily engage two sensory organs, the eyes, and ears, minimally the sense of touch as a click. What needs to be added here is the polysensory and multidimensional engagement in exploring the world when interacting with natural objects [27], which are fundamental to treating speech disorders such as apraxia or dyspraxia. Using telepractice with children or other patients, a family member, supported and guided by the SLT, is required during sessions. It is an opportunity to be more involved in a child's therapy sessions and meet with the therapist. The second benefit of therapy at home is the opportunity to meet with a therapist before or after each session.

The problem with using digital media by speech therapists is also connected with fear (in therapists and parents/caregivers) of children's excessive use of digital media. Today, digital media, including tablets and smartphones, have become essential devices in almost all homes. After all, the proper development of children depends on direct contact with sensitive, physically present people and engagement with the real world through all the senses. With this, parents and therapists face various questions: Should digital media be used in therapy? If so, how much time in therapy should children use digital media? Will the use of media affect the relationship between therapist and child? Will the use of media increase/maintain the child's motivation to work? From what age can technology be used in therapy? [28].

But on the other hand, using digital media in therapy allows patients to learn how to use technology in a productive way and purpose, which relates to developing their media competencies. Moreover, it could motivate them to continue working.

Technology helps to communicate with people with mobility and physical disabilities. It is mainly based on touchscreen speech and eye-tracking technology (a device for measuring eye positions and eye movement, and points of gaze to see where a person is looking on a computer screen). The eye-tracking technology system is C-Eye, developed for patients who cannot communicate due to brain damage [29]. Assistive technology and communication solutions are something that also helps people, for example, with Rett syndrome [30], in need of communication and development. It is one of the best examples, showing the importance of development and technology for improving the quality of human life.

Summing up, using digital media in speech therapy has advantages and disadvantages. Some of the benefits are: 1) saving time on the way to and from therapy, 2) the opportunity to consult with specialists from around the world, 3) the opportunity of recording sessions, 4) reducing stress before meeting someone you know in the waiting room, 5) the opportunity, that a session can take place everywhere and every time, 6) experiencing the effectiveness of using new technology, 7) the chance to develop media competencies, which are very important in the modern world. On the other hand, there are some disadvantages which could be: 1) the need for having devices, the Internet, and special programs or apps, 2) having functional digital skills, 3) ensuring security and privacy, 4) exposure to numerous distractions and disruptors, e.g., at home, 5) limited opportunities for hands-on and polysensory learning, 6) lack of psychical interaction and feedback. The use of digital media in speech therapy should be adequate to the patient's capabilities and difficulties. However, speech therapists should follow technological innovations and allow patients to try different types of therapy.

4   Digital Media in Speech Therapy - Examples

Over the years, numerous applications and computer programs have been developed. They have different functionalities and are tools that adopt game-based scenarios and mechanics to increase motivation and treatment adherence. Here are three examples of programs and applications which can be helpful for children with articulation or other disorders connected with speaking and listening (*Kokolingo* and *mTalent* series) and people with aphasia (*Afast. Powiedz to!*). These programs were chosen for different reasons. First, these programs can support speech therapy with varying speech disorders, showing their diversity. Second is that they are developed by specialists, like pedagogues, speech therapists, and ITC specialists. The other reasons are: 1) *Kokolingo* is a program that uses not only in Poland. It was created in Croatia. It also has an English version, so it is international; 2) *mTalent Logopedia* is a part of one of the most extensive educational and therapeutic series for children. The other details are, for example, Auditory Perception, Visual Perception, and Central Auditory Processing Disorders, and the Polish Dyslexia Association recommends them. Unfortunately, there is no research on the effectiveness of using these specific programs. This is the field that should be thoroughly examined. Examples from different areas, like cognitive, logical thinking, concentration, hand-eye coordination, and achieving goals by using some computer games, give hope that these programs could be helpful because they are something like computer games; 3) *Afast.Powiedz to!* is free to use, and it should be promoted in Poland and the world because it is a comprehensive proposition, supporting work with patients with various types of aphasia.

4.1 Kokolingo

Kokolingo is a program created for preschool and elementary school children (from 4 to 10 years old) with articulation or phonological speech sound disorders. It could be used online on computers, laptops, tablets, and smartphones. *Kokolingo* has got a lot (more than 5000! [31]) of different screens with exercises, like, for example, single syllable speech sound exercises (for example, moving mouth correctly to pronounce single syllable sounds), mouth and tongue exercises (tongue in cheek, feathers blowing, using the tongue to count teeth), differentiation of sounds, correctly articulation, memory exercises, looking for the correct syllables, reading, and so on. Before a patient uses a program, it is recommended to consult a speech therapist, who makes an accurate diagnosis and decides which sound should be trained first. The consultation is also essential because it should exclude other problems and factors that cause wrong articulation.

The authors of this program recommend using it every day for at least 30 min. If the child has better attention, it could be used longer and more frequently. They also suggest that *Kokolingo* should be used with adult supervision because, in some exercises, an adult (parent, caregiver, speech therapist) decides the success of each speech attempt. Moreover, in this way, a child can have an additional opportunity to have fun with adults and experience the educational side of new technology [32].

One of the most exciting facts about Kokolingo is that this program is not only used in one country for one language. Pedagogues, speech therapists, and ITC specialists initially invented it in Croatia. They are united in E-Glass d o. o. founded in July 2009 by a group of scientists from the Faculty of Engineering, University of Rijeka. The author of the Polish version is Katarzyna Łuszczak from ATABI company, a pedagogue and speech therapist interested in Augmentative and Alternative Communication. This program also has an English (American & British) version. The characters in each version are the same – a pirate (in the Polish – Kazik) and a parrot named Koko. The Pirate is like a guide in the world of Kokolingo. He explains exercises and rules and teaches children how to do breathing exercises and produce sounds. Koko motivates children to do the exercises by giving very nice comments, like "Well done!" or "Good job!". During each activity, the users collect some precious, like diamonds, coins, rubies, etc. If they collect enough valuables, it will be an opportunity to visit Koko's shop and buy unique items for her, such as hats, glasses, skirts, and more. The more exercises are done, the more things can be purchased at the shop. The Demo English version is here: https://app.us.kokolingo.com/ [33].

4.2 Afast. Powiedz to!

Afast. Powiedz to! is a free online platform that helps people with aphasia. Aphasia is often a result of a stroke or breakdown of the two-way translation that establishes a correspondence between thoughts and language. A person with aphasia has problems with formulating language or/and an inability to comprehend language [34]. This program was created to help people with speech therapy difficulties because of their living place. People can use it on their computers or tablets. Installation is not required. In the application, there are many exercises (more than one thousand orders), for example: naming objects, building sentences, recognizing colors, recognizing names of the days of the week, or counting.

The authors prepared three rehabilitation programs: 1) for people with sensory aphasia, 2) for people with motor aphasia, and 3) for people with conduction aphasia. Before using the platform, a patient should consult with a specialist. Having an account helps the patient to choose: 1) the right program of therapy, 2) the level of it, and also 3) the right speed of therapy. Moreover, the patient can add their photos (like, for example, favorite/good know items or places) to the platform, which could be helpful in the therapy because of the strong emotional meaning for them. This program was made in cooperation with three institutions: Salus Publica Foundation, Technopark Gliwice, and Jagiellonian University [35].

It was created by Michał Kręcichwost and other scientists (like speech therapists and programmers) for his mother, who had a stroke. She was one of the first people who got the opportunity of using the program. She lived in a small village and had limited access to specialist help. The program was also used, for example, by Krzysztof Globisz, a famous Polish actor, after he had a stroke. According to the creators of the program, Globisz liked the program. Conversations with the actor and his wife allowed the creators to pay attention to some critical issues related to motivation to use this kind of program. Moreover, the authors see some possibilities for using this program with patients with dementia [36].

Currently (as of August 2, 2023), the program has over 85,000 users (speech therapists, carers, and patients). Unfortunately, we were unable to obtain feedback from its users[1]. The program is available here: https://afast.pl/.

4.3 mTalent Series

mTalent series [37] is one the newest and wealthiest therapeutic and educational sets of computer programs on the Polish market to support therapists, speech therapists, educators, and teachers in working with children with special educational and developmental needs. They can be used for various purposes and activities, but primarily for prevention, therapy, and stimulation of preschool and school-aged children during didactic and equalization, remedial, speech therapy, and corrective-compensation classes.

The first publications of the *mTalent* series appeared on the Polish educational and therapeutic market in 2018. It was *Zajęcia Logopedyczne (Speech Therapy)*, created by Monika Zielińska-Miętkiewicz (speech therapist, linguist) and expert Professor Małgorzata Cackowska. This part was divided into two boxes. The first one is prepared to work on 12 sounds (SZ, Ż, CZ, DŻ, S, Z, C, D, Ś, Ź, Ć, DŹ, R, L). The second one is based on T, D, N, K, G, H, B, P, W, F, and voiceless sounds [38]. Children can practice pronouncing sounds in isolation, logotoms, syllables, sentences, and texts. Speech therapists can also print directly from the program worksheets for children. Both program

---

[1] Data provided by the developers of the program.

parts included extra devices like a microphone, headphones, and loudspeakers. More-over, speech therapists can have a free training program, and (after buying the set) they get the methodological guide and instructions for creating their resources. The demo version is available here: https://www.mauthor.com/present/6138183699136512.

There is also a part for teenagers and adults - *Zajęcia logopedyczne dla dzieci i dorosłych*. It included exercises for the R sound, sonority-soundlessness, prosodic fea-tures of speech, vowels, and lengthening of the expiratory phases. According to the authors, it does not contain infantile graphics. It has almost 1,000 interactive screens and a collection of printable worksheets [39].

The programs in the *mTalent* series were created by scientists and experienced SLTs, psychologists, linguists' practitioners [40], and programmers, making the proposed exercises in line with the latest scientific knowledge and enjoyable for children.

The series includes 21 products, such as Auditory Perception, Visual Perception, Speech Therapy Activities, Writing Difficulties, Spelling, Reading with Syllables, Autism, etc. In total, there are more than 20,000 interactive screens. Each program contains about 500 interactive programs and about 100 printable worksheets. A wide range of exercises appears on the interactive screens, such as listening to and recording your version of the language material, connecting items, categorizing comprehension, spotting differences, memory games, connecting the dots, interactive puzzles, picture sudoku, as well as exercises designed for working with groups of children (interactive board games, interactive whiteboard games) and text exercises such as filling in gaps in funny rhymes, completing illustrations, creativity exercises, drawing activities and much.

At www.mTalent.pl, demo exercises allow users to get acquainted with the *mTalent* series for free. Learnetic, the developer of the *mTalent* series, has also created free tools *Logo test* for screening diagnoses for articulation, phoneme hearing disorders, stuttering risk assessment (Polish, Russian, Ukrainian, English), etc. The free version is here: Logotest.pl, https://www.logotest.pl.

The mTalent series is based on HTML5 technology so that the therapist can work on a computer, laptop, tablet, whiteboard and multimedia screen, and even a smartphone, even without Internet access.

In conclusion, all these three programs can be helpful in speech therapy, but in different disorders. *Afast. Powiedz to! i*s dedicated to adult people after strokes, with aphasia. m*Talent. Zajęcia logopedyczne* and *Kokolingo* are generally prepared for chil-dren, especially with articulation problems. The products' strengths are the technical side, namely a straightforward, intuitive interface, high usability, and functionality. In the case of mTalent and Kokolingo, some animations and graphics motivate children to keep going.

More colorful are these, which are prepared for children. Moreover, these pro-grams assumed similar patient activities, like cognitive and motor. They have some exercises that help produce the right sounds and name objects/verbs. *mTalent* also has some activities which can help practice hands work.

One of the disadvantages of *Kokolingo* and *mTalent* programs is that they are not free to use. Users can try demo versions and get to know if this kind of speech therapy practice is comfortable for them and their patients. After using the demo, it is possible to buy the whole program. *Afast. Powiedz To!* is free to use. The user needs to log in.

These programs are prepared mainly for the therapist's work with the child or adult. Using them in group work is difficult, but it is not impossible. If the speech therapist has a giant tablet, interactive screen/whiteboard, or online therapy, it could be an excellent modification of practicing. One of the programs has some ideas for group working - it is *mTalent*.

5 Summary

Digital media can be used in synchronous, asynchronous, and hybrid speech therapy. There is a variety of possibilities: 1) chats, videoconferences, and e-mails can be used to communicate with patients; 2) electronic games/programs and mobile apps can be used to motivate patients and keep their attention; 3) earlier prepared videos, recordings, graphics, interactive worksheets can be used as homework, some extra exercises to achieve therapeutic goals faster. Moreover, it gives patients a chance to practice more, even if the therapist is unavailable (because of diseases, long distance to the speech therapist's office, etc.). Digital media are a real opportunity for patients with articulation, speech sound disorders, aphasia, or other problems. There is a growing evidence base to support telepractice in many areas of SLT [17, 41].

The use of digital media increased during the COVID-19 pandemic. Many speech therapists started online sessions to continue therapy, not to lose their progress. Because of the lockdown, they were forced to look for new solutions to practice their profession. So they began to use online work more intensively, as well as various computer programs/games and applications. Unfortunately, there is not enough research that shows the effectiveness of using digital media in speech therapy. But, focusing on using digital media like some unique apps or computer programs used in other fields of education and therapy, it can be assumed that these kinds of tools will also be effective in the case of speech therapy. Moreover, online video conferences let speech therapists discuss problems or difficulties with specialists worldwide, always and everywhere.

There are few specific studies about the effectiveness of using different digital media during speech therapy. We do not know if it could be helpful to finish therapy faster because there are many individual factors like, for example, media competencies, willingness to repeat exercises, appropriate adjustment of the programs/applications, devices available to the patient out of therapeutic sessions, etc. The research carried out on Romanian speech therapists (N = 244) in 2021 by Viorel Aghena and Doru-Vlad Popovici showed that the effectiveness of online speech therapy is lower due to a lack of direct interaction. Still, in this way, cooperation with the family of the patients is better. 66% of speech therapists rated the collaboration with family as good and very good, 29.5% as satisfactory and only 4.5% as poor, so it could be said that online speech therapy can increase the involvement of the patient's family in the therapy process [42].

There is a high probability that computer programs and applications created in the form of electronic games can help increase the effectiveness of speech therapy. They are attractive, motivate users to achieve goals attractively, and keep them focused. Patients should repeat many things to achieve goals, like in a game. Moreover, repetitions in speech therapy are significant. The research shows that electronic games are a good option in teaching-learning and even psychotherapy [43]. In their study, L. Aghlara and N. H. Tamjid (2011) indicated that children learning vocabulary by playing digital games are more motivated than those taught through traditional methods [44]. Still, their effectiveness depends mainly on teachers [45]. The effectiveness will be higher if speech therapists want or know how to use digital media during speech therapy.

As A. Vaezipour, J. Campbell, D. Theodoros, and T. Russel (2020) [46] point out, there is a need to develop apps that complement traditional speech therapy, but ones that are designed and developed by a multidisciplinary team of experts, including speech pathologists, human-computer interaction experts, user experience designers, and app developers, to ensure a balance between clinically relevant content and a positive user experience. Finally, randomized, controlled trials of adequate power are needed to evaluate the effectiveness of apps developed for long-term use in treating communication disorders. This article presents three programs that help in speech therapy. Unfortunately, there is not enough research that shows the effectiveness of using these programs during speech therapy.

Now we are researching in what ways, what kind of media and devices, and how often Polish speech therapists use them. We also intend to explore what facilitators are important in working with a patient remotely (e.g., ICT infrastructure, professional development, etc.) and whether there are gaps in the ability of SLTs to access facilitators. In addition, we plan to describe and assess the preparation of future SLTs for conducting therapy using digital media during university studies. After that, we would like to do other research focused on specific programs and tools to analyze their effectiveness and ease of use and collect independent opinions from therapists, patients, and caregivers. Our activities will contribute to determining the effectiveness of the use of digital media in speech therapy.

Another interesting problem is connected with artificial intelligence during speech therapy. We could generate perfect articulation that would be a model for patients, or it could be possible to make robots that make unique face, head, and shoulder massages as a part of logopedic therapy. Some researchers have already thought and tried using Virtual Reality (VR), Artificial Intelligence (AI), and 3D game environments for aphasia patients [47, 48]. This has some challenges but also gives some new opportunities. The future will undoubtedly bring the necessity and the possibility of implementing many exciting solutions. Therefore, therapists should not fear new technologies but treat them as complements and new opportunities.

References

1. Goban-Klas, T.: Cywilizacja medialna. Geneza, ewolucja, eksplozja. WSiP, Warsaw (2005)
2. Levinson, P.: New Media, 2nd edn. Penguin Academics, London (2012)
3. Manovich, L.: The Language of New Media. The MIT Press, Cambridge (2001)
4. Hongbo, Y.: The definition, fulfillment and development of digital media. Advances in Economics. Business and Management Research, vol. 651, pp. 138–141 (2022). https://doi.org/10.2991/aebmr.k.220404.026
5. Bhosale, S., Patil, R.B., Karjulkar, J.: Augmented Reality, Contemporary Research in India, Special issue, 57–62 (2021)

6. Vuorikari, R., Kluzer, S., Punie, Y.: DigComp 2.2: The Digital Competence Framework for Citizens - With New Examples of Knowledge, Skills, and Attitudes. Publications Office of the European Union, Luxembourg (2022)
7. European Council Recommendation on Key Competences for Life-long Learning, Luxembourg (2018). https://doi.org/10.2766/569540
8. Patel, R., Loraine, E., Gréaux, M.: Impact of COVID-19 on digital practice in UK pediatric speech and language therapy and implications for the future: a national survey. Int. J. Lang. Commun. Disord. 57(5), 1112–1129 (2022). https://doi.org/10.1111/1460-6984.12750
9. Sikka, K.: Parent's perspective on teletherapy of pediatric population with speech and language disorder during Covid-19 lockdown in India. Indian J. Otolaryngol. Head Neck Surg. 75, 14–20 (2023). https://doi.org/10.1007/s12070-022-03310-y
10. Agheana, V., Popovici, D.V.: Efficiency and results in online speech therapy. In: Rad, D., Dughi, T., Maier, R., Ignat, S. (eds.) Designing for Digital Wellbeing, pp. 175–189. Peter Lang, Berlin (2023)
11. Poh Li, L., Jaladin, R.A.M., Abdullah, H.S.: Understanding the two sides of online counseling and their ethical and legal ramifications. Procedia Soc. Behav. Sci. 103, 1243–1251 (2013). https://doi.org/10.1016/j.sbspro.2013.10.453
12. American Speech-Language-Hearing Association. Professional issues in telepractice for speech-language pathologists (2010). www.asha.org/policy/. Accessed 09 Aug 2023
13. American Speech-Language-Hearing Association. Professional issues. Telepractice. https://www.asha.org/practice-portal/professional-issues/telepractice/#collapse_1. Accessed 09 Aug 2023
14. Weidner, K., Lowman, J.: Telepractice for adult speech-language pathology services: a systematic review. Perspect. ASHA SIGs 5(1), 326–338 (2020). https://doi.org/10.1044/2019_PERSP-19-00146
15. Mohan, H.S., Anjum, A., Rao, P.K.S.: A survey of telepractice in speech-language pathology and audiology in India. Int. J. Telerehabil. 9(2), 69–80 (2017). https://doi.org/10.5195/ijt.2017.6233
16. American Speech-Language-Hearing Association (2016). Special interest group 18: Telepractice survey results. American Speech-Language-Hearing Association. https://www.asha.org/uploadedFiles/ASHA/PracticePortal/ProfessionalIssues/Telepractice/2016-Telepractice-Survey.pdf. Accessed 09 Aug 2023
17. Farren, E., Quigley, D., Lynch, Y.: Telepractice in service delivery: a survey of perspectives and practices of speech and language therapists in Ireland during COVID-19. Adv. Commun. Swallowing 25(1), 5–16 (2022). https://doi.org/10.3233/ACS-210036
18. Karowicz, A.: Przeszkody i wyzwania w pracy zawodowej logopedy podczas pandemii Covid-19. Logopaedica Lodziensia 5, 87–104 (2021). https://doi.org/10.18778/2544-7238.05.06
19. Kwok, E.Y.L., Chiu, J., Rosenbaum, P., Cunningham, B.J.: The process of telepractice implementation during the COVID-19 pandemic: a narrative inquiry of preschool speech-language pathologists and assistants from one center in Canada. BMC Health Serv. Res. 22, 81 (2022). https://doi.org/10.1186/s12913-021-07454-5
20. Całek, G.: Jak się zmieniała edukacja zdalna w czasie pandemii COVID-19. Raport. Warszawa: Uniwersytet Warszawski (2021). https://depot.ceon.pl/bitstream/handle/123456789/22453/Grzegorz%20Ca%C5%82ek%20-%20Jak%20si%C4%99%20zmienia%C5%82a%20edukacja%20zdalna%20w%20czasie%20pandemii%20COVID-19.pdf?sequence=1&isAllowed=y. Accessed 09 Aug 2023
21. Szurek, M.: Czy współczesny logopeda powinien wykorzystywać multimedia w terapii logopedycznej? In: Brzyszcz, E., Koziej, S. (eds.) Zastosowanie nowych mediów w edukacji dzieci i młodzieży, pp. 133–143. Uniwersytet Jana Kochanowskiego, Kielce (2017)
22. Soundshapers website, Sound Shapers offers Smart Palate Speech Therapy. http://soundshapers.org/smart-palate-speech-therapy/. Accessed 09 Aug 2023

23. AFAST (the Facebook profile). https://www.facebook.com/afastpowiedzto/posts/pfbid0 2rYdJgkAg2bGWjVio8anygDoq3X8Yu9UncDeD5u9eUYWLjaGyAa34nb4wkH9GtGrGl. Accessed 09 Aug 2023

24. Chaudhary, T., Kanodia, A., Verma, H., Singh, C., Mishra, A.K., Sikka, K.: A pilot study comparing teletherapy with the conventional face-to-face therapy for speech-language disorders. Indian J. Otolaryngol. Head Neck Surg. **73**, 366–370 (2021). https://doi.org/10.1007/ s12070-021-02647-0

25. Szabó, B., Dirks, S., Scherger, A.L.: Apps and digital resources in speech and language therapy - which factors influence therapists' acceptance? In: Antona, M., Stephanidis, C. (eds.) HCII 2022. LNCS, vol. 13308, pp. 379–391. Springer, Cham (2022). https://doi.org/10.1007/978-3-031-05028-2_25

26. Michniuk, A.: Nowe media w Polskiej szkole. Obecność i zastosowanie. Wydawnictwo Naukowe Akademii im. Jakuba z Paradyża, Gorzów Wielkopolski (2020)

27. Krasowicz-Kupis, G.: Badanie funkcji językowych w dysleksji. In: Krasowicz-Kupis, G. (ed.) Diagnoza dysleksji. Najważniejsze problemy, pp. 188–202. Harmonia, Gdańsk (2009)

28. Jatkowska, J.: Rozwój językowy dziecka a b-learning. Annales Universitatis Paedagogicae Cracoviensis. Studia de Cultura **4**(10), 125–140 (2018). https://doi.org/10.24917/20837275. 10.4.10

29. Lech, M., Kucewicz, M.T., Czyżewski, A.: Human computer interface for tracking eye movements improves assessment and diagnosis of patients with acquired brain injuries. Front. Neurol. **6**(10), 1–9 (2019). https://doi.org/10.3389/fneur.2019.00006

30. Vessoyan, K., Steckle, G., Easton, B., Nichols, M., Siu, V.M., McDougall, J.: Using eye-tracking technology for communication in Rett syndrome: perceptions of impact. Augment. Altern. Commun. **34**(3), 230–241 (2018). https://doi.org/10.1080/07434618.2018.1462848

31. Edupolis. https://edupolis.pl/aplikacja-logopedyczna-kokolingo/. Accessed 09 Aug 2023

32. Kokolingo. https://www.kokolingo.pl/faqs. Accessed 09 Aug 2023

33. Demo version of the Kokolingo. https://app.us.kokolingo.com/. Accessed 09 Aug 2023

34. Damasio, A.R.: Aphasia. N. Engl. J. Med. **326**(8), 531–539 (1992). https://doi.org/10.1056/ NEJM199202203260806

35. Afast.pl. https://afast.pl/Home/About. Accessed 13 May 2023

36. Jasiński, G.: Krzysztof Globisz twarzą aplikacji AFAST, która pomoże w walce z afazją, RMF FM. https://www.rmf24.pl/nauka/news-krzysztof-globisz-twarza-aplikacji-afast-ktora-pomoze-w-walc,nId,2396040#crp_state=1. Accessed 09 Aug 2023

37. mTalent.pl. https://www.mtalent.pl/. Accessed 13 May 2023

38. mTalent.pl. https://www.mtalent.pl/zajecia-logopedyczne-cz-1/. Accessed 09 Aug 2023

39. mTalent.pl. https://www.mtalent.pl/zajecia-logopedyczne-dla-mlodziezy-i-doroslych/. Accessed 09 Aug 2023

40. mTalent.pl. https://www.mtalent.pl/autorzy/. Accessed 09 Aug 2023

41. Morris, J., Jones, M., Thompson, N., Wallace, T., DeRuyter, F.: Clinician perspectives on rehab interventions and technologies for people with disabilities in the United States: a national survey. Int. J. Environ. Res. Public Health **16**(21), 20–42 (2019). https://doi.org/10.3390/ije rph16214220

42. Agheana, V., Popovici, D.-V.: Efficiency and results in online speech therapy (2023). https://www.researchgate.net/publication/369251431_Efficiency_and_results_in_o nline_speech_therapy. Accessed 09 Aug 2023

43. Horne-Moyer, H.L., Moyer, B.H., Messer, D.C., Messer, E.S.: The use of electronic games in therapy: a review with clinical implications. Curr. Psychiatry Rep. **16**(12), 520 (2014). https:// doi.org/10.1007/s11920-014-0520-6

44. Aghlara, L., Tamjid, N.H.: The effect of digital games on Iranian children's vocabulary retention in foreign language acquisition. Procedia Soc. Behav. Sci. **29**, 552–560 (2011). https:// doi.org/10.1016/j.sbspro.2011.11.275

45. Rüth, M., Birke, A., Kaspar, K.: Teaching with digital games: how intentions to adopt digital game-based learning are related to personal characteristics of pre-service teachers. Br. J. Edu. Technol. **53**(5), 1412–1429 (2022). https://doi.org/10.1111/bjet.13201
46. Vaezipour, A., Campbell, J., Theodoros, D., Russell, T.: Mobile apps for speech-language therapy in adults with communication disorders: review of content and quality. JMIR Mhealth Uhealth **8**(10), e18858 (2020). https://doi.org/10.2196/18858
47. Oche, A.E., Asghar, I., Griffiths, M., Warren, W.: Digital speech therapy for the aphasia patients: challenges, opportunities and solutions. In: Proceedings of the 9th International Conference on Information Communication and Management (ICICM 2019), pp. 85–88. Association for Computing Machinery, New York (2019). https://doi.org/10.1145/3357419.3357449
48. Galliers, J., et al.: Accessibility of 3D game environments for people with Aphasia: an exploratory study. In: The Proceedings of the 13th International ACM SIGACCESS Conference on Computers and Accessibility (ASSETS 2011), pp. 139–146. Association for Computing Machinery, New York (2011)

Special Education Teachers' Training Needs on Evidence-Based Practice on Autism in Spain: An Online Program for In-Service Teacher Training

Aitor Larraceleta[1,2]([⊠]) (ⓘ), Luis Castejón[2] (ⓘ), and José Carlos Núñez[2] (ⓘ)

[1] Equipo Regional ACNEAE, Ministry of Education of the Principality of Asturias, Avenida San Pedro de los Arcos, 18, 33012 Asturias, Spain
aitorlg@educastur.org
[2] Department of Psychology, University of Oviedo, Plaza Feijoo s/n, 33003 Asturias, Spain

Abstract. Students with special educational needs associated with autism are ever more present in schools in various countries meaning that teacher training plays a crucial role in offering them appropriate, inclusive education. This chapter discusses the fundamental aspects of a study about a series of variables aimed at achieving that: special education teachers' perceptions of their training needs about evidence-based practices aimed at the socio-communicative dimension of autism, their perceptions of their university and in-service training in these practices, along with the results, and teachers' perceptions, of an online training program for in-service teachers about these strategies. The goal is to use these results as a starting point from which to establish a future online training model based on teachers' thoughts about the training they have had, which may become an effective part of achieving quality, inclusive educational results for these students.

Keywords: Autism · Evidence-based Practices · Professional Development

1 Autism and Its Growing Reality

1.1 A Brief Summary of the Concept of Autism Spectrum Disorder and Its Relationship with Social Communication

When we talk about Autism Spectrum Disorder (ASD) we are using an "umbrella term" that covers a number of neurodevelopmental conditions characterized by the presence of issues in two dimensions of human development: communication and social interaction skills in different contexts—the subject of this chapter—and restrictive or repetitive patterns of behaviour [1]. This means dealing with the behavioural expression of atypical neurodevelopment [2] associated with many possible aetiologies [3], the cause of which has not been fully determined, although there is strong evidence for a genetic origin [4].

It may be expressed in very different ways, on a spectrum of manifestations from a lesser to a greater extent, rather than by presence or absence [5]. It originates in early

Ł. Tomczyk (Ed.): NMP 2022, CCIS 1916, pp. 83–101, 2023.
https://doi.org/10.1007/978-3-031-44581-1_7

infancy, although its diagnostic symptoms may or may not be evident until, with the passage of time, social demands overwhelm capabilities, or it may remain masked by strategies learned in subsequent stages of life [1, 6]. In addition, it must cause a clinically significant deterioration in social or work settings or in other important areas of usual functioning that are not better explained by intellectual disability or global developmental delay [1]. Autism appears in all socio-economic levels and ethnic groups, although in the USA for example, children in poorer social classes or ethnic minorities are usually diagnosed later [7].

In the present study, of the two dimensions in the Diagnostic and Statistical Manual of Mental Disorders (DSM-5) [1] noted above, we focus on aspects related to communication and social interaction.

Social Communication. This can be defined as the use of language and other communicative modalities—such as gestures—in a linguistic, cognitive, and social context—face to face, here and now—[8]. A broad definition would include "a child's understanding of a speaker's intent and verbal and non-verbal signals that indicate these intentions, as well as their interpretation in the environmental context, the social norms and expectations, and how they fuse with the structural aspects of language (for example, vocabulary, syntax, and phonology) to achieve successful communication" [9, p. 204].

Deficits in the pragmatic aspects of language, social interaction, and communication are a well-recognized distinctive mark of autism [10, 11]. This idea of autism, which the scientific literature espoused, appeared in the DSM-5, as social and communicative difficulties were combined into a single domain, recognizing that socialization is inherently linked to the development of communicative skills [1]. Even the different models of intervention, regardless of having a more behavioural or socio-pragmatic approach, focus on improving socio-communicative skills [10]. This is because various studies have indicated that teaching early social communication skills can lead to better development of subsequent socio-communicative behaviours that emerge in autism [10, 12].

In recent years, the scientific literature on development has emphasized a set of early social communication behaviours that are linked to the development of social and cognitive skills in typically developing children, including joint attention, the use of gestures, symbolic play, and imitation [13]. Research in to the autism spectrum has identified a set of socio-communicative deficits grouped in two main areas: the capacity for joint attention, which indicates the difficulty in autism of coordinating attention between people and objects and therefore paying attention to and processing carers' speech, and difficulties in the development of symbolic play, which reflects the difficulty those with autism have acquiring conventional or shared meanings of symbols, and which is clear in issues such as the acquisition of gestures, words, imitation, and play [14, 15].

1.2 The Increase of Autism in Different Societies

For many years, the number of people on the autistic spectrum has been growing in various societies. Research has shown a worldwide increase in the prevalence of autism [16], which has grown from 0.05% in 1966 to current estimates, depending on the study, ranging from 0.9% to 1.5% of the population [17] and even as high as 2% in some studies

[18]. Accepting a true prevalence somewhere between 1 and 2%, which may vary from region to region, at least 78 million people worldwide would be autistic [19].

In the USA, statistical monitoring by the Autism and Developmental Disabilities Monitoring (ADDM) Network indicates that in 2020, in the states which were surveyed—Arizona, Arkansas, California, Georgia, Maryland, Minnesota, Missouri, New Jersey, Tennessee, Utah, and Wisconsin—one in every 36 eight-year-olds was on the autistic spectrum, a prevalence of 2.76% [20]. These figures mean that since 2000 there has been a 317% percent increase in prevalence.

In Europe, and more specifically in Spain, according to the data from organizations such as the World Health Organization [21], one in a hundred births produce a child on the autistic spectrum [22]. Using that figure with the data from 2023, that would mean more than 480,000 people in Spain [23] and more than 4.4 million people in the European Union would have this developmental condition [24].

It is only logical that this clear reality of increasing numbers of people with autism in various societies is reflected in the classroom, as we will see below.

1.3   Increased Numbers of Students with Special Educational Needs Associated with Autism in Educational Settings

The undeniable social reality above has brought with it a number of consequences for education. With the increase in prevalence of autism generally, there have been more children with Special Education Needs (SEN) associated with autism (ASD-SEN) in the classroom who, thanks to their social and communicative peculiarities, need specialist educational responses [25, 26]. We will examine the situation in education in two countries as an example, the United States and Spain.

The United States of America. Looking at the rates of students with ASD-SEN according to the National Center for Education Statistics (NCES), it is clear that autism is the category within the "Individuals with Disabilities Education Act" (IDEA) framework that has increased most and continues to grow, going from 4% of IDEA students in academic year 2006/7 to 12% in 2021/22 [27].

The data published by the NCES from 2008/9 to 2021/22 shows that the total number of students aged between 3 and 21 who received services related to educational needs due to disability associated with IDEA grew from 6.4 million—13.2% of the total number of students in public schools—to 7.2 million—14.7% of the total, an increase of 11.3%. In the same period, the number of autistic students in the same age range rose from 336,000—0.7% of the total student population—to 882,000—or 1.8% of the total—representing an increase of 162.5% in the number of these students attending public schools and an increase of 161.8% in prevalence [27].

In summary, ever greater numbers of students in schools in the USA require educational services related to autism. This growth means that autism is found at a significantly higher rate than changes in educational services for students with any other type of disability [28].

Spain. A review of the figures from the Spanish Ministry of Education and Vocational Training (Ministerio de Educación y Formación Profesional; MEFP) leads to a clear conclusion. The number of ASD-SEN students is growing notably in Spanish schools

[29]. Looking at the data from the MEFP statistics service for academic year 2021/22—the most recent data—about non-university students with SEN, a total of 69,002 students (57,104 boys and 11,898 girls) had SEN associated with ASD. These students represent 28.1% of SEN students, and at the time of publication, that makes them the most common SEN students in the country [29].

Looking at the last eleven academic years—there is no desegregated data prior to that—the percentage increase in ASD-SEN students was 262.73%, calculating from the difference between the 19,023 students there were in 2011/12 to the 69,002 in 2021/22. This is a long way from the 6.05% increase in the school population in general [29], and marks a pattern that should lead educational administrations to carefully consider the educational response.

2   Teacher Training as the Key to Inclusive Education for Students on the Autistic Spectrum

2.1   Evidence-Based Education for These Students

From its initial description in the 1940s, when authors such as Kanner and Asperger [5] laid the foundations of the concept that we understand today as Autism Spectrum Disorder [1], there have been countless educational and therapeutic initiatives in response to the developmental differences presented by those on the spectrum. The increased prevalence of people included within the framework of the autism spectrum has intensified the demand for effective services [30, 31] and in response, research is providing evidence about what practices [31, 32] or programs [33] seem to be most effective.

So which educational practices and models are the most appropriate for these students? Answering this question means intervention models and practices presenting evidence of efficacy through rigorously designed studies [30, 32], since there are a multitude of intervention strategies, methodological approaches, and programs with varying results and different implementations [26]. In order to address this confusion in school settings with regard to interventions with ASD-SEN students, we have to fall back on "evidence-based practice", which refers to the teaching strategies, interventions, and training programs that produce consistent positive results and which have been experimentally proven to be effective for students [32, 34].

Government investment in education for autism has been substantial and has taken various approaches in the school setting [35]. Unfortunately, many educational interventions for ASD-SEN students do not have empirical evidence supporting their effectiveness, and this may mean wasting resources or hindering the provision of other, more valuable interventions in schools [25]. Studies in the USA, for example, have shown that school systems do not provide evidence for the quality of their programs in relation to proper deployment of Individualized Educational Programs (IEP), learning environments, or—the issue the present study focuses on—teacher training [36].

Implementing educational intervention programs aimed at these students needs to be underpinned by proper teacher training, aimed at reducing the gap between research about these interventions and how they are implemented in the classroom [32, 35]. This is especially so when there are multiple difficulties implementation faces: teachers' lack of understanding of causal mechanisms, the need for high-intensity and individualized intervention, variability in how teachers use them, the speed of use and mastery of these practices, and the occasional need to combine them [37, 38].

This training must be based on evidence-based intervention approaches for specific students in various contexts, in other words, tailored to individual needs [35], as there is no single, universal method for all children on the autism spectrum [39–41]. The results of studies about the social validity of these practices between teachers support this [42].

This indicates the need for teachers to have sufficient training related to autism to be able to select the evidence provided by research or practice [33, 35]. This selection would be based on the evidence for the effectiveness of the practice, on evaluation of the cost of implementing it, consideration of its complexity and transferability, and on a contextual determination [43].

Inclusive education must respond to, among other things, the ASD-SEN student's particular cognitive and perceptive processing and learning style [44]. However, certain educational interventions for autism should be avoided. They may occasionally be used in schools with good intentions to "try things out" despite the evidence base for them being poor or controversial [45]. As Marder and deBettencourt [32] noted, the continued growth in the numbers of ASD-SEN students attending ordinary schools means that many teachers are at a disadvantage, as they do not know how to adapt empirically validated teaching strategies or programs that would satisfy the needs of these students, despite being aware of those needs. This led to our region implementing a pilot program to improve training in these aspects.

3   An Online Program to Improve In-Service Training about Autism for Special Education Teachers

3.1   The Importance of Teachers' Professional Development

There are growing numbers of studies, related to both initial training and in-service training or continued professional development, about the need for teachers to adopt practices in education with ASD-SEN students that are evidence-based. This requirement has been incorporated into education policy and legislation, although there are few cases where it is being carried out [25, 46].

Professional development consists of facilitating teaching and learning experiences about various content, designed to support acquisition of knowledge, skills and professional attitudes and to apply them in practice [47]. In general, there are three key dimensions for designing continuing training that should be realized in teaching practice—the *who*, the *what*, and the *how*—the context and target population for the training; the specific content it concerns; and the procedure for organizing and facilitating the experience [48].

Educational intervention aimed at ASD-SEN students must be based on teacher training that seeks to reduce the gap between research about interventions and implementation in the classroom [32]. This means a teacher training system based on the principles of implementation science, in other words, bringing practices that work in the laboratory or in applied research settings under researchers' control into daily use in real-world settings under the control of teachers. That procedure is more likely to lead to teachers adopting and using the innovations they need to improve the quality of services dealing with diversity and the use of evidence-based practices with ASD-SEN students [36, 49, 50], going beyond information from anecdotal reports, case studies, websites, or social networks [32].

3.2 Evidence-Based Practice About Autism in Education

As we have noted above, with autism there has been a tendency to accept certain interventions with the expectation, on the part of teachers and families, of improving these students' education without sufficient evidence of results [25, 35]. This has been happening in a situation where the increased prevalence of children on the autistic spectrum in schools has intensified the demand for effective educational services and therapies [30, 31].

The concern about the quality of psycho-educational practices aimed at these students since the 1990s has led to various international organizations and institutions funding systematic reviews to identify the most effective evidence-based models and practices [e.g., 31, 51–53]. In other words, those backed by evidence of efficacy demonstrated through the use of rigorously designed studies [30, 32] which have produced improvements in a broad range of skills, such as communicative, social, cognitive, and adaptive abilities [30]. These psycho-educational interventions fall into two groups: global or comprehensive models—a set of practices within a conceptual framework designed to achieve a broad impact on learning and the core characteristics of autism, such as TEACCH or SCERTS—and practices based or focused on intervention [26, 30]. The latter are specific learning procedures or techniques that are used to reinforce development or learning of specific behaviours or to reduce problematic behaviours in a short period of time [30]. They are designed for ASD-SEN students to acquire a skill or reach a goal [54] and there is evidence for their efficacy [46].

Two of the reviews of these focused practices had caught the attention of the scientific community when the present research began because of their importance and because they found similar results [31, 46]. The review by the National Autism Center (NAC), which selected 14 focused practices, some grouped together in intervention packages [54]: Behavioural Interventions; Cognitive Behavioural Intervention Package; Comprehensive Behavioural Treatment for Young Children; Language Training (Production); Modeling; Natural Teaching Strategies; Parent Training; Peer Training Package; Pivotal Response Training; Schedules; Scripting; Self-Management; Social Skills Package; and Story-based Intervention.

The review from the National Professional Development Center on ASD (NPDC) [26, 31] selected 27 practices: Antecedent-based Interventions; Cognitive Behavioural Intervention; Differential Reinforcement of Alternative, Incompatible or Other Behaviour; Discrete Trial Training; Exercise; Functional Behaviour Assessment; Functional Communication Training; Modeling; Naturalistic Intervention; Parent-Implemented Interventions; Peer-Mediated Instruction and Intervention; Picture

Exchange Communication System; Pivotal Response Training; Prompting; Reinforcement; Response Interruption/Redirection; Scripting; Self-management; Social Narratives; Social Skills Training; Structured Play Group; Task Analysis; Technology-aided Instruction and Intervention; Time Delay; Video Modeling; and Visual Support.

3.3 An Online, Evidence-Based Program for Teachers of ASD-SEN Students: Developing the Study

In education aimed at ASD-SEN students, evidence-based practices (EBP) should consider the child's characteristics, the context of the intervention, practitioner variables, and research-based knowledge [55]. The work of special education teachers is particularly important. In Spain, they are split into two specialties, Hearing and Language (HL) and Therapeutic Pedagogy (TP) who work mainly with SEN students, including those on the autistic spectrum [56]. Their work may include advising general teachers, who mostly feel undertrained to teach these students [57].

Our study focused on addressing two big issues that are of vital interest for the success of future training programs related to autism:

Understanding the perceptions of special education teachers (HL and TP) about their training in EBP aimed at the socio-communicative dimension of autism and about their training needs in that regard (Phase 1 of the study).

Determining the changes in levels of knowledge and from a procedural and attitudinal perspective in teachers following a pilot study of an online training module (Phase 2 of the study). A summary of the study approach is given in Fig. 1.

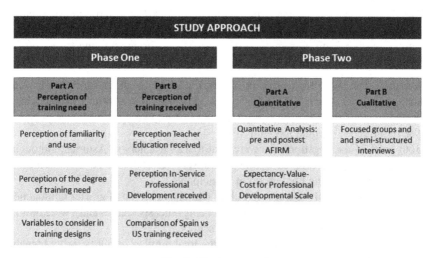

Fig. 1. Study approach

Phase 1. We performed a transversal observational study in two parts via a survey.

Design and Instrument. The instrument was designed based on the practices identified in the NPDC and NAC studies on ASD [31, 54]. Although the two reviews were done independently, and their literature searches covered different periods of time, their findings were very similar and the message was convergence between two independent sources of data [31, 46].

In part A we designed a questionnaire ad hoc, inspired by the work from Borders et al. [58] and Sulek et al. [59], selecting the focused practices appearing in both the NAC and NPDC reviews on ASD [31, 54]. This produced 21 practices and left 6 out— Exercise (ECE); Functional Behaviour Assessment (FBA); Functional Communication Training (FCT); Picture Exchange Communication System (PECS); Structured Play Group (SPG) and Technology-aided Instruction and Intervention (TAII) [60]. Some of the focused practices in the NPDC review were included within more global NAC practices, these included the NAC behavioural intervention packed which included 7 focused evidence-based practices in the NPDC [31].

Following that, we established criteria for inclusion of the 21 practices, which was a relationship to the socio-communicative dimension of autism, in other words, evidence of impact on the three development domains—social, communicative, and joint attention [31, 54]. This led to the selection of 12 practices: Differential Reinforcement of Alternative, Incompatible or Other Behaviour (DRA/I/O); Discrete Trial Training (DTT); Modeling (MD); Naturalistic Intervention (NI); Peer-mediated Instruction and Intervention (PMII); Prompting (PP); Reinforcement (R+); Scripting (SC); Social Narratives (SN); Task Analysis; (TA); Time Delay (TD); and Video Modeling (VM) [61].

The questionnaire had an initial section asking for sociodemographic information, a second section for information about teaching experience with ASD-SEN students or training in that, and a third section asking about their perceptions of familiarity, use and need for training in relation to the practices above [61].

Part B included a questionnaire based on the work by Hsiao and Sorensen-Petersen [39], which in addition to the sociodemographic variables noted above, included questions about teachers' initial training at university or in-service training for each of the indicated practices. [62].

Participants. The study took place in Asturias, a region in the north of Spain with a population of 1,004,686 in 2022 [63] and 134,551 students in non-university education in academic year 2021/22. There were 2,648 students with ASD-SEN, representing 48.69% of the school population with SEN [64].

Both parts of the questionnaire were sent to 128 teachers in Asturias, although in part A, only 116 were special education specialists—HL (50) and TP (66)—which was the number making up the final group of participants.

Part B considered only teachers in public schools, in search of greater homogeneity, resulting in 108 teachers. 12 were removed for being other specialties and 8 were removed as they worked in independent (*concertado*) schools.

The sample represented almost 15% of the total number of public-school teachers in the region at the time of the study [62].

Procedure. Non-probabilistic snowball sampling was used for the two parts of the first phase of the study [65]. The online questionnaires were sent to the directors of the 8 special education schools in Asturias that taught ASD-SEN students to pass on to their teachers. At the same time, the online questionnaires were sent to Dealing with Diversity Advisors at the four Asturian Teacher Resource centres, who passed them on to special education teachers in the specialties noted above during their training activity. The participants had one month to complete the survey [61, 62].

Measures and Analysis. In part A of the study, we calculated descriptive statistics (percentages, frequencies, and statistics of central tendency and dispersion) about the level of familiarity and use. We also performed an analysis of variance and differences of means related to teachers perceived levels of training needs in order to effectively use these practices, and the related variables [61].

In part B we calculated the number and percentage of responses to determine what training teachers were offered in each of the practices and as a whole as part of their initial and their in-service training. Descriptive statistics (means and standard deviations) were also used to summarize the teachers' scores about the training they had received in each practice and overall [62].

Results. The results from this study were published in Larraceleta-González et al. [61] and Larraceleta et al. [62].

Summarizing the most notable aspects of part A [61], related to teachers' perceived needs for training, the practices they were most familiar with were Reinforcement (98.3%), Modeling (96.6%) and Task Analysis (91.4%). They were least familiar with Peer-Mediated Intervention (50%), Discrete Trial Training (48.3%), Time Delay (44%) and Video Modeling (13%). The results for most of the practices differ from similar studies with teachers in other countries [e.g., 45, 58], we found lower levels of familiarity in our study.

There was a similar pattern in the use of the practices. Those used more often were Reinforcement (99.0%), Modeling (93.9%), and Task Analysis (75.5%). Those used less often were Discrete Trial Training (45.9%), time delay (39.8%), peer-mediated intervention (37.8%) and Video Modeling (5.1%). The frequency of use for these practices is also lower than reports from studies in other countries.

In terms of perceived training needs, the mean score was lower in Modeling, Reinforcement, and Task Analysis. The teachers felt a greater need for training in Video Modeling, Peer-Mediated Intervention, Discrete Trial Training, and Time Delay. Teachers' perceptions of general training needs about these practices had a mean score somewhere between "moderate" and "to a large extent".

We also examined the extent to which teachers' perceptions of training about the selected practices were affected by different variables. The results indicate that training designs should be aimed at teachers who have worked with fewer ASD-SEN students, those who have not had specific training, and those with a lower perception of competence and application of evidence in interventions with these students.

Part B, assessing teachers' perceptions about the training they have had, produced the following notable results [62]:

Around 9 out of 10 teachers surveyed (87.6%) indicated having been given little or no training about the practices during their university education, and 99.1% characterized the general training about them "inadequate" or "very inadequate".

Almost three-quarters (73.6%) of the teachers had been given little or no training about the EBPs in their in-service training, and 62.9% considered their general training "inadequate" or "very inadequate".

Almost 70% of the teachers (68.6%) reported not having had any training about autism at university, and 14.8% had received no training in it at all.

The practices that the teachers felt had been taught most comprehensively during their university education were Reinforcement and Modeling, while those that had been taught least were Discrete Trial Training and Video Modeling. In their continuing professional development, the practices that they had been taught more thoroughly were the same, but in the opposite order—Modeling and Reinforcement. The least comprehensively taught were Time Delay and Video Modeling.

In terms of the overall results about evidence-based practices, the percentage that was imparted through direct instruction or debate in the sample of United States students in the study by Hsiao and Sorensen-Petersen [39] was much greater, both at university (63.6% compared to the 12.3% we found) and during in-service training (61.6% compared to our 26.4%).

Phase 2. This involved a mixed qualitative-quantitative study based on the results of the first phase of the study. Those results indicated that special education teachers felt a real need for training about methodological practices that have repeatedly been recommended for students on the autism spectrum, which would supposedly be part of the advice given to other teachers [57]. Secondly, the results indicated that there was felt to be insufficient incorporation of these practices into university and in-service training. This second phase was split into two parts, (A) quantitative and (B) qualitative.

Design and Instruments. Three editions—the second and third quarters of the 2020–2021 scholar year and the first quarter of the 2021–2022 scholar year—of the online training in an asynchronous format were put online using the Moodle platform belonging to the Asturian Education Department [Consejería de Educación del Principado de Asturias (Centro de Profesorado y Recursos de las Cuencas Mineras)]. Three 1-h live sessions—in the beginning, in the middle, and near the end of the training—were also included via the department's Microsoft TEAMS® platform to answer any questions about evidence-based practices aimed at the socio-communicative aspect of autism. Both activities were led by this chapter's lead author. Selection of the practices to be worked on in each of the teaching units considered the new publication of the old NPDC on ASD, now the National Clearinghouse on Autism Evidence and Practice (NCAEP) [55]. The same selection process as in the first phase of the study was followed, this time with evidence-based practices recommended by Naturalistic Developmental Behavioural Interventions (NDBI) approaches, in other words, research-based interventions that include components provided by both developmental and behavioural psychology [66].

Five strategies were ultimately included: Modeling (MD), Peer-mediated interventions (PMII), Video Modeling (VM), Naturalistic Intervention (NI), and Pivotal Response Training (PRT). This last practice, which was part of the NPDC review of ASD, became part of NI in the most recent NCAEP review but was maintained as a teaching unit regardless because of its importance and to include practices from one of the most famous comprehensive models that has been the basis of other models, such as the Early Start Denver Model [67]. An initial teaching unit was also included aimed at understanding evidence-based practice in the framework of inclusive schooling and the NDBI practices. Each of the six units comprised a pdf file and various links to scientific and informative articles and videos etc. Students were given a week to do each unit, although they also had an extra week at the end of the course to finish any units or questionnaires, they had not been able to complete within the set timeframes.

Part A of the study assessed levels of knowledge before and after each of the course units via evaluation questionnaires used in the Autism Focused Intervention Resources and Modules [68]. They each had 10 questions about the teaching unit with 10 points awarded for each correct answer, giving a maximum of 100 points for each test. At the end of each of the three versions of the course, there was a final test with 10 questions about each of the 6 units, with the same scoring. All the tests were translated into Spanish by the investigators.

Each of the practices was also evaluated via the Expectancy-Value-Cost for Professional Development Scale (EVP-PD) [69] to determine participating teachers' expectations of success attributed to each practice, its value, and the cost they see in applying it.

For part B, participating teachers were asked to participate in focus groups or individual semi-structured interviews to make a qualitative analysis of the training.

Participants. A total of 179 teachers signed up to the training announced by the Cuencas Mineras Teacher Resource Center in part A over the three editions. Three dropped out in the first few weeks and one participant's results were rejected as they did not have any scores in the pre-test. 175 teachers completed the training: 65 in the first edition, 68 in the second, and 42 in the third. 157 of the participants were special education teachers from the PT (80) and HL (77) specialties, representing 18% of the active specialist teaching team with these specialties according to the 2020/21 data [70]. Four of the participants were in educational guidance and 14 had other specialties. The vast majority of the participants were women, 172 compared to only 3 men.

All of the participants in part A were offered the chance to participate in part B of this second phase. A total of 28 agreed, although 3 dropped out during the process. Of the 25 remaining teachers, all of whom were women, 14 were HL specialists, 10 were PT specialists and one was an educational guidance teacher.

Procedure. In part A of this second phase, the participants completed an initial questionnaire before beginning each unit and a final questionnaire within three days of completing the unit. Each questionnaire had 10 multiple-choice questions [68] worth 10 points for a correct answer. Participants had to score 50 points or more to pass the post-test, and they could try as many times as they wished—although for the study calculations we took each participant's first attempt at the test as the valid attempt. During the training, in addition to the three live sessions for answering questions, a forum was available. Each edition of the training lasted 6 weeks, one week for each teaching unit plus one final week to finish all the outstanding activities. To make course organization simpler, units were closed each week to maintain the same pace among participants.

For part B, the focus groups and individual semi-structured interviews were held online using the Microsoft TEAMS® platform for a qualitative analysis of the training. There were three, approximately 1-h, sessions every three months.

Preliminary Results. In this section we provide some preliminary results for the quantitative part (part A), specifically about the knowledge teachers acquired through this training. The rest of part A—expectations of success, value, cost, etc.—and part B—transcription and analysis of focus group and semi-structured interview answers—were still being analysed.

Table 1 gives the scores related to knowledge in each of the three editions of the training and the mean score for the three. It indicates an increase in knowledge between the beginning and end of each of the course units, with an increase of 30.39 points (50.96%) in the unit on NDBI and educational inclusion, 15.69 points (19.83%) in the unit on Naturalistic Interventions, 21.82 points (29.58%) in the unit on Modeling, 27.37 points (40.66%) in the unit on Peer-Mediated Instruction and Intervention, 27.13 points (39.83%) in the Video Modeling unit, and 33.06 points (53.37%) in the Pivotal Response Training unit. The mean score in the three editions of the final test was 82.15 points.

Table 1. Results for the three editions of the online course ($N = 175$) about NDBI focused practices: Scores and mean score $\overline{X}$

	ED1 (65)	ED2 (68)	ED3 (42)	$\overline{X}$
Pre NDBI	58.77	62.06	58.10	59.64
Post NDBI	92.15	87.94	90.00	90.03
Pre NI	79.08	82.94	78.33	80.12
Post NI	95.85	95.15	96.43	95.81
Pre MD	72.46	76.91	71.90	73.76
Post MD	96.62	94.41	95.71	95.58
Pre PMII	67.08	71.32	63.57	67.32
Post PMII	94.92	93.68	95.48	94.69
Pre VM	67.08	71.76	65.48	68.11
Post VM	95.69	95.74	94.29	95.24
Pre PRT	62.92	62.21	60.71	61.95
Post PRT	96.62	94.12	94.29	95.01
Final Test	86.09	85.59	74.78	82.15

Note. ED1 = Edition 1; ED2 = Edition 2; ED3 = Edition 3; NDBI = Naturalistic Developmental Behavioural Interventions; NI = Naturalistic Intervention; MD = Modeling; PMII = Peer-Mediated Instruction and Intervention; VM = Video Modeling; PRT = Pivotal Response Training.

Adding together, the mean scores in the three editions of each pre- (68.48) and post-test (94.39) and comparing them to the result of the final test (82.15), there was a 25.91 point (37.84%) increase between the mean pre-test and mean post-test result, an increase of 13.67 points (19.96%) between the mean pre-test score and the mean final score, and a drop of 12.24 points (13.71%) between the mean post-test score and the mean final score.

Discussion. The data analysed so far allow for some interesting preliminary conclusions to be drawn about the knowledge acquired in part A.

Firstly, the results from the pre-tests assessing knowledge about the practices taught in this training were in line with other similarly designed international studies by Morin et al. [71], using the same evaluation instrument. They found that scores in their pre-tests were similar or slightly lower than in our study: 78 points in Morin et al. vs 80.12 points about NI in our study; 63.62 points vs 73.76 about MD; 65.62 vs 67.32 in PMII, and 57.57 vs 68.11 in VM. This point is very important because, as far as we know, there are some studies regarding teachers' knowledge perception about aspects in relation to autism but a few studies exploring the increment of teacher knowledge about educational responses to autism after receiving training–f. e. Giannopoulou et al. [72]–and even less in an online format [71].

Secondly, there was an increase in participants' knowledge following this online training both looking at the mean pre-test compared to post-test results or the mean final results, agreeing with other studies like Sam et al. [46], although caution is advised when interpreting this as different variables might have influenced the results—e.g., having the unit text available to consult. There was a drop of 12.24 points between the mean post-test and the mean final result, which may be explained by the time between the end of the training and the final test, which was about a month.

Lastly, putting the results of the four practices—the initial unit about NDBI and inclusion was an introduction, and PRT would be part of NI, although this was addressed separately in the training—in perspective with the results of the first phase of the study, which was made up of different cohorts of teachers to phase two, raises interesting questions.

On the one hand, there is a consistent line in some practices, such as VM and PMII, in which the participating teachers in our first studies felt a significant training need—to a large extent (4.21) for VM and between a moderate and large extent (3.59) in PMII—[61], poor education or training during their time at university—both "never mentioned and never taught", with a mean of 1.15 for VM and 1.44 for PMII—and in their continued professional development—VM falling within "never mentioned and never taught", with a mean of 1.44, and PMII close to "mentioned incidentally, with a mean of 1.98 [62]. These "low" expectations were confirmed by the results of the pre-test, with the lowest scores—68.11 in VM and 67.32 in PMII.

There was a mean perception of training need for MD of 2.4—between "to a small extent" and "a moderate extent" [61]—and the mean perception of the training they were given at university was 2.26, "mentioned incidentally", rising to 2.47 in their continuing professional development, between "mentioned incidentally" and "mentioned and discussed" [62]. The mean result of the three pre-tests was 73.76 points, which seems to be in line with the expectations indicated by the teachers in the first phase.

However, this consistency between the data was not seen in Naturalistic Intervention. Teachers in the first phase of the study scored their training need as 3.40, close to the mid-point between "a moderate extent" and "a large extent" (3.59) [61], while the mean perception of their university training in this practice was 1.46, "never mentioned and never taught", rising to 2.05 "mentioned incidentally" in reference to their continued professional development [62]. In contrast, the mean result for the pre-test from the three editions was 80.12. In other words, their sense that they needed training in this practice did not agree with their initial knowledge, something that might be explained because they were using this practice in their everyday work without knowing its theoretical definition.

3.4 Conclusions and Future Directions

This chapter has summarized results of research being done about the training situation for special education teachers (PT and HL) in relation to focused evidence-based practices aimed at ASD-SEN students. The aim was to establish the key foundations for future training that would include these practices in teachers' continued professional development.

The idea behind the study was to start from the teachers perceived training needs, as training programs often do not consider the actual situation or the true interests of the audience they are aimed at. Because of that, it was essential to understand the teachers' professional priorities. This meant, on the one hand, starting from their levels of professional training—where there was wide variability. On the other hand it also meant determining how the different evidence-based practices could help satisfy the needs of students on the autism spectrum [73], starting from the premise that pre-service training—university education—and professional support—continued training—could be used to improve how these practices are implemented [39].

So far, our results indicate the need to rethink current university teaching plans and continued professional development due to the perception by a large part of the teachers that there is a need for improved training so that teachers understand EBPs and achieve effective, efficient educational interventions [61, 62]. One cannot forget that such perceptions can influence the processes of inclusion/segregation, as there is evidence that teacher training is a key factor in inclusive processes for students on the autistic spectrum [74]. In fact, our study is part of an analysis via a mixed design of the relevance of a suggested online model, assessing its impact both on knowledge, that we have reported here, and on other variables.

This research will continue with the aim of navigating beyond what we have called the "perfect storm", i.e., a large number of ASD-SEN students in our schools, increasing the pressure for a quality response from the education system, in the face of a pressing need for teacher training which will leave them better educated about autism and evidence-based practices. This will be key to their inclusive processes [61]. We trust we will reach a safe harbour.

Funding. This work was partially funded by the Ministry of Science and Innovation of Spain (Funds from the European Union–NextGenerationEU–); Ref. TED2021-131054B-I00, of the Spanish State Plan for Scientific, Technical Research and Innovation 2021–2023.

References

1. American Psychiatric Association. Diagnostic and Statistical Manual of Mental Disorders, 5th edn. American Psychiatric Publishing: Washington, DC (2013)

2. Peeters, T., Gillberg, C.: Autism. Medical and Educational Aspects. Whurr Publishers, London (1999)
3. Sigman, M., Capps, L.: Niños y Niñas Autistas. Morata, Madrid (2000)
4. Volkmar, F.R., Lord, C., Bailey, A., Schultz, R.T., Klin, A.: Autism and pervasive developmental disorders. J. Child Psychol. Psychiatry **45**, 135–170 (2004)
5. Feinstein, A.: Historia del autismo. Conversaciones con los pioneros. Autismo Ávila, Ávila (2016)
6. World Health Organization.: 6A02 Autistic Spectrum Disorder. In: International Statistical Classification of Diseases and Related Health Problems, 11th edn. (2019). https://icd.who.int/browse11/lm/es#/http%3A%2F%2Fid.who.int%2Ficd%2Fentity%2F437815624. Accessed 29 Apr 2023
7. Mandell, D.S., et al.: Racial/ethnic disparities in the identification of children with autism spectrum disorders. Am. J. Public Health **99**(3), 493–498 (2009). https://doi.org/10.2105/AJPH.2007.131243
8. Andrés-Roqueta, C.: Desarrollo de la Pragmática. In: Aparici, M., Igualada, A. (eds.) El desarrollo del lenguaje y la comunicación en la infancia, pp. 145–166. UOC, Barcelona (2018)
9. Norbury, C.F.: Practitioner review: social (pragmatic) communication disorder conceptualization, evidence and clinical implications. J. Child Psychol. Psychiatry **55**(3), 204–216 (2014)
10. Ingersoll, B.: Teaching social communication: a comparison of naturalistic behavioural and development, social pragmatic approaches for children with autism spectrum disorders. J. Positive Behav. Interv. **12**(1), 33–43 (2010). https://doi.org/10.1177/1098300709334797
11. Tager-Flusberg, H., Paul, R., Lord, C.: Language and communication in autism. In: Cohen, D.J., Volkmar, F.R. (eds.) Handbook of Autism and Pervasive Developmental Disorders, 3rd edn., pp. 335–364. Wiley, New York (2005)
12. Watkins, L., Khun, M., Ledbetter-Cho, K., Gervarter, C., O'Reilly, M.: Evidence-based social communication interventions for children with autism spectrum disorders. Indian J. Pediatr. **84**(1), 68–75 (2015). https://doi.org/10.1007/s12098-015-1938-5
13. Mundy, P., Block, J., Delgado, C., Pomares, Y., Van Hecke, A.V., Parlade, M.V.: Individual differences and the development of joint attention in infancy. Child Dev. **78**(3), 938–954 (2007). https://doi.org/10.1111/j.1467-8624.2007.01042.x
14. Wetherby, A.: Understanding and measuring social communication in children with autism spectrum disorders. In: Charman, T., Stone, W. (eds.) Social and Communication Development in Autism Spectrum Disorders. Early Identification, Diagnosis and Intervention, pp. 3–34. Guilford Press, New York (2006)
15. Wetherby, A., Prizant, B., Schuler, A.: Understanding the nature of communication and language impairments. In: Prizant, B.M., Wetherby, A.M. (eds.) Autism Spectrum Disorders. A Transactional Developmental Perspective, pp. 109–142. Paul H. Brookes Publishing, Baltimore (2001)
16. Zeidan, J., et al.: Global prevalence of autism: a systematic review update. Autism Res. **15**(5), 778–790 (2022). https://doi.org/10.1002/aur.2696
17. Fombonne, E.: Epidemiological controversies in autism. Swiss Arch. Neurol. Psychiatry Psychother. **171**, w03084 (2020). https://doi.org/10.4414/sanp.2020.03084
18. Roleska, M., et al.: Autism and the right to education in the EU: policy mapping and scoping review of the United Kingdom, France Poland and Spain. PLoS ONE **13**(8), e0202336 (2018). https://doi.org/10.1371/journal.pone.0202336
19. Lord, C., et al.: The lancet commission on the future of care and clinical research in autism. Lancet **399**(10321), 271–334 (2022). https://doi.org/10.1016/S0140-6736(21)01541-5

20. Maenner, M.J., et al.: Prevalence and characteristics of autism spectrum disorder among children aged 8 years - autism and developmental disabilities monitoring network, 11 sites, United States, 2020. MMWR Surveill. Summ. **72**(2), 1–14 (2023). https://doi.org/10.15585/mmwr.ss7202a1

21. World Health Organization. Autismo. https://www.who.int/es/news-room/fact-sheets/detail/autism-spectrum-disorders. Accessed 25 May 2023

22. Autismo España. Qué es el Autismo. https://autismo.org.es/el-autismo/que-es-el-autismo/. Accessed 25 May 2023

23. Instituto Nacional de Estadística. https://www.ine.es/dyngs/INEbase/es/operacion.htm?c=Estadistica_C&cid=1254736177095&menu=ultiDatos&idp=1254735572981. Accessed 25 May 2023

24. Unión Europea.: Datos y cifras sobre la vida en la Unión Europea. https://european-union.europa.eu/principles-countries-history/key-facts-and-figures/life-eu_es. Accessed 25 May 2023

25. Hess, K.L., Morrier, M.J., Heflin, L.J., Ivey, M.L.: Autism treatment survey: services received by children with autism spectrum disorders in public school classroom. J. Autism Dev. Disord. **38**, 961–971 (2008). https://doi.org/10.1007/s10803-007-0470-5

26. Wong, C., et al.: Evidence-based practices for children, youth, and young adults with autism spectrum disorder: a comprehensive review. J. Autism Dev. Disord. **45**(7), 1951–1966 (2015). https://doi.org/10.1007/s10803-014-2351-z

27. Irwin, V., et al.: Report on the Condition of Education 2023 (NCES 2023-144). U.S. Department of Education. Washington, DC: National Center for Education Statistics. https://nces.ed.gov/pubsearch/pubsinfo.asp?pubid=2023144. Accessed 25 May 2023

28. Cardinal, D.N., Griffiths, A.J., Maupin, Z.D., Fraumeni-McBride, J.: An investigation of increased rates of autism in U.S. public schools. Psychol. Sch. **58**(1), 124–140 (2021). https://doi.org/10.1002/pits.22425

29. Ministerio de Educación y Formación Profesional.: Servicios al Ciudadano. Enseñanzas no Universitarias. Alumnado con Necesidad Específica de Apoyo Educativo. Alumnado con Necesidades Educativas Especiales. Curso 21–22. Ministerio de Educación y Formación Profesional de España. https://www.educacionyfp.gob.es/servicios-al-ciudadano/estadisticas/no-universitaria/alumnado/apoyo/2021-2022.html. Accessed 26 May 2023

30. Salvadó-Salvadó, B., Palau-Baduell, M., Clofent-Torrentó, M., Montero-Camacho, M., Hernández-Latorre, M.A.: Modelos de Intervención Global en Personas con Trastorno del Espectro Autista. Revista Española de Neurología **54**(1), 63–71 (2012). https://doi.org/10.33588/rn.54S01.2011710

31. Wong, C., et al.: Evidence-Based Practices for Children, Youth, and Young Adults with Autism Spectrum Disorder. University of North Carolina, Chapel Hill (2014)

32. Marder, T., deBettencourt, L.U.: Teaching students with ASD using evidence-based practices: why is training critical now? Teach. Educ. Spec. Educ. **38**(1), 5–12 (2015). https://doi.org/10.1177/0888406414565838

33. Alcantud, F., Alonso, Y.: Modelos y Programas de Intervención Precoz en Niños con TEA y sus Familias. In: Alcantud, F. (coord.) Trastornos del Espectro Autista. Detección, diagnóstico e intervención temprana, Pirámide, Madrid, pp. 207–228 (2013)

34. Torres, C., Farley, C.A., Cook, B.G.: A special educator's guide to successfully implementing evidence-based practices. Teach. Except. Child. **45**(1), 64–73 (2012). https://doi.org/10.1177/004005991204500109

35. Parsons, S., Charman, T., Faulkner, R., Ragan, J., Wallace, S., Wittemeyer, K.: Commentary – bridging the research and practice gap in autism: the importance of creating research partnerships with schools. Autism **17**(3), 268–280 (2013). https://doi.org/10.1177/1362361312472068

36. Odom, S.L., Cox, A.W., Brock, M.E.: Implementation science, professional development, and autism spectrum disorders. Except. Child. **79**(2), 233–251 (2013). https://doi.org/10.1177/001 440291307900207

37. Dingfelder, H.E., Mandell, D.S.: Bridging the research-to-practice gap in autism intervention: an application of diffusion of innovation theory. J. Autism Dev. Disord. **41**(5), 597–609 (2010). https://doi.org/10.1007/s10803-010-1081-0

38. Stahmer, A.C., et al.: Examining relationships between child skills and potential key components of an evidence-based practice in ASD. Res. Dev. Disabil. **90**, 101–112 (2019). https://doi.org/10.1016/j.ridd.2019.04.003

39. Hsiao, Y., Sorensen-Petersen, S.: Evidence-based practices provided in teacher education and in-service training programs for special education teachers of students with autism spectrum disorders. Teach. Educ. Spec. Educ. **42**(3), 193–208 (2019). https://doi.org/10.1177/088840 6418758464

40. Cook, B.G., Odom, S.L.: Evidence-based practices and implementation science in special education. Except. Child. **79**(3), 135–144 (2013). https://doi.org/10.1177/001440291307 900201

41. Stansberry-Brusnahan, L.L., Collet-Klingenberg, L.L.: Evidence-based practices for young children with autism spectrum disorders: guidelines and recommendations from the national resource council and national professional development center on autism spectrum disorders. Int. J. Early Child. Spec. Educ. **2**(1), 45–56 (2014). https://doi.org/10.20489/intjecse.107957

42. Callahan, K., Henson, R.K., Cowan, A.K.: Social validation of evidence-based practices in autism by parents, teachers, and administrators. J. Autism Dev. Disord. **38**, 678–692 (2008). https://doi.org/10.20489/intjecse.107957

43. Leko, M.M., Roberts, C., Peyton, D., Pua, D.: Selecting evidence-based practices: what works for me. Interv. Sch. Clin. **54**(5), 286–294 (2019). https://doi.org/10.1177/1053451218819190

44. Martos, J., Ayuda, R., Freire, S., González, A., Llorente, M.: Trastornos del Espectro Autista de Alto Funcionamiento. Otra forma de aprender. CEPE, Madrid (2012)

45. McNeill, J.: Social validity and teachers' use of evidence-based practices for autism. J. Autism Dev. Disord. **49**(11), 4585–4594 (2019). https://doi.org/10.1007/s10803-019-04190-y

46. Sam, A.M., Cox, A.W., Savage, M.N., Waters, V., Odom, S.L.: Disseminating information on evidence-based practices for children and youth with autism spectrum disorder: AFIRM. J. Autism Dev. Disord. **50**, 1931–1940 (2019). https://doi.org/10.1007/s10803-019-03945-x

47. National Professional Development Center on Inclusion. What do We Mean by Professional Development in the Early Childhood Field? University of North Carolina, FPG Child Development Institute. https://npdci.fpg.unc.edu/sites/npdci.fpg.unc.edu/files/resources/NPDCI_Pro fessionalDevelopmentInEC_03-04-08_0.pdf. Accessed 27 May 2023

48. Buysse, V., Winton, P.J., Rous, B.: Reaching consensus on a definition of professional development for the early childhood field. Top. Early Child. Spec. Educ. **28**(4), 235–243 (2009). https://doi.org/10.1177/0271121408328173

49. Wood, J.J., McLeod, B.D., Klebanoff, S., Brookman-Frazee, L.: Toward the implementation of evidence-based interventions for youth with autism spectrum disorders in schools and community agencies. Behav. Therapy **46**(1), 83–95 (2015). https://doi.org/10.1016/j.beth. 2014.07.003

50. Simpson, R.L.: Evidence-based practices and students with autism spectrum disorders. Focus Autism Dev. Disabil. **20**, 140–149 (2005). https://doi.org/10.1177/10883576050200030201

51. Anderson, S.R., Romanczyk, R.G.: Early intervention for young children with autism: continuum based behavioural models. J. Assoc. Severely Handicapped **24**, 162–173 (1999). https://doi.org/10.2511/rpsd.24.3.162

52. Smith, T., Iadarola, S.: Evidence base update for autism spectrum disorder. J. Clin. Child Adolesc. Psychol. **44**, 897–922 (2015). https://doi.org/10.1080/15374416.2015.1077448

53. Odom, S.L., Collet-Klingerberg, L., Rogers, S.J., Hatton, D.D.: Evidence-based practices in interventions for children and youth with autism spectrum disorders. Prev. Sch. Fail. **54**(4), 275–282 (2010). https://doi.org/10.1080/10459881003785506
54. National Autism Center.: Findings and Conclusions: National Standards Report, Phase 2. National Autism Center. (2015)
55. Steinbrenner, J.R., et al.: Evidence-Based Practices for Children, Youth, and Young Adults with Autism. Frank Porter Graham Child Development Institute, The University of North Carolina: Chapel Hill, NC, USA (2020). https://ncaep.fpg.unc.edu/sites/ncaep.fpg.unc.edu/files/imce/documents/EBP%20Report%202020.pdf. Accessed 29 May 2023
56. Sandoval, M., Simón, C., Echeita, G.: Análisis y Valoración Crítica de las Funciones del Profesorado de Apoyo desde la Educación Inclusiva. Revista de Educación, nº extraordinario, 117–137 (2012). https://doi.org/10.4438/1988-592X-RE-2012-EXT-209
57. Able, H., Sreckovic, M.A., Schultz, T.R., Garwood, J.D., Sherman, J.: Views from the trenches: teacher and student supports needed for full inclusion of students with ASD. Teach. Educ. Spec. Educ. **38**, 44–57 (2015). https://doi.org/10.1177/0888406414558096
58. Borders, C.M., Jones, S., Szymanski, C.: Teacher ratings of evidence-based practices from the field of autism. Deaf Stud. Deaf Educ. **20**(1), 91–100 (2015). https://doi.org/10.1093/deafed/enu033
59. Sulek, R., Trembath, D., Paynter, J., Keen, D.: Empirically supported treatments for students with autism: general education teacher knowledge, use, and social validity ratings. Dev. Neurorehabilitation **22**(6), 380–389 (2018). https://doi.org/10.1080/17518423.2018.1526224
60. National Professional Development Center on Autism Spectrum Disorder.: Comparison of NPDC and NSP EBPs. https://autismpdc.fpg.unc.edu/sites/autismpdc.fpg.unc.edu/files/imce/documents/Matrix%20NPDC%20NSP%20v3.pdf. Accessed 29 May 2023
61. Larraceleta-González, A., Castejón-Fernández, L., Iglesias-García, M.-T., Núñez-Pérez, J.C.: Un Estudio de las Necesidades de Formación del Profesorado en las Prácticas Basadas en Evidencias Científicas en el Ámbito del Alumnado con Trastorno del Espectro del Autismo. Siglo Cero Revista Española sobre Discapacidad Intelectual **53**(2), 125–144 (2022). https://doi.org/10.14201/scero2022532125144
62. Larraceleta, A., Castejón, L., Iglesias-García, M.T., Núñez, J.C.: Assessment of public special education teachers training needs on evidence-based practice for students with autism spectrum disorders in Spain. Children **9**, 83 (2022). https://doi.org/10.3390/children9010083
63. Instituto Nacional de Estadística.: Cifras Oficiales de Población de los Municipios Españoles en Aplicación de la Ley de Bases del Régimen Local (Art. 17). Asturias: Población por municipios y sexo. https://www.ine.es/jaxiT3/Datos.htm?t=2886. Accessed 30 May 2023
64. Ministerio de Educación y Formación Profesional.: EDUCAbase. http://estadisticas.mecd.gob.es/EducaDynPx/educabase/index.htm?type=pcaxis&path=/no-universitaria/alumnado/apoyo/2021-2022/acnee&file=pcaxis&l=s0. Accessed 30 May 2023
65. Goodman, L.A.: Snowball sampling. Ann. Math. Stat. **32**, 148–170 (1961). https://doi.org/10.1214/aoms/1177705148
66. Bruinsma, Y., Minjarez, M.B., Schreibman, L., Stahmer, A.C.: Naturalistic Developmental Behavioural Interventions for Autism Spectrum Disorder. Paul H. Brookes Publishing Co., Baltimore (2020)
67. Rogers, S.J., Dawson, G.: Early Start Denver Model for Young Children with Autism: Promoting Language, Learning, and Engagement. The Guilford Press, New York (2010)
68. Autism Focused Intervention Resources and Modules. https://afirm.fpg.unc.edu. Accessed 29 May 2023
69. Osman, D.J., Warner, J.R.: Measuring teacher motivation: the missing link between professional development and practice. Teach. Teach. Educ. **92**, 103064 (2020). https://doi.org/10.1016/j.tate.2020.103064

70. La Nueva España.: Educación Niega los Recortes en Atención a la Diversidad por los que le Condena el Juez. https://www.lne.es/asturias/2021/04/15/educacion-niega-recortes-atencion-diversidad-48381919.html. Accessed 30 May 2023

71. Morin, K.L., Sam, A., Tomaszewski, B., Waters, V., Odom, S.L.: Knowledge of evidence-based practices and frequency of selection among school-based professionals of students with autism. J. Spec. Educ. **55**(3), 143–152 (2021). https://doi.org/10.1177/0022466920958688

72. Giannopoulou, I., Pasalari, E., Korkoliakou, P., Douzenis, A.: Raising autism awareness among Greek teachers. Int. J. Disabil. Devel. Educ. **66**(1), 70–81 (2019). https://doi.org/10.1080/1034912X.2018.1462474

73. Brock, M.E., Huber, H.B., Carter, E.W., Juarez, A.P., Warren, Z.E.: Statewide assessment of professional development needs related to educating students with autism spectrum disorder. Focus Autism Other Dev. Disabil. **29**, 67–79 (2014). https://doi.org/10.1177/1088357614522290

74. Van Kessel, R., et al.: Inclusive education in the European Union: a fuzzy-set qualitative comparative analysis of education policy for autism. Soc. Work Public Health **36**(2), 286–299 (2021). https://doi.org/10.1080/19371918.2021.1877590

Let's Open the Locker of Creativity - How the Traditional Educational Escape Room Changed into a Virtual Puzzle Game During the COVID-19 Pandemic

Monika Frania[⊠] [iD]

Faculty of Social Sciences, Institute of Pedagogy, University of Silesia in Katowice,
Grażyńskiego 53, 40-126 Katowice, Poland
monika.frania@us.edu.pl

Abstract. This research aimed to analyze the opinions of prospective early childhood and primary school teachers regarding implementing the educational escape room method in the teaching process in three forms: traditional 1:1, miniature version, and virtual. These three forms have been utilized in blended learning sessions since the onset of the Covid-19 pandemic, necessitating alternatives to physical, educational escape rooms. This qualitative study is based on the focus group interview method, conducted in 12 discussion focus groups. The participants consisted of 62 female final-year master's degree students who, over one semester, participated in an elective course designed to familiarize them with the educational escape room (EER) method.

The research findings indicate that most respondents perceive more advantages than disadvantages in the educational escape room method across all its forms. Students observe a positive impact on team building, collaboration, motivation, and satisfaction with task completion. Respondents suggest that puzzle-solving is an activity suitable for individuals of all ages, and they consider creating their own EER project as an effective method of working with youth and adults.

Keywords: Blended Learning · Educational Escape Room · Gamification

1 Introduction

In recent years, gamification has become an increasingly popular strategy for enhancing learning outcomes. Gamification involves using game design elements in non-game contexts to increase engagement, motivation, and learning outcomes [1]. One promising form of gamification is educational escape rooms, which involve the creation of a physical or virtual room from which participants must escape by solving a series of puzzles or challenges [2]. Educational escape rooms offer a unique approach to learning by creating immersive and interactive environments that encourage active learning and problem-solving skills. This article's objective entails examining opinions expressed within focus group discussions conducted among individuals undergoing teacher training regarding

Ł. Tomczyk (Ed.): NMP 2022, CCIS 1916, pp. 102–114, 2023.
https://doi.org/10.1007/978-3-031-44581-1_8

the efficacy of the escape room tool in fostering interpersonal connections, influencing the motivational process in learning, and assessing the merits and demerits associated with its implementation. Additionally, the article seeks to explore perceptions about the offline forms of escape rooms, namely the traditional 1:1 format, the miniature variant, and the online version.

The closure and restrictions associated with the epidemic threat during the Covid-19 pandemic have significantly impacted education [3]. Scientific research emphasizes that teachers, educators, students, and university lecturers face challenges in primary, secondary, and higher education [4]. Many negative aspects and specific positive changes have been discussed, particularly those related to developing and implementing new technologies in teaching. The educational escape room in the classroom typically took the form of a physical space - a room arrangement or a miniature version. Remote teaching has necessitated the search for new solutions.

2 Theoretical Framework

Educational escape rooms, often associated with gamification and the Game Based Learning (GBL) approach, have gained popularity in recent years, although the history and theory of incorporating games into education have a much longer tradition [5]. The use of escape rooms during educational activities and entertainment activities also finds its references in the theories of cooperative learning [6] and Flow Theory [7]. As discussed in the Discussion section, many teachers and researchers have recognized the use of educational escape rooms as a tool for improving learning outcomes and soft skills where students *"(…) enjoyed the activity and was highly engaged during the activity, more than in comparison to regular classes."*[8].

Educational escape rooms can be designed and implemented in various forms for educational purposes. The most common choice is to replicate the commercial entertainment vision of such places in a 1:1 scale classroom, transforming the space into a large-scale game. Another form is the miniature version, where the concept of an escape room is preserved but adapted to a "box" version within a limited space, not necessarily a box. Another form is the online game, which follows similar rules to a physical escape room. In many cases, this virtual form has replaced offline versions during the restrictions associated with the Covid-19 pandemic. Gamification was part of online teaching in many online classrooms where modern and creative teachers and educators were unafraid to cross boundaries. It was indicated that *"(…) it is possible to infer that gamification can be effectively combined with traditional teaching methods, such as online lectures, in order to enhance students' engagement and deliver curricula material that usually is taught through face-to-face education. Likely, technology-enhanced learning initiatives will become more prominent as the education landscape is reorganized following COVID-19, and gamification may therefore be considered as an option to augment traditional learning no longer deliverable at traditional face-to-face classes."*[9]. An online educational escape room can be considered an example of implementing gamification in e-learning.

The effectiveness of educational escape rooms, in general, can be attributed to their ability to create an immersive and interactive learning environment that encourages active participation and problem-solving skills. Educational escape rooms promote critical thinking, problem-solving, and teamwork skills by providing participants with a series of puzzles or challenges to solve [10]. The engaging nature of the game also motivates participants to engage significantly with educational content, leading to increased retention of information, as well as empathy [11].

Furthermore, educational escape rooms can be designed to promote learning in specific subject areas. For example, an educational escape room designed for teaching computational thinking. It is found that: *"(...) educational potential of escape rooms in (...) science education as an engaging, problem-based environment for processing, rehearsing, and formative assessment in which thinking and teamwork skills are required, with the opportunity for teachers to scaffold learning processes without losing students' feeling of ownership, discovery and victory."* [12].

3   Method

In October 2022, 62 early childhood and preschool education students studying at the University of Silesia in Katowice, Poland, were invited to participate in an elective course titled *"Educational Escape Room"*. Throughout the semester and after completing the course, the students were invited to participate in focus group interviews conducted in 12 focus groups. Below are the results of the discourse analysis conducted during interviews, aimed at addressing the research problems derived from the research objectives, which were formulated as follows:

– What are the opinions of participants undergoing teacher training regarding the effectiveness of the escape room tool in fostering interpersonal bonds, influencing motivational processes in learning, and assessing the advantages and disadvantages associated with its implementation?
– How do respondents perceive different Escape Room (EER) forms, namely: the offline version in the traditional 1:1 format, the miniature variant, and the online version?

These research problems are related to three subtopics, which are detailed below. Additionally, the reflection in the Results section has been organized according to these subthemes.

The instructional activities were based on workshops during which the students tested, planned, designed, built, and implemented educational escape rooms. In the final phase, they solved puzzles in their peers' games. The participants could experience and try escape rooms in three forms: 1:1, miniature, and virtual.

All participants were divided into two instructional groups, Group A and Group B, for the research. Group A consisted of 26 women studying full-time, Monday through Friday, in their second year of master's studies. Group B, on the other hand, consisted of 36 women studying part-time, on weekends (Friday to Sunday), and also in their second year of master's studies. In Group A, the respondents were divided into five four-to-five-member focus groups; in Group B, they were divided into seven four-to-five-member focus groups. Each group went through three sessions of focus group interviews.

The research was conducted in 12 focus groups, following the respondent-moderator focus group model [13]. The researcher participated in both the instructional activities phase and the interview phase. However, during the crucial phase, the researcher selected group leaders who moderated the discussions, allowing for more authentic responses. The entire instructional-research process lasted from October 2022 to February 2023.

The focus group interviews aimed to analyze future teachers' attitudes, experiences, and reflections regarding the effectiveness of the escape room method in education and relationship building, depending on the form: 1:1, miniature, or virtual.

The selection criteria for participating in the focus group interviews were as follows: 1) year of study – all students were in their final year of master's studies; 2) specialization/field of study – all students were studying early childhood and preschool education; 3) participation in classes at the university both before and during the COVID-19-related restrictions, experiencing remote education; 4) voluntary choice of elective classes and participation in the study – all students freely chose to participate in the escape room classes; 5) familiarity with all forms of escape rooms – all students had the opportunity to experience both offline and online forms during the semester-long instructional meetings.

After reviewing the relevant literature, the following subtopics were identified, around which the moderators formulated their questions:

- Educational escape room and relationship building within the group at each working stage with this method.
- Evaluation of different escape room forms and a comparison between offline and online forms in terms of selected educational aspects.
- Advantages and disadvantages of the educational escape room method concerning pedagogical work.

Each group consisted of four to five individuals, and the designated moderator was a student and a participant in the discussions. The membership in a specific focus group was identical to the membership in the project group in which students worked on their own 1:1, miniature, and virtual escape room projects throughout the semester. Therefore, participants could exchange their views during the semester-long project work, implementation, and puzzle-solving stages. The duration of each session was flexible for each group and was not time-limited. The researcher played a combined role of an interviewer who intervened and an observer.

The obtained data were qualitatively analyzed and coded according to categories corresponding to the subthemes. The method of focus groups, based on interviews and discussions, which is used interchangeably in this article, is a good choice when qualitatively exploring the participants' perspectives. The main reason for choosing this method was the nature of the topic focused on the five-month cycle of experiencing the pedagogical method of escape rooms by the respondents. The opinion of final-year students, most of whom (66.12% of the participants) are already working (part-time students) or cooperating (full-time students) in the profession, is critical at such an advanced stage.

4   Results

The focus discussions conducted by 62 respondents in 12 focus groups were filled with emotions and complemented the student's experience of various escape rooms, both offline and online. The conclusions drawn from the analyses and several examples of students' statements are organized below according to subthemes. The names of the respondents have been anonymized.

4.1 Educational Escape Rooms (EER) and Team-Building at Every Stage of Using the Method

The conclusions drawn from 11 out of the 12 focus groups created regarding team-building during the escape room method were very similar. Students emphasized the significant role and potential of the puzzle room in fostering community and relationships within project teams. There were no significant differences between groups A and B. They noted that this method requires a high level of collaboration with others. Here are some statements supporting this thesis:

- Student X31: *"Without teamwork, no project could succeed."*
- Student X1: *"It is the perfect method for integrating and building deep relationships. We are faced with a task, an exciting challenge, and it brings us closer together."*
- Student X22: *"The most challenging part for me was the initial phase before we came up with the concept. Later, when we started creating stories, developing the plot, and constructing puzzles, I felt we were inspiring each other. I was so involved that time flew by quickly. I discovered abilities in my classmates that I had no idea about."*

Collaboration with others, and thus establishing and maintaining relationships, is important both in the planning and design stages and in the construction and implementation of the escape room. Respondents also emphasized the ability to negotiate, reach a consensus, and share a common vision regarding the escape room's storyline and content. It was mentioned that every puzzle provides an opportunity to seek common solutions.

- Student X44: *"We spent the longest time working on the puzzles and the logical sequence of events. We needed to have a cohesive vision to achieve the outcome we did. It didn't work out at every moment, but ultimately, we succeeded, and I'm proud of what we created."*

The importance of team cohesion was emphasized when time pressure increased as the deadline for the design phase approached. In 7 teams, it was strongly expressed that the experience of building an escape room had solid emotional potential. Students acknowledged that negative emotions, such as anger or frustration arising from conflicts, and positive emotions, such as joy and pride, emerged during the process. The sense of fulfillment and community was particularly strong when successfully implementing their own project.

- Student X6: *"We argued the most during two moments: the initial conceptual phase and building the specific physical space of the miniature escape room. It was a roller coaster of emotions."*
- Student X32: *"These were the best educational activities this semester. We laughed and argued together. Afterward, I felt a tremendous sense of satisfaction."*

One of the teams, which relied on a clear division of tasks during the creation of the escape rooms, noticed during the discussion that building relationships ultimately depends on the individual personalities and characteristics of the team members, as their sense of community was not particularly highlighted. This team admitted they collaborated to complete the project but *"cooperated out of necessity without significant willingness."*

Significantly, during the discussions, all teams initially focused on emphasizing the importance of relationship building to a greater or lesser extent in constructing their own escape room, and only in the second instance did they consider this issue in the context of solving puzzles created by others.

Among the respondents, it was evident that more emotionally intense relationship building, filled with discussions and internal crises within the team, took place during the design of their own escape room.

- Student X58: *"Building the escape room was more challenging because I had never worked in this way before, but I also enjoyed it more than solving them. Especially in the virtual escape room, solving puzzles was not as exciting as creating."*
- Student X26: *"I thought we would not have enough time to come up with everything and prepare it ourselves, but we managed it with my classmates. When I saw how our converted room looked like a 1:1 escape room, even before other girls entered to take on the challenge, I knew we did a good job. I would gladly do it again."*

Regarding puzzle-solving, collaboration was also intense, but the sense of community manifested particularly after completing the task, often in the form of team satisfaction.

When constructing an escape room in the 1:1, miniature, and virtual formats, most respondents (9 groups) did not perceive a difference in relationship-building stimulation between these formats. However, they did notice a difference when solving puzzles in someone else's escape room and attempting to escape from a different escape room. In these cases, the sense of community, the potential for relationship stimulation, and collaboration were rated highest for the 1:1 and miniature versions while significantly lower for the virtual quest cage game in most focus groups.

4.2 Evaluation of Different Escape Room Forms and Comparison of Offline and Online Formats in the Context of Selected Educational Aspects

Evaluation of different escape room forms and comparison of offline and online formats in the context of selected educational aspects.

In the surveyed focus groups, participants were asked to compare the educational escape room as an offline method (in the 1:1 and miniature versions) with the online format to assess their sense of motivation. Most focus groups (10) rated their level of motivation for creating an offline and online puzzle room equally high. The participants emphasized similar stages of creation, such as the theme selection phase, story selection phase, logical story progression planning, construction of individual puzzles, and the building phase (in the case of offline options, manual preparation of space or interior arrangement, prop preparation; in the case of online options, platform selection, tool familiarization, creation of digital stages). However, when solving puzzles created by others, the motivation level was higher for the offline formats. The virtual version engaged the students, but not to the same extent as the "box" or 1:1 room escape experiences.

- Student X19: *"I was most engaged in the 1:1 escape room - I do not know when time flew. I had so much fun. We had great teamwork with the girls, so we were strongly motivated at every stage of designing, decorating the room, etc., and worked towards our goal."*
- Student X1: *"If I had to choose the most boring stage, it would be difficult for me because I really liked it, but I got a little bored with the virtual one."*

Individual factors also influence motivation.

- Student X59: "I definitely think it is something 'new' and unconventional. I enjoy creating different stories - whether on paper or in life, as part of various activities, etc. So here I have another field to explore. However, I usually have a problem with working in groups (in general) because I often can't collaborate the way I want to - but that is more of a flaw related to the consequences of perfectionism and the desire to perfect everything to the last detail, but not at the expense of fairness (sometimes when I see someone slacking off, I lose motivation to work in a group). So, I definitely have to be careful about that. However, I am glad I can get to know and experience this method, which opens a gateway to my future school practice."

Considering that the respondents are future teachers of grades 1–3 in primary schools and preschool groups, they were asked about this perspective. The conclusion drawn from the analysis of statements and findings in the 12 focus groups is that the offline/physical form is definitely more beneficial for younger children. For older students and adults, the online form is equally good. There were no significant differences between groups A and B.

The students' opinions regarding the role of puzzle rooms in imparting knowledge were inconsistent. Respondents saw the possibility, but at the same time, there were strong voices suggesting that it was primarily just entertainment. Importantly, students rated the online platform game slightly higher as a tool, as it *"does not evoke as many emotions and excitement as physical escape rooms, allowing the student to focus on the content."*

4.3 Advantages and Disadvantages of the Educational Escape Room (EER) Method Concerning Pedagogical Work

Discussions in focus groups were intended to identify the advantages and disadvantages of the educational escape room method in the context of future (or current) professional work. The respondents unanimously expressed high satisfaction with the activities and recognized the immense potential of this creative method in terms of general educational work, knowledge acquisition, and educational goals. The statements made in the focus group interviews later confirmed the results of an anonymous evaluative survey conducted independently by the institution where the session occurred.

The respondents emphasized the educational advantages of escape rooms, both in the form of 1:1, miniature, and virtual formats, in terms of:

- Activating students during lessons or extracurricular activities and diversifying educational tools (emphasizing that it should be "one of the methods" rather than replacing other traditional methods).
- Developing soft skills and serving as a tool for knowledge transfer.
- Flexibility in crisis situations, such as a sudden transition to remote education.

The following statements serve as examples:

- Student x59: *"Working with this method is activating, so I think it would benefit everyone as a way to 'refresh' lessons. Sometimes it can be done individually, and sometimes in groups. Our perception is not yet accustomed to such things during classes, so I believe it is something stimulating and motivating in terms of intrinsic motivation. I think this method should be used to summarize specific subjects or within spelling lessons, which are usually just 'shrouded in boredom.' I also think that EER cannot replace normal lessons. It is rather an addition, something 'extra,' 'festive,' but also something that develops logical thinking or attention."*
- Student x60: *"Escape rooms can teach organization, planning, prediction - which are necessary later, for example, in programming - logical thinking, creativity, attention concentration, and sometimes even technical skills related to construction. It also depends on the type of escape room."*
- Student x7: *"As a future teacher, I believe this method helps conduct in-person and remote classes. The definite advantage is the attractive form of work, which can better motivate students."*
- Student x11: *"I see only the advantages of creating a virtual escape room in education, starting with the accessibility of the tool used. The tool is transparent and well-constructed, so participants enjoy solving tasks that could be discouraging if presented on paper as a quiz. Such an escape room is also a challenge for slightly older people - it does not provide everything on a silver platter; you often have to search for ways to progress to the next slide or ponder over task solutions. For the youngest, this form will also be exciting, especially considering the fact that we are a media society, and children have access to smartphones/tablets/computers from an early age. This educational path - involving a digital screen, the possibility of clicking on specific elements, and playing music during certain tasks - will only enhance knowledge absorption".*

Additionally, respondents identified advantages in increased motivation, digital skill development, creativity, imagination, critical thinking, and collaboration.

The most prominent conclusion regarding the disadvantages in the context of pedagogical work was the significant time investment required by educators or teachers in constructing escape rooms.

- Student x57: "The main disadvantage of creating a virtual version is the time-consuming nature of the work. If we want the escape room to be of the highest quality in content and editing, we must be prepared to spend several hours working with the tool. Traditional version drawbacks: the materials needed to create such an escape room can be costly; it involves working with physical objects."

Other drawbacks mentioned were:

- Material costs for the offline version,
- Lack of access to devices in the online version,
- Logistic difficulties in organizing traditional escape rooms within the school premises,
- Issues of technology overuse and media saturation in the online version, particularly concerning younger children and associated health problems.

The following statements confirm these considerations:

- Student x3: *"Such an experience in the classroom is undoubtedly more memorable. However, the drawback of a traditional escape room is that it involves a large group of children in one room, requiring careful logistical planning to ensure that all students are engaged and have the opportunity to participate."*
- Student x1: *"A disadvantage of using this method online could be eye strain from staring at a computer monitor."*

Students also emphasized that the method and topic should be adapted to the children's age and developmental level, rightly emphasizing that constructing an escape room is a task suited for older children and adolescents. In the case of younger children, it is the teacher's responsibility to ensure their focus on solving puzzles.

In conclusion, despite the various dimensions of the discussions in all focus groups, the students are aware of the drawbacks and weaknesses while emphasizing the numerous advantages they perceive.

5 Discussion

Numerous scientific studies and educational reports have indicated that in many countries, the Covid-19 pandemic, particularly in the years 2020-2021, was a time of significant challenges and changes [14]. The response to the threat was the transition of many schools, universities, and institutions to remote forms of education. However, many institutions sought to overcome these challenges by introducing innovative remote methods [15] and simulations and games [16]. The elective course "Educational Escape Room" existed prior to 2020, only in the form of direct offline contact. At that time, the game format was conducted as a 1:1 escape room, transforming the classroom into an escape room. The second form was the miniature version, symbolically called the educational escape room in a box, which meant limited space but not necessarily a box. In the winter semester of 2020/2021, searching for alternatives and options for similar games to quest cages on online platforms became necessary. One semester was conducted remotely, and after the success of this format, confirmed by evaluation surveys, the entire course remained in a blended learning format, utilizing three forms. Research comparing students' attitudes towards the online and offline versions of educational escape rooms, particularly in chemistry, indicated that both forms support motivation in the learning process [17]. The escape room method has proven adaptable in such crisis situations [18].

The Covid-19 pandemic significantly increased the popularity of online versions of escape rooms [19–21]. For example, during the academic year 2019/2020, the method and research were implemented at the University of Almeria as part of the course "Socio-educational Programs in Children, Youth, Adults, and Seniors" in the Social Education degree. The results essentially confirmed what researchers had demonstrated at that university: virtual escape room games can awaken students' curiosity, participation, and motivation. Furthermore, the cooperative nature of this method was emphasized [22]. Increased team interaction, team-building, and a sense of community were also highlighted in studies conducted among dentistry students [23].

In our own research, future early childhood education teachers primarily appreciated the potential of using this tool as a challenge to solve for elementary school students, where the nature of the teaching content is integrated. At the same time, the respondents emphasized the method as an enriching element for subject lessons in older classes (through puzzle-solving or constructing their escape rooms). The universality of this method, both in its online and classic versions, is demonstrated by an experiment involving implementing an escape room in the STEM field. The research was conducted during two courses of experimental sciences and mathematics in the second year of the Primary Education degree at a Spanish university during the 2020/2021 academic year. The cognitive and affective domains were examined. Positive emotions, motivation, and reduced anxiety were observed. Researchers also noted the advantages in terms of knowledge transfer [24]. The method itself and its added value, such as community-building and teamwork, or, in the case of our research, the didactic component that aimed to familiarize students with the intricacies of the offline and online versions of the method, are just one aspect. The characteristic feature of all 1:1, miniature, and online escape rooms is that they have a narrative and relate to a specific range of knowledge. This range can be arbitrary, making the method universal. Other researchers' studies show that participating in this type of game increases knowledge in the specific subject area addressed by the escape room [25]. My experience implementing this method online during the pandemic allowed me to confirm this during media education classes, where students constructed virtual escape rooms on the Genial.ly platform, focusing on cybersecurity threats [26]. The research has also compared the level of acquired competencies and emotions among students in technical fields and future teachers. In both areas, no significant differences were observed. Positive emotions predominated, and competencies increased [27]. Such positive evaluations of the method and its reception can be attributed to the recipients being representatives of Generation Z, which seeks and expects innovation [28]. In this context, it is justified to implement the educational escape room method in both offline and online versions (not only in crises) in the training and curriculum of future teachers, not only in early childhood education but also in educator training for working with older youth.

In conclusion, numerous scientific studies and reports have highlighted the challenges and changes brought about by the Covid-19 pandemic in the education sector. The response to this situation was the widespread adoption of remote education, including the innovative use of educational escape rooms and online simulations. Research and experiences have shown the positive impact of escape rooms on motivation, knowledge acquisition, teamwork, and community-building. The adaptability of the escape room method in crises and its appeal to Generation Z makes it a valuable tool for both offline and online teaching environments. Future teachers can benefit from incorporating this method into their training and curriculum to enhance student engagement and learning outcomes.

6 Conclusion

In conclusion, it is worth emphasizing that after participating in a semester-long escape room course in three different forms, the surveyed students appreciated this form of educational work and evaluated it positively. They clearly distinguish be-tween their discussions on designing their escape room and solving puzzles created by others. They recognize the method's potential in their future professional work, mainly to diversify lessons, enhance student motivation, develop soft skills, and foster relationship-building within student groups. These advantages are evident both in the process of creating and solving puzzles. However, the participants acknowledge that, in the case of younger students, only the latter option is the appropriate solution. Among the disadvantages of creating an escape room, there is a significant role of the time-consuming and material burden on the educator who initiates such an activity. In the case of solving puzzles, sensory overload may be perceived by the respondents.

The students emphasized that if they had to choose only one form, it would undoubt-edly be the offline version, namely the 1:1 or miniature format. However, they also expressed high satisfaction with the opportunity to experience all three forms, meaning engaging in blended learning. Therefore, escape rooms can be regarded as a method of cooperation and activation, which can utilize the three forms mentioned above, while the virtual version can be considered a crisis-oriented approach in remote education.

Nevertheless, it is essential to acknowledge the limitations of the present study. The research methodology was qualitative, relying on qualitative focus group interviews as the primary data collection method. While this approach offers a rich and nuanced under-standing of the participants' opinions and reflections, it is constrained by the relatively small sample size.

Consequently, it would be beneficial to supplement these findings with experimental investigations that target the cognitive, emotional, and behavioral dimensions. Such a research design would contribute valuable insights and enhance the study's comprehen-siveness. Further research is needed in the Polish educational context to examine the effectiveness of all three methods in primary and secondary school didactics.

It is also worth emphasizing the research and workshops' practical dimension. The Educational Escape Room (EER) module has been permanently integrated into the cur-riculum for students at the Faculty of Social Sciences, University of Silesia in Katowice, and the program has been expanded to include other groups, including international students from social sciences fields, participating in the Erasmus+ exchange program. This expansion was made possible due to the recognition of the course through the *T4EU Innovative Teaching Award 2022* competition. In the 2023/2024 academic year, as part of the master's seminar for early childhood and preschool education students, also a small-scale pedagogical experiment utilizing the EER method is planned among a group of younger elementary school students.

References

1. Deterding, S., Dixon, D., Khaled, R., Nacke, L.: From game design elements to gamefulness: defining" gamification". In: Proceedings of the 15th International Academic MindTrek Conference: Envisioning Future Media Environments, pp. 9-15 (2011). https://doi.org/10.1145/2181037.2181040
2. Wiemker, M., Elumir, E., Clare, A.: Escape room games. Game Based Learn. **55**, 55-75 (2015). https://thecodex.ca/wp-content/uploads/2016/08/00511Wiemker-et-al-Paper-Escape-Room-Games.pdf. Accessed 28 Apr 2023
3. UNESCO. When Schools Shut: Gendered Impacts of COVID-19 School Closures (2021). https://unesdoc.unesco.org/ark:/48223/pf0000379270. Accessed 28 Apr 2023
4. Pokhrel, S., Chhetri, R.: A literature review on impact of COVID-19 pandemic on teaching and learning. High. Educ. Future **8**(1), 133–141 (2021). https://doi.org/10.1177/2347631120983481
5. Clarke, S., Peel, D.J., Arnab, S., Morini, L., Keegan, H., Wood, O.: EscapED: a framework for creating educational escape rooms and interactive games for higher/further education. Int. J. Serious Games **4**(3), 73-86 (2017). https://doi.org/10.17083/ijsg.v4i3.180
6. Doolittle, P.E.: Understanding cooperative learning through Vygotsky's zone of proximal development (1995). https://files.eric.ed.gov/fulltext/ED384575.pdf. Accessed 26 Apr 2023
7. Csikszentmihalyi, M., Rathunde, K.: The measurement of flow in everyday life: toward a theory of emergent motivation. In: Jacobs J.E. (ed.) Nebraska Symposium on Motivation, 1992: Developmental Perspectives on Motivation, pp. 57–97. University of Nebraska Press (1993)
8. Veldkamp, A., van de Grint, L., Knippels, M.C.P., van Joolingen, W.R.: Escape education: a systematic review on escape rooms in education. Educ. Res. Rev. **31**, 100364 (2020). https://doi.org/10.1016/j.edurev.2020.100364
9. Nieto-Escamez, F.A., Roldán-Tapia, M.D.: Gamification as online teaching strategy during COVID-19: a mini-review. Front. Psychol. **12**, 648552 (2021). https://doi.org/10.3389/fpsyg.2021.648552.
10. Bowyer, S.: Learn, play, design: using the escape room concept to teach creativity and innovation in a business course. Bus. Educ. Innov. J. **13**(59) (2021). http://www.beijournal.com/images/V13_N1_draft_9_12.pdf#page=59. Accessed 26 Apr 2023
11. Fotaris, P., Mastoras, T.: Room2Educ8: a framework for creating educational escape rooms based on design thinking principles. Educ. Sci. **12**(11), 768 (2022). https://doi.org/10.3390/educsci12110768
12. Veldkamp, A., Knippels, M.C.P., van Joolingen, W.R.: Beyond the early adopters: escape rooms in science education. In: Frontiers in Education, vol. 6. Frontiers Media SA. (2021). https://doi.org/10.3389/feduc.2021.622860
13. Nyumba, T.O., Wilson, K., Derrick, C.J., Mukherjee, N.: The use of focus group discussion methodology: Insights from two decades of application in conservation. Meth. Ecol. Evol. **9**(1), 20–32 (2018). https://doi.org/10.1111/2041-210X.12860
14. Iivari, N., Sharma, S., Ventä-Olkkonen, L.: Digital transformation of everyday life–how COVID-19 pandemic transformed the basic education of the young generation and why information management research should care? Int. J. Inf. Manage. **55**, 102183 (2020). https://doi.org/10.1016/j.ijinfomgt.2020.102183
15. Gomez, M.: A COVID-19 intervention: using digital escape rooms to provide professional development to alternative certification educators. J. Technol. Teach. Educ. **28**(2), 425-432 (2020). https://www.learntechlib.org/primary/p/216251/. Accessed 02 May 2023
16. Kriz, W.C.: Gaming in the time of COVID-19. Simul. Gaming **51**(4), 403-410 (2020). https://journals.sagepub.com/doi/pdf/10.1177/1046878120931602

17. Ang, J.W.J., Ng, Y.N.A., Liew, R.S.: Physical and digital educational escape room for teaching chemical bonding. J. Chem. Educ. **97**(9), 2849–2856 (2020). https://doi.org/10.1021/acs.jchemed.0c00612

18. Wynn, L.: Adapting the escape room to engage learners two ways during COVID-19. J. Diab. Clin. Res. **3**(1), 6–8 (2021). https://doi.org/10.33696/diabetes.3.031

19. Ross, J.M., Wright, L., Arikawa, A.Y.: Adapting a classroom simulation experience to an online escape room in nutrition education. Online Learn. **25**(1) (2021). doi: https://doi.org/10.24059/olj.v25i1.2469

20. Kretz, C., Payne, C., Reijerkerk, D.: Study room time machine: creating a virtual library escape game during COVID. Coll. Undergraduate Libr. **28**(3–4), 273–295 (2021). https://doi.org/10.1080/10691316.2021.1975341

21. Yllana Prieto, F.; Jeong, J.S. González Gómez, D.: Virtual escape room and STEM content: effects on the affective domain on teacher trainees. JOTSE: J. Technol. Sci. Educ. **11**(2), 331–342 (2021). https://doi.org/10.3926/jotse.1163

22. Manzano-León, A., et al.: Online escape room during COVID-19: a qualitative study of social education degree students' experiences. Educ. Sci. **11**(8), 426 (2021). https://doi.org/10.3390/educsci11080426

23. Zaug, P., et al.: Development of an innovative educational escape game to promote teamwork in dentistry. Eur. J. Dent. Educ. **26**(1), 116–122 (2022). https://doi.org/10.1111/eje.12678

24. Yllana-Prieto, F., González-Gómez, D., Jeong, J.S.: Influence of two educational escape room–breakout tools in PSTs' affective and cognitive domain in STEM (science and mathematics) courses. Heliyon **9**, e12795 (2023), https://doi.org/10.1016/j.heliyon.2023.e12795

25. Iverson, L., Jizba, T., Manning, L.: Beat the clock! implementation and evaluation of an escape Room. J. Nurse Pract. **19**(5), 104523 (2023). https://doi.org/10.1016/j.nurpra.2022.12.007

26. Frania, M.: Educational E-escape room as an educational method of media literacy training for future teachers during the COVID-19 pandemic. Media Educ. (Mediaobrazovanie) (3), 452-459 (2021). https://doi.org/10.13187/me.2021.3.452. https://me.cherkasgu.press/journals_n/1630960618.pdf. Accessed 02 May 2023

27. Sánchez-Martín, J., Corrales-Serrano, M., Luque-Sendra, A., Zamora-Polo, F.: Exit for success. Gamifying science and technology for university students using escape-room. A preliminary approach. Heliyon **6**(7), e04340 (2020). https://doi.org/10.1016/j.heliyon.2020.e04340

28. Wintheiser, K., Becknell, M: A guide for facilitating an escape room for undergraduate nursing students. Teach. Learn. Nurs. **18**(1), 181-184 (2023). https://doi.org/10.1016/j.teln.2022.08.006

The OH!BUG App: Learning to Identify Plants Through Their Characteristics

Sara Martins[1]([⊠]) [iD] and Carlos Santos[2] [iD]

[1] University of Aveiro, 3810-193 Aveiro, Portugal
`saracristiana@ua.pt`
[2] DigiMedia, Department of Communication and Arts, University of Aveiro, 3810-193 Aveiro, Portugal
`carlossantos@ua.pt`

Abstract. Urban migration has resulted in a disconnection from the natural world and consequently a lack of knowledge about other living beings. Since the creation of Sustainable Development Goals (SDGs) there have been made efforts to inform and educate citizens, especially the youngest, in pro-environmental attitudes and behaviours by promoting critical thinking about our world through environmental education. With the continuous digitalization of information, mobile apps and games with narratives around climate change and environmental issues, have gained a place in this mission. In this paper, we present the creation process and the results of the first usability tests of the OH!BUG app, a digital product developed to connect young learners to plants, by helping them to identify the species through their characteristics.

Keywords: Mobile Application · Sustainable Development · Environmental Education · Biodiversity · Species Identification · Gamification

1 Introduction

At the same time as the world's population tends to move away from natural environments, living mostly in urban areas [1], humanity faces sustainability challenges that require the protection and preservation of the ecosystems that are essential to life on planet Earth. The industrialized world and urban migration have led us to a disconnection from other living things which has implications for our understanding of them [2]. Reports show that biodiversity is declining faster than at any other time in human history with an irreversible effect of species extinction, which makes ecosystems more fragile and less resistant to disruptions [3]. Human activities and decisions have been recognized as a part of the problem [4] so it became clear, over the last few decades, that it's fundamental to promote pro-environmental and sustainable values, attitudes and actions in our society.

To answer this problem, the United Nations has defined a global agenda to reach until 2030 that includes a framework of sustainability goals that has been universally accepted and includes the need to take action in raising awareness for environmental issues and

© The Author(s), under exclusive license to Springer Nature Switzerland AG 2023
Ł. Tomczyk (Ed.): NMP 2022, CCIS 1916, pp. 115–124, 2023.
https://doi.org/10.1007/978-3-031-44581-1_9

climate change [5]. Among them, goal 15 points out the importance of managing and restoring forests, combating desertification and reversing biodiversity loss, reinforcing the idea that living species such as humans depend on the balance of nature and its ecosystems.

On the other side, the Sustainable Development Goals (SDGs) acknowledge the potential of education as a means to achieve sustainability referring in Goal 4, Quality Education, the need to "ensure that all learners acquire the knowledge and skills needed to promote sustainable development" [5].

Education has been revealed to be a key factor to respond climate change as long as behavioural change cannot occur without environmental knowledge [6]. As the United Nations themselves refer:

> "Sustainable development cannot be achieved by technological solutions, political regulation or financial instruments alone. We need to change the way we think and act. This requires quality education and learning for sustainable development at all levels and in all social contexts." [7].

However, studies reveal that have been discrepancies and deficits in Education for Sustainable Development (ESD), for example, UNESCO reports that only 20% of teachers can explain well how to take action against climate change [8]. This could be linked to the fact that the concept of sustainability has been taught from a particular point of view [9] rather than allowing students to reach their own conclusions based on critical reflection which leads to a disconnection between environmental education and personality responsibility [10]. For this reason, it has been considered a reassessment of the educational efforts to improve the process of teaching environmental education [11].

So, in the last decade, we have assisted a new approach to ESD by adopting progressive pedagogical methods such as critical thinking, participatory decision-making, value-based learning and social learning so that learners understand of the world based on their own observations and develop competences to take action [12]. These methodologies attempt to go beyond the "exposure to information to the transformation of values and behaviours in order to contribute to solutions for environmental problems" [13]. Environmental awareness and education must approach real-life problems that are easier for people to relate to, by reflecting on their surroundings and learning from their own experiences [14].

At the same time, technological developments gave us the opportunity to create new forms of engaging young learners in environmental subjects based on these new pedagogical methods. Smart technological tools have proved to be an important and alternative resource concerning to achieve the SDGs goals [15] with the potential to engage and educate young learners in scientific concepts and topics, promoting their motivation, curiosity and critical reflection on the environment [16].

This paper presents the case study of the mobile application OH!BUG, an app developed to connect young learners and the natural world of plants. The theoretical framework addresses the technological development of mobile apps and their role in achieving environmental sustainability to change environmental values and behaviours in younger citizens. Following we explain the thinking process of designing the OH!BUG app, the implication of scientific research to build an identification system using the characteristics of different species and the feedback of young citizens on the first version of the application.

1.1 Species Identification and Sustainable Development

As Kaplan and Kaplan [17] referred to in their book "The Experience of Nature: A psychological perspective." people often see Nature or the natural world as an external part of human beings, something away from us. Recognising the role of biodiversity as a fundamental part of life on planet Earth and the need to protect the diversity of living species is a starting point to understanding the complex concept of sustainability [18]. Although the knowledge about biodiversity and its importance is seen as a basic link to achieving sustainable development or an essential goal in environmental education [19], over the last few decades we assisted a phenomenon of significantly decreasing understanding of ecological processes and the natural world referred as ecological illiteracy [20]. An environmentally literate citizen "is an individual who is, most importantly, informed about environmental issues and problems and possesses the attitudes and skills for solving them" but also someone who "takes action in terms of changing his or her own behaviours in order to remediate or prevent further environmental problems" [19].

Skills such as the identification of species are important for people to develop an interest in environmental issues and sustainability [21]. This could be related to the simple reason that the identification of plants requires to have contact with the natural world. This kind of experience may develop a "possible emotional and/or cognitive relationship between the individual and nature" [2] and therefore with environmental issues.

1.2 Mobile Apps and Games for ESD

In a digital era of information where we use technological devices every day, mobile apps and games gain users' attention with billions of apps downloaded worldwide in online stores [22]. The rising of new forms of communication has been reflected in the daily life of our society, with apps and games transcending to sectors beyond entertainment [23]. Some of these mobile applications include gamification methods and mechanisms, with the use of game elements in contexts considered non-game ranging from themes such as productivity, finance, health, education and sustainability [24]. In education, studies report a significant increase in motivation and learning achievements of students using digital game-based applications [25]. That's why gamified mobile applications and games have gained popularity in educational programs as an alternative tool to traditional methods of teaching, having the potential to engage young learners on issues related to climate change and sustainability [6]. For that reason, we have witnessed in the last few years a growing development of mobile apps and games with narratives around climate change and environmental issues, such as the need to protect wildlife, reduce atmospheric pollution, litter and energy consumption, food waste or management of natural resources [26].

Apps and games have the ability to engage users in environmental behaviours users by reducing the perceived risks of those same behaviors and giving tangible pro-environmental goals to achieve [27]. These apps and games often appeal to users' emotions as part of the gamified experience, promoting sensitivity towards ecology and developing empathy with the visualization of different negative scenarios and future implications of their acts [28]. On the other hand, some apps try to have a positive approach to sustainability placing the users in the role of a scientist giving them the mission to search and discover scientific observations of living beings such as animals and plants, allowing them to participate in collective data in the fields of biology and ecology [29].

2   The OH!BUG App

By acknowledging the background theoretical framework, we decided to develop a mobile app that aims to engage young users in the role of an explorer by encouraging them to identify the plants in their surroundings.

The OH!BUG app was originally designed in 2020 during the Startup Voucher Portugal Program 2019–2022 in which the designer of the OH!BUG app participated and was later developed in collaboration with a outsourcing development team in 2021. The OH!BUG app is now available in Google Store and App Store.

At the origin of the mobile app is the constructionism methodology, as it is believed that app users can (re)construct their knowledge about plants as they build their maps. Starting from the idea that if we recognize the plants that we observe in our daily lives and realize their value, we will be more sensitive to their existence and will be able to protect and preserve them. Furthermore the OH!BUG application aims to contribute to environmental literacy by teaching about the different characteristics of plants, shapes and colours, to understand the diversity of the living beings that share this planet with us.

The target audience for this mobile application is children from 8 years old. However, it can be used by younger children as the description of different plant characteristics is always accompanied by several illustrations (Fig. 1). To appeal to this specific audience, the design of the application uses colourful graphic elements and visual references from the natural world such as insects. The insects play a role in the narrative of the application and are used as avatars, comparing the users to little bugs on a journey of discovering plants and being an important part of the well-being of the ecosystems.

2.1   Georeferenced Map

Users have access to a personal georeferenced map where they insert the plants that they can identify. The plants identified by the users are shown by the location where they were found through an icon where can access their name and information (Fig. 2). The user can search for how many specific species they have found to see their geographical distribution on the map.

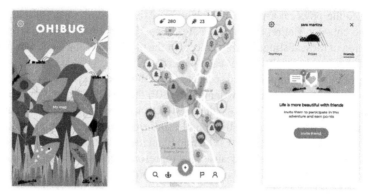

Fig. 1. Colourful illustrations are used in OH!BUG application aims to attract young users.

Fig. 2. Georeferenced map in the OH!BUG app.

2.2 Designing a Species Identification System

The species identification system in the OH!BUG application is inspired by the dichotomous scientific method of species identification. Dichotomous keys are usually used in botany or zoology to classify or identify living organisms and are based on a decision between two alternatives in a series of questions until the species name are identified [30]. The selection of possible answers is based on the physical characteristics of the species, which requires attention to the detail of the plant and the critical thinking of the observer.

The identification of species in the OH!BUG app is carried out through an interactive system of filters by a combination of characteristics - the type of plant, type of leaf, flower, fruit and habitat (Fig. 3). For each section there are several options to be selected according to the physical aspect of the plant, for example, in the type of leaf, the user can choose between Entire; Lobed; Dentate; Long; Compound; Palm Tree or Needle. The selection of these distinguishable aspects of the plant allows the user to be presented with a list of possible results that fit each pattern.

As species identification is often seen as a difficult process because is compared with the learning of new words of a new language [30], the OH!BUG app uses illustrations and icons to help the user to identify the most detectable elements of the plant. Visual communication is used to simplify the complex information related to botanical subjects and demystify the challenging process behind plant identification. Icons are an essential part of the identification system because they represent a quick and easy way to convey information and make decisions about the plant found.

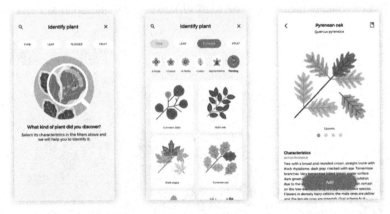

Fig. 3. Final design wireframes of the identification system in OH!BUG application.

2.3 Gamification

Gamification has been used in mobile apps to motivate users in non-game activities by communicating their progress in the accomplishment of sustainable actions [32]. So as a form of engagement, gamification mechanisms and components were included in the OH!BUG application such as points, levels, rewards, challenges and avatars. The integration of game elements in the application aims to turn the process of identification playful and fun, providing a ludic experience that appeals to the user's emotions in the achievement of progressive states in the game.

For each plant that users insert in their map, they gain points and level up the game. The levels of the game are shown in the user's journey on their profile. While challenges are based on concrete goals or tasks that users must complete. These challenges increase in difficulty, beginning with tasks such as "Identify a tree" to "Find a species with lobed leaf". The conclusion of a challenge ensures a reward that users can access in their profile.

The gamification methods and dynamics are limited only to the user and cannot be seen by other participants of the OH!BUG application. However, this represent a potential grow for these gamification systems in the future, with the collaboration between users, creation of team players or even collaborative maps.

3   Results

Based on the results obtained in a pilot study, the Beta version of the mobile app was developed. This version was tested in July of 2021 with 3 children from the 3rd grade to 6th grade and the results obtained allowed the mobile application to be improved, to obtain a version close to the final one.

Usability tests were realized using a high-fidelity prototype including all interactive features of the OH!BUG app. The tests include an introduction about the purpose of this study and a quick explanation of how to proceed, followed by a script with multiple tasks to complete. To simulate the identification of the plants were shown a sequence of pictures with key elements that allowed the identification of common trees and shrubs. In the end, the participants had to answer a questionnaire about their experience using the application, based on the five-level Likert scale (Fig. 4). The results were positive in the answers given by the participants, giving rise to the following diagram:

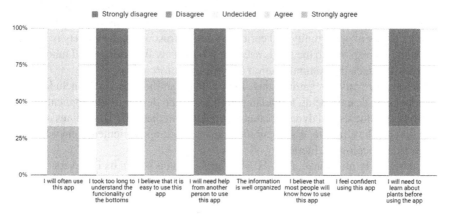

Fig. 4. Answers of the participants to the usability questionnaire.

At the same time, the test was observed from an external point of view making it possible to analyse the reaction and emotions of users attempting to complete the requested tasks and classify them within the following parameters: completed without difficulty; completed with some difficulty; undecided; completed with great difficulty; does not complete the task. The majority of the assignments were completed quickly without apparent difficulty and the use of the application took place continuously and fluidly. However, just one participant was able to identify all of the plants without any help. The remaining participants showed difficulties in interpreting the images in order to characterize the different properties of the plants. Besides that, the participants show a preference for the use of the interactive system of plant identification, referring to it as fun and colourful showing the plant's characteristics with simplicity and creativity.

The fact that they had to interpret the image of the plant and search for the right icon or characteristic in the system, by comparing different illustrations and the possible results presented, reveals to be a game side of the app that was not considered at the beginning of its creation.

4 Limitations

Although the results of the usability test were useful to review specific aspects of the application that should be improved, both in terms of the graphical look and the user's experience, there are a few points that should be considered in future research related to the OH!BUG app. First, this initial study used a small sample for testing the technology and covered an age group very close. With this limitation, it became difficult to compare different points of view on the application and the results were quite similar. A larger sample of users should be used in further studies to achieve significant statistical results and allow a detailed comparison of distinct approaches to the OH!BUG app. Another aspect to be enforced in future groups of participants is the cross-cultural and generational diversity to understand the effectiveness of the application in different cognitive and social developments.

A second limitation was the content of the usability test itself. The following researchers should explore the different triggers in the emotions of the participants, detecting points of opportunity and curiosity or even frustration and anxiety of the user. The emotional response to the app is necessary to improve both design and functionality but also to enhance the communication of botanical information.

The final limitation regarding this study is that gamification is not included in the questionnaires, despite being a fundamental part of the design of the application. The game-based elements and dynamics that are included in the OH!BUG defines an opportunity to study the effectiveness of gamification in mobile apps oriented to environmental education and ecological literacy.

As previously mentioned, the OH!BUG application is still in its Beta version which implies that the application itself has limitations and issues to solve. Currently, the database contains 38 registered species that are found mainly in Portuguese territory, where the application was developed. However, we assume these limitations as research opportunities and possibilities to grow and improve this digital product.

5 Conclusions

Taking into consideration the presented theoretical contextualization, ecological knowledge can guide citizens to have pro-environmental attitudes and actions by helping to understand the importance of ecosystems and biodiversity. This way, the objective of the OH!BUG application of teaching about vegetal species reveals to be promising in a way that can lead users to care for and preserve the plants identified. The interactive identification system reveals to be an essential feature of the app because of its playful and game-like design. Future research must cover a wider and more diverse audience of participants, their emotions and their response to the gamified mechanisms of the app.

References

1. United Nations: Revision of World Urbanization Prospects (2018)
2. Beery, T., Ingemar Jönsson, K., Elmberg, J.: From environmental connectedness to sustainable futures: Topophilia and human affiliation with nature. Sustainability **7**, 8837–8854 (2015). https://doi.org/10.3390/SU7078837
3. United Nations: Life on land: Why it matters?. https://www.un.org/sustainabledevelopment/wp-content/uploads/2019/07/15_Why-It-Matters-2020.pdf. Accessed 10 Aug 2023
4. United Nations: The Sustainable Development Goals Report (2022)
5. United Nations: Transforming our world: the 2030 Agenda for Sustainable Development Transforming our world: the 2030 Agenda for Sustainable Development Preamble (2015)
6. Boncu, S., Candel, O.S., Popa, N.L.: Gameful green: a systematic review on the use of serious computer games and gamified mobile apps to foster pro-environmental information, attitudes and behaviors. Sustainability **14**, 10400 (2022). https://doi.org/10.3390/su141610400
7. UNESCO: Building more inclusive, sustainable and prosperous societies in Europe and Central Asia, vol. 54 (2017)
8. UNESCO: Getting every school climate-ready: how countries are integrating climate change issues in education (2021)
9. Carew, A.L., Mitchell, C.A.: Teaching sustainability as a contested concept: capitalizing on variation in engineering educators' conceptions of environmental, social and economic sustainability. J. Clean. Prod. **16**, 105–115 (2008). https://doi.org/10.1016/J.JCLEPRO.2006.11.004
10. Kioupi, V., Voulvoulis, N.: Education for sustainable development: a systemic framework for connecting the sdgs to educational outcomes. Sustainability **11**, 6104 (2019). https://doi.org/10.3390/SU11216104
11. de Pauw, J.B., Gericke, N., Olsson, D., Berglund, T.: The effectiveness of education for sustainable development. Sustainability **7**, 15693–15717 (2015). https://doi.org/10.3390/su71115693
12. Ouariachi, T., Li, C.Y., Elving, W.J.L.: Gamification approaches for education and engagement on pro-environmental behaviors: searching for best practices. Sustainability **12**, 4565 (2020). https://doi.org/10.3390/SU12114565
13. Thor, D., Karlsudd, P.: Teaching and fostering an active environmental awareness design, validation and planning for action-oriented environmental education. Sustainability **12**, 3209 (2020). https://doi.org/10.3390/SU12083209
14. Mondejar, M.E., et al.: Digitalization to achieve sustainable development goals: steps towards a smart green planet. Sci. Total Environ. **794**, 148539 (2021). https://doi.org/10.1016/J.SCITOTENV.2021.148539
15. Tavares, R., Vieira, R.M., Pedro, L.: Mobile app for science education: designing the learning approach. Educ. Sci. **11**, 1–23 (2021). https://doi.org/10.3390/educsci11020079
16. Kaplan, R., Kaplan, S.: The Experience of Nature: A Psychological Perspective. Cambridge University Press, Cambridge (1989)
17. Palmberg, I., Hofman-Bergholm, M., Jeronen, E., Yli-Panula, E.: Systems thinking for understanding sustainability? Nordic student teachers' views on the relationship between species identification, biodiversity and sustainable development. Educ. Sci. (Basel). **7**, 72 (2017). https://doi.org/10.3390/educsci7030072
18. McBride, B.B., Brewer, C.A., Berkowitz, A.R., Borrie, W.T.: Environmental literacy, ecological literacy, ecoliteracy: what do we mean and how did we get here? Ecosphere **4**, 1–20 (2013). https://doi.org/10.1890/ES13-00075.1
19. Puk, T.G., Stibbards, A.: Systemic ecological illiteracy? Shedding light on meaning as an act of thought in higher learning. Environ. Educ. Res. **18**, 353–373 (2012). https://doi.org/10.1080/13504622.2011.622840

20. Palmberg, I., et al.: Nordic-Baltic student teachers' identification of and interest in plant and animal species: the importance of species identification and biodiversity for sustainable development. J. Sci. Teacher Educ. **26**, 549–571 (2015). https://doi.org/10.1007/s10972-015-9438-z

21. Annual number of mobile app downloads worldwide 2022---Statista, https://www.statista.com/statistics/271644/worldwide-free-and-paid-mobile-app-store-downloads/. Accessed 08 May 2023

22. Fernández, A.H., Camargo, C.D.B., Do Nascimento, M.S.L.: Technologies and environmental education: a beneficial relationship. Res. Soc. Sci. Technol. **4**, 13–30 (2019). https://doi.org/10.46303/RESSAT.04.02.2

23. Deterding, S., Dixon, D., Khaled, R., Nacke, L.: From game design elements to gamefulness: defining "gamification." In: Proceedings of the 15th International Academic MindTrek Conference: Envisioning Future Media Environments, MindTrek 2011, 9–15 (2011). https://doi.org/10.1145/2181037.2181040

24. Hussein, M.H., Ow, S.H., Cheong, L.S., Thong, M.K., Ale Ebrahim, N.: Effects of digital game-based learning on elementary science learning: a systematic review. IEEE Access. **7**, 62465–62478 (2019). https://doi.org/10.1109/ACCESS.2019.2916324

25. Brauer, B., Ebermann, C., Hildebrandt, B., Remané, G., Kolbe, L.M.: Green by app: the contribution of mobile applications to environmental sustainability (2016)

26. Douglas, B.D., Brauer, M.: Gamification to prevent climate change: a review of games and apps for sustainability. Curr. Opin. Psychol. **42**, 89–94 (2021). https://doi.org/10.1016/J.COPSYC.2021.04.008

27. Torres-Toukoumidis, A., Vintimilla León, D., De-Santis, A., Carlos López-López, P.: Gamification in ecology-oriented mobile applications—typologies and purposes. Societies **12**, 42 (2022). https://doi.org/10.3390/SOC12020042

28. Holmgren, S.: Gamified Citizen Science: A Study of Expert Users in the Field of Biodiversity (2020)

29. Randler, C.: Teaching species identification-a prerequisite for learning biodiversity and understanding ecology. Eurasia J. Math. **4**, 223–231 (2008)

30. Ro, M., Brauer, M., Kuntz, K., Shukla, R., Bensch, I.: Making cool choices for sustainability: testing the effectiveness of a game-based approach to promoting pro-environmental behaviors. J. Environ. Psychol. **53**, 20–30 (2017). https://doi.org/10.1016/J.JENVP.2017.06.007

Evaluating Digital Resources in Teaching History

Miljenko Hajdarovic(✉) 🄳

Faculty of Education, J. J. Strossmayer University, Osijek, Croatia
mhajdarovic@foozos.hr

Abstract. This research article underscores the critical role of specialized digital literacy in history education for both teachers and students, with a specific focus on primary and secondary educational levels. Drawing upon a comprehensive review of existing literature, the article illuminates the essential digital literacy skills required to evaluate online information credibility. Furthermore, the article critically assesses different models of online information assessment and examines empirical research on user approaches to determining internet information credibility. The authors underscore the need for students to acquire the fundamental skills necessary for proficient digital resource evaluation before any expected academic improvement. The authors also introduce disciplinary literacy as a tool to enable readers to inquire and acquire knowledge. In sum, this research article underscores the vital importance of digital literacy in history education and offers valuable insights for educators and researchers.

Keywords: Digital Literacy · History Didactics · History Teaching

1 Introduction

In the realm of education, a diverse array of teaching materials and methodologies exist with the aim of achieving desired educational objectives. When it comes to instructing students in the discipline of history, a key emphasis centers on the analysis of sources. Within this context, students are expected to engage with primary and secondary sources either autonomously or in a collaborative setting, with or without guidance from the instructor. By working on sources, students practice historical skills by collecting sources, analyzing them, and creating conclusions or historical narratives. The precise form of pedagogical instruction is contingent on the accessibility and familiarity of the sources at hand to the instructor. At present, sources can be accessed not only through traditional books, textbooks, and printed materials but also via an array of digitized archives, digital libraries, and repositories. The available sources have expanded beyond printed materials over the past few decades and now encompass a range of multimedia formats, such as documentaries, feature films, newsreels, and audio recordings, as well as contemporary 3D objects and immersive technologies, including augmented and virtual reality.

Ł. Tomczyk (Ed.): NMP 2022, CCIS 1916, pp. 125–133, 2023.
https://doi.org/10.1007/978-3-031-44581-1_10

The advent of the digital age has transformed the way in which information is produced and disseminated. The digital environment has enabled anyone to be an author, which poses a significant challenge to information credibility. The lack of oversight and editorial review on many websites, combined with the ease with which digital information can be altered, plagiarized, misrepresented, or created anonymously under false pretenses, compounds the problem of credibility. While the body of written sources has continuously expanded throughout history, the advent of the internet has facilitated self-publishing on an unprecedented scale, with speed, and with minimal regulation. However, the abundance of digital sources has introduced challenges in navigating through the sheer volume of available sources, making the scrutiny of source material and its veracity a pivotal issue [1]. Despite these challenges, the increase in available source material has facilitated the discovery of new insights into the past. The imperative to ascertain the authenticity of sources in contemporary times has led to the emergence of a distinct subfield of historical scholarship known as diplomatics.

The body of written sources that have informed our understanding of the past has been expanding continually, irrespective of the medium on which it is inscribed. Two historic events in particular stand out as being especially transformative: the introduction of movable type printing in the 15th century and the advent of the Internet into society towards the end of the 20th century. In relation to the printing press, its most significant consequence was the marked reduction in the cost of book production, which facilitated wider access to literacy for both publishers and readers alike. Nonetheless, the potential pool of publishers remained relatively limited. The revolutionary nature of the Internet, on the other hand, stems from its capacity to enable every user to become a content creator, thereby facilitating self-publishing on an unprecedented scale, speed, and with minimal regulation. Nevertheless, the utopian vision of media democratization appears to be mutating into a dystopia. The process of digitization has impacted not only the pedagogical practices of history teachers, but also the research methodologies of historians. While the dramatic increase in available source material has facilitated the discovery of new insights into the past, it has simultaneously introduced challenges in navigating through the sheer volume of available sources. Today, the number of digital titles on a researcher's computer or in the cloud can easily exceed the number of books available in the local public library. The scrutiny of source material and its veracity has been a concern since the inception of written records, with the detection of fraudulent documents being a pivotal issue. The imperative to ascertain the authenticity of sources in contemporary times has led to the emergence of a distinct subfield of historical scholarship, known as diplomatics.

An increasing number of books are being published without the involvement of professional editors or reviewers. The most recent approximation suggests that there are approximately 1.7 million self-published book titles produced annually [2]. Additionally, the total number of websites in existence worldwide is estimated to be around 1.14 billion, of which only 17% are deemed to be active, with the remaining 83% deemed inactive [3]. It is noteworthy that the majority of these websites are not created by established legacy institutions, such as museums, libraries, or archives, nor are they published by prominent publishing houses [4]. The potential of artificial intelligence for the analysis of sources and the synthesis of research results will significantly increase the number of historical research and the dissemination of their results in the coming years. Thus, it is quite appropriate that the recommendations of the Council of Europe on the teaching of history in twenty-first-century Europe establish that digital resources have become an essential part of historical education. When used effectively, such resources invite questions about the authority and reliability of information and significantly increase access to historical information and multiple interpretations of the past. They can also contribute to the development of students' critical faculties, intellectual autonomy, and resistance to manipulation [5].

The proliferation of the internet has fundamentally altered the way individuals access information, and the vast quantity of information available online raises issues of both credibility and quality. As a result, the responsibility of ensuring the reliability of information has shifted from professional gatekeepers to individual information seekers, underscoring the necessity of critical evaluation of online sources. However, despite the paramount importance of developing the requisite skills for evaluating web-based information, extant research provides evidence of a knowledge gap among internet users regarding the assessment of online sources [1, 6]. In addition to the problem of choosing the appropriate source, there is a growing problem of distortion of historical narratives and falsification of sources.

Information technology is of no value in itself or by itself: it needs questions to drive it and disciplined forms of thinking to make sense of the answers that it can provide [7]. The pace of technological development has been so rapid that teachers have found it difficult to find time to reflect fully on how best to incorporate new applications into their teaching [8].

2 Plethora of Literacies

So-called digital natives know how to use ICT and the Internet, but this does not mean that they are critical in their use. There are many similar models for assessing the credibility of information found on the Internet: information literacy, digital literacy, digital citizenship, media literacy, news literacy, online reading comprehension ability, etc. The competence to proficiently search for, appraise, and authenticate social and political information online, referred to as civic online reasoning, is an essential skill set in today's digital age. Its mastery is crucial for individuals to make informed judgments about the reliability of the available information and prevent the formation of conclusions solely based on personal beliefs. However, it is essential to note that civic online reasoning is a distinct skill from other related digital competencies, such as digital literacy and online citizenship [6]. Efforts to educate and train users on establishing credibility in the online environment began soon after the issue was recognized, and many of these efforts were associated with the "digital literacy" movement. The literature outlines five criteria that users should apply when assessing the credibility of online information: accuracy, authority, objectivity, currency, and coverage. Accuracy pertains to the freedom from errors, the verifiability of information, and the reliability of the information on a website. Authority is assessed by examining the author's credentials, qualifications, affiliations, and whether the website is recommended by a trusted source. Objectivity involves identifying the purpose of the website, whether the information provided is fact or opinion, and whether there is commercial intent or a conflict of interest. Currency refers to the timeliness of the information, while coverage pertains to the comprehensiveness or depth of the information provided on the website [1].

Navigating and engaging effectively in a digital world is crucial for individuals to become empowered citizens. While there is no single definition of digital literacy, numerous international, national, and local frameworks have been developed to promote and assess this skill, particularly among educators and students at various educational levels and citizens. Open, distance, and digital education has a lengthy track record of exploring and incorporating digital literacy into teaching and learning practices. However, due to the extensive research conducted on digital literacy since its inception in the late 1990s, comprehending the vast amount of information on the topic can take time and effort. Despite abundant research, there is still no universally accepted definition of digital literacy, and the concept continually evolves within the ever-changing digital landscape [9].

As one of eight key competencies for lifelong learning recommended by the European Commission, Digital competence involves the confident, critical, and responsible use of and engagement with digital technologies for learning, work, and participation in society. It includes information and data literacy, communication and collaboration, media literacy, digital content creation (including programming), safety (including digital well-being and competencies related to cybersecurity), intellectual property-related questions, problem-solving, and critical thinking [5]. Individuals should be able to use digital technologies to support their active citizenship and social inclusion, collaboration with others, and creativity toward personal, social, or commercial goals. Skills include the ability to use, access, filter, evaluate, create, program, and share digital content.

3   Criteria for Evaluating Sources in Teaching History

Diplomatics is an interdisciplinary subfield of historical scholarship that deals with the study of documents and their authenticity, origin, form, and purpose, as well as the institutions and practices involved in their creation, transmission, and preservation. It seeks to understand these documents' historical context and significance, including the individuals and institutions involved in their creation and use, the social and political contexts in which they were produced, and the broader cultural and intellectual currents that influenced their development.

For the past decade, Dr. Simon Bates, the Associate Provost of Teaching and Learning at the University of British Columbia, has given a series of lectures that elucidate the role of teachers in the digital age [10]. Dr. Bates' "Anatomy of 21st Century Educators" model comprises six key roles educators must fulfill. Firstly, they must be proficient in facilitating learning by comprehending how students learn and devising practical learning activities. Secondly, they must act as curators by generating and consuming appropriate educational resources. Thirdly, they should possess technical skills to effectively use learning technology. Fourthly, they must collaborate with colleagues from diverse fields to enhance their educational approaches. Fifthly, they must remain abreast of research-based and appropriate pedagogical methods to act as scholars. Finally, they must be willing to experiment with new pedagogical approaches and technologies, reflecting upon their efficacy and learning from their experiences.

We can enable students to search for information and sources freely or let them work under the "glass bell" of pre-prepared controlled sources. Stradling (2003) suggests that the teacher should carefully choose internet sites to give students [11]. A positive consequence of that model is the complete control of the content, but the negative aspect is that students need to prepare for the real world. He advised the teacher to evaluate the websites based on their intended purpose, source, access, ease of navigation, design, and content. According to Stradling, an internet researcher must consider the following:

is it a primary or secondary source

who wrote the document

what does the document tell us about the author's position and thinking

for whom it was written

why was it written

what kind of document is it

what are the main messages the author wants to convey

can other sources confirm the information in this document

whether the information is correct

which the document does not tell us

is there evidence of the impact of this document on the people for whom it was written

have any documents have been produced in response to this

why the document was saved

why the document is included on this website

Based on his model Hajdarovic (2010) proposed criteria for the evaluation of websites on historical topics: credibility, accuracy, objectivity, content and functionality, and age appropriateness of students [12].

Fundamentally, the evaluation of digital resources for teaching history relies on the fundamental historical skills students acquire from their earliest exposures to history. In order to highlight the particularities of the digital world that contemporary students inhabit and operate within, these skills must be augmented with elements of digital literacy. Therefore, to ensure a high evaluation standard, it is recommended to structure the evaluation model into two distinct categories: activities designed for the teacher and activities intended for the student.

Metzger proposed four methods for evaluating the credibility of online information in the literature. These include [1]:

1) The checklist approach involves users asking and answering a set of questions to evaluate each criterion. However, this can be time-consuming and labor-intensive for individuals to perform for every website they visit.

2) Ascribing cognitive authority to internet information encompasses both credibility and quality.

3) In the iterative model, the seeker assesses the authority and credibility of the author, document, institution, and affiliations, combined into a global judgment of credibility. Strategies such as verifying a website's author and institutional identity through reputation or qualifications, considering the factual accuracy of the document and its presentation, and examining overt and covert affiliations of the website contribute to an overall impression of cognitive authority.

4) The contextual model, which focuses on external information to the site, recommends three techniques to determine the quality of online information, including promoting peer- and editorially reviewed resources available online, comparing information found on a website to other web sources or offline sources such as newspapers, peer-reviewed articles, or books, and corroboration, which involves seeking more than one source to verify information on a given topic.

3.1 Student-Oriented Criteria

In light of digital media's challenges, it is worth acknowledging that today's students are exposed to a diverse array of narratives, historical accounts, and social and political discourses that transcend national borders. This is facilitated mainly by the formidable influence of digital tools, which offer unparalleled power compared to traditional paper books. Multimedia in nature, digital resources seamlessly integrate audio-visual and written formats and enable users to perform cognitive operations related to information organization and retrieval effortlessly [13]. The widespread availability of applications and websites that offer visually-rich graphics and video sequences has led students to prefer them over text-heavy sites. While digital media offers students and citizens an extensive array of visual materials, there is no guarantee that they will accurately interpret them in line with their historiographical significance. Pre-existing knowledge, which can often manifest as prejudice or stereotypes, plays a vital role in the learning process, underscoring the importance of comprehending how historical concepts can be elevated to more intricate and disciplined representations of the past. Conversely, the historical concepts held by students and citizens frequently stem from national master narratives constructed from idealized and essentialist depictions, resulting in overly simplified representations [13]. Undoubtedly, students require fundamental techniques to decipher the text. Disciplinary literacy reinstates control to the reader. Sourcing demands that readers interact with authors, questioning their qualifications, investment in the narrative, and stance regarding the event they describe [14].

Gathering information online poses several challenges for students, particularly concerning searching for and assessing the credibility of sources. In the context of an unregulated internet search, young individuals tend to view the order of search results as a reliable indicator of the trustworthiness of websites. Instead of meticulously assessing information based on its source's credibility or the accuracy of its evidence, students rely on several heuristics commonly used by adults. These include website design, navigability, and how well the content aligns with the information sought by the students [6]. McGrew et al. (2018) conducted a study where 15 tasks were created, and 2,616 responses from middle school, high school, and college students were collected. The findings reveal that students needed help performing fundamental assessments of authors, sources, and evidence. History teachers must aid them in acquiring the skills essential for locating dependable sources. When considering the criteria for evaluating digital sources, a fundamental question arises regarding the skills and abilities students can apply before and after acquiring knowledge of the topic. Before acquiring basic knowledge about a topic, it is crucial for students to investigate the source's credibility. This involves asking questions such as who is behind the information and not only considering the author but also the creator and maintainer of the website. Once students have

acquired basic facts, they can utilize adapted historiographical content analysis to evaluate sources based on various factors, including the type of source (primary, secondary,
encyclopedias, dictionaries, textbooks, and other reference materials), the presence of a
reference list, the use of professional or scientific formatting, the objectivity of the text,
and the inclusion of different perspectives.

Novice readers often rely solely on the information presented within the text, while
historical readers view the text as a gateway to a different era. Contextualization establishes the setting and time frame for the text. Disciplinary literacy requires that students
utilize their total intellectual capacity while reading. In addition to sourcing and contextualization, corroborating details and closely examining the text are essential components
in comprehending historical literature [14]. The Stanford History Education Group's
curriculum, "Reading Like a Historian," centers around the duty of citizenship rather
than the profession of history. This approach is particularly relevant in the digital age.

Digital misinformation has been a concern since the medium's inception, prompting extensive research to develop critical approaches for evaluating online information.
Despite these endeavors, recent studies indicate that students need help critically analyzing digital information. One of the contributing factors to this issue is the need for
more emphasis on critical analysis in the early stages of the educational system, as well
as an insufficient emphasis on these concepts throughout secondary school. Although
fake news has been a persistent problem, the failure to incorporate critical analysis in
the curriculum exacerbates the challenge of digital misinformation [15, 16].

3.2 Teacher Oriented Criteria

The term "digital teacher competencies" refers to a collection of skills, attitudes, and
knowledge that educators must possess to facilitate student learning in a technology-
driven world, transform classroom practices, and enhance professional development.
Educators must be able to evaluate digital texts critically and make connections within the
school context, especially given the rise of fake news and the abundance of information
accessible online [17]. Research has indicated that when deciding on the credibility of
a website, adults rely on cues and heuristics such as the search engine's authority, the
design and functionality of the website, previous experience or referrals to the website,
and perceived expertise [6].

Research has demonstrated that the skills cultivated in historical inquiry, known
as historical thinking, align with informed and critical digital citizenship principles.
Historical thinking encompasses proficiencies in information assessment and analysis
[15]. When researching the evaluation of websites, Goulding combines the research of
Hilligoss, Rieh, Metzger, Wathen & Burkell. Heuristic assessments allow quick judgments without deep engagement with information and are used when cognitive load or
motivation is high. Hilligoss and Rieh identified four categories of heuristics in online
evaluation: media-related, source-related, endorsement-based, and esthetics-based. Disciplinary heuristics of sourcing, corroboration, and contextualization were of limited
value in evaluating websites. Wineburg and McGrew suggested going beyond the website
and using tools like Google Search to corroborate and contextualize the site.

Kelly used the deliberate creation of fictional historical narratives as a teaching
method on two occasions [4]. As part of the Lying About the Past course, Kelly's students

created the Edward Owens hoax in 2008 and the Reddit serial killer hoax in 2012. While the ethical implications of such an assignment can be questioned, Kelly utilized this unconventional method to transform the creation of forgeries into an educational tool. In doing so, his students enhanced their historical and digital skills through group work while honing their creativity. Historians often stress the importance of teaching students to think historically, and Kelly's approach to this assignment allowed his students to do just that.

4 Conclusion

In conclusion, the democratizing potential of the Internet has brought forth a critical responsibility for individuals to evaluate the veracity of online information carefully. Social studies classrooms are crucial in equipping students with digital literacy skills to navigate this challenge [6]. As online sources increasingly become the first choice for students, historians need to consider the many ways students use these sources to create new forms of history. While the limitations of textbooks restrict their format, online resources can aid in students' historical research and broadening of historiographical horizons. However, caution must be exercised as online material can be selective, intentionally spread misinformation, or promote specific ideas or political groups [11]. Applied digital literacy is essential for developing historical literacy and critical thinking. Despite the increased workload on history teachers due to digitization and technological progress, addressing this issue has become unavoidable in the fake facts and post-truth era.

References

1. Metzger, M.J.: Making sense of credibility on the web: models for evaluating online information and recommendations for future research. J. Am. Soc. Inf. Sci. Technol. **58**(13), 2078–2091 (2007). https://doi.org/10.1002/asi.20672
2. How Many Books Are Published Each Year? [2022 Statistics]. Toner Buzz. https://www.tonerbuzz.com/blog/how-many-books-are-published-each-year/. Accessed 09 May 2023
3. How Many Websites Are There in the World? (2022). Siteefy. https://siteefy.com/how-many-websites-are-there/. Accessed 09 May 2023
4. Kelly, T.M.: Teaching History in the Digital Age. University of Michigan Press, Ann Arbor (2013). https://doi.org/10.2307/j.ctv65swp1
5. Recommendations of the Committee of Ministers to member states on history teaching in twenty-first century Europe. https://search.coe.int/cm/Pages/result_details.aspx?ObjectId=0900001680909e91. Accessed 09 May 2023
6. McGrew, S., Breakstone, J., Ortega, T., Smith, M., Wineburg, S. Can students evaluate online sources? Learning from assessments of civic online reasoning. Theory Res. Soc. Educ. **46**(2), 165–193 (2018). https://doi.org/10.1080/00933104.2017.1416320
7. Walsh, B.: Stories and their sources: The need for historical thinking in an information age. Teach. Hist. **133**, 4–9 (2008)
8. Arthur, J., Phillips, R. (ed.).: Issues in History Teaching. Routledge, Milton Park (2000)
9. Marín, V.I., Castañeda, L. Developing digital literacy for teaching and learning. In: U Handbook of Open, Distance and Digital Education (str. 1–20). Springer, Cham (2022). https://doi.org/10.1007/978-981-19-0351-9_64-1

10. Bates, S.: The 21st Century Educator—Students as partners in teaching and learning. In: 8th Excellence in Teaching Conference, London (2014)
11. Stradling, R.: Nastava europske povijesti 20. stoljeća. Srednja Europa (2003)
12. Hajdarović, M.: Vrjednovanje internet stranica povijesne tematike. Historijski Zbornik **63**(2), 561–569 (2010)
13. Carretero, M., Cantabrana, M., Parellada, C. (eds.).: History Education in the Digital Age. Springer, Cham (2022).https://doi.org/10.1007/978-3-031-10743-6
14. Wineburg, S., Reisman, A.: Disciplinary literacy in history a toolkit for digital citizenship. J. Adolesc. Adult Literacy **58**(8), 636–639 (2015). https://doi.org/10.1002/jaal.410
15. Goulding, J.: Historical thinking online: an analysis of expert and non-expert readings of historical websites. J. Learn. Sci. **30**(2), 204–239 (2021). https://doi.org/10.1080/10508406.2020.1834396
16. Berghel, H.: Lies, damn lies, and fake news. Computer **50**(2), 80–85 (2017). https://doi.org/10.1109/MC.2017.56
17. Key competences for lifelong learning. Publications Office. https://data.europa.eu/doi/10.2766/569540. Accessed 09 May 2023

A Systematic Literature Review of Digital Storytelling for English Language Speaking and Writing Skills

Saima Khan(✉) ⓘ, Azidah Abu Ziden ⓘ, and Alla Baksh Bin Mohamed Ayub Khan ⓘ

Universiti Sains Malaysia, Gelugor, Penang, Malaysia
saimakhan@student.usm.my

Abstract. There is an increased interest in the use of digital storytelling (DST) in English language education to assist learners in improving their language skills by writing and narrating stories using multimedia tools. This necessitates the exploration of the research focus to understand the current practice and future scope of DST-based research. Extant review studies are unable to address this niche specifically in relation to English language speaking and writing skills. The present study conducts a systematic review of articles published between January 2010 and February 2023. Following the PRISMA-P framework, 33 studies on the use of DST for improving English language productive skills of speaking and writing were selected for review. The findings are presented to understand the research objective, outcome, and methodological approach. Based on cross-analysis and synthesis, the paper foregrounds some considerations on 'research direction' where past studies are directed towards evaluating the effectiveness of DST intervention while ignoring the process of it; the 'nature of the task' where findings seem to be over shadowed by novelty effect; and the 'nature of the result' where studies lack elaboration on non-significant findings. Suggestions and implications of this systematic review would support DST based research and its use in English language education.

Keywords: Digital Storytelling · English Language Productive Skills · Speaking Skills · Writing Skills · Technology-based Intervention · Systematic Review

1 Introduction

In recent years, digital storytelling (DST) has taken a prominent position in the language education as it is considered an effective tool for technology-enriched learning [1]. DST is storytelling carried out by using technology. It is a process where short narratives are formed through text, graphics, video, audio, music, and other digital elements [2]. Digital stories are like short videos with narration of events, stories, or any other information. DST in education often occurs as an individual learning activity or as a collaborative task [3]. Moreover, it can take the form of a teacher-generated DST, where teachers deliver lessons using digital stories, or a student-generated DST, where students are given tasks to create digital stories [4]. The process of creating digital stories involves

Ł. Tomczyk (Ed.): NMP 2022, CCIS 1916, pp. 134–151, 2023.
https://doi.org/10.1007/978-3-031-44581-1_11

pre-production, production, and post-production. These stages include gathering and preparing content, producing the story through narration and combining content, and finally editing and publishing the story. In classroom setting, the post-production stage takes the form of students sharing their digital stories with their peers and instructor [3].

According to Ohler [5], DST promotes the integration of digital and language literacy within a task along with a holistic coverage of the content, cognitive engagement, and learning motivation. [6] highlighted that DST promotes convergence of learner engagement, critical thinking, and task-oriented learning. This promotes opportunities for collaboration and enables students to construct their knowledge [7]. By harnessing students' creativity, DST encourages students to utilize various resources to access comprehensive and diverse information which supports students' learning process [1]. It is an effective tool in language education settings as it enables learners of all ages to create and present stories while gaining content knowledge and skills. The interplay between technology and language skills in DST is crucial in enhancing learners' language capabilities [8].

In today's times, DST is being implemented in different settings, with a particular emphasis on improving English language in the classroom environment [9–12]. In English language education, DST is used for enhancing various aspects of the language learning process, such as motivation in language learning, interaction, engagement, and creativity among others [13, 14]. It is also used as a technology-based tool to assist learners in improving language proficiency using multimedia support to narrate stories [15]. Since the productive language skills of speaking and writing form an integral part of the process of creating stories, studies are extensive to gauge the impact of DST on these skills. The use of DST allows learners to engage in repeated speaking practice while recording, which facilitates English oral proficiency [9]. Language educators view DST as an attractive opportunity for learners to build their writing skills as learners engage in prolonged and continuous writing sessions to build the story [16]. Therefore, the focus of DST rests on productive language skills and it is considered suitable for improving speaking and writing skills [5].

In order to gain a comprehensive understanding of the research focus and the present use of DST in improving English language productive skills, a comprehensive overview of studies is timely. The extant review studies have explored DST in education. Wu and Chen [17], Quah and Ng [18], and Rodriguez et al. [19] reviewed studies that highlighted the pedagogical implications of DST. These reviews provided an overall idea of the use of DST in general education settings without exploring the nuances of English language education. There are quite a few systematic reviews that have explored studies focusing on DST in English language teaching and learning, however, these reviews are limited in their implication by only addressing the affective factors in English language education [13], not identifying the adequate language constructs [14], demonstrating error in following the review protocol [20], and missing the review framework [21].

As highlighted above, there is a dearth of systematic review studies that could potentially provide a holistic overview of the research focus of past studies related to the use of DST for English language productive skill development. It is essential to explore this niche because the skills of speaking and writing form the core of the process of DST.

Therefore, informed implications are necessary to validate the current practice of DST in English language education and to direct future research in the field.

1.1 Aims and Objectives

We began by analyzing the lacunas in the extant review studies to develop appropriate research questions. The goal of the present study is to highlight the research focus and research methods used in previous studies related to the use of DST for English language productive skill development. This would assist in delimiting the research gap for future studies. The following research questions have guided this study:

1. What is the objective of previous research that used DST for the development of English language productive skills?
2. What is the outcome of previous research that used DST for the development of English language productive skills?
3. What are the methods and research designs used to explore the effect of DST on English language productive skills in previous research?

2   Methodology

The present systematic literature review was framed according to the Preferred Reporting Items for Systematic Review and Meta-Analyses Protocols (PRISMA-P) [22]. PRISMA-P framework provides inclusive directions for designing and conducting rigorous literature reviews. This systematic literature review was based on empirical articles published from January 2010 to February 2023. These articles were retrieved from journals indexed in the Web of Science (WoS) database. A framework was established following the PRISMA-P guideline to monitor the review process of this study. The research included four major phases – the identification phase, screening phase, eligibility phase, and the inclusion phase.

The first phase was the identification phase where the academic databases were selected and relevant articles were searched using keywords. We selected the WoS database and the search process was conducted on March 01, 2023. The Web of Science (WoS) database core collection includes the Social Science Citation Index (SSCI), Emerging Source Citation Index (ESCI), Arts & Humanities Citation Index (A&HCI), and the Science Citation Index Expanded (SCI-EXPANDED), which covers only high-quality journals with good impact factor and citescore. Suitable query strings, within the scope of the study, were used to retrieve the articles from the WoS Core Collection (see Table 1). A total of 706 articles were identified in this phase. Then an initial assessment was conducted to eliminate the duplicates before the screening. Out of the total articles, 81 articles were removed for being duplicates.

The second and third phases were guided by the inclusion and exclusion criteria (see Table 2). Two coders were involved in the screening and eligibility check of the articles. This was later validated by the third coder during the final assessment.

The screening phase included an initial screening to ensure that only empirical articles published in peer-reviewed journals were included. Further, articles published beyond the selected timeline were removed. The second part of this phase involved the

Table 1. Query string used for article retrieval.

Database	Keywords	n
WoS	((digital storytelling AND speaking) OR (digital storytelling AND vocabulary) OR (digital storytelling AND pronunciation) OR (digital storytelling AND fluency) OR (digital storytelling AND oral))	316
	((digital storytelling AND writing) OR (digital storytelling AND written composition) OR (digital storytelling AND writing AND composition))	390

screening of abstracts to ensure that they met the inclusion and exclusion criteria. A total number of 462 articles were removed during the screening phase.

Further, in the third phase, full-text eligibility was examined to ensure that the articles met the criteria. A total of 130 articles were excluded during this stage.

Table 2. Inclusion and exclusion criteria.

Inclusion Criteria	Exclusion Criteria
• Timeline - January 2010 and February 2023 • Peer-reviewed articles in the journal • Focus on speaking and/or writing skill • Use of DST in the educational setting • Use of DST for English language teaching • Articles written in the English language • Full text of article available	• Timeline - January 2010 and February 2023 • Articles published in conference proceedings, books, and reports • Articles not focusing on speaking and/or writing skill • Use of DST in non-educational setting • Use of DST for languages other than English • Articles written in other languages • Full text of article not available

Finally, 33 articles qualified for the inclusion phase of the present systematic review. An in-depth analysis and review of the selected articles was conducted. Figure 1 explains the procedure of selecting the articles based on the PRISMA-P.

3   Findings

The present study analyzed 33 articles retrieved from the WoS database published from January 2010 to February 2023 to understand the research focus of the past empirical studies specifically focusing on English language productive skills of speaking and writing. To answer the research questions, we analyzed the research objective, outcomes, the nature of methodology, the research design of the selected studies.

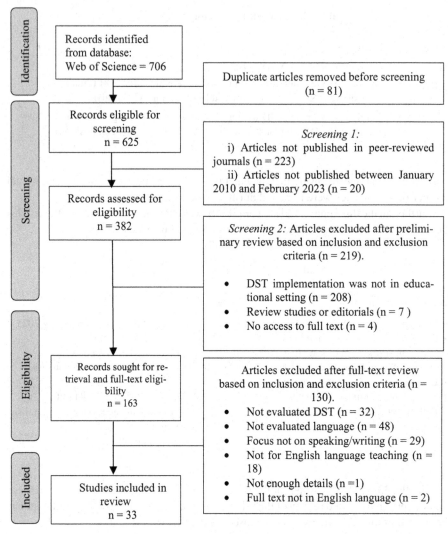

Fig. 1. The process of article selection based on PRISMA-P.

3.1 What is the Objective of Previous Research that Used DST for the Development of English Language Productive Skills?

Table 3 presents the objective and outcomes of the studies. The selected studies aimed to develop English language skills of speaking and writing by adopting DST. Predominantly, student-generated DST was used in these studies as the tasks were focused on engaging students to create digital stories. In the reviewed studies, most of the studies aimed at 'evaluating the effectiveness' of the DST-based intervention in improving English language speaking or/and writing skill.

Table 3. Details of the research objective and outcome of the reviewed studies.

Author	Research Objective	Focus*	Sample	Findings
[1]	To explore the benefits and challenges of participating in DST projects	W	University students (n = 60)	It was found that DST promoted academic writing skills
[8]	To investigate the effects of online and offline DST on literacy skills	W	High school students (n = 42)	Results reveal a significant improvement in reading and writing with online DST
[9]	To provide ways and effectiveness of integrating IWB, podcast, and DST for language proficiency development and students' perception regarding it	S and W	Third and fourth grade students (n = 11)	DST was effective in improving writing and speaking. Repeated practice while creating DST in building speaking ability. The repeated revisions of the draft helped in developing writing skills
[10]	To investigate whether DST improves oral proficiency and motivation	S	College students (n = 5)	Results show improvement in oral proficiency. The study reports no improvement in terms of discourse and grammar
[11]	To explore learners' perception of using the DST application for language learning	S and W	Primary students (n = 6)	Learners were positive about using the DST application as it helped them improve speaking and writing skills
[12]	To examine the use of local culture-based DST in meaning-making in English	S	Junior high school (n = 30)	DST was an effective tool to help students make meaning in English language and improving their vocabulary

(continued)

Table 3. (*continued*)

Author	Research Objective	Focus*	Sample	Findings
[15]	To investigate the effect of DST on boosting language literacy	S and W	11th grade students (n = 48)	Students developed writing and speaking manners in terms of oral production. DST also helped them gain more understanding of the process of writing
[16]	To investigate the level of engagement, writing quality, interaction patterns, and perception of students during the DST writing task	W	Principals, teachers, and primary students (n = 264 primary students)	DST writing tasks were engaging and students demonstrated fewer mistakes, but teachers had concerns over interaction and shift in focus from writing to decorating the story during DST tasks
[23]	To investigate the effect of DST in promoting language skills for English for Tourism courses	S and W	University students (n = **)	Students had positive attitude towards improving their speaking and writing skills with DST. Some students had concerns regarding the amount of time DST-based activities require
[24]	To investigate the effects of collaborative DST on writing skills, and students' perception regarding it	W	University students (n = 38)	The use of a collaborative DST improved students' writing skills. Students faced a few technological and pedagogical challenges during the task
[25]	To examine students' perception of DST chatbot in increasing language output	W	University students (n = 37)	The students reported having improved their writing skills with storybot

(*continued*)

Table 3. (*continued*)

Author	Research Objective	Focus*	Sample	Findings
[26]	To investigate any significant difference in vocabulary with online tools –Wikis, YouTube, and DST	W	Ninth grade students (n = 70)	Results reveal a improvement in EFL students' vocabulary achievement with the innovative learning environment of DST
[27]	To investigate the effect of listening to digital stories on pronunciation	S	Secondary students (n = 40)	A significant difference was found between the control group and the experiment group. DST was effective in motivating students to improve their pronunciation
[28]	To investigate the effect of DST on reading and writing skills	W	High school students (n = 51)	Post-test results show improvement in students' writing skills, motivation, and confidence with DST
[29]	To investigate the use of DST on student achievement	S and W	Level not specified (n = 20)	Students spent more time on the language aspect while creating DST which provided good practice for speaking and writing skills
[30]	To investigate the effect of DST on students' writing skills and their perception regarding it	W	Pre-service teachers (n = 101)	Findings reveal DST improved students' writing skills in terms of grammar and vocabulary

(*continued*)

Table 3. (*continued*)

Author	Research Objective	Focus*	Sample	Findings
[31]	To explore the effectiveness of DST in developing communicative competence (written and oral) and narrative competence	S and W	Pre-service teachers (n = 143)	Significant increase in written competence with DST, but a low level (3.4%) decrease in oral competence and a significant decrease in narrative competence of the learners. The negative effect on competencies was related to extraneous cognitive efforts while using digital tools
[32]	To investigate the effect of using DST on students' English speaking ability	S	University students (n = 40)	DST was effective in improving students' overall English speaking ability. Participants also had a positive perception of using DST
[33]	To investigate the effects of Toontastic as a DST tool on learners' speaking competence and to find any correlation between speaking competence	S	University students (n = 100)	DST had significantly improved speaking competence in terms of fluency and language use. Topic familiarity and scaffolding while carrying out the DST task led to an improvement in speaking competence and engagement
[34]	To examine the effect of the podcast, DST, and a short film with PBL on oral skills	S	University students (n = 15)	Results show an observable effect on developing students' oral production and positive affective factors

(*continued*)

Table 3. (*continued*)

Author	Research Objective	Focus*	Sample	Findings
[35]	To evaluate the effect of DST on EFL students' motivation, satisfaction and their opinion regarding the use of DST in EFL education	S and W	University students (n = 60)	Findings reveal that students believed to have developed their speaking ability with DST. 16% of students expressed a negative opinion about the use of DST to learn English
[36]	To explore the process of writing development of pre-service teachers through DST	W	Pre-service teacher (n = 1)	The study highlights that the recursive nature of DST composition helped in improving writing structure and in reimagining the writing process
[37]	To examine how predicting factors of English writing ability are associated with DST task outcome	W	High school students (n = 48)	English writing proficiency and L1 narrative skills were found to have significantly predicted DST task outcomes in terms of the quality of language use and task fulfillment
[38]	To examine the effects of DST on students' writing skills	W	Junior College students (n = 2)	After the extended engagement, a significant improvement in students' writing was observed
[39]	To investigate the effect of grouping patterns in DST tasks on learning outcomes	S	Sixth grade students (n = 55)	Students working cooperatively during DST performed better with increased interaction which had a positive effect on speaking anxiety in the EFL setting

(*continued*)

Table 3. (*continued*)

Author	Research Objective	Focus*	Sample	Findings
[40]	To examine student involvement and the effect of Web 2.0 DST activities on student language proficiency	S	Third grade students (n = 24)	Students' vocabulary and oral fluency improved. Several phases of disengagement were reported because of the repetitive nature and task difficulties
[41]	To investigate the impact of DST on literacy learning	S and W	5-year-old learners (n = 53)	The use of DST improved oral language, social interaction, and writing
[42]	To explore the effectiveness of DST in improving writing and speaking	S and W	University students (n = 21)	Learners improved speaking skills with DST, but no improvement in pronunciation and intonation
[43]	To examine the effect of Digital composition on students' perception and academics	W	University students (n = 9)	The study provided evidence for the use of DST in promoting reflective avenues in process-based writing
[44]	To investigate the effects of DST on speaking skills and creativity	S	Seventh grade students (n = 54)	DST had a significant effect on improving spoken fluency, accuracy and creative thinking skills
[45]	To investigate the effect of DST on students' narrative writing skills and their perception regarding it	W	Secondary students (n = 52)	A significant difference in narrative writing skills was observed, but no difference between the score of the experiment and treatment groups

(*continued*)

Table 3. (*continued*)

Author	Research Objective	Focus*	Sample	Findings
[46]	To explore the use of DST to support the learning of content, language proficiency, and academic English	W	University students (n = 203)	DST encouraged learners to become critical users of knowledge and promoted English language writing skills
[47]	To investigate the effect of DST using Toontastic 3D on students' speaking skills	S	11-year-old learners (n = 35)	Results highlight that DST assisted in improving students' speaking skills, motivation, and confidence

S = Speaking; W = Writing
**Not specified*

3.2 What is the Outcome of Previous Research that Used DST for the Development of English Language Productive Skills?

As highlighted in Table 3, the results of the analyzed studies show a positive effect of DST-based intervention on students' English language productive skills. All of the studies reported favorable outcomes with the use of DST, however along with presenting positive outcomes, only a few studies [10, 16, 23, 31, 35, 40, 42, 45] presented non-significant results or concerns with DST in some aspects.

3.3 What are the Methods and Research Designs Used to Explore the Effect of DST on English Language Productive Skills in Previous Research?

The articles reviewed indicated a balance of methodological approaches. Studies were broadly classified into three categories according to their methodological paradigm – qualitative, quantitative, and mixed-method study (see Table 4). Qualitative design was employed in 36.36% of the studies, while 30.30% of studies were quantitative. 33.33% of studies employed a mixed-method design. As presented in Table 4, case study was the most common among qualitative studies, while quantitative studies primarily adopted the quasi-experimental design. As for the studies with a mixed-method design, a combination of quasi-experiment and qualitative questionnaire, observation, and/or interview was used. However, mixed-method design was dominated by quantitative analysis. Overall, most studies were dedicated to using quantitative research approach with a quasi-experimental research design.

Table 4. Details of research methods and designs used in the reviewed articles

Method	Research design	References	n
Qualitative	Case study	[11, 12, 29, 36, 38, 42]	12
	Descriptive	[15]	
	Exploratory	[16]	
	Qualitative pre-test post-test	[34]	
	Case study + ethnography	[43, 46]	
	Qualitative without specific design	[1]	
Quantitative	Quasi-experimental	[8, 23, 26, 27, 33, 39, 44, 47]	10
	Case study	[31, 40]	
Mixed	Quasi-experiment + survey	[10, 30]	11
	Quasi-experiment + Interview	[45]	
	Quasi-experiment + Interview, observation, document analysis	[41]	
	Quantitative pre-test post-test + survey	[37]	
	Quantitative pre-test post-test + interview	[32]	
	Quantitative pre-test post-test + interview, questionnaire	[28, 35]	
	Quantitative pre-test post-test + interview, observation	[9]	
	Quantitative pre-test post-test + Interview, observation, document analysis	[24]	
	One-sample qualitative participation analytics + survey	[25]	

4 Discussion

This systematic review aims to provide insights into the research that deal with DST in English language education focusing on productive language skills of speaking and writing. Using cross-analysis and synthesis, we analyzed the research objectives, outcomes, and methodology used across the studies to understand the research focus in the field and to foreground the future direction of DST-based research. From our analysis, we discovered potential areas in terms of the research direction, the nature of task, and the nature of result that seek further consideration.

4.1 Research Direction

The research direction of the past studies rested on evaluating the effectiveness of DST for improving English language productive skills. Besides addressing the level of effectiveness of DST on speaking and writing, a few studies explored why any significant increase and/or decrease in skills occurred. Study Hur and Suh [9] recognized that repeated practice of speaking and recursive draft composition while creating DST assisted in improving the speaking and writing skills of the learners. The study conducted by Del Moral et al. [31] identified the extraneous cognitive efforts while using digital tools as the reason that caused a negative effect on English as a foreign language (EFL) learners' speaking skills. Some studies identified motivation, engagement, and interaction as factors associated with DST that help learners improve their productive language skills (e.g. [16, 24, 27, 33, 41, 45]).

However, these studies were predominantly directed toward exploring the level of language improvement that resulted from DST-based intervention. We observed an outcome-oriented research trend with a heavy focus on the outcome of DST by answering 'how much' or 'why' any significant change occurs. This can be related to the selection of research design in the reviewed articles. Quantitative and mixed method studies employed research designs such as the quasi-experimental method, pre-test and post-test analysis, and survey to explore the extent of effectiveness of DST-based intervention. Using these research methods, studies on learning the English language are primarily concerned with determining the degree to which productive language skills have improved as a result of various pedagogical approaches, learning modules, activities, and even web applications based on DST. These studies aim to quantify the degree of improvement, any significant variation between intervention recipients and non-intervention recipients, or variation pre and post DST intervention. Here, it is essential to highlight that none of the studies provided insights on 'how' the process of creating DST enhances English language productive skills. We suggest that future research can be directed towards looking into the improvement patterns using in-depth qualitative approach to foreground the effective and/or ineffective elements embedded in the process of creating digital stories.

4.2 Nature of the Task

As can be seen from the analysis (see Table 3), only few studies reported negative findings (e.g. [16, 31, 35, 40]). However, the positive findings can be due to the novelty of the nature of the task. Many studies introduced DST to the participants as a new technological intervention that results in increased motivation and engagement (e.g. [28, 33, 42, 47]). This novelty effect [48] captures learners' interest when exposed to new technology. This observation is in line with the review conducted by Wu and Chen [17] which observed a similar novelty effect among the studies. We recommend that future research must adopt repeated intervention of the tool for the corroboration of the positive results of DST in improving English language productive skills.

4.3 Nature of the Result

Based on our analysis it was found that the focus of the studies is on significant results but they fall short in reporting non-significant findings. Parallel to Wu and Chen [17] a file-drawer effect was observed from the analysis. The File-drawer effect occurs when the researcher assumes that non-significant results would cause publication bias. This often leads to risking the objectivity of the study and not accounting for the errors in initial statistical reports [49]. In the present review, studies were found to present details about the significant results while lacking reasons and elaboration on the negative and non-significant findings (see Table 2). Prima facie, studies portray DST as an inclusively effective tool for English language productive language skills development. It is highly encouraged that researchers must report details on non-significant findings and present rigorous critique to direct improvements in tools, methodologies, as well as practice.

5 Future Research and Implications

This systematic review presents a comprehensive overview of the extant literature on the use of DST in English language pedagogy. The analysis was conducted to highlight the focus of DST-based research in improving productive language skills of speaking and writing. It was found that a large number of studies confirmed the effectiveness of DST, while only a few had negative results and mixed perceptions. As highlighted in the discussion, the present analysis strongly encourages the use of DST for improving productive language skills. However, there are a few considerations that require attention from future researchers. It is recommended that there is a need for studies that could highlight how these positive outcomes of language improvement occur with DST. Such insights would be beneficial for language instructors and instructional technologists in refining and designing new pedagogical approaches. Since DST is also widely practices in language education other than English, it would be prudent to undertake systematic review of the use of DST in other language setting. Such studies could possibly highlight shared implications across language teaching and learning with DST.

References

1. Al Khateeb, A.A.: Socially orientated digital storytelling among Saudi EFL learners: an analysis of its impact and content. Interact. Technol. Smart Educ. **16**(2), 130–142 (2019). https://doi.org/10.1108/ITSE-11-2018-0098
2. Lambert, J.: Digital Storytelling Cookbook. Digital Diner Press (2010)
3. Robin, B.R.: Digital storytelling: a powerful technology tool for the 21st century classroom. Theory Pract. **47**(3), 220–228 (2008)
4. Kearney, M.: A learning design for student-generated digital storytelling. Learn. Media Technol. **36**(2), 169–188 (2011). https://doi.org/10.1080/17439884.2011.553623
5. Ohler, J.: The world of digital storytelling. Educ. Leadersh. **63**(4), 44–47 (2006)
6. Barrett, H.: Researching and evaluating digital storytelling as a deep learning tool. Presented at the Society for Information Technology & Teacher Education International Conference (2006)
7. Robin, B.R.: The power of digital storytelling to support teaching and learning. Digit. Educ. Rev. **30**, 17–29 (2016)

8. Rahimi, M., Yadollahi, S.: Effects of offline vs. online digital storytelling on the development of EFL learners' literacy skills. Cogent Educ. **4**(1) (2017). https://doi.org/10.1080/2331186X. 2017.1285531

9. Hur, J.W., Suh, S.: Making learning active with interactive whiteboards, podcasts, and digital storytelling in ELL classrooms. Comput. Sch. **29**(4), 320–338 (2012). https://doi.org/10.1080/ 07380569.2012.734275

10. Kim, S.: Developing autonomous learning for oral proficiency using digital storytelling. Lang. Learn. Technol. **18**(2), 20–35 (2014)

11. Amelia, L.C.H., Abidin, M.J.Z.: Young ESL learners' perception on the effects of using digital storytelling application in English language learning. Pertanika J. Soc. Sci. Humanit. **26**(T), 179–198 (2018)

12. Kristiawan, D., Ferdiansyah, S., Picard, M.: Promoting vocabulary building, learning motivation, and cultural identity representation through digital storytelling for young Indonesian learners of English as a foreign language. Iran. J. Lang. Teach. Res. **10**(1), 19–36 (2022). https://doi.org/10.30466/ijltr.2022.121120

13. Khan, S., Ziden, A.A.: A systematic review of the effect of digital storytelling on affective factors in improving speaking skills. In: 2022 IEEE 2nd International Conference on Educational Technology (ICET), pp. 81–85 (2022)

14. Nair, V., Yunus, M.M.: A systematic review of digital storytelling in improving speaking skills. Sustainability **13**(17) (2021). https://doi.org/10.3390/su13179829

15. Mesa, P.A.G.: Digital storytelling: boosting literacy practices in students at A1-level. HOW **27**(1), 83–104 (2020). https://doi.org/10.19183/how.27.1.505

16. Cheung, A.: Digitizing the story-writing process for EFL primary learners: an exploratory study. Lang. Teach. Res. (2021). https://doi.org/10.1177/13621688211027772

17. Wu, J., Chen, D.-T.V.: A systematic review of educational digital storytelling. Comput. Educ. **147**, 103786 (2020)

18. Quah, C.Y., Ng, K.H.: A systematic literature review on digital storytelling authoring tool in education: January 2010 to January 2020. Int. J. Hum.-Comput. Interact. **38**, 851–867 (2022). https://doi.org/10.1080/10447318.2021.1972608

19. Rodríguez, C.L., García-Jiménez, M., Massó-Guijarro, B., Cruz-González, C.: Digital storytelling in education: a systematic review of the literature. Rev. Eur. Stud. **13**(2), 13–25 (2021). https://doi.org/10.5539/res.v13n2p13

20. Lim, N., Zakaria, A., Aryadoust, V.: A systematic review of digital storytelling in language learning in adolescents and adults. Educ. Inf. Technol. **27**, 6125–6155 (2022). https://doi.org/ 10.1007/s10639-021-10861-0

21. Abderrahim, L., Cigerci, F.M.: A systematic review of research undertaken into the use of digital storytelling as a pedagogical tool in the language classroom. In: AICMSE & AICBEM 2018 (Oxford) Conference Proceedings, pp. 113–124. FLE Learning, Oxford (2018)

22. Moher, D., et al.: Preferred reporting items for systematic review and meta-analysis protocols (PRISMA-P) 2015 statement. Syst. Rev. **4**, 1–9 (2015). https://doi.org/10.1186/2046-405 3-4-1

23. Alcantud-Díaz, M., Vayá, A.R., Gregori-Signes, C.: 'Share your experience'. Digital storytelling in English for tourism. Ibérica, Revista de la Asociación Europea de Lenguas para Fines Específicos 185–204 (2014)

24. Azis, Y.A., Husnawadi: Collaborative digital storytelling-based task for EFL writing instruction: outcomes and perceptions. J. Asia TEFL **17**, 562–579 (2020). https://doi.org/10.18823/ asiatefl.2020.17.2.16.562

25. Bailey, D., Southam, A., Costley, J.: Digital storytelling with chatbots: mapping L2 participation and perception patterns. Interact. Technol. Smart Educ. **18**(1), 85–103 (2021). https:// doi.org/10.1108/ITSE-08-2020-0170

26. Baniabdelrahman, A.: The effect of using online tools on ninth grade Jordanian students' vocabulary learning. Arab World Engl. J. (AWEJ) **4**(1), 175–188 (2013)
27. Bashirnezhad, H., Yousefi, A.: Digital storytelling listening influence on Iranian intermediate EFL learners' pronunciation. QUID: Investigación, Ciencia y Tecnología (1), 1702–1707 (2017)
28. Batsila, M., Tsihouridis, C.: "Once upon a time there was…" a digital world for junior high school learners. Int. J. Emerg. Technol. Learn. (iJET) **11**(03), 42–50 (2016). https://doi.org/10.3991/ijet.v11i03.5370
29. Peñuelas, A.B.C.: The use of glogs in the English language classroom. @tic revista d'innovació educativa **10**, 68–74 (2013). https://doi.org/10.7203/attic.10.1775
30. Castillo-Cuesta, L.M., Quinonez-Beltran, A., Cabrera-Solano, P., Ochoa-Cueva, C., Gonzalez-Torres, P.: Using digital storytelling as a strategy for enhancing EFL writing skills. Int. J. Emerg. Technol. Learn. (iJET) **16**(13), 142–156 (2021). https://doi.org/10.3991/ijet.v16i13.22187
31. Del Moral-Pérez, M.E., Villalustre-Martínez, L., del Neira-Piñeiro, M.: Digital storytelling: activating communicative, narrative and digital competences in initial teacher training. Ocnos **15**, 22–41 (2016). https://doi.org/10.18239/ocnos_2016.15.1.923
32. Eissa, H.M.S.: Pedagogic effectiveness of digital storytelling in improving speaking skills of Saudi EFL learners. Arab World J. **10**(1), 127–138 (2019)
33. Fu, J.S., Yang, S.-H., Yeh, H.-C.: Exploring the impacts of digital storytelling on English as a foreign language learners' speaking competence. J. Res. Technol. Educ. **54**(5), 679–694 (2021). https://doi.org/10.1080/15391523.2021.1911008
34. Gonzalez, D., Molina, J.C., Cardona, B.S.R.: Project-based learning to develop oral production in English as a foreign language. Int. J. Educ. Inf. Technol. **11**, 87–96 (2017)
35. Hava, K.: Exploring the role of digital storytelling in student motivation and satisfaction in EFL education. Comput. Assist. Lang. Learn. **34**(7), 958–978 (2019). https://doi.org/10.1080/09588221.2019.1650071
36. Hicks, T., Turner, K., Stratton, J.: Reimagining a writer's process through digital storytelling. Learn. Landsc. **6**(2), 167–183 (2013). https://doi.org/10.36510/learnland.v6i2.611
37. Kang, S., Kim, Y.: Examining the quality of mobile-assisted, video-making task outcomes: the role of proficiency, narrative ability, digital literacy, and motivation. Lang. Teach. Res. 13621688211047984 (2021). https://doi.org/10.1177/13621688211047984
38. Lee, H.-C.: Using an arts-integrated multimodal approach to promote English learning: a case study of two Taiwanese junior college students. Engl. Teach. Pract. Crit. **13**(2), 55–75 (2014)
39. Liu, M.-C., Huang, Y.-M., Xu, Y.-H.: Effects of individual versus group work on learner autonomy and emotion in digital storytelling. Educ. Tech. Res. Dev. **66**, 1009–1028 (2018). https://doi.org/10.1007/s11423-018-9601-2
40. Liu, C.C., Wang, P.C., Tai, S.J.D.: An analysis of student engagement patterns in language learning facilitated by Web 2.0 technologies. ReCALL **28**(2), 104–122 (2016). https://doi.org/10.1017/S095834401600001X
41. Oakley, G., Wildy, H., Berman, Y.: Multimodal digital text creation using tablets and open-ended creative apps to improve the literacy learning of children in early childhood classrooms. J. Early Child. Lit. **20**(4), 655–679 (2020). https://doi.org/10.1177/1468798418779171
42. Pardo, B.S.: Digital storytelling: a case study of the creation, and narration of a story by EFL learners. Digit. Educ. Rev. **26**, 74–84 (2014)
43. Stewart, K.D., Ivala, E.: Silence, voice, and "other languages": digital storytelling as a site for resistance and restoration in a South African higher education classroom. Br. J. Edu. Technol. **48**(5), 1164–1175 (2017). https://doi.org/10.1111/bjet.12540
44. Yang, Y.-T., Chen, Y.-C., Hung, H.-T.: Digital storytelling as an interdisciplinary project to improve students' English speaking and creative thinking. Comput. Assist. Lang. Learn. **35**(4), 840–862 (2020). https://doi.org/10.1080/09588221.2020.1750431

45. Zakaria, M.A., Aziz, A.A.: The impact of digital storytelling on ESL narrative writing skill. Arab World Engl. J. **5**(5), 319–332 (2019)
46. Fan, Y.-S.: Facilitating content knowledge, language proficiency, and academic competence through digital storytelling: performance and perceptions of first-year medical-related majors. J. Res. Technol. Educ. 1–21 (2022). https://doi.org/10.1080/15391523.2022.2110337
47. Nair, V., Md Yunus, M.: Using digital storytelling to improve pupils' speaking skills in the age of COVID 19. Sustainability **14**(15), 1–19 (2022). https://doi.org/10.3390/su14159215
48. Clark, R.E.: Reconsidering research on learning from media. Rev. Educ. Res. **53**, 445–459 (1983)
49. Sterling, T.D.: Publication decisions and their possible effects on inferences drawn from tests of significance—or vice versa. J. Am. Stat. Assoc. **285**, 30–34 (1959)

Greek Kindergarten Teachers' Perceived Barriers in Using Touchscreen Tablets in the Post-pandemic Era: An Intersectional Study

Emmanouela V. Seiradakis[1,2]([envelope]) [ID]

[1] Technical University of Crete, 73100 Chania, Greece
eseiradaki@tuc.gr
[2] Hellenic Open University, 26335 Patras, Greece

Abstract. The purpose of this work was to identify Greek kindergarten teachers' perceived barriers in using touchscreen tablets for educational purposes in the post-covid era through an intersectional lens. Twelve Greek kindergarten teachers participated in in-depth interviews. Thematic content analysis informed by intersectionality was adopted. Analysis revealed a range of first and second-order personal, professional and contextual barrier themes in the interrelationships of gender, class, family status and professional identity. First-order barrier themes included (1) "School barriers", (2) "Endless low-quality training", (3) "Lack of time and feelings of devaluation", (4) "Nomad life and low pay" and (5) "Parents' resentment". Second-order barriers included (1) "Screen guilt and Covid" and (2) "Preschoolers are experts". Findings suggest main post-covid barriers to integrating tablets in Greek kindergarten schools are the invisible ones and no longer focus on equipment or connectivity. Implications for educational policy, kindergarten teacher professional development and screen media integration are discussed in conjunction to limitations of the study.

Keywords: touchscreen tablets · barriers · kindergarten · teachers' perceptions · post-covid · intersectionality

1 Introduction

Extensive research prior to the Covid-19 pandemic [1–3] has shown Greek kindergarten teachers seem more hesitant in integrating technology-enhanced pedagogies as compared to their primary and secondary education counterparts. Major barriers reported in these works are related to poor funding, lack of equipment and connectivity, lack of teachers' training and teachers' beliefs regarding the importance of hands-on learning experiences in kindergarten. The emergence of the Covid-19 pandemic back in 2020 radically changed the Greek educational technology landscape as the then newly elected neoliberal Greek government invested substantial capitals on connectivity, equipment and particularly tablets which were distributed to all schools around the country, teachers' training and passed emergency legislation allowing online teaching and mobile

Ł. Tomczyk (Ed.): NMP 2022, CCIS 1916, pp. 152–167, 2023.
https://doi.org/10.1007/978-3-031-44581-1_12

devices use in K-12 which up until then was prohibited [4]. Despite the effort, the single post-pandemic work exploring tablet and mobile phone use barriers in K-12 [4] shows Greek kindergarten educators still lag in implementing technology-enhanced pedagogies and cite similar pro-covid concerns. Nikolopoulous' study [4] provides us with valuable information on Greek kindergarten teachers' perceived barriers in using mobile phones and tablets in the post-covid era yet its quantitative design fails to capture more fine-grained information on the underlying "whys" they still seem reluctant in integrating touchscreen devices in their teaching even though at least some of the pre-covid barriers have or should have been removed.

The present qualitative work sought to fill this current gap by identifying factors that Greek kindergarten teachers identify as barriers to implementing touchscreen-enhanced pedagogies through an intersectional lens [5]. Back in 1989, Crenshaw used the term intersectionality to explicate and analyze the multifaceted and hidden forms of marginality women of color experienced within the US legal system due to gender, class and race identity intersections. Since then, intersectionality has been employed as an analysis tool for exploring women's as well as other marginalized groups' experiences in multiple fields for diverse forms of hidden barriers in society. Intersectionality highlights the interaction of social identities that function within various social frameworks at the individual, relational, and institutional planes, which eventually emerge at the individual level [6]. Thus, research conducted from this standpoint may be able to shed light on the abstract intricacies of the intersections among barriers to technology integration, Greek kindergarten teachers' social identities, and diverse formulae of disguised barriers linked with the Greek kindergarten context that still hold teachers back even though some of the issues related to equipment, training and connectivity have now been resolved.

Early childhood education (ECE) is pertinent to intersectionality for a number of reasons. ECE educators as opposed to other teacher disciplines are almost exclusively women in Greece [7] and worldwide [8–10] yet relevant research on technology integration barriers hasn't taken this fact under consideration. Compared to other educational grades, teaching in kindergarten still is perceived as a feminized profession [11, 12] and teachers are often seen as "glorified babysitters" (:11) [13]. Their role in society is perceived as more relevant to providing children of this age with care and love and less to education, which in turn triggers feelings of devaluation [9, 14] and some would argue that this perception is translated into concrete systemic inequalities. For example, in Greece kindergarten teachers and headteachers have by law the longest weekly teaching hours compared to all other state teachers with no provision for breaks during their 8–13:00 classes [15]. This perception which views the kindergarten teacher as an expansion of the mother's role and less as a professional combined with Greek teachers' current financial struggles, their widespread internal migration for securing a teaching position and poor working condition issues in post-covid, post-crisis Greece may have implications on their use of technology in classroom. Accordingly, using qualitative accounts grounded in some of these teachers' experiences the present study aimed to obtain fine-grained data hidden in the interrelatedness of gender, family-status, social class, professional identity and teachers' perceived barriers in touchscreen tablet use within Greek kindergarten classroom settings. More specifically, the leading question of this interview-based study was:

What are Greek kindergarten teachers' perceived barriers in using touchscreen tablets for educational purposes in the post-covid era?

1.1 Barrier Categorization

Technology integration barriers refer to conditions that hinder the effective use of ICTs in educational settings [16]. Based on Ertmer [16] technology integration barriers can be categorized as first and second-order barriers. First-order barriers are linked to external obstacles teachers encounter in using technologies. Common first-order barriers based on relevant findings include issues in access, lack of resources, deficits in technology leadership and in technical support, insufficient training and time constraints [17–20]. Second-order barriers encompass teachers' attitudes and beliefs towards technology, their confidence in using it and willingness to change their teaching patterns and routines [17–22]. According to Ertmer [16, 17], first and second-order barriers are interrelated. A teacher who argues he/she doesn't use technology due to external obstacles (first-order barriers) such as lack of equipment or time pressure may actually hold negative beliefs on the appropriateness or effectiveness of technology. Likewise, a teacher who constantly finds ways to integrate technology, a teacher who devotes personal time and effort to resolve issues related to equipment or design technology-enhanced lessons may also hold strong beliefs on educational technology use.

First and second order barriers are influenced by other contextual factors such as rurality, school size and community. Teachers in remote rural schools often have limited access to technologies and make less use of technologies despite their positive attitudes and willingness [23]. Findings further suggest different perceived barriers and technology integration patterns among urban, suburban and rural school teachers with suburban teachers adopting a more active approach in using technology in their classrooms. Social class and the socioeconomic status of the area teachers work also generate different types of perceived barriers. Teachers from affluent suburb schools appear to be more confident in implementing sophisticated technology-based pedagogies compared to educators in disadvantaged areas. Age of students and different educational grades are also associated to different types of barriers. For example, compared to kindergarten, secondary education teachers hold more positive attitudes towards technology integration [24, 25].

2 Materials and Methods

2.1 Context

Teachers' wider cultural and social context significantly influences both their practices and perceptions regarding the use of technology in their classrooms [21]. Therefore, in order to grasp Greek kindergarten teachers' perceptions on the use of tablets in their classrooms, the wider Greek educational context must be taken under consideration. Greece is a country that has just overcome a painful decade of financial crisis and austerity measures which inevitably triggered negative effects in public education funding. Weekly teaching hours increased but teachers' salaries were cut around 30%, permanent teacher appointments froze from 2009 to 2019 and the system became largely dependent on substitute teachers with yearly contracts [26]. The crisis also had a significant impact on funding for technological equipment and teachers' training in state schools.

The Covid-19 pandemic which emerged right at the time when Greece was recovering from the crisis changed everything as state funding both for technological equipment and teacher training sharply increased. The pandemic also had an effect on official national-level ICT policies in education. The then newly elected neoliberal government Nea Dimokratia changed the previous legislation which prohibited mobile phone and tablet usage in K-12 classrooms and modified the curriculum which until then ignored mobile learning all together [4]. Online learning became obligatory for several months for K-12 classes across the country and the Ministry of Education distributed tablets to all schools both for teachers and students. State-school teachers received obligatory training on the use of mobile technologies. Simultaneously, the national-level recruitment legislation changed and national-level exams were replaced by a point system based on formal qualifications such as postgraduate diplomas and training certificates. This in turn prompted a sharp influx of literally hundreds of thousands of Greek teacher candidates obtaining qualifications, including ICT - related programs. In addition, in 2021 the government brought an Education Bill which included multiple evaluation and accountability measures for schools and teachers which in turn triggered union mobilization and conflict which continues until today [27]. One of the axes state teachers are evaluated is the integration of technologies in their teaching. Overall, Greek teachers have gone through intensive training on ICT by their own means in order to secure a teaching position in state schools or obligatory training by the Ministry of Education. They currently are under a lot of stress and pressure due to the new evaluation legislation and also because a large percentage of them work away from home, in remote areas of Greece such as islands struggling to make ends meet [27, 28].

Structure wise, the Greek education system is highly centralized, in fact the Ministry of Education regulates everything related to schools from curriculum and budgeting to teacher recruitment procedures and textbooks. School autonomy is essentially non-existent and schools are obliged to comply with directives issued by the ministry's regional directorates [29]. In terms of curriculum, one of the ministry's scientific agencies, the Institute of Educational Policy (IEP) issues detailed curriculums for K-12. Regarding ICT in the kindergarten, IEP issued a new curriculum in 2021 [30] based on which teachers should design and implement technology-enhanced pedagogies regularly in order to help their students develop into digitally literate citizens. The new curriculum includes three long, distinct yet theoretical sections on preschoolers' familiarization with ICTs, the use of ICTs for research, discovery, problem solving, programming and digital creativity.

2.2 Participants and Procedure

Twelve female state kindergarten teachers participated in the study. Participants' ages ranged from 30–41 years old. Their teaching experience ranged between 4–9 years. All participants had a bachelor's in ECE from a Greek state university, a master's degree and one of them a PhD. Nine of them were married with one child or more, one of them was a single mother. Four of them had just gained a permanent teaching position while the rest were substitute teachers. At the time, seven participants worked away from their hometowns in three Greek islands, two of them worked in Athens and the other three at smaller towns in northern Greece. Participants were recruited via purposive sampling and the snowball sampling procedure. The researcher who also was their tutor during their online postgraduate degree at the Hellenic Open University contacted two of her ex-students and then through them contacted other kindergarten teachers. Recruitment continued until the desired number of participants were recruited for the study. Informed consent was obtained in writing from all participants and the significance of maintaining anonymity and confidentiality was highlighted. To ensure participants' anonymity, numbers are used throughout this paper (e.g., P1, P2).

Interviews were conducted via Zoom and ranged in length from one to two hours. They had the form of an open conversation nonetheless they focused on the same topics with each teacher. These included (i) their perceptions of first and second order barriers in using touchscreen devices in their classrooms; (ii) the relevance of their identities (e.g., woman, mother, state kindergarten teacher, Greek) to their experiences of barriers in implementing touchscreen-informed pedagogies.

2.3 Data Analysis

This work employed content thematic analysis [31] in order to analyze interview data. Analysis further aimed to recognize barriers at the intersections of participants' social identities simultaneously but also separately [6]. Initially transcribed interviews were repeatedly read and early themes were acknowledged for each participant's perceived barriers in integrating touchscreen tablets in their teaching. Data were subsequently refined and categorized under first and second order barriers. First -order barriers themes include (1) "School barriers"; (2) "Endless, low-quality training" (3) "Nomad life and low pay", (4) "Lack of time and feelings of devaluation" and (4) "Parents' resentment". Second-order barriers include (1) "Screen guilt and Covid" and (2) "Preschoolers are experts".

3 Results

3.1 First-Order Barriers

First-order barriers in the current work are defined as participants' perceived obstacles in using touchscreen tablets in their classrooms. These barriers refer to perceived problems created by school, lack of time, national-level policies, parents and gender/class intersections. By contrast, second-order barriers derive from teachers' internal beliefs and attitudes towards touchscreen tablets.

School Barriers

The number of students per class emerged as a major obstacle for participants to make use of tablets in their classrooms. Variations in students' number per class was related to school location with urban preschools having 20–23 students with no teaching assistants. Participants expressed frustration and sometimes anger for the fact that both legislators and parents are unable or unwilling to comprehend the difficulties and peculiarities of having so many preschoolers instead of older children in class. For many participants, the number one priority in the classroom is ensuring preschoolers' safety and not integrating technology:

My priority is to hand them back to their parents safely […]. I've heard of a lot of stories with colleagues having ended up at court or listen to threats when something happens. […]. Two -three months ago, I had given them the tablets, I was concentrated on the screen to show them how the game works, in front of my eyes, one of them takes the tablet out of another girl's hands, knocks her down and throughs the tablet on the floor. (P2)

Lack of technology leadership and support was another school-related barrier mentioned by participants which often discouraged them from using technology in their teaching. Most participants attributed this leadership deficit to systemic ECE barriers in Greece. Greek kindergarten teaching stuff includes by law only preschool teachers and as a result the headteacher of every school is usually in charge both for equipment and contacting the corresponding municipality if there is a technical difficulty. There are no ICT teachers like in primary and secondary education schools and the actual number of teachers is usually smaller. To make things worse, kindergarten headteachers in Greece are also the only administrators in Greek education who have all the responsibilities of managing a school but have no reduction in their weekly teaching hours:

To be fair, they can't really support us because they have more serious things to do, like teaching their own class for 24 hours a week, deal with parents, do the administrative work, so they prioritize, a broken tablet for example or the WiFi can't be their number one priority when they have to deal with students' who have serious family issues, do budgeting and so on. (P1)

Other participants encountered headteachers who were intrusive and they themselves resented the use of touchscreen devices due to their belief that teachers who use them are lazy or due to parents' interreference or their own lack of knowledge and skills in touchscreen technologies. P7 painted a rather cynic picture of the multiple concealed barriers created by lack of technology leadership in Greek kindergartens:

Some of them (headteachers) don't care, some of them think it's a sign of laziness, some of them don't know how to use them cause they are older and some of them don't want us to use them because parents don't want us to use them […] and since we are their babysitters we do as they tell us. (P7)

Participants' reflections indicated that post-covid external barriers related to the existence of devices and connectivity decreased yet they didn't vanish. These difficulties were related less to the absence of technological means and mostly to insufficient maintenance of the existing equipment. They stated that these difficulties are in some cases an inhibitory factor for using technology yet they pointed that post-covid problems related specifically to tablet shortages lessened. Most participants' worries as kindergarten teachers were school infrastructures in terms of space and run-down buildings which are not appropriate for preschoolers rather than the technological equipment:

Educational technology is just a buzzword in Greece right now […] the ministry is obsessed with technology and tablets and interactive whiteboards but for me the real problem is our students don't have space to run and play, many kindergartens are in dark depressive buildings with ceilings leaking in the first rain [...]. (P11)

Endless, Low-Quality Training

Although the majority of participants had qualifications related to educational technologies and attended numerous training programs provided both by the agencies of the Ministry of Education and universities, some of them did not succeed in gaining concrete creative skills for designing touchscreen-enhanced lessons. The quality of the majority of these programs was heavily criticized due to two main reasons. The first reason was related to relevance, as the majority of ICT training programs failed to respond to kindergarten teachers' specific needs and the second one was related to poor design. Most of these programs were asynchronous MOOCs with pdfs, videos and multiple-choice quizzes. The few programs which comprised synchronous learning modes included large numbers of participants, with switched-off cameras and a trainer presenting a PowerPoint with theoretical knowledge that could not easily be implemented in realistic settings:

> *We have had endless training on technologies, we did it during Covid, we do it now but we do not have the time to self-reflect and practice what we learn, if we learn something, that is. Everything is really fast-paced.* (P6)

> *I can tell you with certainty that the problem is not lack of training but the quality of training, we have all had hundreds of hours of training for educational technologies, we have all done countless quizzes, listened to the same and same theoretical stuff we cannot really apply in our classrooms because most of them are not even related to kindergarten.* (P4)

Other than the perceived low-quality of training there also was resentment regarding the endless training courses some participants had to attend both before, during and after covid on the use of educational technologies as well as other subjects. Once again, intersections of gender and social class emerged as participants reflected on their constant daily struggles to cope with online training, workload, housework and childcare:

> *The word training has lost its meaning in this country. Yes, I have had training on ICTs. We do online training non-stop, nobody pays attention any more, it's just papers for extra points. I have three children, I have downloaded Teams, Zoom, Webex on my phone, I drive my kids to their swimming classes, I do laundry, I cook and I'm on the phone for training. It's frustrating and ridiculous. They probably think we have nannies, servants, drivers like them at home.* (P11)

Nomad Life and Low Pay

Another barrier that emerged was job insecurity and lack of feelings of belonging in the school especially from participants who work as substitute teachers. In Greece, substitute teacher contracts are terminated in June and teachers usually spend a stressful summer waiting till they are hired back again most probably not at the school they were and often not at the same city, municipality or even island. This constant insecurity triggers feelings of resentment for P3 who felt that it really wasn't worth it to invest capital at her school since she really wouldn't be a part of it in a couple of months:

> *Every year, a different school, you never know what you'll find here, what equipment, headteachers, other teachers, parents [...]. In the beginning I remember I used to devote time and energy to fix my classroom, I had arguments with head-teachers asking for equipment, then I would leave and felt like all my work was wasted, I had to start all over again.* (P3)

P10 a young substitute teacher who this year moved to the touristic island of Crete due to scarcity of teaching positions in Athens, mentioned time and financial struggles:

> *I borrow from my parents to be here, I make almost 850 euros, my rent is 450[...]. I also work at a restaurant in the evenings because if I didn't, I literally wouldn't be able to fill my gas tank [...]. It's not that we are lazy, we are burnt out and poor, teachers in Greece used to be middle-class, not anymore.*

Other participants also reflected on their economic hardships and the low salaries in relation to the workload and the level of education required in order to become a kindergarten teacher in Greece. All of the participants had a master's degree and one of them had a doctoral degree. P7 talked about the cost of acquiring advanced degrees and the lack of associated financial reward:

> *Greek teachers make peanuts; it didn't use to be like that but the crisis changed everything [...]. I went to school for close to 6 years to get my bachelor's and my master's because that's the minimum requirement for state teachers in Greece and I spent a lot of money to be here and teach because I love it but now I have to work a second job as a private tutor every single afternoon in order to be able to survive and I end up being exhausted[...].I don't have the energy or the time to design lessons, I return home at nine o'clock at night because I need to pay rent, it's as simple as that.*

Lack of Time and Feelings of Devaluation

Lack of time was mentioned by all participants as the main obstacle in integrating technology in their teaching. Most participants appeared confident in using touchscreen devices for personal purposes but not as confident when integrating it with very young children for educational purposes. They exhibited heightened awareness regarding educational technologies and clearly distinguished between their ability to use phones and tablets or giving their students an application to occupy them for a bit as opposed to designing a proper technology-enhanced lesson incorporating developmentally appropriate activities with specific learning outcomes. As P1 noted: *Integrating technology in our lesson sure isn't handing them a tablet to play a stupid game or watch a video to shush them, it requires a lot of time and preparation.*

Burdensome directives and bureaucratic procedures that take up valuable time of teaching emerged as an extra barrier. Recent reforms and policies related to state teachers' evaluation and accountability voted by the Greek neoliberal government [27] were mentioned by several participants who seemed frustrated and upset by the lack of respect and trust towards their profession. Four participants referred to the current government's effort to copy paste punitive teacher evaluation systems similar to the ones in the US and the UK but as P4 commented: *just the accountability systems-not the salaries.* On top of bureaucratic procedures related to the new education bill, kindergarten teachers in particular also have to deal with issues related to students' cyber and physical safety and parents' aggressiveness:

> *Imagine having twenty five-year olds all alone with no break, imagine you aren't allowed even to go to the toilet if the colleague next door can't cover for you. Imagine having constant anxiety if one of them gets hurt and you end up in court [...]. On top of this, imagine having endless paperwork for meaningless administrative procedures for your evaluation after seven years of teaching, please tell me if you were in my position would using tablets and games be your number one priority?* (P2)

Mother-participants' reflections regarding time were even more intense. Combined with motherhood, unbending work arrangements, exhaustion, extreme difficulties in arranging childcare especially for those working away from their hometowns dominated their accounts. Three participants stated that household work and childcare were divided equally with their partners and husbands, but the rest described doing more than their share. P5 a mother of two toddlers, at the junction of having no other family support for childcare and a husband working long hours stated:

> *Greece is no Sweden, it's a bit better than the previous generations but women still do almost everything at home and there's no support from the state. I feel tired all the time, other mothers I know say they actually relax at work, I have fifteen preschoolers at work all alone, then I go home and I have two toddlers, again all alone, when exactly am I gonna find the time to sit at my computer and do lesson planning and find apps and games for school?*

Parents' Resentment

Parental concerns regarding young children's technology use especially after the pandemic emerged as a major first-order barrier. According to participants, Covid-19 created new behaviors and habits for young children and their parents who used mobile phones and tablets as a babysitting device to survive long shutdowns. These habits didn't vanish after Covid and parents still use screen media in order to wind their children down but at the same time they feel guilty about their parenting and worry about their children's well-being. Participants reported they often have parents talking to them about children's tantrums at home or confessing fears they may have developed mobile phone addiction in order to convince them not to use screen media at school:

> *They give children their phones watching all sort of garbage UTube videos to keep them busy when they do housework, they use them for making them eat breakfast quickly, they use them when they are out for coffee to keep them quiet but they don't want them to spend any screen time here.* (P9)

Some participants suggested social class and educational background positioning influence parents' views on the use of touchscreen technologies in the classroom. The higher the education level of parents, the bigger the resentment of using screen-media at school. Participants from two urban kindergartens in affluent areas encountered multiple parental interventions and prescriptions regarding the use of tablets and videos in the classrooms. Parents' negative attitudes were underpinned by stereotypes of public sector employees and especially teachers being lazy and using technology in order to avoid interactive engagement in the classroom:

Doctors, engineers, lawyers are the worst [...]. Constantly intervening, complaining to the headteacher, gossiping on Viber with other parents, treating us like we are their employees, implying we are lazy [...]. Because they are educated and have money they think they know everything and because they work long hours and their children are constantly in front of a screen at home they don't want them to use tablets here. But it's not the same thing is it? We are educators and we use tablets and specific applications for specific reasons. They don't get that. (P8)

3.2 Second-Order Barriers

Screen Guilt and Covid

Second-order barriers identified in the current study were linked to participants' negative beliefs regarding the use of technologies and screen time for young children. They all alleged educational technologies are useful and necessary for preschoolers to evolve into digital citizens but thought this post-pandemic generation of young children spends extraordinary amounts of time in front of a screen which in turn may harm their cognitive and socioemotional development. Mother-participants in particular, stated they often experience feelings of guilt when their own children use tablets and phones at home yet they considered these devices as a "necessary evil". Their accounts revealed their roles as mothers and teachers overlapped and combined with the negative memoirs from the long pandemic shutdowns, they sketched a picture full of worries, fears and guilt for the consequences of long screen time for both their students and their own children. Similarly to parents at their schools, these mothers were concerned about issues like screen addiction and the overall effect the past three years have had on their children's well-being. P1, a single mother with two young children felt guilty as she believed that touchscreen devices are really just a way of "parking" children and keeping them quiet even for applications she thought were of high-quality and developmentally appropriate for her students:

Kindergarten is about hands-on experiences, no matter how good quality apps and games we are using this generation is deprived of real playtime, playing with their peers, getting their hands dirty with mud. Covid left us with bad habits, I also let my kids use my phone to get work done at home for example but I do feel guilty [...] four-year olds shouldn't be using tablets and phones 24/7. (P1)

Preschoolers are Experts

All participants portrayed the majority of Greek preschoolers as capable technology users who can effortlessly and autonomously use technologies, especially mobile touchscreen devices. Their view of Greek preschoolers as digital natives existed even before the pandemic but post-covid this perception was further reinforced. This assumption seemed to act as an internal barrier as some of them explicitly underestimated their role in helping their students developing digital skills at school. Three participants further reflected on colleagues and headteachers of older age who actually experienced challenges in keeping up with their students' digital skills in class as P2 jokingly remarked: *Sometimes it's the other way around, four-year olds give the teachers instructions.*

4 Discussion

This work aimed to gain a deeper understanding of the barriers in using tablets for educational purposes among Greek kindergarten teachers in the post-covid era using an intersectional lens. Data analysis suggests teachers' perceived first-order barriers are related to their heightened awareness of the complexity of implementing high quality technology-enhanced pedagogies rather than to quantity of equipment or connectivity. The shift of first-order barrier focus from quantity to quality in relation to technology use is in line with the few post-covid works in the relevant literature across educational grades [32]. The pandemic prompted a series of radical changes in educational technology use as governments around the world provided both equipment and training to teachers in order for them to cope with the sudden switch to remote education. Regarding availability of equipment and access, participants painted a quite different picture of the Greek kindergarten landscape [1] compared to pro-covid works which described teachers struggling to share one desktop computer, usually slow with preschoolers ending up getting bored. Current findings are also in contrast to more recent findings from Greek primary and secondary education [3] which suggested legal barriers hindered the use of mobile technologies including tablets yet these studies were conducted prior to the pandemic and the change of Greek legislation on touchscreen devices use.

First-order barriers associated to overcrowded run-down schools and large classes, preschoolers' challenging behaviors and disruption in class are in line with findings across K-12 in Greece [1–4] but in the current study fear of damaging equipment and most importantly teachers' anxiety for ensuring students' physical safety, even fear of parents taking legal action in case a student had an accident in class arose as major impediments in using tablets. This finding is also related to national-level policies and systemic barriers as in mainstream classes there is no provision for teaching assistants or support teachers except for the cases where a student has been diagnosed with a disability [33].

An unexpected outcome was the power of Greek parents' interference on teachers' practices related to technology. It seems that the pandemic strengthened parents' beliefs extended screen time hampers young children's health and as a result their explicit resentment to tablet use puts pressure and discourages even the teachers who are willing to devote time and effort to implement technology-enhanced pedagogies. This finding is also related to the profession's feminization and devaluation and agrees with findings in other contexts [34] but it hadn't emerged in studies in Greece previously. Findings related to feelings of depreciation and frustration also emerged towards policymakers and the neoliberal government which has just implemented its new educational bill [27] on teachers' evaluation which also assesses ICT integration. Participants feel that the government not only fails to appreciate their problematic working conditions but intentionally attempts to depict them as lazy state school teachers [35] and as a result they exhibit a negative attitude towards devoting personal time on designing technology-enhanced lessons.

In line with previous works in the Greek K-12 [1–4] lack of time emerged as one of the most dominant barriers in integrating technologies however in the current study it seemed to be even more valuable due to participants' intersections of gender and social class. Participants described current Greek state teachers as belonging to lower rather than middle class due to the cuts in their salaries during the crisis [26] and the extreme rise of living costs especially in the capital Athens and the touristic Greek islands. These financial difficulties force them to find additive employment elsewhere and combined with their motherhood and household obligations render out-of-school engagement related to technology integration prohibitive. In fact, most of the teachers in the current study seemed confident and familiar with the principles of pedagogical design and methods of evaluating and using educational technologies appropriate for kindergarten settings, yet their accounts clearly described draining daily routines which simply are incompatible with time-consuming procedures such as creating appropriate materials or assessing and adapting of existing materials to the needs of their students.

Barriers related to lack of time also emerged in relation to the endless low-quality, low-relevance ICT training participants have received during the past three years. This finding agrees with previous works within the ECE context both in the pre and post-covid era [21, 22, 36] which suggest that kindergarten teachers' main concerns related to training is that these courses often take place after school hours which can affect their family life and usually do not correspond to their professional needs.

Findings associated to time concerns may also be related to the wider Greek socio-cultural context and the professional identity of Greek kindergarten teachers. Results from studies on pre-service kindergarten teachers' identities in Greece has shown that one of the main reasons they opted to become teachers is the wider perception in Greek society that the specific profession is "suitable" for women who at some point will become mothers due to child-friendly working hours, lack of anxiety and stress [7]. The latest changes however in the post-crisis Greek society and the Greek ECE landscape seem to have canceled these expectations.

Second-order barrier findings revealed how the complex and multifaceted intersections of participants' gender and teacher identities in the post-covid era function as barriers in using screen media technologies with young children. Covid-19 seems to have nurtured even more preexisting feelings of guilt among kindergarten teachers many of whom are also mothers for the consequences of extended screen time on this generation of preschoolers. The global contradiction between educational policies pushing for technology integration in ECE and public health agencies fiercely advocating for minimizing screen time due to its negative effects on young children's cognitive, emotional, social and physical health [37, 38] is at the heart of this internal conflict and even though it is by no means new, current work findings suggest it has been magnified in the post-covid era. Similarly to previous works in other kindergarten contexts [22, 39], some of the participants in the current study clearly felt an urge to "protect" their students' health because despite their educational technology formal qualifications they still conceptualize traditional play-based pedagogies as healthy whereas they see screen-time as harmful. Moreover, participants' view of their students as "digital natives" who sometimes are even better than the teachers' themselves is in agreement with previous findings within the ECE field [21] and the wider misconception of policymakers, researchers, teachers and parents that contemporary preschoolers are all confident and skillful users of technology [40].

4.1 Implications

Findings suggest Greek policymakers should legislate the provision of teaching assistants or support teachers in mainstream kindergartens in order for educators to be able to cope with the demands of the specific context and the highly-demanding age-group of preschoolers. Providing extra support will contribute in technology integration and it will also contribute in improving the quality of ECE offered. Greek legislators should also form conditions whereby kindergarten teachers work and receive training within school hours without taking it home. In addition, the Greek Ministry of Education should implement bottom-up reforms that will reduce weekly teaching hours at the national level and design a more structured technology-enhanced curriculum which will lessen kindergarten teachers' burdens and leave them more time to be with their families since women still constitute the main providers of primary childcare and household work in Greek society [41, 42].

Reducing weekly teaching hours for teachers and legislating breaks equivalent to other state teachers is not only a matter of safety for preschoolers, it is also is a way to lessen kindergarten teachers' feelings of devaluation. Headteachers weekly teaching hours should also be reduced to the level of primary and secondary education administrators and principals in order for them to be able to develop technology leadership and actively support technology integration. Regarding ICT training, teachers in the ECE context need continuing professional development which can be in the form of formal courses or informal learning from colleagues or mentors but these courses have to be adjusted to their specific needs and include educational technology models and approaches that can be translated into practical classroom strategies linked to preschoolers' development [43]. Training courses targeted to parents at the national level are also required in order to raise their awareness on the differences between educational uses of touchscreen media as opposed to their use as an alternative babysitting mode. Kindergarten teachers themselves are also parents and current work findings clearly indicate that the pandemic influenced their attitudes and beliefs on screen time effects on young children's well-being. Kindergarten teaching as a profession both in Greece and globally should attempt to overcome the wide post-covid supposition of screen-media technologies as being "harmful" yet this demands top-down and bottom-up educational policies that will take under consideration the needs of teachers, parents and preschoolers holistically.

4.2 Limitations

Small sample size, purposive sampling and lack of triangulation limit the generalizability of findings to a larger population of kindergarten teachers in Greece. Future works in the post-pandemic ECE landscape should explore types and frequency of barriers in relation to socioeconomic status of schools, parents, students and teachers at the national level. The Covid-19 pandemic acted as a catalyst for barriers related to equipment and connectivity yet other barriers related to kindergarten teachers' working conditions, family/work balance and negative personal beliefs and attitudes got deeper. Future studies must investigate the underlying reasons Greece's investment on educational technologies during the pandemic does not translate into innovation in kindergarten classrooms in the post-covid era.

References

1. Nikolopoulou, K., Gialamas, V.: Barriers to the integration of computers in early childhood settings: teachers' perceptions. Educ. Inf. Technol. **20**, 285–301 (2015). https://doi.org/10.1007/s10639-013-9281-9
2. Nikolopoulou, K.: Mobile devices in early childhood education: teachers' views on benefits and barriers. Educ. Inf. Technol. **26**(3), 3279–3292 (2021). https://doi.org/10.1007/s10639-020-10400-3
3. Nikolopoulou, K.: Secondary education teachers' perceptions of mobile phone and tablet use in classrooms: benefits, constraints and concerns. J. Comput. Educ. **7**(2), 257–275 (2020). https://doi.org/10.1007/s40692-020-00156-7
4. Nikolopoulou, K., Gialamas, V., Lavidas, K.: Mobile learning-technology barriers in school education: teachers' views. Technol. Pedagog. Educ. **32**(1), 9–44 (2023)
5. Crenshaw, K.: Demarginalizing the intersection of race and sex; a black feminist critique of discrimination doctrine, feminist theory and antiracist politics. Univ. Chicago Legal Forum (1), 139–167 (1989)
6. Collins, P.H.: Intersectionality's definitional dilemmas. Ann. Rev. Sociol. **41**, 1–20 (2015)
7. Androusou, A., Tsafos, V.: Aspects of the professional identity of preschool teachers in Greece: investigating the role of teacher education and professional experience. Teach. Dev. **22**(4), 554–570 (2018)
8. Nicholson, J., Maniates, H.: Recognizing postmodern intersectional identities in leadership for early childhood. Early Years **36**(1), 66–80 (2016)
9. Gomez, R.E., Kagan, S.L., Fox, E.A.: Professional development of the early childhood education teaching workforce in the United States: an overview. Prof. Dev. Educ. **41**(2), 169–186 (2015)
10. Warin, J., Wilkinson, J., Greaves, H.M.: How many men work in the English early years sector? Why is the low figure so 'stubbornly resistant to change? Child. Soc. **35**(6), 870–884 (2021)
11. Yang, Y., McNair, D.: Male teachers in Shanghai public kindergartens: a phenomenological study. Gend. Educ. **31**(2), 274–291 (2019)
12. Xu, Y., Schweisfurth, M., Read, B.: Men's participation in early childhood education and care (ECEC): comparative perspectives from Edinburgh, Scotland and Tianjin, China. Comp. Educ. **58**(3), 345–363 (2022)
13. Abawi, Z., Eizadirad, A.: Bias-free or biased hiring? Racialized teachers' perspectives on educational hiring practices in Ontario. Can. J. Educ. Adm. Policy **193**, 18–31 (2020)

14. Whitebook, M., Phillips, D., Howes, C.: Worthy work, STILL unlivable wages: the early childhood workforce 25 years after the National Child Care Staffing Study (2020)
15. Rentzou, K.: Prevalence of burnout syndrome of Greek child care workers and kindergarten teachers. Education **43**(3), 249–262 (2015)
16. Ertmer, P.A.: Addressing first-and second-order barriers to change: strategies for technology integration. Educ. Tech. Res. Dev. **47**(4), 47–61 (1999). https://doi.org/10.1007/BF02299597
17. Ertmer, P.A., Ottenbreit-Leftwich, A.T., Sadik, O., Sendurur, E., Sendurur, P.: Teacher beliefs and technology integration practices: a critical relationship. Comput. Educ. **59**(2), 423–435 (2012)
18. Hsu, P.S.: Examining current beliefs, practices and barriers about technology integration: a case study. TechTrends **60**, 30–40 (2016). https://doi.org/10.1007/s11528-015-0014-3
19. Liu, X., Pange, J.: Early childhood teachers' perceived barriers to ICT integration in teaching: a survey study in Mainland China. J. Comput. Educ. **2**, 61–75 (2015). https://doi.org/10.1007/s40692-014-0025-7
20. Tondeur, J., Van Braak, J., Ertmer, P.A., Ottenbreit-Leftwich, A.: Understanding the relationship between teachers' pedagogical beliefs and technology use in education: a systematic review of qualitative evidence. Educ. Tech. Res. Dev. **65**, 555–575 (2017). https://doi.org/10.1007/s11423-016-9481-2
21. Dong, C.: 'Young children nowadays are very smart in ICT'–preschool teachers' perceptions of ICT use. Int. J. Early Years Educ. 1–14 (2018)
22. Dong, C., Mertala, P.: It is a tool, but not a 'must': early childhood preservice teachers' perceptions of ICT and its affordances. Early Years **41**(5), 540–555 (2021)
23. Goh, D., Kale, U.: The urban–rural gap: project-based learning with Web 2.0 among West Virginian teachers. Technol. Pedagogy Educ. **25**(3), 355–376 (2016)
24. Kormos, E.: The unseen digital divide: urban, suburban, and rural teacher use and perceptions of web-based classroom technologies. Comput. Sch. **35**(1), 19–31 (2018)
25. Kormos, E.: Technology as a facilitator in the learning process in urban high-needs schools: challenges and opportunities. Educ. Urban Soc. **54**(2), 146–163 (2022)
26. Traianou, A.: The intricacies of conditionality: education policy review in Greece 2015–2018. J. Educ. Policy **38**(2), 342–362 (2023)
27. Traianou, A.: Evaluation and its politics: trade unions and education reform in Greece. Educ. Inquiry 1–20 (2023)
28. Anastasiou, S., Belios, E.: Effect of age on job satisfaction and emotional exhaustion of primary school teachers in Greece. Eur. J. Invest. Health Psychol. Educ. **10**(2), 644–655 (2020)
29. Papazoglou, A., Koutouzis, M.: Educational leadership roles for the development of learning organizations: seeking scope in the Greek context. Int. J. Leadersh. Educ. **25**(4), 634–646 (2022)
30. IEP, Curriculum of Preschool Education - Kindergarten. Ministry of Education, Greece (2021)
31. Creswell, J.W.: Educational Research: Planning, Conducting, and Evaluating Quantitative and Qualitative Research. Pearson Education, Inc. (2012)
32. Schmitz, M.L., Antonietti, C., Cattaneo, A., Gonon, P., Petko, D.: When barriers are not an issue: tracing the relationship between hindering factors and technology use in secondary schools across Europe. Comput. Educ. **179**, 104411 (2022)
33. Koutsoklenis, A., Papadimitriou, V.: Special education provision in Greek mainstream classrooms: teachers' characteristics and recruitment procedures in parallel support. Int. J. Inclusive Educ. 1–16 (2021)
34. Schriever, V.: Early childhood teachers' perceptions and management of parental concerns about their child's digital technology use in kindergarten. J. Early Child. Res. **19**(4), 487–499 (2021)

35. Glaveli, N., Manolitzas, P., Tsourou, E., Grigoroudis, E.: Unlocking teacher job satisfaction during the COVID-19 pandemic: a multi-criteria satisfaction analysis. J. Knowl. Econ. 1–22 (2023). https://doi.org/10.1007/s13132-023-01124-z
36. Blau, I., Shamir-Inbal, T., Avdiel, O.: How does the pedagogical design of a technology-enhanced collaborative academic course promote digital literacies, self-regulation, and perceived learning of students? Internet High. Educ. **45**, 1–12 (2020)
37. Straker, L., Zabatiero, J., Danby, S., Thorpe, K., Edwards, S.: Conflicting guidelines on young children's screen time and use of digital technology create policy and practice dilemmas. J. Pediatr. **202**, 300–303 (2018)
38. Liu, J., Riesch, S., Tien, J., Lipman, T., Pinto-Martin, J., O'Sullivan, A.: Screen media overuse and associated physical, cognitive, and emotional/behavioral outcomes in children and adolescents: an integrative review. J. Pediatr. Health Care **36**(2), 99–109 (2022)
39. Schriever, V., Simon, S., Donnison, S.: Guardians of play: early childhood teachers' perceptions and actions to protect children's play from digital technologies. Int. J. Early Years Educ. **28**(4), 351–365 (2020)
40. Kirschner, P.A., De Bruyckere, P.: The myths of the digital native and the multitasker. Teach. Teach. Educ. **67**, 135–142 (2017)
41. Minguez, A.M., Crespi, I.: Gender equality and family changes in the work–family culture in Southern Europe. Int. Rev. Sociol. **27**(3), 394–420 (2017)
42. Daskalaki, M., Fotaki, M., Simosi, M.: The gendered impact of the financial crisis: struggles over social reproduction in Greece. Environ. Plann. A Econ. Space **53**(4), 741–762 (2022)
43. Markowitz, A.J., Seyarto, M.: Linking professional development to classroom quality: differences by ECE sector. Early Child Res. Q. **64**, 266–277 (2023)

Playing, Discovering, and Learning in Corfu Old Town

Sofia-Maria Poulimenou[1]([⊠]) [iD], Polyxeni Kaimara[2] [iD], and Ioannis Deliyannis[2] [iD]

[1] Department of Tourism, Ionian University, 4 Vraila Armeni Str, 49100 Corfu, Greece
poulimenouf@ionio.gr
[2] Departement of Audio and Visual Arts, Ionian University, Tsirigoti Sq. 7, 49100 Corfu, Greece

Abstract. Sustainable development of the world's cultural heritage heavily relies on the acquisition of knowledge about its values and ethics. United Nations' 4th Sustainable Development Goal refers to ensuring inclusive education and promoting equal opportunities for lifelong learning for all. Sustainable development through education requires the design, development, implementation and validation of sustainability competencies to contribute to the monitoring of initiatives in the field. Considering the above, the purpose of this chapter is to underline the significance of educational documentation in preserving and promoting cultural heritage using a gamification approach, based on established learning theories derived from the field of educational psychology, including but not limited to behaviorism, constructivism, social constructivism, activity theory, and discovery learning. More specifically the chapter introduces the design of a game named "Discover Corfu old town" (DisCot), which integrates certain United Nations' SDGs. The game refers to the exploration of the Old Town of Corfu, a multicultural World Heritage Cultural Monument and encourages the protection of shared heritage, fostering intercultural dialogue between the players. The gameplay and the ideas behind the design are being presented, emphasising on the diversity understanding, mutual comprehension of the different aspects of the monument's history as well as inclusiveness, all of which can enhance the societal needs for peace and prosperity, which are the basic goals of United Nation's Agenda 2030.

Keywords: Cultural heritage management · Educational Theories · Educational Psychology · Gamification · Sustainability

1 Human Participation - Cultural Heritage - Inclusive Societies

Human participation in the modern knowledge society presupposes the recognition of the value of the past and the consideration of cultural heritage as a fundamental foundation of our identity [1]. The utilization of technologies and multimedia content in the dissemination, communication, promotion and learning of cultural heritage has begun for years to acquire the necessary momentum, at least at a research level. The use of modern and combined media improves the way humans experience and perceive culture [2] and transforms the way history is perceived through research data exchange [3]. The digitisation of cultural elements causes both pleasure for the public and usability for

Ł. Tomczyk (Ed.): NMP 2022, CCIS 1916, pp. 168–185, 2023.
https://doi.org/10.1007/978-3-031-44581-1_13

heritage experts [4]. Visitors of a cultural heritage site create expectations for the enjoyment and knowledge they will acquire during an on-site visit [5]. In addition, the use of new technologies allows the presentation of cultural heritage focusing on the users themselves and their personal needs [6]. Cultural learning is enhanced through methods of interaction with collaborative features, which can be a practical approach to digital cultural heritage applications and enhance the social dimension in the experience created [7]. Nowadays, the learning process is being intertwined with the use of new technological tools, which are widely used in the tourism and cultural industry and which have been used by all learners, students and non-students. The visitor of a destination also acts as an apprentice [8, 9] as the knowledge acquired expands with the use of technology, creating greater connectivity and personal relationship with the destination visited.

In the same direction, museums are immensely related to education and heritage preservation. They serve as custodians of cultural heritage, preserving art and historical records that reflect local identities and societal development. In addition, they offer unique experiences that go beyond the traditional classroom. New technological tools that used to promote artifacts, interactively engage visitors and promote experiential learning and critical thinking. In the framework of museum education, the organization of educational programs foster deep communication and understanding of different cultures, traditions, and values between the visitors. Museum education makes cultural heritage accessible to audiences and activates individuals to participate in a self-interpreting procedure of heritage, ensuring cultural continuity and inclusion.

Inclusion is not just about disability, nor is it just about education. Inclusion is about social justice and equal opportunities. At the same time, education is not the end in itself but the means of contributing to the realization of an inclusive society with human rights to be the compass of policy making. Inclusive education is the broadest concept that encompasses all efforts to reduce exclusion from school programs, culture and community. Therefore, the issue is about equality, free access, social justice and the struggle for a society without discrimination. These principles must be at the heart of all policies and practices for sustainable development as underlined by United Nation's Agenda 2030.

1.1 Quality Education and Sustainable Cities and Communities

The United Nations Sustainable Development Goals (SDGs) cover a comprehensive set of 17 goals designed to pave the way towards a sustainable future for all individuals and the planet [10]. Among these goals, the 4th and 11th SDGs specifically target inclusive societies and inclusive education as crucial pillars for achieving sustainable development worldwide. Inclusive societies are characterized by a deep appreciation for diversity and the promotion of equal opportunities for individuals, irrespective of their background, identity, or circumstances. Inclusive education stands as a vital component of fostering inclusive societies. It embraces an educational approach that acknowledges and addresses the diverse needs of all learners [11]. The 4th SDG "Quality Education" strives to ensure inclusive and equitable quality education while promoting lifelong learning opportunities for everyone. To accomplish this goal, efforts have been initiated for an inclusive education system that uproots any kind of disparities in education and guarantees equal access to all levels of education and vocational training for vulnerable populations, such as persons with disabilities, indigenous peoples, and children facing challenging circumstances. Additionally, it necessitates the construction and enhancement of educational facilities that are sensitive to the needs of children, disabilities, and gender, providing safe, non-violent, inclusive, and effective learning environments for all. Inclusive education bears numerous benefits for individuals and society as a whole. It fosters individuals' socio-emotional growth, self-esteem, and peer acceptance, diminishes discrimination, and helps fight stigma, stereotyping, discrimination, and alienation in schools and societies, cultivating social cohesion and a sense of belonging [12].

The 11th SDG "Sustainable Cities and Communities" aims to cultivate cities and human settlements that are inclusive, safe, resilient, and sustainable. Achieving this objective entails ensuring access to secure and affordable housing, basic services, and public spaces for all individuals. Moreover, it calls for the promotion of social inclusion and the reduction of inequalities, particularly among marginalized and vulnerable groups. Inclusive societies and inclusive education are indispensable components for the realization of the 4th and 11th UN Sustainable Development Goals. Attaining these goals necessitates the establishment of an inclusive education system that eradicates gender disparities, guarantees equal access to education and vocational training, and provides safe, non-violent, inclusive, and effective learning environments. Simultaneously, it requires the creation of inclusive, safe, resilient, and sustainable cities and human settlements by ensuring access to secure and affordable housing, basic services, and public spaces, and by actively promoting social inclusion while reducing inequalities. By collectively pursuing these aspirations, we can make significant strides towards building a sustainable future where no one is left behind.

The importance of learning in the sustainable management of cultural heritage is also evident through UNESCO's Thematic Indicators on Culture, which were designed in 2019 as an Annex to the 2030 Agenda for Sustainable Development. These indicators are divided into 4 categories: a) environment and resilience, b) well-being and livelihood, c) knowledge and skills, and d) inclusion and participation. The third category clearly refers to the contribution of culture to the enhancement of learning and the creation of knowledge and competencies, focusing, among others, on the transmission of local cultural values, the promotion of empowerment through the educational process that can foster cultural diversity and a deeper comprehension of sustainability. The social implications and the active involvement of local communities in cultural management are often overlooked by decision-makers and are not always included in their strategic objectives. In this direction, UNESCO has established another initiative, the Global Network of Learning Cities, which is oriented to the exchange of expertise and good practices between the participating cities.

1.2 Cultural Management: Museum Education and Digital Games

Museum education refers to the applied pedagogy that constitutes the methodological framework for the pedagogical use of the museum. That is, it simultaneously constitutes a research field of cultural management and an innovative educational practice without setting restrictions on the target groups. Thus, museums have the potential to become key public pedagogies for sustainable development [13].

Museum-pedagogical activities play a catalytic role in the learning process:

- learning becomes an "active" process based on the active participation of visitors
- active learning takes place through the transformation of ideas-information and the creation of meaning
- transformation of ideas-information is based on learning theories

The museum education practice aims to obtain an attractive and memorable experience for the visitors, emphasising both the individual and social dimensions of this experience in an inclusive learning environment. Visitor participation is widespread in museum pedagogy, making it a best practice for transmedia learning [14, 15].

Current literature shows that digital educational games have a significant role to play in museum education [16]. Digital educational games offer an engaging and dynamic learning environment, as they promote information understanding by actively involving learners in problem-solving and decision-making. Cultural digitisation may bring exhibitions to life and make historical, cultural, or scientific topics more approachable and engaging in museum education. Visuals, sound and motion sensors are common features in digital games. This multisensory technique simplifies complicated subjects and may be tailored to different learning styles making applications inclusive. This function may be used by museums to provide an engaging inclusive learning environment for visitors and adapt to a player's preferences and needs.

2 Gamified Transmedia Educational Applications for Cultural Heritage: A Dynamic Interplay of Pedagogy and Technology

An educational application or platform for cultural assets that utilize cutting-edge technology affordances such as Augmented Reality (AR), combined with traditional materials including maps, flashcards, and compass, as well as techniques of gamification and transmedia storytelling, can offer users a comprehensive learning experience that fosters active involvement with cultural heritage. This approach can engage users in meaningful discovery to gain a profound understanding of cultural heritage by adhering to sound pedagogical principles. These principles are derived from well-documented learning theories, such as behaviorism, constructivism, and social constructivism which are related to other theories including, activity theory, and discovery learning. These related theories are branches of constructivism and contribute to the overall effectiveness of the approach [17, 18]. This section demonstrates how the learning process can effectively promote and protect cultural heritage by integrating diverse theories into the design of educational applications, utilizing gamification and transmedia storytelling techniques.

2.1 Principles Based on Behaviorism

Behaviorism principles are incorporated into gamified transmedia applications, especially AR applications, to encourage users to explore cultural heritage sites and artefacts by providing positive reinforcement for their engagement in an incidental and effortless learning process [19]. AR can monitor user progress and motivate them to continue exploring by supplying structured and clear feedback. AR applications enhance users' understanding by presenting visual and audio cues that highlight important aspects of the heritage site or artefact. Additionally, research has shown that game-based learning environments that incorporate elements of behaviorism can be effective in promoting learning outcomes. For example, a study by Plass et al. [20] found that a game-based learning environment that used a reinforcement-based approach improved students' performance on a post-test compared to a traditional lecture-based approach. The combination of positive and negative consequences is more effective than a traditional classroom-based approach. Although behaviorism principles can be used as a theoretical framework for developing AR educational gamified applications, other theoretical foundations can also be applied to create engaging and interactive experiences that promote cultural heritage, such as constructivism and social constructivism.

2.2 Principles Based on Constructivism and Social Constructivism

AR experiences that integrate constructivist and social constructivist principles can provide captivating and immersive learning opportunities that inspire users to investigate cultural heritage. Constructivist principles emphasise the importance of active, experiential learning in which learners construct knowledge and meaning from their interactions with the environment [21]. AR applications have been shown to enhance learning outcomes and engagement by encouraging users to interact with cultural assets dynamically and engagingly, promoting deeper levels of learning and understanding [22]. Furthermore, games and other interactive media can be effective tools for promoting constructivist learning, as they provide chances for users to experiment, make decisions, and receive feedback in a low-risk environment. AR games merge game structures with AR technology's immersive potential, allowing users to connect with cultural artefacts or monuments. This dynamic relationship is influenced by the interplay between constructivism and behaviorism. Vygotsky [21] also emphasises the importance of social interaction and collaboration in the learning process, arguing that learning is a social activity that occurs through dialogue and interaction with others. AR experiences can incorporate social features, such as multiplayer games or shared storytelling. By integrating elements of both constructivism and social constructivism, AR designers can create immersive and interactive experiences that encourage users to explore cultural heritage in a meaningful and engaging way.

2.3 Principles Based on Activity Theory

"Tools are created by societies over the course of human history and change with the form of society and the level of its cultural development" [21]. The principles of activity theory emphasise the importance of understanding the context of an activity, including the social interactions, tools, resources, goals and motivations that drive the activity [23]. Thus, the impact and social relevance of activity theory are based on our ability to understand how objects and activities change over time. In the context of cultural heritage, activity theory emphasises the importance of understanding the social interactions, tools, and resources that are used and re-used in the preservation and interpretation of cultural artefacts. Research has demonstrated that the use of mobile technology and AR in cultural heritage can lead to positive experiences for visitors and confirmed a strong positive correlation between motivation and learning outcomes [24]. Studies on visitors to museums are found that the use of their smartphones to access information about exhibits, take photos, and share videos and their experiences on social media is very motivating [25]. To sum up, mobile technologies and AR have the potential to enhance the visitor experience and promote learning in cultural heritage contexts. By designing mobile applications that take into account how visitors engage with cultural artefacts through technology, museums can better meet visitors' needs and support human activities.

2.4 Principles Based on Discovery Learning

Bruner [14] who was increasingly influenced by Lev Vygotsky, stated that if individuals can approach learning as a task of "discovering something" rather than "learning about it" then they carry out their activity with the autonomy of self-reward. Discovery learning theory, as proposed by Bruner, prioritizes active student engagement in the learning process and emphasises the importance of experiencing success or failure as a means of obtaining information and the significance of context and social interaction. This approach contrasts with behaviorist principles, which rely on reward and punishment to motivate learning. By promoting student exploration and investigation of topics, providing opportunities for hands-on experimentation, and fostering critical thinking and problem-solving skills, discovery learning can facilitate deeper conceptual understanding and more effective retention of information. Additionally, this approach can promote student curiosity and enthusiasm for the subject matter by allowing learners to take an active role in their own education. The educational framework of AR relies predominantly on principles of discovery learning and behaviorism. AR applications stimulate users to explore hidden components of an image, QR code, or any other identifier, while the strictly linear sequence of AR connections links distinct elements or points. As a result, users are required to utilize prior knowledge and not simply engage in a process of trial and error. Discovery learning is the foundation of a pedagogical approach that enables users to engage with and experience cultural heritage through interactive activities.

2.5 Principles Based on Gamification

Less structured game applications that incorporate features such as rewards, points, prizes, and leaderboards are often referred to as gamification [26]. Gamification is rooted in applied behavioral psychology and relies heavily on motivation, feedback, progress, and reward, making it an integral part of any game, whether digital or not [27]. Gamification is a widely used technique with applications in many domains, including health services, education, and cultural heritage studies, as it is effective in promoting behavioral change and learning [28]. Inserting gamification techniques in educational materials is a complex process that requires collaboration among experts from various fields, including psychologists, educators, game designers, and programmers. Game elements, such as scenarios, rules, challenges, conflict, problem-solving, interactivity, social interaction, and win state, are incorporated into educational materials to enhance social interaction and improve student performance by motivating them to participate in learning activities that are typically perceived as tedious, demanding, or boring [20].

One of the main benefits of gamification is that it provides a virtual environment that encourages exploration, experimentation, and action-taking without the fear of negative consequences associated with making mistakes [29]. By creating a safe and supportive learning environment, gamification can help users overcome the fear of failure and increase their willingness to take risks and try new things. In the context of cultural heritage, AR applications overlay digital information and interactive elements onto real-world artefacts and cultural sites, such as museums and archaeological sites. Users can explore and learn about these sites in a fun and engaging way, by completing challenges, solving puzzles, and unlocking rewards. For example, users may be prompted to find hidden clues or answer trivia questions about the artefacts they encounter. By gamifying learning experiences, AR applications motivate users to engage with the cultural heritage material in a way that is both entertaining and educational.

2.6 Principles Based on Transmedia Storytelling and Transmedia Learning

Transmedia storytelling is a narrative technique that uses multiple platforms and media formats to tell a story [30]. This approach creates a more immersive experience for the audience by offering different perspectives, insights, and experiences through each medium [31]. By expanding across different media, such as books, films, pictures, flashcards, video games, and social media, transmedia storytelling can also create a more comprehensive, inclusive and nuanced understanding of the story and its characters. In summary, transmedia storytelling is a powerful tool for creating dynamic and captivating narratives that can inspire audiences across different platforms and media formats. Transmedia storytelling supports the implementation of innovative educational practices that prioritize student-centred learning and collaborative skills development. Warren et al. [32] contended that "a transmedia story is never-ending, and it is continuously reshaped with the help of peer constative feedback". Therefore, it can be considered a continuous learning process where linear learning is no longer applicable (Fig. 1).

Furthermore, knowledge is constructed through social interaction based on pre-existing knowledge. Transmedia, as a storytelling technique, served as the foundation for a novel pedagogical approach known as "transmedia learning". Transmedia learning combines traditional learning theories such as behaviorism, constructivism, and social constructivism with contemporary inclusive educational approaches and methods such as Differentiated Instruction and Universal Design of Learning. This approach uses all the available, platforms, media and tools, under the prism of multimedia learning and cutting-edge technology, such as AR, to provide a more engaging and interactive learning experience [33, 34].

3 Discovering Corfu Old Town Through a Gamified Transmedia Application

The Old Town of Corfu has been a recognized as historical monument by the Greek state since 1980 [35] and has been a UNESCO World Heritage Site (decision 31 COM 8b.40) since 2007 [36]. The Old Town of Corfu is the only Greek historic city of this size that is

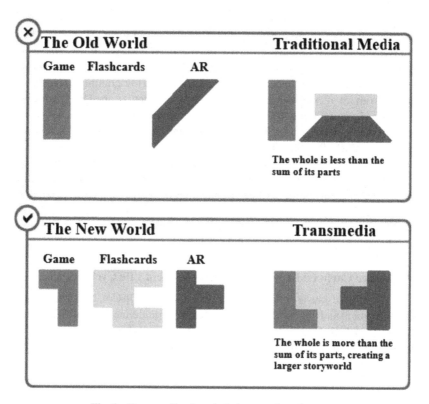

Fig. 1. Transmedia: the whole is more than the sum

mostly preserved unchanged from the Middle Ages until today, expressing with authenticity in the area, the particular historical conjuncture that shaped it. Special features of many different periods are combined in a cultural mosaic that includes fortresses, monuments, archaeological sites, historical sites, small squares, small and large parks, a road system of characteristic roads (kantounia), mansions with heterogeneous style (neoclassical, Venetian, modern, etc.), churches and other religious places, historical buildings, museums, residences, schools, shops and public and private services. The Old Town remains the main attraction of the island as a complex space and a unique cultural entity of high aesthetic values, while at the same time, it is a vibrant city that hosts the vast majority of cultural institutions and activities of the local cultural economy [37].

The Corfu old town acquires characteristics of an open-air museum, thanks to its vast expanse and multicultural character. Cultural elements, natural beauty, and the historicity of private and public spaces are harmoniously integrated with the contemporary activities of users, including permanent residents, professionals, and visitors. This creates the impression of a "living museum". As mentioned, sustainable development of the world's cultural heritage heavily relies on the acquisition of knowledge about its values and ethics. In this context and taking into account that Corfu old town is one of the most popular destinations for both formal and informal educational trips, attracting visitors from Greece and abroad as well, our team has developed a gamified museopedagogical application named "Discover Corfu old town" (DisCot). The gamified museopedagogical application "DisCot" has been designed in the framework of the project "Hologrammatic Corfu" which has been funded by the Operational Program "Ionian Islands 2014–2020" and the European Union. "Hologrammatic Corfu's" goal was to create an interactive touristic guide for the monument of the Old Town of Corfu, using transmedia storytelling techniques. One of the main deliverables of the project was to present touristic walking tours that were accessible to people with physical barriers in mobility. More than 80 points of interest were inspected and characterised according to their accessibility status. DisCot was not an initial deliverable of the project but during the implementation phase, the vast amount of information and multimedia produced by the project led to the inspiration of this application in order to a gamification approach in the process also be included. When the game was being designed, one of the aspects assessed for the choice of the points of interest involved was the accessibility status, so that no player is left behind due to mobility restrictions.

3.1 "Discover Corfu Old Town" Game Development Life Cycle

Creating a gamified museopedagogical application, like DisCot, follows the steps of game development and requires a specific process with guidelines, called Game Development Life Cycle (GDLC) that includes the following phases (Fig. 2): (1) *Concept/Design*, (2) *Alpha version*: (i) pre-production, (ii) production, (iii) testing, (3) *Beta version*, and (4) *Release* [38].

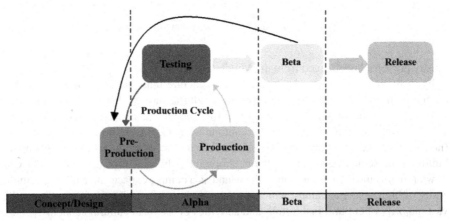

Fig. 2. Game Development Cycle (GDLC). (Source: Content Design for Inclusive Educational Environments [11])

3.2 Concept of the Museopedagogical Application DisCot

"Discover Corfu old town" (DisCot) integrates certain United Nations' SDGs. The game refers to the exploration of the Old Town of Corfu through twelve (12) selected landmarks, a multicultural World Heritage Cultural Monument and encourages the protection of shared heritage, fostering intercultural dialogue between the players. The gameplay and the ideas behind the design are being presented, emphasising on the diversity understanding, mutual comprehension of the different aspects of the monument's history as well as inclusiveness, all of which can enhance the societal needs for peace and prosperity, which are the basic goals of United Nation's Agenda 2030.

The multiculturalism of the Old Town of Corfu is due to the historical imprint of different peoples, such as Venetians, English, and French, but also religions, such as Orthodox and Catholic Christians, Anglicans and Jews, etc. The current physiognomy of the old town incorporates the creative coexistence and inclusion of many different cultures.

Two characteristic locations-monuments of the Old Town of Corfu out of the twelve included in the game are then described, which are symbols of the city. These imposing monuments signify the city's multicultural character, as well as their reuse for the current needs of a living city. The Palace of St. Michael and St. George accommodates the Museum of Asian Art, while in Liston, many cultural and religious events take place, such as the processions of Saint Spyridon, the Patron Saint of the island. One of the most famous events is "The Breaking of Botis" on Holy Saturday during Easter. The breaking of botis (botis is the ceramic pot in Corfiot dialect) symbolises the victory of life over death.

Palace of St. Michael and St. George. Palace of St. Michael and St. George is an impressive neoclassical building which was built in the 19th century (1819–1823) during British rule in the Ionian islands, under Sir Thomas Maitland (1759–1824), the first High Commissioner of the Ionian Islands (Fig. 3). The building was designed by British Army engineer and architect Sir George Whitmore (1775–1862) and is made of Maltese tufa. In 1864, following the Union of the Ionian Islands with Greece, it became the property of the Greek state and today houses the Museum of Asian Art. The palace comprises a central three-storey p-shaped building which connects to two side wings through an outer Doric peristyle. Two gates surround the building, the gate of St. Michael and the gate of St. George. The main entrance leads to the ground floor which includes a magnificent staircase leading to the first floor where the monumental halls of the Order of St. Michael and St. George are housed. The permanent exhibitions of the museum are showcased in these halls. The exhibition extends to the second floor of the building.

Liston. Liston, one of the most important sights of Corfu, is located in the western part of Spianada Square (Fig. 4 and 5). It is a residential complex and its construction began during the French Empire (1807–1814). It was built by the French diplomat Matthieu de Lesseps (1771–1832). The Corfiot engineer and military officer, Ioannis Parmesan (1748–1826) drew up the plans and partly undertook construction supervision. The external features of Liston are slightly inspired by the Rue de Rivoli de Paris and the Napoleonic architecture of the period. At the same time, care was taken to maintain its uniformity and to be consistent with the prominent buildings of the previous Venetian historic town, such as the Kompitsi mansion and the building of San Giacomo theatre which today houses the Town Hall.

The incorporation of these particular landmarks into the gamification approach is crucial for promoting intercultural understanding. These well-known locations, rich in historical and cultural significance, may assist people from different backgrounds to

Fig. 3. Palace of St. Michael and St. George

Fig. 4. Liston

Fig. 5. The Breaking of Botis

interact meaningfully and learn from one another. People can have a greater understanding of various cultures, traditions, and values by visiting these places, which promotes respect and regard for one another. The sharing of thoughts, experiences, and viewpoints on these websites aids in shattering stereotypes, bridging cultural divides, and fostering a sense of interconnectedness across cultures. In the end, the Old Town of Corfu might act as a compelling symbol that brings people together, encouraging harmony and intercultural understanding. As it emphasises the significance of inclusive and diverse educational approaches in attaining sustainable development, intercultural understanding is directly related to learning theories and the United Nations Sustainable Development Goals. Learning theories encourage including different experiences and cultural views in the learning process. They place a strong emphasis on how interaction, communication, and cooperation between people from various backgrounds may advance information sharing and promote cross-cultural understanding.

3.3 Designing the Museopedagogical Application "DisCot"

DisCot aims to enrich visitors' experience and facilitate learning about the historical and cultural significance of the Old Town of Corfu. In addition, DisCot has the potential to contribute to visitors' comprehension of the artworks and history presented in Corfu's museums. Regarding organized educational school trips, students explore the selected monuments of Corfu's Old Town alongside their educators. In this way, they can learn basic historical information effortlessly and through playful methods. At the same time, they cultivate a set of "transferable" skills, such as spatial orientation, compass use, reading a traditional map, and getting accustomed to AR applications. Similarly, individual visitors, whether they belong to a special category such as a family or a group of visitors with particular characteristics such as a group of students-tour guides from other areas, explore and delve deeper according to their interests. They can discover Corfu's Old Town through the lens of history and culture.

Scenario – Rules. Visitors explore twelve (12) selected landmarks of the Old Town of Corfu through the process of the "Treasure Hunt Game" and discover hidden information. The twelve (12) selected landmarks of the Old Town of Corfu through which the game of hidden treasure unfolds are (Fig. 6):

1. Old town's fortresses
2. Statue of Schulenburg
3. Palace of St. Michael and St. George
4. Liston
5. Saint Spyridon church
6. Well mouth in Kremasti Square (campo veneziano)
7. The Metropolitan Church of Our Lady Spilaiotissa, St Vlasios and St Theodora Augusta
8. Gate of the New Fortress
9. Jewish synagogue "Sinagoga Vecchia"
10. Annunziata Bell Tower
11. "Duomo" Cathedral of Saints James and Christopher
12. Town hall (Loggia Nobilei-The Nobles Arcade)

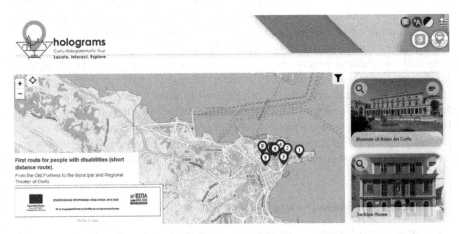

Fig. 6. Discovering the hidden information about Corfu old town

DisCot begins at the hotel where the guests are staying, to directly involve local professionals in the procedure. The teacher or the team leader picks up the game material from the reception, which is a chest including 60 folders (5 per location), a compass and

Fig. 7. DisCot material

a vintage map of Corfu (Fig. 7), and informs the group that they are going to play a game. Until then, the students or the team are not aware that they are going to participate in game activities. The first folder, which is also known as the folder of point 0, includes a QR code that, when scanned, provides players with the necessary information to find the Old Fortress. Old Fortress is point 1 which is the first of the twelve points of interest and the action begins. To connect the twelve points, players must answer questions that utilize their knowledge and the various tools provided, including AR overlays, flashcards, the compass, and the map. After reaching point 12, the game is complete. While the game is well-organized, both team leaders/educators and players may expand the activities by exploring other aspects of the points.

Challenges, Conflicts, and Problem-Solving of DisCot. The challenges, conflicts, and problem-solving refer to the issues that players attempt to address and resolve, such as the correct sequence of activities that will lead them to the right point.

Interactivity - Social Interaction of DisCot. Successful interaction is achieved through computer-mediated interaction (smartphone/tablet), narration, pedagogical agents (who confirm answers and reward students), and peers who act as pedagogical agents as well (peer mentoring).

Win-State of DisCot. DisCot is a game that can be played by a single team or by multiple teams, depending on the players' number. The game's competitive nature, with the winning team being the one that completes the game first, serves as a motivational factor for students to achieve success in addition to the completion of the museum education application.

3.4   Assessing the Museopedagogical Application "DisCot"

Any product, especially when it comes to an educational application, requires evaluation before release. The development of DisCot relies on the dynamic composition of the members of a transdisciplinary design team consisting of a historian, a tour guide, a cultural heritage manager, a psychologist, an educator, and IT/game developers. According to the Game Development Life Cycle, a series of internal evaluations will take place during the development of the prototyping, both for issues related to the gameplay experience and the sequence of points of interest, as well as for technological issues. The app will then be given to potential users, such as teachers and students with and without mobility and learning difficulties, to evaluate. Their evaluations will be taken seriously to improve the application to be distributed to the hotels and then to the participants of organised educational tours as well as individual visitors. Also, the application will be distributed to schools in Corfu, so that locals can also engage in a playful learning experience and get to know aspects of their city that they might not be aware of.

4   Conclusion

The unique capabilities that each component of the gamified transmedia educational application offers to create an engaging and interactive learning experience for users are referred to as the component's dynamic affordances. The above-described application takes advantage of different media and technologies to create a seamless and immersive learning experience that motivates users to interact with the information and actively participate in the learning process by employing a gamified and transmedia approach. Interactivity, feedback, personalisation, and social interaction are just a few examples of the dynamic affordances that each component can offer. These elements all help to make learning more effective and interesting. The integration of gamification into tourism experiences can be a powerful tool for incorporating learning theories and promoting the United Nations Sustainable Development Goals (SDGs) in the context of sustainability. Overall, this chapter illustrated how the learning process may be a useful tool when integrated with a gamified transmedia application and how gamification can improve travellers' engagement and knowledge acquisition by implementing learning theories like game-based learning or experiential learning.

Acknowledgements. The game DisCot has been designed in the framework of the project "Hologrammat-ic Corfu" which was funded by the Operational Program "Ionian Islands 2014–2020" and the European Union.

We would also like to thank the artist Nikolaos Mamalos for offering the use of Corfu photographs.

References

1. Ott, M., Pozzi, F.: Towards a new era for Cultural Heritage Education: discussing the role of ICT. Comput. Hum. Behav. **27**, 1365–1371 (2011). https://doi.org/10.1016/j.chb.2010.07.031
2. Guttentag, D.A.: Virtual reality: applications and implications for tourism. Tour. Manag. **31**, 637–651 (2010). https://doi.org/10.1016/j.tourman.2009.07.003
3. Hansson, K., Cerratto Pargman, T., Dahlgren, A.: Datafication and cultural heritage: provocations, threats and design opportunities. In: Proceedings of 18th European Conference on Computer-Supported Cooperative Work, Siegen, Germany, 13–17 June 2020. European Society for Socially Embedded Technologies (EUSSET) (2020)
4. Cucchiara, R., Grana, C., Borghesani, D., Agosti, M., Bagdanov, A.D.: Multimedia for cultural heritage: key issues. In: Grana, C., Cucchiara, R. (eds.) MM4CH 2011. CCIS, vol. 247, pp. 206–216. Springer, Heidelberg (2012). https://doi.org/10.1007/978-3-642-27978-2_18
5. Chandini Pendit, U., Zaibon, S.B., Abu Bakar, J.A.: Conceptual model of mobile augmented reality for cultural heritage site towards enjoyable informal learning aspect. J. Teknol. **77**(29), 123–129 (2015). https://doi.org/10.11113/jt.v77.6847
6. Levy, S., Gvili, Y.: Online shopper engagement in price negotiation: the roles of culture, involvement and eWOM. Int. J. Advert. **39**(2), 232–257 (2020). https://doi.org/10.1080/02650487.2019.1612621
7. Bekele, M.K., Champion, E.: A comparison of immersive realities and interaction methods: cultural learning in virtual heritage. Front. Robot. AI **6**, 91 (2019). https://doi.org/10.3389/frobt.2019.00091
8. Gössling, S.: Tourism, tourist learning and sustainability: an exploratory discussion of complexities, problems and opportunities. J. Sustain. Tour. **26**, 292–306 (2018). https://doi.org/10.1080/09669582.2017.1349772
9. Moorhouse, N., tom Dieck, M.C., Jung, T.: Augmented reality to enhance the learning experience in cultural heritage tourism: an experiential learning cycle perspective. e-Review Tour. Res. **8**, 1–5 (2017)

10. United Nations: Transforming Our World: The 2030 Agenda for Sustainable Development. A/RES/70/1 (2015)

11. Kaimara, P., Deliyannis, I., Oikonomou, A.: Content design for inclusive educational environments. In: Daniela, L. (ed.) Inclusive Digital Education, pp. 97–121. Springer, Cham (2022). https://doi.org/10.1007/978-3-031-14775-3_6

12. UNESCO: Global education monitoring report 2020: inclusion and education: all means all. United Nations Educational, Scientific and Cultural Organization (2020)

13. Hansson, P., Öhman, J.: Museum education and sustainable development: a public pedagogy. Eur. Educ. Res. J. **21**, 469–483 (2022). https://doi.org/10.1177/14749041211056443

14. Bruner, J.S.: The act of discovery. Harv. Educ. Rev. **31**, 21–32 (1961)

15. Schunk, D.H.: Learning Theories: An Educational Perspective. Pearson Education, Boston (2016)

16. Beavis, C., O'Mara, J., Thompson, R.: Digital games in the museum: perspectives and priorities in videogame design. Learn. Media Technol. **46**, 294–305 (2021). https://doi.org/10.1080/17439884.2021.1896539

17. Kaimara, P., Poulimenou, S.M., Deliyannis, I.: Digital learning materials: could transmedia content make the difference in the digital world? In: Daniela, L. (ed.) Epistemological Approaches to Digital Learning in Educational Contexts, pp. 69–87. Routledge (2020)

18. Poulimenou, S.M., Kaimara, P., Deliyannis, I.: World heritage monuments management planning in the light of UN sustainable development goals: the case of the Old Town of Corfu. Acad. Res. Community Publ. **7**, 73–81 (2022). https://doi.org/10.21625/archive.v6i1.881

19. Poulimenou, S.M., Kaimara, P., Papadopoulou, A., Miliotis, G., Deliyannis, I.: Tourism policies for communicating world heritage values: the case of the Old Town of Corfu in Greece. In: IAFeS (ed.) 16th Netties Conference: Access to Knowledge in the 21st Century the Interplay of Society, Education, ICT and Philosophy Old Town of Corfu in Greece, pp. 187–192 (2018)

20. Plass, J.L., Homer, B.D., Kinzer, C.K.: Foundations of game-based learning. Educ. Psychol. **50**, 258–283 (2015). https://doi.org/10.1080/00461520.2015.1122533

21. Vygotsky, L.S.: Mind in Society: The Development of Higher Psychological Processes. Harvard University Press, Cambridge (1978)

22. Garzón, J., Pavón, J., Baldiris, S.: Systematic review and meta-analysis of augmented reality in educational settings. Virtual Real. **23**, 447–459 (2019). https://doi.org/10.1007/s10055-019-00379-9

23. Engeström, Y.: The future of activity theory: a rough draft. In: Sannino, A., Daniels, H., Gutierrez, K.D. (eds.) Learning and Expanding with Activity Theory, pp. 303–328. Cambridge University Press, Cambridge (2009)

24. Xu, N., Li, Y., Wei, X., Xie, L., Yu, L., Liang, H.-N.: CubeMuseum AR: a tangible augmented reality interface for cultural heritage learning and museum gifting. Int. J. Hum.-Comput. Interact. 1–29 (2023). https://doi.org/10.1080/10447318.2023.2171350

25. Wang, D., Park, S., Fesenmaier, D.R.: The role of smartphones in mediating the touristic experience. J. Travel Res. **51**, 371–387 (2012). https://doi.org/10.1177/0047287511426341

26. Deterding, S., Dixon, D., Khaled, R., Nacke, L.: From game design elements to gamefulness. In: Proceedings of the 15th International Academic MindTrek Conference: Envisioning Future Media Environments, pp. 9–15. ACM Press (2011)

27. Walther, B.K., Larsen, L.J.: Gamification and beyond: the case of ludification. In: Marfisi-Schottman, I., Bellotti, F., Hamon, L., Klemke, R. (eds.) Games and Learning Alliance: 9th International Conference, GALA 2020, Laval, France, December 9–10, 2020, Proceedings, pp. 125–134. Springer, Cham (2020). https://doi.org/10.1007/978-3-030-63464-3_12

28. Deliyannis, I., Kaimara, P., Poulimenou, S.M., Lampoura, S.: Introductory chapter: games, gamification, and ludification, can they be combined? In: Deliyannis, I. (ed.) Gamification. IntechOpen, Rijeka (2023)

29. Fabricatore, C.: Learning and videogames: an unexploited synergy. In: 2000 Annual Convention of the Association for Educational Communications and Technology (AECT). Workshop: In Search of the Meaning of Learning (2000)
30. Jenkins, H.: Transmedia storytelling and entertainment: an annotated syllabus. Continuum **24**, 943–958 (2010). https://doi.org/10.1080/10304312.2010.510599
31. Scolari, C.A.: Transmedia storytelling: implicit consumers, narrative worlds, and branding in contemporary media production. Int. J. Commun. **3**, 586–606 (2009)
32. Warren, S.J., Wakefield, J.S., Mills, L.A.: Learning and teaching as communicative actions: transmedia storytelling. In: Wankel, L., Blessinger, P. (eds.) Increasing Student Engagement and Retention Using Multimedia Technologies Video Annotation, Multimedia Applications, Videoconferencing and Transmedia Storytelling, pp. 67–94. Emerald Group Publishing Limited, Bradford (2013)
33. Fleming, L.: Expanding learning opportunities with transmedia practices: inanimate alice as an exemplar. J. Media Lit. Educ. **5**, 370–377 (2013)
34. Kaimara, P., Deliyannis, I., Oikonomou, A., Miliotis, G.: Transmedia storytelling meets Special Educational Needs students: a case of Daily Living Skills Training. In: Kotopoulos, T.H., Vakali, A.P. (eds.) 4th International Conference on Creative Writing Conference, Florina, Greece, 12–15 September 2019, pp. 542–561 (2021)
35. Hellenic Government Gazette: Presidential Decree Dated 22.4/5.5.1980, Issue 274D
36. UNESCO-WHC: Old Town of Corfu: A UNESCO World Heritage Site. Nomination file 978. UNESCO World Heritage Committee (2007)
37. Mariani, M.M., Buhalis, D., Longhi, C., Vitouladiti, O.: Managing change in tourism destinations: key issues and current trends. J. Destin. Mark. Manag. **2**, 269–272 (2014). https://doi.org/10.1016/j.jdmm.2013.11.003
38. Ramadan, R., Widyani, Y.: Game development life cycle guidelines. In: 2013 International Conference on Advanced Computer Science and Information Systems, ICACSIS 2013 (2013)

Interactive Museums - New Spaces
for the Education of Children and Adolescents

Joanna Sikorska(✉) ⓘ

Adam Mickiewicz University, Wieniawskiego 1, 61712 Poznań, Poland
joannas07@amu.edu.pl

Abstract. The discussion of the importance of museums, their status, their functions, and the transformations taking place in these areas has been going on for a long time. The changes taking place in postmodernity mean that museums will not escape new challenges and will be transformed more and more, becoming not only a place for the reception of art or other artifacts but also spaces for lifelong learning, enabling the development of individual passions and fascinations of visitors, places of meeting with other people and dialogue.

The purpose of this article is to highlight the role that interactive museums can play in the process of educating children and adolescents to function in the digital society of the 21st century. Referring to the new culture of learning based on the idea of STEAM and the assumptions of constructivism and connectivism, the article attempts to analyze the category that interactive museums represent, suggesting, based on the example of Tokyo's TeamLab and Poland's Funzeum, selected motives that can make an interactive museum a space for experiencing and learning. The art-based research used structuralist narratology, focusing on qualitative analysis of the content and forms of interactive communication of interactive exhibitions in selected museums.

The results of the analysis show that interactivity has revolutionized the museum space, arousing curiosity in the visitor and creating new opportunities for multisensory learning, individual experiences, interpretation, and deciphering the meaning of artifacts.

Keywords: interactive museums · educational spaces · learning by doing · digital art-based research

1 Introduction

Over the past few decades, the image of museums as passive forms of a collection made available to the public has continuously been transforming, and the substitute for the museum understood in this way is a creative institution that stimulates the development of culture and science, combines education and entertainment, conducts research activities, and is at the same time a perfectly organized organization, increasingly closer to the Turquoise model [1]. The transformations taking place in museums are related to the acceptance of the fact that visitors, among whom a significant group are children and young people, themselves functioning in the constantly evolving, expansive world of

Ł. Tomczyk (Ed.): NMP 2022, CCIS 1916, pp. 186–199, 2023.
https://doi.org/10.1007/978-3-031-44581-1_14

digital technologies, expect that museums, which for years have turned from places of passive contemplation of art into spaces of learning, will inspire this process according to their needs. The observation of educational experiences and practices in museums and the transformations in this area thus prompts an analysis of contemporary modern interactive museum spaces. The starting point here is the following search for answers to the questions: Does learning in interactive museum spaces make it possible to acquire and develop the competencies needed by modern man? How can education in a museum enrich the learning process and translate it into other areas of life? Can it help respond to dynamic changes, and thus meet the challenge of the 21st century? The questions posed in this way are significantly related to the question underlying the signaled problems: What theories and assumptions about learning should be the starting point for creating museum spaces conducive to optimizing learning in an era in which globalization and the rapid evolution of digital technologies such as the Internet of Things (IoT), artificial intelligence (AI), and robotics are bringing significant changes to society [2]?

Making certain assumptions about the process of learning in postmodernity, this is important because, according to the latest learning theories, the educational process cannot be limited to educational institutions alone; for learning in both the instrumental and directional spheres of personality, it is vital to go beyond the walls of the school, however, as J. Rekus and T. Mikhail write it is no longer enough to demand "Open the school, let life enter because life enters it with the changed, "new" children, but rather: Open the school, enter life(…)" [3]. Education in the spaces of interactive museums is becoming such an entry into a life increasingly dominated by new technologies, examples of which include the exhibitions created by TeamLab Tokyo or Funzeum in Gliwice - chosen because they differ significantly from traditional museums and those in which, on par with the presentation of the collection, it is crucial to organize activities that facilitate the audience's contact with the object. However, multimedia only makes the message form more attractive, allowing information about the exhibits to be acquired.

2 Learning in the Museum Space - Perspectives Determined by New Approaches to Learning

Contemporary approaches to learning vigorously promote 21st century competencies as a combination of knowledge, skills, and attitudes [4]. Jérémy Lamri draws attention to the so-called 4Cs – critical thinking, creativity, communication, and cooperation [5] and stresses that it is becoming necessary to rethink our learning style because the current one, based on knowledge accumulation and storage, is ineffective. 4C competencies can also develop in various situations when we learn to use the resources of the digital world thoughtfully. Currently, reflexivity becomes essential to increase the individual's autonomy in regards to his development, unlimited access to information, and ambiguity. Nowadays, every person can build personalized knowledge resulting from learning about reality, analyzing, understanding, and interpreting the content he learns. Understanding the opportunities that interactive museums create for potential learning participants is related to defining them as a category of museums that encourages visitors to actively participate in the expositions and exhibitions and not just look at them. It can be achieved through touch screens, virtual reality, and practical actions. The goal of an interactive museum is to make the museum more interesting, intriguing, exciting, and memorable for visitors.

It is worth noting at this point that one of the most critical moments, from the perspective of the concept of museum education, was the turn to the constructivist approach. Georg E. Hein [6], the forerunner of this approach in museum education, was inspired by John Dewey's method of "learning by doing," whose conception of experience is the source of acquisition and verification of knowledge, and the development and growth process takes place through the accumulation and exchange of ideas because people live in such a reality as they experience [7]. Education should refer to the experience of everyday life in the broadest sense. In this case, the most important is the notion of human experience, which is the acquisition of knowledge by a person about the world and himself. In the constructivist concept of education in the museum space, G. Hein sees that the learning-teaching process should be an enabling experience of the work of the museum object – appropriate museum education thus includes various skills that should open the viewer to a broader experience. Hein's concept points to three skills relevant to optimizing learning:

1. the recognition of knowledge as subjective and thus constructed in the process of human cognition. Therefore, it is more relative than universal. Education here is not limited to activities with the public, but also directly impacts the nature of exhibitions and the relationship between the visitor and the object. Thus, it is necessary to pay attention to the preparation of the museum space and educational materials so that they stimulate the visitor to ask questions and seek answers;
2. emphasizing that education is one of the tools that allow democracy to flourish;
3. to propose the idea of a "progressive" museum education, which aims to break down the divisions between high art and applied art, theory, and practice, or between different categories of viewers (differences have the effect of increasing social inequality).

Museum education, understood in this manner, points to the constant need to enrich knowledge through successive experiences. According to the constructivist concept, knowledge should be built by constantly asking questions and seeking answers from the viewer to ask further questions and create a reflective approach.

Approaches to learning regarding the importance of reflexive learning in interactive museum spaces relating to both the learner and the contexts that determine learning, which is used in creating activities in these spaces, perfectly correspond not only to the views of John Dewey and Georg Heim, but also models of Donald Schön [8], Terry Borton [9], David Kolb [10] and Graham Gibbs [11].

To understand the potential attributed to interactive museums, reference should also be made to connective theories. Connectivism is sometimes presented, as George Siemens did [12], as "a theory of learning for the digital age". The development of digital technology has influenced the emergence of connectivism, and it is not a response to digitization but rather a way of using insights from digitization to solve multi-wave problems in learning and development. Stephen Downes emphasizes that central to this theory is an understanding of the term knowledge as a way of understanding the world. People are familiar with two types of knowledge: qualitative knowledge based on properties such as shape, color, or size, and quantitative knowledge, which can be found in the mass or weight of something, volume or size, or quantity or number of things. Connectivism argues that a third type of knowledge, cumulative knowledge, is based on organization and structure [13]. The result of a connectivist learning activity is then the kind of knowledge that involves recognizing relevant phenomena and responding to those phenomena, and connectivist pedagogy can be described in terms of the ARRFF method, where ARRFF stands for aggregation, remixing, repurposing, and feedforward [14].

This pattern is not unique to connectivism and can be found in many other sources. It combines the idea of accumulating things, remixing them, adopting them for personal use, translating them into one's language, and then sharing them. Connectivism, like many other learning theories, is sometimes subject to criticism, being accused, for example, of not adequately explaining how we learn [15]. However, it combines essential elements of many learning theories, social structures, and technological tools to form a solid theoretical foundation for understanding learning in the digital age. What seems crucial, for example, is to point out the importance of being able to see connections between sources of information (including sensory information) and make decisions, even in rapidly changing environments, based on the ability to recognize things and to be able to constantly update and change knowledge based on new phenomena that are presented. So, it is not simply "Can you repeat something?" but "Can you learn in a rapidly changing and dynamic environment?". Downes notes that in connectivism, "to teach is to propose a model and experience, to learn is to practice and reflect" [14].

Interestingly set against this background is a presentation posted by Downes online, in which he presented an intriguing picture of Education 2050. His vision for future education is based on technologies and discoveries that are becoming important in learning, such as semantic networks, learning communities, creative teaching, and practical approaches to knowledge and learning. The author predicts that this will bring about changes in learning, which will take on the formula of long-life learning. Still, the process will be based primarily on people sharing knowledge regardless of age or stage of education. Learning will be a "stream" (practical knowledge that is frequently updated and renewed) rather than the creation of a closed resource (the so-called "reservoir of retention") that we use throughout our lives. The essence of the education process will be acceptance of change and the ability to acquire the new knowledge needed to function in life. His outlook shatters thinking about learning and becomes a kind of invitation to rethink the learning process of the current and future generations of children and adolescents [16].

It is worth emphasizing here that learning is understood in this context as a network of complementary forms of learning (formal, non-formal, and informal), developing synergistically throughout life and in all areas of education.

This aspect is evident in the tenets of STEAM education, indicating the importance of perceiving and interpreting the world holistically and using it in interactive museums. It should be noted that initially the concept of STEM was used, which, limiting itself to science, technology, engineering and mathematics and omitting the concept of art, turned out to be inadequate because STEM partially corresponded to reality, requiring much more than an understanding of these areas. Modern people (at every stage of life) also need creativity, ingenuity, and the skills to use ideas. STEAM has taken STEM to a new level by combining science learning with artistic practices, elements, and design principles, equipping the individual with many learning opportunities. The transformation of STEM to STEAM (proposed by the Rhode Island School of Design in 2010 [17]) is one of the fundamental changes in education. It is because in learning, skills related to, among other things, sensory learning are essential – the lack of these skills makes a person a passive recipient who becomes helpless in the face of stimuli that attack him, unable to perceive and analyze phenomena and thus unable, per his value system, to respond to them [18]. In STEAM, preparation for the active perception of all wonders of nature, art, and technology plays an important role that cannot be overestimated. Furthermore, the problem, as Hanna Krauze – Sikorska points out, is that when analyzing the essence of sensory learning, the role of perception of visual phenomena is emphasized, but "too little emphasis is placed on the fact that in the process of activating a vision and thinking with these categories, it is important to actively perceive phenomena not only with the help of vision but also with the help of other senses" [18]. In this kind of activity, active observation is thus necessary, "because the need for visual perception must also assume the existence of non-traditional situations related, for example, to movement or space-time" [18].

Education using the STEAM approach remains open to these dimensions of learning and thus prepares for the active perception of all phenomena of nature, art, and technology because "progress does not come from technology alone, but from the fusion of technology and creative thinking through art and design" [19]. The multidisciplinary and interdisciplinary approach in STEAM education, which combines elements of science, technology, engineering, art, and mathematics, remains open to the dimensions of art, creativity, and innovation and can be applied not only in formal but also in informal settings (e.g., museum spaces) – the recipients of this approach are students at the primary, secondary, and post-secondary levels [20], who, while seeking innovative solutions, at the same time have the opportunity to verify their ideas practically, and making mistakes and verifying hypotheses enables effective learning by doing. It should be noted that the use of interactive STEAM activities in museum educational practices can also significantly develop students' social skills. Collaborative problem solving allows them to form teamwork, discussion, and mediation skills. They have the opportunity to motivate themselves and develop self-efficacy, reflective and flexible thinking, and cognitive curiosity. STEAM education is implemented entirely in line with the requirements of postmodernity, the progressive development of technology, and the growing demand for people with scientific, mathematical, and technological competencies [21] – because of all these competencies students can develop in interactive museum spaces.

3   Interactive Museums TeamLab and Funzeum - The Answer to the Challenges of the Digital World

3.1   Purpose and Method of the Study

Interactive museums, although they do not take a uniform form and are redefined continuously (divisions can be made here due to the type of interactivity, content or form of exhibitions, and even the specifics of building interactive spaces due to the age of the audience and their needs, e.g., interactive art museums, narrative museums), can be generally characterized as museums where visitors can touch, feel, and experience exhibits. There are several types of interactive environments. One is the recreation of 3D space with visual representations of the museum using a 3D architectural metaphor that provides a sense of place using various spatial references. 3D modeling, VRML (Virtual Reality Modeling Language), and now X3D (successor of VRML) are typically used for viewing exhibits. Multiple imaging techniques, such as infrared reflectography, X-ray imaging, 3D laser scanning, and IBMR (Image-Based Rendering and Modeling), have also been introduced to build interactive museums. Thus, there is no single answer to the question of museum interactivity because different museums present different approaches to interactivity.

The educational potential of interactive museums is demonstrated by installations available for viewing in many European and non-European museums – as interactivity in museum spaces is an increasingly strong trend worldwide.

The research represented in this article aimed to reflect on how a space that makes a museum fully interactive fits into the culture of learning in a digital world: encouraging hands-on or participatory learning, enabling questions or opinions, but also showing how offering digital or technological elements allows children and young people to build new experiences.

In pursuing such an objective and the resulting research questions, the focus was on a qualitative analysis of the content and forms of interactive communication in the spaces created at Teamlab in Tokyo and Funzeum in Gliwice – they were chosen not only for their interactivity but also for the fact that the exhibitions proposed by these museums use a specific type of visual language with a peculiar formal structure, and thus are part of the area of relevance for modern man, functioning in the era of image culture, related to visual literacy [22]. In describing the projects of the exhibitions held at Teamlab and Funzeum, art-based research methods were used, within the paradigm of qualitative research, with structuralist narratology as the basis for analysis. By analyzing the form and content of the exhibitions, it was assumed that narrativity is not only a characteristic of written [23] or spoken texts but also of artifacts created with the help of digital media, which made it possible to take into account the context of their representational and creative power, showing possible ways of constructing messages and communicating values by creators and audiences of interactive visual realizations. In doing so, the narratological description is not an end in itself, but rather a starting point for further explication.

3.2 TeamLab Tokyo

Since its inception, TeamLab, an interdisciplinary creative group that brings together professionals from various fields related to digital society: artists, programmers, engineers, CG animators, and mathematicians, has revolutionized digital art and broken world records for the number of visitors. In its first year, TeamLab Borderless received 2.3 million visitors from 160 countries, and 1.25 million people from 106 countries used TeamLab Planets. Lucia Tsujiguchi, referring to her experiences in the halls of teamLab, writes: "If we had been told a few decades ago that one day there would be a place that would allow us to go barefoot while climbing waterfalls, chasing Japanese koi carp that turn into flowers when trying to catch them, or even wandering through sparkling crystals in a distant galaxy, we would have thought it was a crazy idea" [24].

When creating interactive spaces, TeamLab uses Epson 3LCD projectors to project extraordinary digital installations and refers to its employees as "ultra-technologists" as they strive to combine and achieve a balance between art, science, technology, creativity, and the natural world. The museum features eight works by TeamLab, centered in four massive workspaces. Visitors have the opportunity to immerse their entire body (together with others) in these enormous works of "Body Immersive" art – where the boundary between the body and the artwork disappears and the boundaries between the individual, others and the world become something continuous, a new relationship is discovered without boundaries between man and the world [24].

An unusual experience is an encounter with others in the *Soft Black Hole*, where the body becomes a space that affects another body (see Fig. 1).

Fig. 1. Soft Black Hole experience, TeamLab Tokyo

Visitors have to escape the gravitational force of the black hole as their feet sink into the soft surface with every step, so the task is not as easy as it seems. The shape of the entire space is constantly changing and transforming into something completely different, not only due to the actions of the participant, but also the actions of other visitors in the same situation. After exiting the black hole, visitors enter the next room through a dimly lit corridor. The path ends where the galaxy begins. Unexpectedly, the visitor finds himself in a maze of crystals and lights reflecting on all sides and in all directions. In this room, the ceiling, walls, and floor are covered with mirrors – the impression of an infinite and magical world is created. Drawing on the surface created by the *Dance of Koi and People - Infinity* is also an unusual experience. In this space, visitors must immerse themselves in the artwork by entering a knee-deep pond with hundreds of digital koi carp swimming in it. If visitors try to catch and touch them, they explode, turning into flowers that change according to the season. The koi can also turn into colorful lines that illuminate the room every seven minutes. *Cold Life* is a graphic hidden in a small space, accessed directly from the koi room. Visitors also have to walk on water here, but they can also sit back and enjoy a modern digital interpretation of Japanese calligraphy. Visitors can see the kanji strokes on the screen, for example, 生, meaning "life", turning into a tree full of flowers and butterflies. Another room is filled with giant colored spheres of light reflected in mirrors on the floor and floating around visitors. If one touches one of them, it changes color. The space will gradually transform depending on the visitor's interaction with the spheres. In another space, one can sit freely on the mirrored floor. The magic of silence makes visitors feel like they are floating in a universe of changing digital flowers. One can also use the TeamLab app to launch butterflies that fly toward the flowers, making them sprout, grow, and bloom. Then their petals will begin to fall until they wither and die. Being in this space is an excellent and beautiful representation of the cycle of life.

TeamLab's concept of body immersion aims to make visitors experience art through their bodies. The lighting of a visitor's route, the sounds, textures, and even the smells constantly changing so that each space can be experienced differently. This multisensory experience stimulates touch, sight, hearing, smell, and imagination. It allows visitors to immerse themselves in the world of art literally – this world comes to life and is constantly changing. In 2021 a new *Garden Area* was opened at TeamLab. The area consists of one garden filled with countless orchids blooming in the air, and the other is a moss garden with metallic egg-shaped sculptures. By adding this space to the existing *Water Area*, TeamLab Planets has become a museum that integrates water and flora with digital art in one place. (see Fig. 2).

3.3 Funzeum

Poland's largest interactive museum offering multimedia installations inspired by the magic of light and color, using modern digital technology to offer visitors extraordinary visual, auditory, and kinesthetic effects and experiences, from optical illusions to visual designs. The Funzeum website proclaims, "When visiting the Funzeum, be prepared for a completely unfamiliar experience. Here, visitors can unleash their imagination and create on their terms. An ordinary visit will become a unique and exciting adventure while systematically exploring our magical world" [25]. More than 50 multisensory interactive installations are divided into two main exhibitions: Light and Color – where physics, biology, history, and art integrate, and the whole exhibition is planned in such a way that it stimulates activity, inspires, develops the imagination, and creativity of visitors, although the creators of Funzeum are not afraid to refer to its entertainment function – in the spaces of this museum, children, teenagers (but also adults) play while learning and learn while playing, and the experiences and lessons learned encourage further exploration of the topics after the visit.

The Color exhibition consists of 36 exhibits in 12 rooms; this is the first exhibition visited in the Funzeum, where guests can immortalize their stay on the selfie walls

Fig. 2. Interactive Kinetic Installation, TeamLab Tokyo

scattered throughout the facility. The exhibit aims to draw attention to the essence of the colors surrounding people, which significantly impact emotions and often contribute to decisions. The Color Exhibition begins by entering a completely white room where visitors can listen to stories about colors. Visitors can learn from this part of the exhibition about, among other things, how certain dyes were once produced, how specific colors affect our mood, and what each color symbolizes. In practice, it is also possible to see what mixing of individual colors looks like: interactive installations, such as "sliding glass" and "color projectors", are used for this purpose. The interiors change colors as visitors learn more color trivia, and when the narrative is over, one can move on to another small room where it can be seen how colors form. The subsequent spaces are a journey through each color with several different color arrangements. Each section also has an information board about the color (including how it comes into being and some trivia about it).

An unusual space is built by the Prism exhibit (see Fig. 3) – visitors can admire it in all its glory, understand its principles, and then at a table with smaller prisms, they have the opportunity to play with the light and learn how many colors white, "colorless" light contains. Visitors can immerse themselves in the colors of the rainbow as much as possible when dealing with light.

Fig. 3. The Prism exhibit, Funzeum in Gliwice

Multimedia installations and interactive elements encourage the discovery of color, and by interacting with each of the colors shown, one can discover surprising visual effects. Spaces dominated by color allow visitors to play and learn – they can take photos, dress up, pose, and create new arrangements. There are some unusual installations, such as walls with flowers or a huge inflatable dog. Visitors can sit on a snowy throne, hide between sunflowers, swing among the clouds, and even cause storms. There are also frames, armchairs, loungers, cages, backlights, unicorns, rainbows, and colorful ribbons for public use, so that visitors, limited only by their imagination, can also participate in creating an artistic installation.

The Light exhibition is a three-dimensional space where visitors must wear special 3D glasses to experience it fully. Upon entering, one can find oneself in a dark room full of bright, fluorescent, glowing shapes and paintings. To the left is a cat straight out of Alice in Wonderland; to the right, one can dive into an underwater marine world.

The Light exhibition is also comprised of a fluorescent zone, illuminated by UV light and viewed through 3D glasses, the effect of depth from the various elements of the exhibition, i.e., a planet of overgrown flowers, an infinity room, a moon room, and an interactive aquarium, is enhanced. From mirrors to natural and artificial light sources, visitors can learn and experience light from an entirely new side, immerse themselves in their reflections, go inside a kaleidoscope, or "get lost" in a magical fluorescent forest (see Fig. 4).

The subsequent rooms have more luminous installations: crystals and lanterns separated into two infinity rooms, creating the illusion of endless space. Although only two main exhibits are made available to the public, the Funzeum also offers a space for

Fig. 4. Fluorescent forest, Funzeum in Gliwice

gaining other experiences, such as playing the floor piano or creating artwork that comes to life on a giant screen.

4   Discussion and Conclusion

Interest in the development of virtual museums is growing rapidly. In recent decades there have been numerous efforts to develop interactive museums. The realistic result is, of course, always a real challenge, especially in the field of education [28], but interactivity should become an immanent component of the tasks of museums. Many studies confirm that the active use of various multimedia technologies that inform, educate and provide information in a playful way increases the interest and experience of museum users [29] while stimulating discussions among educational researchers and practitioners about the potential of interactive experiences and contextual learning in museums in the process of lifelong education, but also questions about interactive design solutions in line with the needs of museum users of different ages [30].

The article attempts to show that the use of interactive digital installations is an excellent tactic that captures the attention and interest of viewers, providing a potentially effective way to promote art to children and adolescents, but also to indicate how significantly art can be linked to various fields of science. While creating innovative works of art, artists also explore the boundaries of art itself. These advances offer greater accessibility to people's art experiences, and integrating interactive digital installations can improve the effectiveness of learning outcomes such as collaborative skills and critical and creative thinking. It is worth highlighting the openness of interactive learning spaces in museums open to different learning styles. In the interactive spaces of museums, the process of multisensory cognition is stimulated and direct viewing and experience become possible. By building an enthusiastic attitude and participation in the process of cognition, children and adolescents can feel themselves equal recipients of culture, its co-creators, creators, or actors, but also learn to cope with cognitive and aesthetic challenges, experience new things, and by exploring the museum space, develop cognitively, emotionally and socially. Indeed, it becomes crucial in the education process that new digital technologies, new teaching systems, and the changing expectations of the new generation of students resulting from their interaction with virtual reality (VR), augmented reality (AR), artificial intelligence (AI), gamification, allow digital natives to become "digitally smart".

Interactive museums can effectively support the acquisition of new knowledge and the creation of new values, the creation of connections between people and things, and between the real and cyber worlds, they can also be an effective and efficient way to solve problems. In this way, children and adolescents can learn to read the world through "glasses of human culture" – symbolic tools transmitted through cultural development – visual signs, plans, symbols, texts, and language in an ever-evolving society, for which knowledge has become a strategic resource, (not only its acquisition but also learning to understand world phenomena, behavior, skills, values, attitudes, and preferences), related to the human personality [4].

The use of new technologies in museum spaces brings significant benefits to children and young people (though not only to them, as education in museum spaces meets lifelong learning requirements). It can be described as "catalytic" [26] as the digital revolution has clearly "helped shift museography from object-oriented design to experience-centered design" [27].

Interactive museums are becoming new places of cultural education, meeting zones of science with art, spaces where the viewer, becoming an active co-participant in the meeting, can experience new perceptual, cognitive, emotional, and social experiences.

Sometimes, they are the space that initiates the first contact of children and adolescents with science and art, creating the interactive experience model assuming that the museum experience is constructed from the visitor's perspective. To fully realize the interactive experience model, it is necessary to move away from informational museology to performative museology, in which the museum becomes an ensemble of techniques, skills, and methods designed to have an impact on visitors.

The attractiveness, but also the impact of interactive exhibitions, is due to the fact that they activate not only multisensory experiences but also thought processes and emotions, drawing the visitor into the depths of the story they propose and do not allow him to remain indifferent to new sensations. Therefore, analyzing narrative exhibitions from an educational perspective, it is clear that their design aligns with ideas that indicate the need for changes in education, enriching the learning process for students visiting the museum, and can be highly effective in developing the competencies needed in a new culture.

References

1. Laloux, F.: Reinventing Organizations. A Guide to Creating Organizations Inspired by the Next Stage of Human Consciousness. Nelson Parker, Brussels (2014)
2. Fukuyama, M.: Society 5.0: aiming for a new human-centered society. Jpn Spotlight **37**(5), 47–50 (2018)
3. Rekus, J., Mikhail, Th.: Neues schulpädagogisches Wörterbuch. Beltz-Juventa, Weinheim/Basel (2013)
4. Gross, R.: Psychology: The Science of Mind & Behaviour, 6th edn. Hodder Education Publishers, London (2010)
5. Lamri, J.: Kompetencje XXI wieku. Kreatywność, Komunikacja, Krytyczne myślenie, Kooperacja [Competencies of the 21st Century. Creativity, Communication, Critical Thinking, Cooperation]. Wolters Kluwer, Warsaw (2021)
6. Hein, G.E.: John Dewey's 'Wholly Original Philosophy' and its significance for museums. Curator **49**(2), 181–202 (2006)
7. Dewey, J.: Democracy and Education & Experience and Education: How to Encourage Experiential Education, Problem-Based Learning & Pragmatic Philosophy of Scholarship. E-artnow, Chicago (2017)
8. Schön, D.: The Reflective Practitioner. Temple Smith, London (1983)
9. Borton, T.: Reach, Touch and Teach. Hutchinson, London (1970)
10. Kolb, D.A.: Experiential Learning, Experience as the Source of Learning and Development. Prentice-Hall Inc., Englewood Cliffs (1984)
11. Gibbs, G.: Learning by Doing: A Guide to Teaching and Learning Methods. Further Education Unit, Oxford Polytechnic, Oxford (1988)
12. Siemens, G.: Connectivism: a learning theory for the digital age. Int. J. Instr. Technol. Distance Learn. **2**(1) (2005). http://www.itdl.org/Journal/Jan_05/index.htm. Accessed 28 Apr 2023
13. Downes, S.: Connectivism. Asian J. Distance Educ. **17**(1), 58–87 (2022)
14. Downes, S.: An introduction to connective knowledge. In: Hug, T. (ed.) Media, Knowledge & Education – Exploring New Spaces, Relations and Dynamics in Digital Media Ecologies, pp. 77–102. Innsbruck University Press, Innsbruck (2008)
15. Kop, R., Fournier, H., Mak, J.S.F.: A pedagogy of abundance or a pedagogy to support human beings? Participant support on massive open online courses. Int. Rev. Res. Open Distrib. Learn. **12**(7), 74–93 (2011)
16. Krauze-Sikorska, H.: Cyfrowa epoka - nowe wyzwania dla procesu edukacji dzieci i młodzieży [The digital era – new challenges for the educational process of children and adolescents]. In: Jaskulska, S., Jankowiak, B., Sikorska, J., Klichowski, M., Krauze–Sikorska, H. (eds.) Proces uczenia się przed, w trakcie i po pandemii COVID-19.Badanie VULCAN [Learning Process Before, During and after the COVID-19 Pandemic. VULCAN Study], pp. 23–29. Adam Mickiewicz University Press, Poznan (2021)
17. Rhode Island School of Design. https://www.risd.edu/steam. Accessed 20 Apr 2023
18. Krauze-Sikorska, H.: Edukacja przez sztukę. O edukacyjnych wartościach artystycznej twórczości dziecka [Education Through Art. On Educational Values of Artistic Creativity of a Child]. Adam Mickiewicz University Press, Poznan (2006)
19. Land, M.H.: Full STEAM ahead: the benefits of integrating the arts into STEM. Procedia Comput. Sci. **20**, 547–552 (2013)

20. Güleryüz, H.: The importance of 3D design in science education within STEM education. In: Yalçın, P. (ed.) Focus of Educational Sciences and Future Perspective, pp. 1–18. SRA Academic Publishing, Klaipeda (2023)
21. Chyrk P.: Nauki ścisłe, technologia, inżynieria i matematyka [Science, technology, engineering, and mathematics]. In: Księga Trendów w Edukacji 2.0 [The Book of Trends in Education 2.0], pp. 162–164. Young Digital Planet a Sanoma Company, Gdynia (2015)
22. Serafini, F.: Visual Literacy. Oxford Research Encyclopedia of Education. https://oxfordre.com/education/view/10.1093/acrefore/9780190264093.001.0001/acrefore-9780190264093-e-19. Accessed 30 Apr 2023
23. Bal, M.: Narratology: Introduction to the Theory of Narrative, 4th edn. University of Toronto Press, Toronto (2017)
24. Tsujiguchi, L.: teamLab Planets: An Immersion into Another Planet Inside Tokyo, https://voyapon.com/teamlab-planets-tokyo/. Accessed 30 Apr 2023
25. Funzeum Homepage. https://funzeum.pl/. Accessed 30 Apr 2023
26. Parry, R.: Recoding the Museum: Digital Heritage and the Technologies of Change. Routledge, London, New York (2007)
27. Falk, J.H., Dierking, L.D.: The Museum Experience Revisited. Routledge, New York (2013)
28. Brüninghaus-Knubel, C.: Museum education in the context of museum functions. In: Bojlan, P.J. (ed.) Museum: Running a Museum a Practical Handbook, pp. 119–132. ICOM – International Council of Museums, Paris (2004). https://unesdoc.unesco.org/ark:/48223/pf0000 141067. Accessed 26 July 2023
29. Ser, S.H.: Engagement with interactive museum collections: the rise and development of interactive museum exhibitions in Thailand (2000–2019). Connexion J. Humanit. Soc. Sci. 8(2), 77–86 (2019). https://so05.tci-thaijo.org/index.php/MFUconnexion/article/view/241041. Accessed 26 July 2023
30. Moury, A.J.: Interactive elements in museum design: why new generation are less interested in visiting a museum. https://www.researchgate.net/publication/354652278_Interactive_Elements_in_Museum_Design_Why_new_Generation_are_less_interested_in_visiting_a_museum. Accessed 26 July 2023

Remix Exquisite Bioethics Transcultural Dialogues

Richard Kabiito[1] and Karen Keifer-Boyd[2(✉)]

[1] Makerere University, Kampala 08544, Uganda
[2] The Pennsylvania State University, University Park 16802, USA
ktk2@psu.edu

Abstract. Exploring new media, Penn State art education students in the USA working in conjunction with art students at Makerere University in Kampala, Uganda, collaborated in a process akin to the early 20th Century Surrealist Art Movement's "exquisite corpse" collaborative art practice. Together, they created a "Remix Exquisite Bioethics" online exhibition, which is also a teaching resource of transcultural dialogues. Students from Uganda and the United States discussed and collaboratively produced bioethic narratives in which their remixed assemblages inspired the stories and became characters in the stories. The assembled characters were comprised of their drawings of body components such as eyes, neck, waist, and feet. As collaborating facilitators, we present how we generated transcultural dialogues. Our new media pedagogy guided the creation of bioethic narratives based on students conceptualizing their remix characters' personality, beliefs, and history. We discuss their audio-visual multimedia bioethic narratives as examples of our new media pedagogy. Annually, for more than 15 years, we have collaboratively developed new media transcultural dialogue pedagogy.

Keywords: Remix Aesthetics · Bioethic Narratives · Collaboration

1 Introduction to Facilitating Transcultural Dialogues

Each year since 2007, we, the co-authors[1] of this essay, have facilitated arts-based transcultural dialogues between students in our courses at Makerere University in Kampala, Uganda and The Pennsylvania State University (Penn State) in the United States [1, 2]. As we plan and schedule the next transcultural dialogue with new media (e.g., 360-degree filming and editing, mixed reality, virtual worlds) critical reflections on our transcultural dialogue new media pedagogy helps us refine goals and improve facilitation and student motivation. While project themes have varied each year (e.g., house, place, idioms, visual culture), underpinning our more than 15 years of annual collaborative teaching projects are theories of intertextuality, transcultural, remix, feminism, indigeneity, and more recently bioethics. In Fall 2022, we centered remix aesthetics and bioethics as

---

[1] There is no first author as we each contributed to all stages of writing and rotate the order of our names for each co-authored article.

Ł. Tomczyk (Ed.): NMP 2022, CCIS 1916, pp. 200–220, 2023.
https://doi.org/10.1007/978-3-031-44581-1_15

the theoretical lens to guide the making and discussion of art collaboratively created by students in Uganda partnered with students in the United States. In this essay, we present our new media pedagogy in facilitating remix exquisite bioethics transcultural dialogue.

Infused in our pedagogy is attention to multidirectional dialogue among participants to learn about themselves and each other, to broaden ways of knowing, and disrupt assumptions that marginalize and bring about inequities. The dialogues happen in multimedia ways in which drawing, interpreting images, and imagination are integral. We encourage students to expand their knowledge of local narratives and images into a new world of interrelated ways of knowing by investigating each other's systems of knowledge. This leads to collaborative construction of knowledge and shared experiences that influence the making of new worldviews. Students from the United States have learned new perspectives about themselves and about Uganda from the students based in Uganda; likewise, students from Uganda learned much about the United States quite different from portrayals in movies, news, and other prevalent media. Many of the small group dialogues were about real-life situations through the narratives of everyday experiences. Further, through the making of art collaboratively, students from both countries learn about each other as they reconstruct their worldviews.

By emphasizing collaboration and dialogue, as facilitators we demystify the artistic genius narrative that separates art from life. Instead, from a transcultural dialogue perspective, art becomes a communal engagement. In the local life of an Indigenous Ugandan, art serves the purpose of mediating local forms of knowledge ranging from divination to intellectual engagements often in the form of game-like cultural teaching of literacy. These recreational forms are relatable to the collaborative play of the Surrealist way of making art that brings community together [3]. Multidirectional engagements in art making are important in the making of a just society since a multiplicity of voices is present and heard.

Bioethics is pursuit of life well lived toward creating a socially just world. Principles of bioethics include transparency, integrity, and respect for the rights and welfare of all people. Bioethical questions ask: How do stories told, written, or expressed in multimodal forms by individuals and groups define and structure morals? [4]. What are the normative narratives pervasive today? Whose norms are reflected, whose are marginalized or absent? What are some examples of counter-narratives that address interconnected systems of oppression? [5] How does place, placement, context, and juxtaposition impact bioethic narratives?

1.1   Transcultural Dialogue Pedagogy

Transcultural dialogue in our project focuses on exploring bioethics as a lens that focuses on contemporary visual culture as geo-cultural practices. We facilitate toward goals of eroding assumptions, ignorance, and misunderstandings, and building rapport and care about the wellbeing of each other. Pedagogical strategies of transcultural dialogue consider positionality, community, voice, relationality, and reciprocal-reflexivity. The dialogic process elicits micro-cultural views that are specific and unique yet are shared within or are part of macro-cultural knowledge. The act of meaning-making from microcultural practices can sustain as well as change the macro-cultural. Transcultural dialogue is conversational performative cultural critique, collaborative artmaking, and commentary surrounding artworks by those involved in our transcultural dialogic projects [6]. As critical methodology, the purpose of transcultural dialogue is to promote "a reflexive discourse constantly in search of an open-ended, subversive, multivoiced, participatory epistemology" [7, p. x]. In order to develop a pedagogical process to engage reflexive dialogue, the cultural knowledge and experiences of diverse students are validated in the learning environment. In what follows, we describe how we facilitated transcultural dialogic new media pedagogy in Fall 2022.

We begin with an overview of the process and project. Each student created an image of a section of the body. The images were then shared, and students remixed and assembled the drawings into characters for an online exhibition. Students from Uganda and the U.S. then discussed and created stories together with the characters in response to the following prompts.

1. Imagine the character in different places. How might the **surroundings** shape the meaning of the character?
2. Give your character a **personality**, a tone of voice, and an attitude. Experiment with speaking from the character's perspective. What does the character know? What kinds of **adventures** has it had? What is the character's **history**? What does the character **believe**?
3. Imagine a **conversation** between two or more characters. What would they say to each other?
4. How would you **feel** being the character? How might it affect your body, thoughts, or emotions? How might it affect your relationship with others?
5. Which drawing **surprised** you and why?

Through dialogue and reflexivity, students creatively explored their remix bioethic narratives in a back-and-forth exchange using Zoom and WhatsApp as the platforms to connect with each other. The Makerere University students were introduced to the remix bioethics project through an art history class taught by Kabiito. In Fall 2022, Ugandan students considered remix aesthetics, narrative inquiry in bioethics, and exquisite engendering to expand their knowledge of artistic theories. Kabiito's art history course focused on art that was made collaboratively as a counternarrative to the longstanding concept of art by a 'genius' individual artist. A learning objective was to understand the functionality of group processes in collaborative artmaking. The students, as they contributed to an ongoing artistic process, could revision a local narrative, the Nakayima story, they have known from the past by reframing the narrative through collaborative art making. The Nakayima story is well-known among Ugandans and is intriguing from a bioethical standpoint with its geo-historical and cultural structuring that offered a viewpoint of how to approach art making through a collaborative process.

1.2 Remix Aesthetics

A remix is a critical art practice in which cultural elements from pre-existing sources are creatively reassembled to critique socially normalized beliefs about gender, race, ableness, among other identity constructions and normative social narratives. Remix aesthetics within the visual arts reveals "cultural-intertextuality" as "visual archives within a cultural space" [8, p. 179]. The original source is recognizable, yet the meaning is changed by what is added before or after the source. "Remixed media succeed when they show others something new; they fail when they are trite or derivative. ... A remix draws upon the work of others in order to do new work" [9, p. 82]. In our remix project, the body is fragmented into artworks in which the fragments from the body context become bioethical narratives and then are reassembled—offering new cultural tropes. Emphasizing remix aesthetics has been a fruitful artistic approach for students to release their drawing and allow it to be brought into another's artwork. Remix is a process of critical reworking of existing material making 'participation' a compelling aspect of remix art [10]. Participation, in our project, occurs when all involved set the ground rules to create a level ground (i.e., a level playing field of respect for each other) and seek to disrupt the vertical power dynamics that are inherent in racism, sexism, and ableism.

New media digital technologies make the basic remix processes of cut and paste more accessible, although hand-cut collage is a forerunner of the digital remix as artistic expression [11]. Similar to culture, remix tools and intertextualities are never static but rather the cut and paste technologies and their accessibility change, along with shifting cultural references that become less familiar as new context-bound tropes arise [12]. Although the remix music genre originated in Jamaica in the 1960s, remix as an art form has roots traceable as far back as the early 20th century with Dada, Conceptualism, and Surrealism. The Surrealists' *exquisite corpse* artistic game-like practice of each drawing a portion of a human body on the same accordion-folded paper without seeing the prior drawings collapses the notion of artist as genius and unfolds art as collaborative play in producing the unexpected [13].

Intertextuality is an important component of remix culture, due to the recyclability and appropriation of digitized visual, written, and audio texts [14]. This technologically enhanced ability to recycle texts offers multiple layers in remix productions to interface at different levels of cultural complexity. Remix, a phenomenon of recycling cultural material, functions as feedback loops to critique what has become normative cultural texts [15]. In ever emerging cultural practices and age-old traditions of cultural practices, culture is understood and carried forward with the recycling of texts. Remix work can begin to dismantle canons of coloniality and restore Indigenous autonomy from conquers' and settlers' enforced cultural practices such as art produced by an individual creative genius whose visions are novel [16]. Instead, remix aesthetics values intertextuality, which dismantles authority of texts in favor of plurality of meanings.

2 Drawing Bioethic Narratives

Bioethic visual narratives generated by students in Uganda and the United States involved students assigned a number that corresponded to a section of a body. The division of body segments was based on the number of students. Using their number in the alphabetized class roster, each did a drawing for that section of body so that lines in their drawing extend off the top and bottom of the drawing as it would be connected to another's drawing. For example, if a student is listed as number 1 in the course roster, the student would have the top of the head and forehead to draw, if #2 then the eyes, if #3 nose, #4 mouth, #5 neck, #6 shoulders and arms, #7 chest, #8 waist, #9 pelvic and hips, #10 thighs,

#11 knees and calves, #12 ankles and feet. Their drawings could be abstract, symbolic, or metaphoric. The drawings were placed in a shared online folder to assemble as exquisite bioethic narratives of the body. Both classes had access to the shared folder of drawings to assemble into their remix. As part of the exhibition website, each team was responsible for collaboratively developing a webpage to include a slide presentation of the images from a student at Penn State and their Ugandan partner, a title, an audio/zoom recording of dialogue about the individual work and assemblage, the duration of recording, keywords, and a question for discussion.

Uganda's Approach to Bioethic Narratives.   Students in Kabiito's course at Makerere University were divided into groups to allow the formation of collaborative instances of artmaking and to share knowledge they learned from the stories reiterated to them since childhood. Kabiito introduced bioethics through the story of Nakayima.[2] The image is a geo-historical site located in Mubende on a hill with a big tree into which it is believed Nakayima disappeared. This tree has been visited by people from all walks of life. Nakayima is not portrayed as an evil spirit and all religions are accommodated at the site. Nakimaya is a powerful feminist story about leadership and divination. The Nakayima story brings both (ideological) feminist and (procedural) remix structures of narrative and approaches to art making. Framed around a powerful character—Nakayima—this historical narrative of gender and divination helped the students to develop two lines of collaborative thought: students were mindful of maintaining the femininity

---

[2] Here is the story of Nakayima: Legend has it that there was once a powerful Chwezi king named Ndahura born of a woman named Nyamwezi and father named Isingoma. Ndahura was believed to be a polite and kind king who did not discriminate among his subjects. The native people asked the king to marry. He married a woman called Nalongo. She was as powerful as the king. The king and queen were liked by the people for their good deeds. This led the people to offer tithe of their crop harvests as a thanksgiving to the king. Ndahura later disappeared as the Chwezi often did. They disappeared in trees, lakes, hills, rocks, and forests. The ancestors were depressed because of the king's disappearance, so they planted a tree in remembrance of his good rule. After Nalongo ruled for a while, she asked the people to appoint another king because there were a lot of cattle raids. The people appointed Kitaka brother to Ndahura as the *Kabaka* (i.e., the local title for 'king').He came with a different style of rule; he had such power that he knew whomever did wrong despite the distance between him and the people. He punished people by sending them *walumbe* (disease) to kill them. This upset Nalongo since she did not love Kitaka's rule; this was not the way her husband ruled. She made sure she stood up for the innocent people to prevent them from the harsh rule of Kabaka Kitaka. Whenever one did wrong, she pleaded another punishment for them but the king did not listen.This led to less population, the ancestors disappeared to different places in Rwanda, Tanzania, and Kenya. The few that remained only offered gifts to Nalongo instead of the king. Kabaka Kitaka was angry; he felt he was losing power due to Nalongo. He planned on killing her. When Nalongo knew she was going to be sentenced to death, she ran to the present day Fort Portal and hid at "Amabere ga Nyinamwiru" (i.e., Nyinamwiru's breasts). Kiwanuka, one of the elders, later organized the army to fetch Nalongo from Fort Portal to get back to the kingdom because of her good rule. When she returned, she disappeared into the tree planted in remembrance of Kabaka Ndahura, her husband. She started coming in dreams as a sign to help people. She often asked people to pray from the tree and seek her aid. When rumor spread everyone in the kingdom came to the tree to seek aid. This resulted into the name Nakayima meaning the "Savior.".

and feminist leadership characteristics of Nakayima throughout their artistic constructions; and secondly, through the reconstruction of divination, students were compelled by the collective action of worship and thanksgiving to work collaboratively.

The collaborative approach is quite significant in the way the students set up their artwork and how they related to the other groups. Through worship and cultural norms, pilgrims construct elaborate artforms that develop into vast artistic installations over time. These artistic practices are evident at the Nakayima site, and they formed part of the many constructions of Nakayima as a goddess and as a historical character. The collaborative nature of the pilgrims in constructing the powerful character of Nakayima through art making was adapted by the students in building their collaborative works. The iterations, methodologies, and technologies employed by the Ugandan students created a new dimension to which the narrative of Nakayima, as a fable, was reconstructed. Each student group constructed an artwork based on their reinterpretation of the Nakayima narrative, which had been a story of sorcery and deception. It was a new revelation to perceive Nakayima as a good spirit who welcomed every person to her fortress.

Set up as pilgrimages, the Ugandan student groups developed images and artwork based on their interpretation of their trip to the Nakayima tree. The main aim was to track and reconstruct the story of Nakayima based on the idea of feminism and remix and how this could be translated in a visual way and then transformed into a visual phenomenon—a counter narrative that erases the assumptions built around Nakayima based on place and context.[3] Thus, the students would ask the question: in which ways does Nakayima become a remix structure and a feminist ideology rather than a local everyday narrative construed as sorcery and witchcraft? Through a tour guide that retold the story of Nakayima during the pilgrimage, students made recordings (video and audial), drawings, sketches, acts, and choreographed reconstructions of the story into their own interpretations. These were discussed further before embarking on any definitive form or action among the group members. The students later analyzed the videos, audios, drawings, acts, and reconstructions of their tale as narrative inquiries for their visual interpretations as collaboratively created art installations. These visual interpretations would form the basis for their group art making and actions.

Ugandan students created collaborative artworks as visual interpretations of the Nakayima narrative. For example, the purpose of the 2022 artwork titled *Bare Respect* (see Figs. 1, 2, and 3) involved people walking on the art in an interactive way through removal of shoes, which were placed on the side of the walkway, as if walking towards the projection of the Nakayima tree to show respect. The authors (Makabayi Herbert, Mugalu Hakeem, Naginda Lydia Cindy, Namutosi Rebecca, Apio Caroline Sherry, Atekaniza Nelson, Kalungi Edwin, Lubega Farouk, Luyimbazi Ibrahim, and Wantimba Swaibu, 2022) explained their art as follows:

---

[3] Feminism, particularly ecofeminism, raises feminist bioethic questions with regards to gender bias and power imbalances, and human rights and environmental crises [17]. Early works revealed how capitalist domination hierarchies equated women with nature, and the patriarchal view that both need to be controlled and subordinated by men [18, 19]. With a posthumanist turn, ecofeminist bioethics rejects conceptions of ecofeminism based on the beliefs of biological determinism and essentialist naturalism and instead seeks to decenter human domination of nature and work toward rights of nature [20–24].

The title takes the inspiration from the fact that people have to walk "bare-foot" as a sign of "respect" as it's a taboo for one to approach the Nakayima tree with their shoes on their feet. This project is an interactive art piece that even the viewer can contribute. This is because the project gradually builds up as viewers take off their shoes adding them along the aisle. This is a repetitive process that leaves the artwork building and breaking down simultaneously. However, the main emphasis of this artwork is to stress the taboo of not removing shoes while approaching the Nakayima tree. The taboo applies for all groups of people from different backgrounds, religions, and social status.

The students built a collection of images, videos, audio, and interview scripts with which they drew inspiration about bare respect. From these materials, they developed processes through which they were able to reconstruct the Nakayima narrative. They bought a piece of white cloth, sixteen meters long, and lay it almost the whole length of the gallery. They chose white as the color of the cloth to symbolize purity. On this piece of white cloth, the students reconstructed the pathway to the Nakayima tree. Shoes, both physical and implied, modelled out of clay, lay along the trajectory of the white piece of cloth. Not only does Nakayima presuppose remix culture, Nakayima epitomizes equity and bioethics. Ethical dilemmas—the do's and don'ts that apply to everyone—in Nakiyama narratives address taboos from a feminist equity lens. Kabiito emphasized that the purpose of the Ugandan students' collaborative art was to develop equitable perspectives based in the bioethics of the Nakayima narrative.

Fig. 1. *Bare Respect* portrays one of the most significant taboos at the Nakayima tree in that pilgrims should remove their shoes to access the grounds and most especially the main room where Nakayima is said to have disappeared.

In *Rooms of Mystery*, the Ugandan students based their interpretation on the belief that goddess Nakayima is a mediator between the gods and the people. This is symbolically depicted in their artwork (see Figs. 4 and 5). They placed the calabash in the center of

Fig. 2. A student walks on the run-way piece of cloth. Shoes are placed on the side of the white runway as symbol of respect. This artwork is dynamic as it develops with the continued traffic on the "runway."

the main room of the gallery right below the light (the light standing in for Nakayima) to show that the source of power and connection is drawn from the goddess Nakayima. The light symbolizes the goddess Nakayima, yet the calabash symbolizes the nine rooms surrounding the Nakayima tree. The shields, on the other hand, represent the protection offered by the Kiganda god of war, Kiwanuka. The shields surround the tree to protect from all evil-hearted people that might want to deface the tree or cut it down and represent the intercessory protection given by Maama Nakayima toward her believers and the innocent but accused. Notable too, the shields symbolize how African traditions, norms, and beliefs are not taught to other societies, but have been preserved and maintained among people with a common ancestry. There are also significant representations derived from shapes such as the circle, rectangle, and triangle. Circles represent the gathering and unity that is created by the faith. Many people come to the Nakayima tree to get psychological, spiritual, and physical alignment and refreshment. Triangles symbolize strength. The triangle, being the strongest shape and form, is associated with the goddess Nakayima since she is the highest being known by her believers; she is their source of strength. Lines suggest service to the goddess Nakayima that are performed by people upon dreaming or receiving visions of instructions to perform the required tasks.

Maama Nakayima was a woman who is believed to have disappeared into a tree in Mubende district and currently the tree is known as "Omuti gwa Maama Nakayima". Ugandan students created an haute couture dress as a representation of Maama Nakayima's femininity, showing both a modern and traditional representation of "Omuti gwa Maama Nakayima" (see Fig. 6). An haute couture is the creation of exclusive custom fitted high-end fashion design that is constructed by hand from start to finish. The ideology

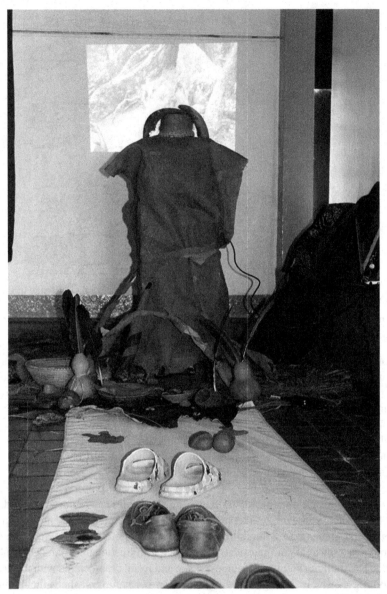

Fig. 3. *Bare Respect* (2022), an art installation, is composed of fabric and traditional artifacts, grass, and shoes. The installation art is 16 × 0.5 m.

of feminism (e.g., women's equal rights) is intended in their representation: although the students decided to create a dress to show her femininity as well. At the base of the dress students made it look like the roots of the actual tree while depicting the nine rooms at the tree. The nine rooms represent the ninety-nine gods that carried out different purposes.

Fig. 4. Makerere University art students created Rooms of Mystery (2022) using metal, barkcloth, bulbs, and gourds.

Maama Nakayima, being a female and a mother, was honored by the Ugandan students for being a selfless provider.

The Ugandan student group (Namirembe Mary Josephine, Nadunga Cynthia, Namuddu Sylvia, Mirembe Faith, Nampeera Tracy Christine, Nanvuma Esther, Ageno Naome, Namulema Anita, and Nassuuna Mariam) added both contemporary (i.e., imported fabrics) and traditional (i.e., Kikooyi, the striped piece of apparel juxtaposed with plain white cloth, and other cultural paraphernalia) materials to symbolize the good side of Maama Nakayima instead of the negative views typically espoused by people that do not believe in the Nakayima spirit. Followers of Nakayima, treat her like a goddess, who brought only good hence the majestic yet traditional appearance. The sculptural installation depicts some of what she bestows to her believers and devotees such as jobs, marriage, love, success, health, among other qualities of life, which are symbolized on the sleeve extension. The crown on her head and the back of the dress have leaves and branches that represent the tree and nature. The head wrap is to show the mixture of different religions since all religions are welcomed at the shrine. The mask is placed on her face as a camouflage since nobody knows her true facial identity. The different fabrics are those worn by the different people present at the tree. The base of the dress which is in the form of roots holds different artifacts that are important to the culture and the people visiting the site. Lastly, the grass on the ground with shoes at the edge shows that the tree area is a holy ground and shoes should be removed before stepping on the grass. The group also performed a short skit, *SEEK AND YOU SHALL FIND*, which incorporated many of the fascinating stories they learned in the midst of their research and exploration of the culture at Nakayima tree in Mubende (see Fig. 7). Additionally, they also acted as pilgrims going to Nakayima to pray for different needs in hopes of receiving them and then later returned to give thanks to her with offerings after receiving what they wanted.

Fig. 5. The *Rooms of Mystery* (2022) close-up shows the shields with circles, triangles, and lines. The installation is made from metal, barkcloth, bulbs, and gourds.

From these three art installations by Ugandan students, the character of Nakayima emerged as a feminist. Further, Kabiito introduced bioethics with the framing of Nakayima as an equitable character. The students considered themselves pilgrims with needs and desires that Maama Nakayima would help to resolve. This would place them at the center of a new frame of mind with which to approach and develop the character of Nakayima. They were then required to construct a character based on their interpretation of Nakayima. Their interpretation would form the basis for construction of an artwork using forms and meanings derived from their expedition. This collaborative knowledge was later transferred to defining different body parts as a larger construction of the Nakayima tree. Each group focused on a segment of the Nakayima tree and collaboratively created works also exhibited in the Makerere Art Gallery as an "exquisite corpse." Students also digitally shared their artworks, as sections of Nakayima tree, with students in Keifer-Boyd's class at Penn State University.

Fig. 6. Students in Makerere University's Bachelor of Industrial and Fine Arts created this haute couture artwork, Obulungi Bwa Maama Nakayima (The Beauty of Maama Nakayima) in 2022.

U.S. Approach to Bioethic Narratives. Keifer-Boyd in the United States introduced bioethics through an activity in which students drew bioethic glasses, first the frames and then bioethical concerns for lenses. Students were able to reflect on bioethical issues important to them as they drew and designed a pair of glasses, like worn to improve vision, or protect eyes (from the sun or dust), or to look "cool." Students shared their drawings as a bioethics lens and then Keifer-Boyd asked that students in her class bring a bioethics perspective into their drawing of a body segment assigned according to how their name was in the alphabetized roster of students, so the first on the list had the top of the head, next had the eyes, another the nose, and so on until the last in the list had feet assigned to draw. For example, how a bioethical lens both influenced what was drawn and how the drawing was interpreted, is conveyed in Riley Cullen's description of his drawing of eyes (see Fig. 8). He stated that the eyes see the world, and the world can see emotions

Fig. 7. One of the students that created this artwork models their haute couture to display the messages about the good deeds of Maama Nakayima.

of the person by looking into their eyes. He shared a story about rude behavior involving a shopping cart and questioned the morals of a person who does malicious acts when thinking they are not being watched, instead of in essence being a caring person.

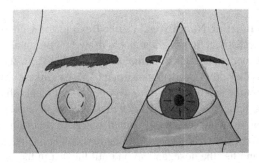

Fig. 8. Riley Cullen's drawing of eyes watching and being watched.

Another example of a bioethics visual narrative is Teghan McIntrye's drawing "Fluidity of the Chest" (see Fig. 9), which concerns how society defines and confines gender as a binary construction of what men's and women's chest should look like. She describes that her drawing of a chest raises the bioethical issue of gender fluidity and how in the medical field there is much discrimination about sexuality and gender, and an increasing socio-political control of the body in the United States and Uganda.

Fig. 9. Teghan McIntyre used markers to draw the chest. Her drawing is one of the elements shared for a bioethics remix of the body.

2.1 Teams Imagine Their Assembled "Remix" Characters' Personality, Beliefs, and History

After the Ugandan and U.S. students created drawings of the body section assigned to them, as facilitators we made sure they uploaded their drawings to a shared online space and labeled the digital file with a number and the name of the body segment. We set up a folder for each class so students could select from each set of body drawings to assemble their character using an image application of their choice to create their remixed assemblage of a character that would be in a story they would collaboratively create.

Students in Keifer-Boyd's class presented their drawings from bioethics perspectives in-person in class and Zoom recorded their presentation as well as the discussion that followed facilitated by Keifer-Boyd. They edited their recording to capture the essence of a bioethics narrative and included the audio and drawing on their page of the exhibition website. Since the pandemic, the use of Zoom has become familiar and even when all are present in class, rather than move to a podium to present, students sit around a large seminar table and no matter where a student sits, they can join the class Zoom link and present their work from their laptop on the larger monitor in the room via Zoom screen sharing.

We organized teams comprised of one or two students from Penn State (as there were more students in the new media course than in the Makerere University course) and a student from Makerere University. We asked the teams to schedule times to meet and record the bioethic narratives of their body segment drawing. The recordings were also included on the team's page of the exhibition website. Students could listen to the audio recordings by the artist in discussion of their work in the process of selecting drawings to assemble into a character.

Once each student in both the Makerere and Penn State courses had a remix character, the Penn State student team member added to their team's webpage using a template Keifer-Boyd had set up with a slider for images and audio-track sections; and a text box to add title, team members' names, keywords, and a question in relation to their bioethics audio-visual narratives (see Fig. 10). The teams scheduled one to three Zoom meetings to record the Makerere student discussion of their body segment drawing. Next, each team member contributed to the development of their remix characters in terms of imagining the characters' personality, history, and beliefs from its visual features and bioethics intent as previously recorded, and finally with shared constructions of the remix characters' personality, history, and beliefs, they recorded a story they generated together. As they met to Zoom record, they could screenshare and look closely at the body segment drawings and their remix characters.

2.2   Teams Imagine Place, Time, Action of Characters, and Create a Story

When schedules did not allow time to meet for Zoom recordings, which was a challenge to find given the time zone difference of seven hours and different holiday schedules. The Ugandan team member sent text responses to include in the image slider or elsewhere on the team's webpage as part of the exhibition website. In what follows are three examples of the process of teams co-creating bioethic narratives.

Teghan McIntyre from Penn State and Claire Nakaddu from Makerere University, as a transcultural team, found time to meet and record their dialogue via Zoom [25]. Claire's drawing of a sad face with tear looks directly at the viewer and wears a mask of a bashful smile covering half of the sad face. The face with mask has Medusa-like hair of snakes and a dragon ferocious face with sharp fangs suggesting power to petrify viewers. In discussion of her remix character's personality that includes Claire's drawing of a head, Claire describes that in the Baganda culture, one should not cry unless there is good reason. If one cries without reason, Claire explains, it is like you want everyone in your family to die. Teghan stated that she agrees with Claire that both of their remix characters appear to be strong with two sides to themselves, and perhaps came from a place where they needed to have strength as well as be able to shield and protect themselves. Teghan speculates that both their characters are from ancient histories and is reminded of images she has seen in art history texts. Further, she suggests that their remix characters might be like them with personalities that are versatile, some days sad, other days happy, or sad on the inside yet show a happy person on the outside. Maybe, she posits, their remix characters, and their selves, believe in being strong for others.

Teghan McIntyre & Claire Nakaddu

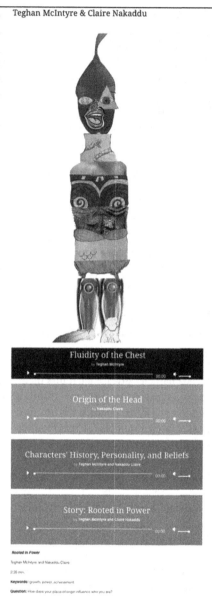

Fig. 10. A screenshot of one team's webpage for the online exhibition shows one of the images of a remix character by a team member, as well as the audio-tracks for each in the team's audio description of their drawing of a body section (e.g., chest by Teghan McIntyre and head by Claire Nakaddua), an audio-track for their recording of character development, and an audio-track for their co-created story involving their remix characters. Under the four audio-tracks the students included their names, keywords, and a question to engage viewers.

Their story begins with where their remix characters came from, which they decided was from an ancient tree. They emerged as tiny organisms that began to grow from their feet up suggested by the roots that entangle their feet and legs. Their lives were not easy, but they were important people because they were rulers of kingdoms. The kingdoms waited a long time for these leaders as they knew they would be slowly growing out of a tree. However, when they did fully develop, they were more powerful than the people of the kingdom imagined they would be. The leaders warn the people if they have anything that disturbs them, they should stand strong rooted in their power. The remix characters' achievements and successes are all rooted in where they came from, which enabled them to know the people (read their minds) and to lead the kingdoms to success. The bioethics type question they pose on their webpage is: How does your place of origin influence who you are?

The transcultural team comprised of Jessica Wilde and Makenna Sterling from Penn State and Wanyama Boniface from Makerere University posted statements and questions on their exhibition page as well as recorded their meeting together discussing their drawings from bioethical perspectives, their remix assembled characters, and a story with the characters. The team asked: Have you ever met someone that is two-faced who smiles while hiding secrets from you? Boniface responds that some men believe women are snakes, they can change all the time. Jessica adds a visible glow surrounding her remix character to challenge the assumption that women are snakes. She further adds light to the characters hands to suggest a superhero (see Fig. 11). Working to develop a bioethics narrative with their remix characters, they emphasized, as did several of the other groups, a two-faced character. However, each group had different interpretations and versions of the two-faced character given each remix incorporated different drawings of body segments. This team discussed that one face is smiling at the viewer and another is thinking otherwise. With the mask, the character is not sure whether she wants to be a villain or superhero. The assembled remix character's bioethical choice is between being good or evil [26]. The team also asked: "Do you abide by socio-cultural expectations for use of right or left hands for certain activities?" In Uganda, hands are used for particular activities, especially the right hand is usually used for domestic activities. It would actually be strange for one to greet with the left hand, even in the United States, just as it is in Uganda where the right hand is used in many cultural activities as normative. Indeed, the drawing portrays a left hand that would be turned back to the right hand, lest it becomes a curse in African tradition.

Alien Remix Character Goes to Earth, is the title of the collaboratively created story by Kisakye Damawe Eve from Makerere University and Samantha Reilly and Kelsey Over from Penn State in Fall 2022 [27]. Their story involves two characters, a male alien whose parents brought him to Earth and a two-faced young woman. Kelsey described the exposed ribs of the character in their story, possibly from starvation or malnutrition, is a reason that he is ridiculed at school because he looked different. Samantha described the hip of a mermaid tail that disappears into the ocean. Damawe stated that her drawing of a chest both front view and side view had no story. Because the remixed body appeared disjointed and yet connected in random ways, Damawe felt the character looked like it was out of this world. As they shaped their story from a close read of the remix characters, they conceptualized a talkative alien with mouth open that could live under the sea. The

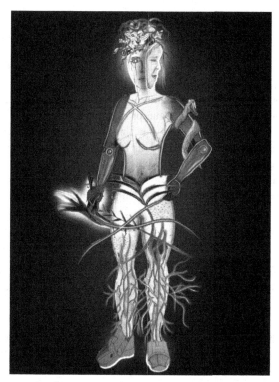

Fig. 11. The digitally created remix by Jessica Wilde (2022) is comprised of drawings from students at Penn State in the U.S. and Makerere University in Uganda.

two-faced woman character they perceived was shy, wearing a mask that covers the face. They speculated the character could be a queen with a good and bad side. Each in the team of three students contributed, in a remix style of character and story development, to raise bioethical issues of alienation, homelessness, and conditions that might make a person both good and evil. The discussion demonstrates how the remix new media collaborative art process generated multifaceted ideas, yet the group seemed to agree with each other's portrayal and were inclusive of all the ideas. In the end, they asked how could the classroom be more inclusive?

3   Exhibition

The exhibition [18] with stories collaboratively created involving remix characters by students in the United States and Uganda motivated transcultural dialogue with new media. Holding an opening event for the exhibition of the Remix Exquisite Bioethics Transcultural Dialogue project required scheduling when both classes could attend, collaboratively creating a poster to announce the opening of the exhibition, and completing all work for the exhibition.

Due to a seven-hour time difference, it was challenging to find a time for all students to meet via Zoom for the online opening of the exhibition. Students in the United States were scheduled to attend Keifer-Boyd's class sessions in the evening, which was the middle of the night for Ugandan students. During the day U.S. students had other classes and work schedules. Likewise, it was difficult to have the students at Makerere University attend via Zoom when scheduled late in their day as some live off-campus without Internet access. The seven-hour difference was overcome with use of social media platforms, such as Whatsapp, which does not require synchronistic meeting. However, we have discovered in prior transcultural dialogue projects that the live real-time sessions are rewarding for students in Uganda and the United States as they seem to appreciate interacting in a classroom situation where both facilitators are present even though online. Nevertheless, coordinating everybody to be present at the same time is a difficult task. Many times, we have had students not able to join due to the time difference. Therefore, we record the meetings for review by those unable to attend and students have been able to communicate asynchronistically through other means such as WhatsApp, email, blogs, and Google Drive. However, as facilitators, we met periodically via Zoom to coordinate and collaborate with the transcultural dialogue new media project.

Kabiito's group concluded the project by holding a local exhibition and an online exhibition. The Nakayima pilgrimage amounted to an exhibition of 12 collaborative multimedia artworks that was shown at the Makerere Art Gallery. The students expressed an upbeat attitude as did the facilitator. The exquisite bioethics remix characters and stories culminated into an online exhibition with the Penn State students. In both instances, the ideas of collaboration and remix were well-received by the students. Through these collaborative works, students have expanded their knowledge of how their counterparts conducted narrative inquiry of bioethics in their remix art.

For the Penn State students, the opening of the online exhibition, while scheduled at noon on a Friday with some Ugandan students conveying that they could attend, none did. Although disappointing to not have their team member present, the Penn State students presented their work to each other, listened to the recorded presentations of Ugandan students, and provided a link to a recording of the opening event to their collaborators. Moreover, the exhibition is available to visit beyond the opening and for many years ahead. Having an exhibition and opening event brought excitement and commitment to the project.

One Penn State class session was devoted to collaboratively creating a poster to announce the exhibition opening event (see Fig. 12). Working together around the seminar table, each student volunteered for a task that drew upon their strengths such as writing about the exhibition, gathering the remix characters, designing the title, finding a police lineup height measuring wall chart, and assembling the parts together. Perhaps the remix process throughout the semester brought a sense of comfort and joy in working together toward a shared goal. There was laughter and appreciation expressed for each other during the poster making class session.

To conclude the exhibition, and this essay, we invite readers to visit the exhibition and leave comments on the exhibition blog responding to the prompt: What ethical concerns are raised in the bioethic narratives in this exhibition? [28]. A conversational performative recording is linked on the discussion board, which is a form of cultural critique in that more than one perspective is included, often as counterpoints, and readers are invited to participate in the dialogue.

Fig. 12. The Penn State student co-created poster to announce their exhibition was a play on a popular 1995 film, *The Usual Suspects*, nominated for two Academy Awards.

References

1. Keifer-Boyd, K., Kabiito, R.: Uganda-US creative collaborations in media arts. In: Knochel, A.D., Sahara, O. (eds.) Global Media Arts Education: Mapping Global Perspectives of Media Art Education, pp. 267–283. Springer, Cham (2023). https://doi.org/10.1007/978-3-031-05476-1_16
2. Kabiito, R., Liao, C., Motter, J., Keifer-Boyd, K.: Transcultural dialogue mashup. J. Interact. Technol. Pedagogy 6 (2014). http://jitp.commons.gc.cuny.edu/transcultural-dialogue-mashup/
3. Kochhar-Lindgren, K.: Towards a communal body of art: the exquisite corpse and Augusto Boal's theatre. Angelaki J. Theor. Humanit. **7**(1), 217–226 (2002)
4. Gotlib, A.: Feminist ethics and narrative ethics. In: The Internet Encyclopedia of Philosophy (2022)
5. Keifer-Boyd, K.: Feminist counter-narratives in visual culture. Vis. Cult. Gender **17**, 1–5 (2022)
6. Keifer-Boyd, K.: Transcultural dialogues. Revista Gearte **5**(3), 439–448 (2018)
7. Denzin, N., Lincoln, Y.: Handbook of Critical and Indigenous Methodologies. Sage, Thousand Oaks (2008)

8. Thomas, T.: Race and remix: the aesthetics of race in the visual and performing arts. In: Navas, E., Gallagher, O., Burrough, X. (eds.) Routledge Companion to Remix Studies, pp. 179–191. Routledge, New York (2015)
9. Lessing, L.: REMIX: Making Art and Commerce Thrive in the Hybrid Economy. The Penguin Press, London (2008)
10. Ibid
11. Keifer-Boyd, K., Liao, C.: Feminism. In: Navas, E., Gallagher, O., Burrough, X. (eds.) Keywords in Remix Studies, pp. 147–157. Taylor & Francis/Routledge, New York (2018)
12. Paatela-Nieminen, M., Keifer-Boyd, K.: Transcultural intra-action. In: Kallio-Tavin, M., Pullinen, J. (eds.) Conversations on Finnish Art Education, pp. 304–317. Aalto ARTS Books, Helsinki (2015)
13. Laxton, S.: Surrealism at Play. Duke University Press, Durham (2019)
14. Navas, E., Gallagher, O., Burrough, X. (eds.): Routledge Companion to Remix Studies. Routledge, New York (2015)
15. Keifer-Boyd, K.: Immersive feminist remix: an affect dissonance methodology. In: Navas, E., Gallagher, O., Burrough, X. (eds.) The Routledge Handbook of Remix Studies and Digital Humanities, pp. 80–94. Routledge, New York (2021)
16. Russell, B.: Appropriation is activism. In: Navas, E., Gallagher, O., Burrough, X. (eds.) Routledge Companion to Remix Studies, pp. 217–223. Routledge, New York (2015)
17. Ryder, S.S.: A bridge to challenging environmental inequality: intersectionality, environmental justice, and disaster vulnerability. Soc. Thought Res. **34**, 8–115 (2017)
18. Nelson, H.L.: Feminist bioethics: where we've been, where we're going. Metaphilosophy **31**(5), 492–508 (2000)
19. Plumwood, V.: Feminism and ecofeminism: Beyond the dualistic assumptions of women, men and nature. Ecologist **22**(1), 8–13 (1992)
20. Cuomo, C.J.: Feminism and Ecological Communities: An Ethic of Flourishing. Routledge (1998)
21. Estévez-Saá, M., Lorenzo-Modia, M.J.: The ethics and aesthetics of eco-caring: contemporary debates on ecofeminism(s). Women's Stud. **47**(2), 123–146 (2018)
22. Foster, E.: Ecofeminism revisited: critical insights on contemporary environmental governance. Fem. Theory **22**(2), 190–205 (2021)
23. Gaard, G.: Ecofeminism revisited: Rejecting essentialism and re-placing species in a material feminist environmentalism. Fem. Form. **23**(2), 26–53 (2011)
24. Kheel, M.: Nature Ethics: An Ecofeminist Perspective. Rowman & Littlefield (2008)
25. McIntyre, T., Nakaddu, C.: Rooted in power (2022). https://sites.psu.edu/uganda/prompts/teghan/. Accessed 9 June 2023
26. Kisakye, D.E., Reilly, S., Over, K.: Alien remix character goes to Earth (2022). https://sites.psu.edu/uganda/prompts/kelsey/. Accessed 7 June 2023
27. Remix exquisite bioethics transcultural dialogue exhibition (2022). https://sites.psu.edu/uganda/. Accessed 7 June 2023
28. Remix exquisite bioethics transcultural dialogue exhibition discussion board (2022). https://sites.psu.edu/uganda/2022/12/02/stories/#comments. Accessed 9 June 2023

Using Web Analytics Methods to Design Open Web-Based University Courses: Case Study on Creative Work with Information Course

Michal Černý[✉] [iD]

Masaryk University in Brno, Brno, Czech Republic
mcerny@phil.muni.cz

Abstract. Hypertext-based or web-based courses are a specific category of e-learning courses for which students do not have to register anywhere. For the actual operation, content management systems (CRM systems) are used to structure the content graphically and efficiently, work quickly with the universal design concept, or ensure responsive course design. While with conventional e-learning platforms or MOOC course tools, content creators can work with relatively well-structured data from their analytical tools and rely on standard web analytics methods. The study analyses the use of Google Analytics for the design of web-based courses using the example of one hypertext course (Creative Information Work). The study answers questions about how web analytics metrics can be used to design course content and format and to support the search for appropriate synchronous educational supplements. The study highlights the variability of each category and the potential of Google Analytics to serve as a tool for a design approach to developing educational objects of this kind.

Keywords: web-based courses · OER · Google Analytics · Learning analytics · hypertext textbooks · design process

1 Introduction

Web-based courses are a specific form of e-learning. Andreson [1] sees them as an evolutionary form of educational content that continues the text, which is understood in a new and more profound way. Thurmond [2] discusses the web becoming a primary asynchronous learning site. McKimm et al. [3] point out that when using web-based courses, learners can access a vast amount of additional information through hypertext, fundamentally transforming the whole nature of learning [4]. Hodges [5] arguments out that such courses require different competencies and skills than regular study. Brown [6] points out in his study that web-based courses can be more easily designed to meet the needs of learners and educators because they allow for a differentiated approach to learning content. Although some authors understand the concept of web-based courses to include courses in tools such as Zoom [7], our idea will more closely follow what is sometimes referred to as hypertextbooks [8–10]. The referenced authors see these as a standard form of university educational content that must be created, designed and evaluated in a specific way [11, 12].

Ł. Tomczyk (Ed.): NMP 2022, CCIS 1916, pp. 221–236, 2023.
https://doi.org/10.1007/978-3-031-44581-1_16

The methodological approaches we analyse are specific in that we systematically work with open courses [13]. The availability of online educational content allows us to adapt the content to a known target audience [14, 15] and a more comprehensive range of random visitors. Thus, principles describing the appropriate design of learning objects based on micro-learning [16, 17] or nano-learning [18, 19] enter the design process of the whole course. When we work in the text with the concept of "learner", we mean every site user, as we cannot differentiate between them.

Standard tools for working with learning analytics [20–22] rely on students logging into a particular system and their authorisation and authentication data, forming a basic structure that allows for linking data about a specific user's behaviour into a single entity. In this way, a reasonably comprehensive picture can be obtained of why students fail courses [23] or how they interact with interactive elements [24, 25]. In the case of web-based coursework, we have no such information, and standard learning analytics practices must be re-evaluated. Consistent data on student behaviour is relatively scarce, which leads to the need to choose other means of analysing learning behaviour.

Essentially, web analytics tools are the only tools to work with data on student interaction with course websites. Their use for many standard commercial situations is well described in the literature [26, 27]. Still, using Google Analytics in education is relatively limited and often associated with their implementation in MOOCs [28, 29]. However, this implies an entirely different situation, or we may see their use in marketing educational activities [30].

Mc Guckin & Crowley [31] were among the first to develop the concept of using Google Analytics for website-based courses. Moissa et al. [32] have published their analytics solution, an approach that may seem suitable in the context of European (and from 2022 onwards, Czech) policies related to cookie bars. According to the current European legislation, using Google Analytics with user approval on the website is only possible. In the case of our courses, it constitutes a drop of more than half of the visitors in visible data. Luo et al. [33] offer the first systematic use of Google Analytics, and in many ways, we will build on this study, however trivial its practical empirical conclusions. Romanowski and Konak [34] consider web analytics a relevant, albeit interpretation-intensive, tool for studying user behaviour.

This study will describe the metrics and concepts associated with web analytics tools that can be applied to open web or hypertext courses concerning their design. We will be interested in what tools and metrics can be followed to create a course that is of high quality and whose design is based on available data. As we follow the general design process [35] for web-based courses, we will illustrate each metric with some of the data we have been able to collect during the development of such courses. Their role will be illustrative, and our goal will not be to analyse specific data but to develop a methodological approach.

2   Methodology

We will use data from a web-based "Information Work Course" course. The course is offered at the university as a required elective or elective course, is fully distance learning, and makes full use of the essential characteristics of a web-based course -

it works with a variety of media, individual texts are hyperlinked and linked to other materials, and students complete assignments and tests (once every 14) as part of their study, but the study is primarily asynchronous. The course is built on the Umbraco content management system, corresponding to the university's unified CRM system. Assignments and tests are implemented in the university's proprietary system.

The course is designed as an open course; it is free to follow and can be accessed from the website https://kisk.phil.muni.cz/kreativita. Google Analytics 3 was used for data collection, which can be considered a standard in this field. The main disadvantage of this tool is the need to transfer data to Google, which complicates the work with analytics cookies. The estimated losses of between 50–60% are also reflected in the data presented in Table 1. Since we have data from the beginning of 2021, we will focus our analysis on data for the last three years (2021–2023). If we talk about the total amount of data (without distinguishing the years), we can say that the sample size corresponds to 20 789 users and 101 994 course pages viewed (Fig. 1). Thus, we have relatively large data collected over a time scale of three years. In this respect, the data and our findings are unique.

The numbers of students are shown by the years we worked with them in Table 1. The discrepancy between the data for 2021 and 2022 is due to the national implementation of the European Directive on protecting users' data, which means that students must agree in the cookie bar to use cookies. The look and feel of the website have undergone a graphical redesign (from 2021 to 2022), but the website's structure, the number of pages and the content (apart from minor updates) have remained the same.

Table 1. Data from Google Analytics and University Information System for 2021–2023. Data are for the first month of study (always February 20 - March 20). The number of students corresponds to the number of university students enrolled in the course.

Year	Number of students	All users			Without immediate abandonment		
		Users of	Pages per 1 session	Session duration	Users of	Pages per 1 session	Session duration
2021	63	1823	3,09	3:58	445	7,21	11:49
2022	90	676	4,62	6:44	240	8,51	13:58
2023	134	748	4,42	5:58	298	7,61	12:11

Table 1 proves two data types from Google Analytics - all and no immediate abandonment. The second category shows (with some degree of imprecision) the behaviour of those who study the course. In the first group, we must include users who visit the site for one specific topic or information. Both groups of users are methodologically valuable to us.

In formulating the research questions, it was worked primarily with inspiration from the studies of Luo et al. [33] and Romanowski and Konak [34]. Combined with the data we had available from Google Analytics, the following three research questions were formulated.

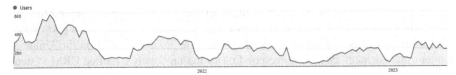

Fig. 1. Weekly course user numbers between 1 January 2021 and 19 April 2023. The decrease between 2021 and 2022 is due to a change in the acceptance of cookies and tracking codes. However, it is realistically associated with the increased number of courses students.

1. What data can be used to design course content?
2. What data can be used for the look and feel of the course?
3. What data can be used to support learning in the course further?

The results section is structured according to these three questions.

2.1　Limits and Ethics of Research

The fundamental limitations of our research are related to the instrument itself or instead to the combination of the instrument and European and Czech regulatory standards. The user must explicitly allow cookies to work with the data. In other websites operated by the university, this means a drop in data of about half, which reduces representativeness (specific user demographics are more likely to agree than others) and the overall explanatory power of the data. At the same time, the bar does not address a significant part of the problems associated with GDPR.

This limit is evident when comparing Fig. 1 and Table 1 - although the number of students more than doubles between 2021–2023 (213%), the number of measured Google Analytics users is only 67%. This difference may be significant in identifying selected trends, but the data collected over a long time is sufficient for the actual course design. The data allows the parameters discussed (Results section) to be monitored with the knowledge that they may be burdened with systematic error. On the other hand, we are still working with at least a third of the users, which creates sufficient data support for most educational design activities.

Therefore, the university plans to gradually migrate the Matomo analytical tool running on local servers, but this does not mean our research conclusions are irrelevant. Working with their simple transfer will be challenging and methodologically trivial. The university environment is one of many that are gradually moving away from working with Google Analytics or supplementing it with other tools.

The data from our research can thus be adjusted (in future) by the correction offered by data collection in local tools (Matomo). It is impossible to estimate the error rate precisely - we know that we measure between a third and half of the users, but the specific selection function of this selection is unknown. Methodologically, however, Matomo and Google Analytics can follow identical approaches.

Another limitation is the issue of data reliability - for example, if users use a VPN, they can influence the geolocation data. Our research data shows that users use a variety of locations or connections with dynamic IP addresses to access the course, which makes it difficult to build models of individual user behaviour.

Regarding research ethics, we are working with a technical solution (it is impossible to operate data collection without cookie approval). All data is fully anonymised, and linking it to specific users is impossible. This means that Google Analytics can effectively work with course design rather than a specific user or model their behaviour.

3 Results

The results of the study will be structured through individual research questions. The chapter's structure corresponds to the study's aim - to illustrate ways to use web analytics tools to work with web-based course design using specific data. While we will present parameters that are relevant for medium-sized courses, such as our test course "Creative Information Work", it is clear that for significantly more minor courses, it would be necessary to choose different metrics and tools and that for courses, on the contrary, that have more users (students), it would be possible to work more with tools such as A/B testing or more careful analysis of individual segments of interest for which we do not have - given the size of the course - sufficient data.

3.1 Data Can be Used for Course Content Design

The first metric offered for content analysis is time spent on a particular page. If the individual pages were balanced in terms of content (number of videos, length of texts, etc.), it would be possible to compare the time users spend on them. Our previous results suggest that, given these conditions, time correlates relatively strongly with student success on tests. Given that we do not have a sufficiently homogeneous course (individual topics vary in length, some contain videos, and others do not), we can orient the content in terms of the number of visits to each topic - those with a high number of visits will be more attractive than those with fewer. However, we have to be cautious in analysing the results. As the semester progresses, the number of users who study the course decreases (dropout, decreasing motivation), and the question for designers is how to set the time window appropriately. Some content pages may engage in the long term, others only if the student attends the course. The situation is illustrated in Table 2, which again takes data from the first month of the semester, i.e. from February 20 to March 20.

Table 2. The table shows the percentages of traffic from the total site traffic. The five monitored sites are selected based on 2023 and its five most visited content sites.

Topic/year	2023	2022	2021
How to create mind maps	4,98	4,26	17,34
What is this teaching	4,31	3,33	3,01
Creativity	3,75	4,33	3,42
Continuous learning	3,52	3,22	2,61
Drill	3,47	3,58	2,51

To make it easier to compare courses, we work with percentages of total traffic in Table 2. Interpreting the data is not trivial. For example, the enormously high traffic to "How to create mind maps" in 2021 is since an external source (a Google Classroom course from an unknown institution) linked directly to the page. Still, this overview provides interesting data, especially if we can look away from individual years and the traffic in a longer-term perspective (1/1/2021–19/4/2023), as shown in Table 3.

Table 3. Characteristics of the most visited content pages in the course between 1/1/2021 and 4/19/2023. In the context of other data, the table shows the attractiveness of practical, creative techniques and practices well known to the public.

Topic/year	View	Display in %	Average time on page	Percentage of departures
How to create mind maps	15847	15,57	3:48	78,88
RWCT	3414	3,36	1:47	54,66
Creative diary	2784	2,74	4:16	62,57
What is creative writing?	2309	2,27	2:47	50,41
Automatic writing and rhythm writing	2066	2,03	3:02	41,63

Table 3 shows several vital elements. The high dropout rate means that students and casual visitors (for the former, about 80% are visitors going directly to the site, not systematically studying students) often enter the content from external sources (dominated by Google or links from articles on other sites or educational environments). Interestingly, these are also the sources from which visitors to the content are generated. In general, the data in our case allow us to formulate the following conclusions:

- There is a demand from external visitors for specific practical, general knowledge topics. It works more with other interesting topics than content-related ones but is not so attractive or well-known.
- For internal students, there is not a sharp distinction between more theoretical and more practical topics, but they need to be linked.
- The popularity of topics among students changes over time.
- Suppose we follow the topic of information architecture. In that case, it is possible to say that it would make sense to work both with thematic structuring (logical construction resulting from a general pedagogical conclusion) and with linking more generally known topics for specific categories of visitors.

Although it is not explicitly shown in the data, our previous research shows that two other factors have an extreme influence on how visited each page is - the location on the page, which partially constrains the design of this course, and most importantly, the topic title. The choice of title is a crucial factor that academics may underestimate, but it plays a vital role in the design of course content.

In terms of content, it may be interesting to observe two more essential parameters. The first is externally conceived interest, i.e. what keywords users search for when they get to the site. In our case, however, the relevant data is unavailable - 99.75% have the parameter set to (not provided). The second source is Google's analysis focused on user interests. The data yield could be higher, but it provides insight into the underlying user interests.

Table 4. The table captures the ten most essential segments of user interest and the basic characteristics of their study between January 1 2021, and April 19 2023.

Category	Users of	Visit	Immediate abandonment	Average session duration
Food & Dining/Cooking Enthusiasts/30-min Chefs	4 400(4,69%)	6 427(4,25%)	71,70%	3:03
Media & Entertainment/Book Lovers	4 230(4,51%)	6 856(4,53%)	66,61%	3:35
Lifestyles & Hobbies/Green Living Enthusiasts	3 586(3,83%)	5 748(3,80%)	68,35%	3:10
Media & Entertainment/Music Lovers	3 488(3,72%)	6 198(4,10%)	65,12%	3:52
Media & Entertainment/Movie Lovers	3 077(3,28%)	5 533(3,66%)	64,41%	3:53
Lifestyles & Hobbies/Art & Theater Aficionados	2 954(3,15%)	5 210(3,44%)	64,51%	3:49
Shoppers/Shopping Enthusiasts	2 886(3,08%)	4 719(3,12%)	66,69%	3:51
Shoppers/Value Shoppers	2 822(3,01%)	4 613(3,05%)	67,37%	3:42
Travel/Travel Buffs	2 779(2,96%)	4 503(2,98%)	67,36%	3:33
Beauty & Wellness/Beauty Mavens	2 726(2,91%)	4 350(2,88%)	68,02%	3:17

Table 4 shows that in the top ten areas of user interest (drawn from 38% of visitors), there is a reasonably significant balance in the proportions of users, visits, immediate abandonment and average length of visit. The parameter variability appears more due to random variation or different landing pages than the site's content suited to a particular target group. Nevertheless, looking at the structure, it is easy to construct the personas for which the content is shaped - most users are (given the university nature of the course) from cities in the Czech Republic (the course is in Czech, which represents a significant limit for external visitors), 68% are female, and 32% are male. In terms of age, most users are in the 25–34 age range (25%), followed by 18–24 (22%) and 35–44 (18%). Therefore, this data allows the content creators to think relatively plastic about the course's language, style, examples or visual design. The ability to draw on examples from culture or cooking provides exciting information for our particular course.

3.2 Data Can be Used for Course Design and Features

The second group of data that we can use to work with the course are those related to the technical equipment of the learners. A basic understanding of these can be critical, for example, for thinking about the importance of responsive elements or what technologies can be used for online course design.

Our course shows an exciting characteristic regarding data on user behaviour with mobile devices and desktops. The overall data return rate is about 52% - overall, mobile is more significant when comparing visits (34.2%) versus 17.7% for desktop. Students use the desktop more during the semester (due to the need to complete assignments and tests), but mobile phone access is dominant outside of that. Self-interest is, therefore, more associated with mobile phone visits. This is even though the time spent on the site is significantly shorter on mobile phones (1:43) compared to 11:33 on desktop, and the number of pages per session is significantly lower for mobile devices 1.75:7.39. The data from previous research shows that mobile users go to a course for specific information (they need to follow the broader context or the content they are currently looking for). In contrast, a traditional computer is used for focused and systematic reading or study, often in a broader context. This finding is interesting in the context of studies pointing to the fact that reading on a computer is not focused and ideal for many reasons.

In this context, web design must be constructed responsively to meet the needs of mobile users (for whom good structuring of content on the page itself is crucial) and desktop users.

Regarding the screen resolution for which the course needs to be adapted, we will work with the data in Table 5. It shows that the dominant resolutions are 1536×864 and 1920×1080, both for working with content (widescreen) and the need to work with responsive design. Dominant means less than 40%. In terms of colour depth, monitors with 24-bit colour depth are still the most represented (88% in 2021, 81% in 2022 and 78% in 2023). Even though the number of devices with higher colour depth is increasing, working with graphics of such quality could be more meaningful (yet), considering the high share of mobile devices and the data intensity of such elements.

Chrome has a substantial share among browsers, ahead of Safari, Edge and Firefox. We typically use this information in the course to recommend specific browser extensions or workflows. The data also shows that Firefox's share is low, and realistically it only makes sense to optimise for the kernels associated with Chrome and Safari. Of similar relevance to us is that the information system information and recommendations on selected Windows software had shares of 55% in 2023 (83% on desktop, however), 57% (or 85%) in 2022 and 65% (or 86%) in 2021. It is apparent that Windows is holding its

Table 5. The table shows the percentage of users with a screen resolution each year.

Resolution/year	2023	2022	2021
1536 × 864	19,58	20,95	20,42
1920 × 1080	18,13	13,01	15,75
1280 × 720	6,96	8,67	7,93
1440 × 900	6,7	6,07	6,08
414 × 896	4,6	3,18	1,74
1366 × 768	3,55	7,66	12,2
390 × 844	3,55	2,17	0,16

share on desktop, and the increase in mobile traffic drives the decline. For Android, for example, we can see a high level of fragmentation between versions 10–13 (in shares between 16–28%) in 2023, which significantly reduces the possibility of working with structured instructional content or for app development, for example.

3.3   Data Can be Used to Support Learning in the Course Further

Google Analytics also allows working with selected data valid for blended coursework or working with certain synchronous phases. These are mainly two data sources. The first one is the distribution of users by time of day. We get significantly different results for different years. However, in general, students take the course in the first half of the week (Sunday to Wednesday) and mainly in the afternoon or morning, which could provide information for times when some synchronous part of the course could be implemented. The fact that a relatively large proportion of users work in the course at 8 am is relatively surprising in the context of everyday teaching.

At the same time, it can be seen that these time preferences change over time. The COVID-19 pandemic influenced the year 2021, and studying between 8–10 am can be attributed to an attempt to establish a daily routine or regimen. The focus on Monday's work is due to the deadline for assignment submission. In 2022, there is still a noticeable emphasis on working on Mondays. However, much less so, and it is evident that students also work on assignments on Sundays, and to a lesser extent, on other days, without a sharper preference. The preferred time for students to work is between 10–13 and 4 pm to 9 pm. The year 2023 is then characterised by a significant shift in the centre of gravity, even into the evening hours from 10 am to 10 pm. There are relatively slight variations and work between Sunday and Wednesday, with little variation between Monday and Wednesday. These data show that while students are accommodating the time requirements of the course, finding a date that would suit most of them would be challenging.

The second vital data is geography, i.e. information about the locations users connect, captured in Table 6 and Fig. 2. In the context of this table, it is significant that while the university is located in Brno, the percentage of this city is lower than that of Prague. The data clearly illustrate that while online meetings might be possible, physical meetings would mean that many learners would need to change their location, which may be problematic. In terms of countries, the Czech Republic has a share of 91% (2023), 93% (2022) and 93% (2021), which is a relatively stable figure. In the table, let us also draw attention to the overall column, which aims to capture some global characteristics for the course - the data show that in the non-semester data, there is a substantial share of those educated in Prague and other larger cities, probably at the expense of villages and smaller settlements.

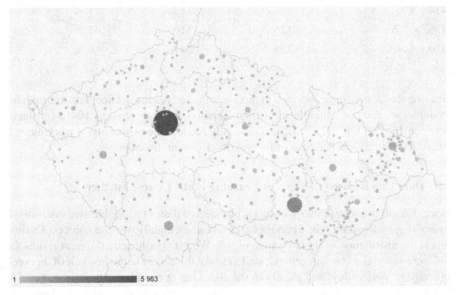

Fig. 2. Map of the distribution of users in cities in the Czech Republic.

On the other hand, in the overall total, large settlements do not have a majority - if we count the shares of the ten largest Czech cities, we get to a share of 50%. About a quarter of the total population of the Czech Republic lives in these cities. Even looking at the data from the larger unit areas, the course has a relatively statistically representative distribution corresponding to the population of the regions in the Czech Republic.

Table 6. The table captures the percentage of essential accesses from cities to the course each year. Data for other locations also show that the course is predominantly an urban affair rather than a university town location.

City/year	2023	2022	2021	Average
Prague	27	29	29	30
Brno	10	19	10	11
České Budějovice	3	3	4	3
Ostrava	3	4	3	3
Olomouc	2	2	2	2
Pilsen	2	1	2	2

4 Discussion

Google Analytics is used in different ways in education and its analysis. Sheu and Sgih [36] offer a similar perspective to this study in that they work with the essential characteristics provided by the tool, such as the age or gender structure of users, mobile versus desktop accesses, etc. In contrast to our results, it is interesting to note that students in Taiwan use significantly fewer mobile devices for learning, and tablets account for almost the same proportion as mobile phones. In our sample, tablets are at the level of statistical error.

Compared to Luo et al. [33], there is a significant shift in the information available in the data. For example, the authors state that one of the limitations is the lack of demographic data that is already available, and the availability of information regarding user interests makes Google Analytics provide a sociological tool that can significantly help with course evaluation and design. This study strongly influenced our selection of sub-tools and metrics that can be used to work with Google Analytics in online course evaluation. At the same time, it is evident that some of the author's interpretations of the learning behaviour pages are simplistic. Our study, therefore, attempts a more nuanced approach to the essential characteristics of attendance (session time, immediate dropout, and interaction). Methodologically, however, we follow a similar approach. We leave aside the flow of visitors to the site from the metrics they examine, as this metric is only partially appropriate given the characteristics of our particular course.

Rohloff et al. [29] point out that Google Analytics can provide relevant information about learning and that in the context of more significant course complexities, a very targeted analogy between buying goods in an e-shop and choosing a course can be used. However, the critical problem lies in the overly complex environment. Regarding the study's findings, Google's new version of Analytics significantly strengthens the ability to create specific views and dashboards, so this criticism partially disappears. However, the requirement to work with and interpret data effectively remains. However, working with a simple course/e-shop analogy is inappropriate as it does not reflect the learning process as a multi-layered complex form of information interaction. Our data show the fundamental possibilities of online course design, especially concerning the appropriate choice of topics and non-linear learning paths, technologies or student interests, allowing for the customised tone of voice. We do not identify and reflect these aspects in the current e-shop in such a way.

Horowitz [37] states in his course evaluation that there is no relationship between the weeks of the semester and page views (literally, he writes: "Table 1 demonstrates the most popular weekly topics were weeks 7, 1, and 13; and that the least engaging weekly topics were weeks 6, 15, and 10." p. 51). Our findings are different in this regard, however - it appears that the relationship is almost inversely proportional, with the possibility that specific factors that disrupt the sequence, such as national holidays (typically Easter, the end of World War II, and Labor Day in the spring semester), or special assignments or other circumstances, may enter into it. However, otherwise, we can observe a gradual decline in all interactions over the semester in all of the courses we observed (not just the "Working with Information" course). This is not just a dropout but a general decline in motivation over the semester.

Research [38] has yielded different results than ours in several respects. First, students study longer from a mobile phone than a desktop in their courses, which is the opposite of our research. Our research shows that studying from a mobile phone leads to fundamentally different study strategies than working with the web. Students often search for one specific piece of information on a mobile phone and scroll quickly otherwise. They also typically follow a linear progression through a course. In contrast, learning on a computer is (on average) more complex and involves searching for broader contexts. Similarly, the authors [38] point to a strong correlation between the choice of web browser and time spent on the site, which needs to be borne out in our case. The distribution of available technologies is similar to our contemporary habits. Contrary to the research [38], our course has more geographically distributed users, unlike Luo et al. [33], primarily within a single country. Here, we lean towards the interpretation of Luo et al. [33] that language accessibility is a crucial parameter.

The selection of the above four studies against which we conducted the discussion was not random. All authors agree that Google Analytics data can be used for effective online course design. If we return to the three research questions we analysed, they can be summarised as follows. In this respect, we substantially extend the essential findings formulated by research [33], which offered a rather general characterization of some web analytics metrics.

Data for course design in terms of content:

- In the case of open web courses, there can be a significant disparity between regular university students and those who come to the web for other reasons or sources. Both target groups must be considered in the environment's design.
- The placement of a particular booth in the site's information architecture and the choice of the title can be a significant source of traffic to individual topics. Working with keywords (especially in the title) is not a matter of SEO but a regulator of learning behaviour.
- Google Analytics provides comprehensive data on user interests, preferences and demographics, allowing for effective didactic choices of examples or adjustments in a tone of voice.

- Essential metrics: time spent on site per session, landing and exit pages, number of pages per interaction, site visitors' interests and demographics.

  Data for the look and feel of the site:

- The data clearly shows that the critical parameter is responsiveness. Users use a variety of screen resolutions as well as desktop and mobile phones as necessary technologies for working with content. Work is needed to balance web development for mobile (and its specific uses) and desktop.
- Mobile users engage with content fundamentally differently than desktop users. This technical knowledge should also be reflected in the information architecture of the entire course.
- The data shows that developing a website on just one technology solution is impossible. Typically, for the desktop, there is a dominant twin of Windows and Chrome (Edge, but technically built on the same core) and Mac OS X and Safari.
- Essential metrics: technology, mobile devices.

  Data for course organisation and study support:

- From the data provided by our research, it can be concluded that users' time preferences change over the years. A crucial piece of information is that Sundays constitute the standard school day. Therefore, students do not perceive it as a day off.
- In terms of geographic location, students make substantial use of the online nature of their studies. Only around 10% of students study long-term in the city where the university runs the course.
- Essential metrics: geographic location, number of users by time of day.

The study demonstrated that Google Analytics data could be used for evaluation, but more importantly, to support the design of web-based courses even outside environments where thousands of users can be counted [29, 33] and, at the same time, go deeper in the analyses than the simple evaluation report of Horowitz [37] does. The study shows that many of the necessary inputs for course design, as considered by design approaches [39–41], can be obtained from Google Analytics, even in courses with less than a hundred students. We see the ability to track student demographics, interests and preferences as key, from general characteristics to selecting topics they work on within their studies. This allows course designers to work effectively with examples, tone of voice [35], and other educational content design practices.

The second aspect that we would like to highlight in the conclusion of the study is the fact that while common approaches to learning analytics [42, 43] track the work of university students, the approach of using web analytics forces designers to work towards a more general barrier removal with universal design in mind [44] - removing barriers or improving a course for the entire student population may be more effective and meaningful than supporting individual students. At the same time, such an approach has many benefits in working with open educational resources [45, 46] and impacting the perception of universities in a socio-cultural context [47].

5 Conclusion

The research has been able to demonstrate unequivocally that data from web analytics can help online course designers to create online courses without the need to burden students through questionnaires or interviews. At the same time, it allows an empirical look at student behaviour and the possibilities of optimising the overall graphic and educational design.

The research identified data sources for all three research questions that can be used in web analytics to measure learning behaviour. The information obtained and discussed in this way is relevant to the work of other designers or researchers who want to focus on designing and developing web-based courses.

There is potential for the methodological approaches we have analysed in the development of open educational resources, where web analytics allows us to track the needs of all users (students) and provide an OER design that allows for the actual implementation of these resources to target groups that would otherwise remain invisible in conventional pedagogical research.

A key challenge in the European environment will be the search for additional tools for obtaining web analytics and their comparison and methodological link with data from Google Analytics. While it is clear that they can still help design web-based courses, having more complete data will represent a significant advance across the European environment.

Acknowledgements. I want to thank Barbora Fukárková for creating the graphic design of the course and the tutors who take care of the students during the course. Without their help, this study could not have been made.

References

1. Anderson, M.D.: Individual characteristics and web-based courses. In: Learning and Teaching on the World Wide Web, pp. 45–72. Academic Press (2001)
2. Thurmond, V.A.: Defining interaction and strategies to enhance interactions in Web-based courses. Nurse Educ. **28**(5), 237–241 (2003)
3. McKimm, J., et al.: Web-based learning. BMJ **326**(7394), 870–873 (2003)
4. Candy, P.C.: Linking thinking: self-directed learning in the digital age. Department of Education, Science and Training (2004)
5. Hodges, C.B.: Self-regulation in web-based courses. Q. Rev. Distance Educ. **6**(4), 375–383 (2005)
6. Brown, J.L.: Online learning: a comparison of web-based and land-based courses. Q. Rev. Distance Educ. **13**(1), 39 (2012)
7. Iida, H., et al.: Satisfaction with web-based courses on clinical practice guidelines for psychiatrists: findings from the "Effectiveness of Guidelines for Dissemination and Education in Psychiatric Treatment (EGUIDE)" project. Neuropsychopharmacol. Rep. **43**(1), 23–32 (2023). https://doi.org/10.1002/npr2.12300
8. Podvorna, L.: Principals of creation of electronic textbooks for higher educational establishments. Sci. Collect. "InterConf." **142**, 130–136 (2023)

9. Ubaydullayeva, D., et al.: The development of electronic educational resources is an important step towards the digitalisation of the agricultural economy. In: AIP Conference Proceedings, vol. 2432, no. 1, p. 040022 (2022)
10. Khmiliarchuk, O., et al.: Analysis of technologies for the creation electronic, multimedia textbooks. Sci. Collect. "InterConf." **134**, 389–393 (2022)
11. Okhunov, A.O.: Smart Textbook-A New Level in the Modern Educational Process (2022)
12. Murodova, Z.R., et al.: Creating an electronic textbook in a programming environment. Eur. Multi. J. Mod. Sci. **4**, 536–544 (2022)
13. Paskevicius, M.: Book review-an introduction to open education. Int. Rev. Res. Open Distrib. Learn. **23**(4), 183–185 (2022)
14. Torkar, G.: Interview with Richard E. Mayer about multimedia materials and textbooks. Center Educ. Policy Stud. J. **12**(2), 189–195 (2022)
15. Aripov, M.M., Tillaev, A.I.: General rules for creating and using multimedia electronic textbooks on "Digital and information technology" in higher education. Acad. Res. Educ. Sci. **3**(4), 112–116 (2022)
16. Mery, Y.: A case for microlearning. Libr. Technol. Rep. **58**(5), 10 (2022)
17. Zarshenas, L., et al.: The effect of micro-learning on learning and self-efficacy of nursing students: an interventional study. BMC Med. Educ. **22**(1), 664 (2022)
18. Frantuzan, L., et al.: The strategic concept of meritology in learning. Revista Romaneasca pentru Educatie Multidimensionala **15**(1), 310–330 (2023)
19. Aburizaizah, S.J., Albaiz, T.A.: Review of the use and impact of nano-learning in education. In: 4th International Conference on Research in education, Nice (2021)
20. Lluch, L., Cano, E.: How to Embed SRL in Online Learning Settings? Design Through Learning Analytics and Personalized Learning Design in Moodle (2023)
21. Gamage, S.H., et al.: A systematic review on trends in using Moodle for teaching and learning. Int. J. STEM Educ. **9**(1), 1–24 (2022)
22. Ji, Y.P., et al.: Activity and dropout tracking in Moodle using UBUMonitor application. IEEE Revista Iberoamericana de Tecnologias del Aprendizaje **17**(3), 307–317 (2022)
23. Poellhuber, L.V., et al.: Cluster-based performance of student dropout prediction as a solution for large scale models in a Moodle LMS. In: LAK23: 13th International Learning Analytics and Knowledge Conference, pp. 592–598 (2023)
24. Rama Devi, S., Subetha, T., Aruna Rao, S.L., Morampudi, M.K.: Enhanced learning outcomes by interactive video content—H5P in Moodle LMS. In: Suma, V., Baig, Z., Shanmugam, S.K., Lorenz, P. (eds.) Inventive Systems and Control: Proceedings of ICISC 2022, pp. 189–203. Springer, Singapore (2022). https://doi.org/10.1007/978-981-19-1012-8_13
25. Nwachukwu, U., et al.: inDash: An Interactions Dashboard to Analyze Moodle Logs (2022)
26. Griva, A.: I can get no e-satisfaction. What analytics say? Evidence using satisfaction data from e-commerce. J. Retail. Consum. Serv. **66**, 102954 (2022)
27. Even, A.: Analytics: turning data into management gold. Appl. Mark. Analytics **4**(4), 330–341 (2019)
28. Romero, C., Ventura, S.: Educational data mining and learning analytics: an updated survey. Wiley Interdisc. Rev Data Min. Knowl. Discov. **10**(3), 1355 (2020)
29. Rohloff, T., et al.: Utilising web analytics in the context of learning analytics for large-scale online learning. In: 2019 IEEE Global Engineering Education Conference (EDUCON), pp. 296–305 (2019). **58**(1), 470–489
30. Camilleri, M.A.: Higher education marketing: opportunities and challenges in the digital era. Academia 16–17, 4–28 (2019)
31. Mc Guckin, C., Crowley, N.: Using Google analytics to evaluate the impact of the cybertraining project. Cyberpsychol. Behav. Soc. Netw. **15**(11), 625–629 (2012)

32. Moissa, B., Carvalho, L.S., Gasparini, I.: A web analytics and visualization tool to understand students' behavior in an adaptive e-learning system. In: Zaphiris, P., Ioannou, A. (eds.) LCT 2014. LNCS, vol. 8523, pp. 312–321. Springer, Cham (2014). https://doi.org/10.1007/978-3-319-07482-5_30

33. Luo, H., et al.: Using Google analytics to understand online learning: a case study of a graduate-level online course. In: 2015 International Conference of Educational Innovation through Technology (EITT), pp. 264–268 (2015)

34. Romanowski, B., Konak, A.: Using analytics to improve the course website of a database course. In: ASEE Mid-Atlantic Regional Conference Papers, pp. 21–22 (2016)

35. FAO: E-learning methodologies and good practices (2021). https://doi.org/10.4060/i2516e

36. Sheu, F.R., Shih, M.: Evaluating NTU's OpenCourseWare project with Google analytics: user characteristics, course preferences, and usage patterns. Int. Rev. Res. Open Distrib. Learn. **18**(4), 100–122 (2017)

37. Horowitz, D.: Course evaluation with Google analytics. Marketing **10**, 4 (2014)

38. Yamba-Yugsi, M., et al.: Using Google analytics to analyse users of a massive open online course. In: 2019 International Conference on Information Systems and Computer Science (INCISCOS), pp. 280–285 (2019)

39. Lenane, H.: Instructional Designer Perspectives of the Usefulness of an Instructional Design Process when Designing e-Learning. Walden University (2022)

40. Sedio, M.: Teaching of make prototype step of design process by e-tutors in open and distance e-learning context. Int. e-Journal Educ. Stud. **6**(12), 202–211 (2023)

41. Ooge, J., et al.: Steering recommendations and visualising its impact: effects on adolescents' trust in e-learning platforms. In: Proceedings of the 28th International Conference on Intelligent User Interfaces, pp. 156–170 (2023)

42. Deho, O.B., et al.: Should learning analytics models include sensitive attributes? explaining the why. IEEE Trans. Learn. Technol. **16**(4), 560–572 (2023). https://doi.org/10.1109/TLT.2022.3226474

43. Sghir, N., et al.: Recent advances in predictive learning analytics: a decade systematic review (2012–2022). Educ. Inf. Technol. **28**(7), 8299–8333 (2022). https://doi.org/10.1007/s10639-022-11536-0

44. Beck Wells, M.: Student perspectives on the use of universal design for learning in virtual formats in higher education. Smart Learn. Environ. **9**(1), 1–12 (2022)

45. Divjak, B., et al.: Flipped classrooms in higher education during the COVID-19 pandemic: findings and future research recommendations. Int. J. Educ. Technol. High. Educ. **19**(1), 1–24 (2022)

46. Rets, I., et al.: Accessibility of open educational resources: how well are they suited for English learners? Open Learn. J. Open Distance e-Learning **38**(1), 38–57 (2023)

47. Akgün-Özbek, E., Özkul, A.E.: e-transformation in higher education and what it coerces for the faculty. In: Research Anthology on Remote Teaching and Learning and the Future of Online Education, pp. 1086–1111. iGI Global (2023)

Technology Usage and Students Performance: The Influence of Blended Learning

Sedigheh Moghavvemi[1(✉)], Seuk Wai Phoong[1], and Seuk Yen Phoong[2]

[1] Department of Decision Science, University of Malaya, Kuala Lumpur, Malaysia
{Sedigheh,phoongsw}@um.edu.my
[2] Faculty of Science and Mathematics, Sultan Idris Education University, Tanjong Malim, 35900 Perak, Malaysia
phoong@fsmt.upsi.edu.my

Abstract. COVID-19 has accelerated technology usage in education. While educators have historically relied on traditional methods, scholars have explored technology's effectiveness in enhancing students' performance. They have also explored its potential as a complementary tool for teaching and learning. Recently, there has been a noticeable shift towards technology to personalize learning. The emergence of COVID-19 compelled the education system and instructors to rapidly transition to online teaching and learning, on an untested and unprecedented scale. This has inspired current research to investigate online teaching trends. It also aims to understand students' and lecturers' perspectives on technology's role in online education and its impact on academic performance. This paper explores university lecturers' technology usage and views on technology effectiveness for teaching. Additionally, the study examines students' satisfaction with technology usage and its influence on academic performance through qualitative research. Nine university lecturers and six students participated in interviews for this study, and the obtained data was analyzed thematically. The results indicated that both lecturers and students believe that technology, when used as a complementary tool, can significantly improve students' academic performance. However, the abrupt transition to a fully online process without proper preparation and a long-term plan may lead to challenges for both educators and students, emphasizing the need for careful planning in such transformations.

Keywords: Online teaching and Learning · Facebook · Game · Academic Performance · Students Engagement

1 Introduction

Education plays a vital role in enhancing countries' economic growth through human capital development. An interactive teaching and learning process is one of the most cost-effective ways of improving education quality [1]. However, this is not easy to achieve with the traditional teaching method, which is teacher-oriented and inflexible. The "chalk and talk" method with the teacher as the single speaker cannot attract and engage the new digital native students in the classroom. Erdama [2] criticised traditional

Ł. Tomczyk (Ed.): NMP 2022, CCIS 1916, pp. 237–253, 2023.
https://doi.org/10.1007/978-3-031-44581-1_17

learning and deemed that the constructivist, student-centred approaches adopted in education produce better performance on tests and better equip students with necessary employment skills. Chatti et al. [3] argued that, in contrast to the traditional method of one size fits all, a fundamental shift is needed towards a more personalised, open, dynamic, and knowledge-pull model, as learning is personal and dynamic. These arguments present convincing justifications for research to investigate the use of technology in teaching, its capability to transform the education system, its role in creating more student engagement, and its impact on students academic performance [4–6]. Empirical evidence indicated that many technologies support teaching and learning, with several instructors using certain technologies to improve students learning. However, there is little evidence of technology's significance and positive impact on teaching and learning [7].

Chatti et al. [3] suggested that new learning designs grounded in effective technology usage would aid learners. In comparative research, Menon [8] highlighted the influence of information and communication technology (ICT), which enabled the creation of new techniques in curriculum development and delivery systems for teachers and learners, nearly transforming the education system. Many studies also investigated the effectiveness of particular technologies on students' performance [9–13]. Nevertheless, the noticeable absence of studies that investigate the types of technologies, the purposes of their use, and the effectiveness of different technologies on students' engagement and learning is evident. For example, although research indicates that incorporating social media in a classroom setting could potentially enhance students' academic performance, the precise mechanism behind this connection remains incompletely explored [14].

The education system was transforming slowly, and for years researchers were figuring out how technology could improve students' performance and the quality of teaching and learning. However, COVID-19 and the subsequent movement control order (MCO) created a sudden change in the condition, and the response to it was a reminder that there is a need for transformation. The sudden change to fully online teaching and learning surprised students and lecturers. Online classes via communication technologies such as Zoom, Google Hangout, Microsoft Team, and WebEx have become the most suitable solution for teaching and learning. Social media channels such as Facebook, WhatsApp, and YouTube were utilised to address the remote learning challenges. The assessment also moved online, with much trial and error and uncertainty. The transformation was troublesome for some institutions, universities, and students due to a lack of infrastructure, resources, and facilities. Students with limited access to the internet or without laptops or desktop computers had difficulty accessing the course material. The same condition existed for the instructors who did not have facilities or whose course content was not designed for online methods. Some studies such as Gopika and Rekha [15] revealed that there was a substantial increase in students' utilization of digital learning resources following the COVID-19 outbreak, and they expressed higher satisfaction with the available digital learning facilities. Yee [16] indicated that it is difficult to assume that all the students have access to unlimited internet or possess laptops, as a study conducted by the Malaysian Communications and Multimedia Commissions in 2018 shows a sizable disparity between urban (70%) and rural internet users. Besides, the coverage and speed of the internet depend on one's budget and location, and the students living in rural areas are at risk of being left behind if the classes are entirely online.

Taking into account how well technology works for teaching and learning in general and during COVID-19, this study aims to find out how instructors and lecturers used technology during COVID-19, how well the technologies helped students do, and what problems they ran into. Additionally, this study examines students' satisfaction with technology usage in learning. In conclusion, the goal of this study is to first determine the type of technology that lecturers use and how well it works for teaching the subject. Second, to explore the influence of online teaching methods and the usage of complementary teaching techniques on students' engagement and academic performance. Third, to examine students' satisfaction with online learning.

The results of this study will give the Ministry of Education (MoE) and academic institutions more information about how technology is used and how well it works in teaching and learning. It will create an overview for after COVID-19 and how the education system should plan for the long term. Malaysia has not been the exception where the traditional mode of instruction is predominant [17, 18]. Traditional teacher-centred learning in the classroom with students listening passively to teachers produces students with little high-order thinking and motivation and results in low classroom participation rates. Overall, this lowers the quality of education and causes dissatisfaction among employers with graduates that lack soft skills. This suggests a need to transform the system into one that is more student- and technology-based.

By making changes to its education system, the Malaysian government has recognised how important student-centered learning is. Introduced in 1988, the Integrated Secondary School Curriculum (ISSC) comprises the integration of theory and practise, knowledge, skills, and values, and the integration of the curriculum and co-curriculum. Additionally, technology-supported smart schools" were also introduced and recognised as bringing a significant change in the education system of Malaysia. The Malaysian Smart School Implementation Plan [1997] was realised in collaboration with technology providers through the implementation of 1000 smart schools that aimed to improve the quality of the education system and provide personalised teaching in school. Malaysia's shift from traditional education is evident with the new focus on technology and blended learning. The implementation of COVID-19 and compulsory online teaching and learning increased the speed of transformation; however, there are few studies about the instructors' challenges and their satisfaction with the online system, as well as students perspectives. This information will provide the academic managers with the knowledge they need to plan for the future.

2 Background of the Study

2.1 The Challenges of the Traditional Approach

The traditional method of teaching and learning has been used since the early days, with the teacher as the centre of the classroom. Classrooms are generally teacher-centric, and teachers are usually the mode of knowledge dispensers via chalk and talk methods instead of being facilitators in the classroom [19]. Spahiu and Spahiu [20] explained three main teaching methods in the history of education, including methods such as "teacher talking time (TTT)," "seatwork," and listening and observation. The first method consists mainly of lectures and direct instructions. It is a standard classroom-based method with direct instructions from the teacher or lecturer known as "teacher talking time," which involves teachers conveying information and teaching in the classroom. The second method, the "seatwork" method, allows the teacher to focus on groups or individuals with varying needs and abilities [21] and track the students' performances. The "listening and observations" method involves students' learning from teachers, with students concentrating in class and listening to the lesson taught by the teachers.

According to Liu and Long [22], the traditional method restrains the creativity and personality of students in the classroom. Students tend to be passive as their initiative and potential are not discovered, with teachers being the centre of the lessons and teachings. There is great emphasis on education and its completion, resulting in few thinking opportunities and little enhancement of their critical thinking. Spahiu and Spahiu [20] highlighted that these weaknesses of traditional teaching and learning methods eliminate students' interest in education as their initiative and enthusiasm are not empowered in classrooms. Studies also concluded that the teacher-centric approach is the least effective teaching method and indicated that student-teacher interaction would improve teaching and learning [9, 10]. Bamwesiga, Dahlgren, and Fejes [23] conducted a qualitative study among 25 students in Rwanda, Central Africa. The study explored higher education teachers' perceptions of students' learning problems and revealed that students are teacher dependent on learning. Students view teachers' work and materials as sufficient for their learning; thus, they find no value in going beyond classroom notes. In a separate study, Bamwesiga et al. [23] indicated that students' perceptions of the education system and teaching methods will influence their engagement and willingness to use complementary learning methods.

2.2 Impact of the Technology

Researchers also identified methods of improving the education system [10, 12, 24]. These researchers argued that using technology can be a solution to improving students' performance and the quality of teaching. According to Saba [25], the benefits of technology integration in education include improving student achievement on tests and the quality of student work. Additionally, technology provides individualised learning and acts as a catalyst for change as it facilitates student-centric approaches. Learning via technology can occur regardless of time and location as technology encompasses various tools and learning styles, such as formal and informal, as well as social and personal learning [24]. Menon [8] argued that learning through technology could be fun and entertaining for the students and enrich learning as it engages both the students and the teacher, creating a student-teacher connection.

A study on 4374 students in the US conducted by ECAR in 2004 shows that almost 41.2 percent of respondents prefer classes with technology usage as technology helps them communicate better with their instructor. The study found that students' interests in technology usage in learning are due to their different learning skills and abilities. Their learning is enhanced through complementary methods such as videos that visualise learning content. Technology usage in education motivates students to concentrate on learning [6, 13, 26, 27]. However, essential success determinants in technology usage are students' engagement and the effectiveness of technology as a medium of instruction [28]. The student engagement determinant improves students' understanding of the course content, improves their critical thinking, and influences academic achievement [28]. The technology determinant, in turn, creates more engagement and increases students' independence to explore and analyse the context and understand the content better [24, 29].

2.3 Benefits of Blended Learning

More recent research introduced the integration of old and new approaches combining the elements of the smart classroom, smart learning, and smart education [24, 30]. Generally, smart education is defined as the use of intelligent technology for teaching and training the future workforce to meet the needs and challenges of society [24]. Smart learning means providing the right technology and personalising adaptive content based on the needs and capabilities of the learner. Smart education is the design of an intelligent, adaptive, and personalised system to fit the different needs of entities and educational conditions [24]. Smart classrooms are equipped with computers and audio-visual equipment that facilitate teaching through various media [30]. This method is known as blended learning. It refers to the combination of technology and traditional methods that help students achieve their goals [30] and improve their academic performance. It creates an environment that caters to students with different learning abilities to share, collaborate, and access online sources, instilling confidence to discuss and absorb the information [26].

Aksoy [31] looked at how animation techniques work in the classroom and came to the conclusion that animation techniques are better than traditional methods. Moghavvemi et al. [11, 12] looked into how social networks (like YouTube and Facebook) are used as a way to help teach and learn, and they said that students are happier when they use technology to learn. Both groups of researchers said that students' use of Facebook and YouTube led to more engagement and sharing of knowledge, which helped their grades. In similar research, Siddiqui and Masud [32] indicated that internet usage in education had caused education to become universal, with students now looking forward to simplicity in learning via more interactive and attractive methods.

The literature review demonstrated that researchers investigated the effectiveness of specific technology on teaching and learning in different contexts and settings from both students' and instructors' perspectives. However, there is a noticeable lack of research that identifies the different types of technology usage by instructors and lecturers, its effectiveness on students' learning, and the students satisfaction with and perceptions of technology usage. There is, therefore, an urgent need for research to investigate these issues from both the instructor's and students' perspectives to further inform existing knowledge.

3 Methodology

3.1 Sampling Procedures

Nine university lecturers and six students from two public universities in Kuala Lumpur, Malaysia, participated voluntarily in this research, sharing their experiences with online classes and technology usage in learning and teaching. As the research objective was to identify the type and usage of the various technologies for inline teaching among university lecturers, purposive sampling was used to select the lecturers. The lecturer's participants were educators who use different technologies during online teaching. Interviews were conducted online. One male and eight female lecturers were participants, of which eight were Malaysians and one foreigner. The lecturer's participants had a diverse number of years of work experience ranging from two to twenty years (Table 1).

Table 1. Lecturer Participants Profiles

Participant	Gender	Nationality	Work Experience (No. of years)	Courses
R1	F	L	9	Statistics
R2	F	L	10	E-commerce
R3	F	L	22	Research Methods
R4	F	L	4	Digital business
R5	F	L	15	Management Information System
R6	F	L	3	Online Business
R7	F	F	5	Management
R8	F	L	5	Quantitative analysis
R9	M	L	6	Mathematics

Note: F: Female, M: Male; Nationality: L: Local, F: Foreign

A team of researchers coded and created themes based on the study's objectives and existing literature. The student's participants interviewed consisted of six local undergraduate students (a mix of males and females) randomly selected from the lecturers' classes to evaluate the effectiveness of the methods and their satisfaction. The third- and fourth-year students were selected because they had been studying at the university for a longer period, and the probability of knowing both face-to-face and online teaching methods among them was higher (Table 2). The use of the lecturers' students will ensure lecturer-student information consistency. All interviews were recorded with participants' permission, and participants' names were kept anonymous to adhere to respondents' requests for confidentiality.

Table 2. Students Participants Profiles

Participant	Gender	Year of study	Area of the study
R1	F	Third year	E-commerce
R2	F	Third year	Digital Business
R3	F	Third year	Digital Business
R4	F	Fourth year	Management
R5	M	Fourth year	Management
R6	M	Fourth year	E-commerce

Note: F: Female, M: Male

Interviews

This is inductive research, and we used interviews to identify the factors that are important for blended learning. Semi-structured interviews were guided by open-ended questions designed to provoke spontaneous responses, uncover a diverse range of experiences, and reduce interviewer bias. The lecturer's participants were first questioned on their overall teaching experiences and perceptions of teacher-centric and student-centric approaches. This is followed by questions on their experience of online teaching, the types of technology used, the purpose of the technology usage, the effects of technology on students' performance, and the limitations faced during online teaching. Once interviews with lecturers have been completed, six students randomly selected from three lecturers classes were interviewed on their experiences with technology usage in learning university courses conducted by their respective lecturers. Three sample questions are: how has the use of technology improved students' concentration and learning experiences compared to traditional methods? to what extent do students believe that access to complementary information online has positively impacted their academic performance? In what ways has technology usage contributed to increased cognitive presence among students, and how has this influenced their academic achievements?". Each interview lasted about an hour on average for the lecturer participants and about ten minutes on average for the student participants. All interviews were conducted in English.

4 Data Analysis and Results

Interview data were transcribed and analysed thematically, guided by a coding scheme developed from extant literature collaboratively by the research team. The coding scheme incorporated key concepts from the previous literature related to technology usage in teaching and learning in accordance with the study objectives. New codes were permitted to emerge. After the initial coding, the interview transcripts and thematically coded remarks were reviewed by a second member of the research team. Microsoft Excel was used to analyse the data since it provides more flexibility for changes in ideas. Lecturer participants' data were mapped to six categories within the themes of student engagement, student performance, limitation of technology, type of technology, student-centricity, and teacher-centricity. In contrast, the student participants' data were mapped into four categories: the themes of the effectiveness of the online methods, resources, concentration and learning, availability of complementary information online, and enjoyment. The following section discusses themes that emerged from interviews with lecturer participants.

4.1 Results from Instructors

Technology Usage Before and During COVID-19
The lecturer's data showed that all of the participants thought that online teaching was good, but that it couldn't be the only way to teach, and that a mix of online and in-person teaching was better. Diverse online platforms used included, Zoom, Google Hangout, Google Classroom, Microsoft Team, Skype, Blog, Forum, WhatsApp, Facebook, Game (Padlet and Kahoot), an internal university online platform named "Spectrum," and Wiki to conduct the online course and improve students' engagement and academic performance. During the COVID-19 pandemic, lecturers considered online technologies as the central platform to teach students compared to before the pandemic, a complementary tool that attracted, engaged, and enhanced students' performance. They noted that before movement control order (MCO), some students were unwilling to use technology because they perceived its usage as "creating extra work for them," as well as their unfamiliarity with the technology. However, the condition changed during MCO, and the online platform was the only way to communicate.

"Before MCO, some of them, especially undergraduates who were from schools, did not like to use an online platform such as "Forum," because it was an extra effort for them, but during MCO, all the students have to use the online platform. However, some were never active, and some disappeared; it was difficult to engage some of the passive students". (R2).

They highlighted that students' perception of technology usage depends on their perception that "they just need to attend the class and all the other things are extra work for them."

Motivation to Use
Lecturers said that whether they teach in person or online, students' interest continues to challenge them. The use of some technology, such as games (Padlet and Kahoot), is a way to engage students, especially timid students who are unwilling to talk and discuss in class. Many students that were uncomfortable discussing or asking questions in class may be more active online, as they can remain anonymous when asking questions online.

"Getting students to contribute during class was always a challenge. Some are very shy, or they probably feel insecure, think they know something but not conceptually, and are unsure about the answer. They like to be anonymous and attend online when they can hide behind the screen, and even when you ask a question, they excuse that their mic does not work. However, some students are always quiet, and it gets worse when the class is online; I have to search for them and make sure that they are listening." (R4).

On the other hand, some students are more involved and active when it comes to using technology to teach and learn. Hence, the lecturers must use different methods to encourage them to participate in learning.

"Some students like online activities, especially now with digital natives on Facebook, and they are so used to things online" (R3). "Social media and gamification are good ways to get them involved" (R5).

Teacher-Centric or Student-Centric

Lecturer participants believed that the choice to implement a teacher-centric or student-centric method depends on the level of students learning efficacy. The student-centric method is suitable for students with higher levels of self-efficacy and better learning strategies. In contrast, the lecture-centric method is suitable for students who need more guidance and coaching. Students will benefit from the technique that meets their needs.

"As I mentioned previously, both teacher- and student-centric methods are important. Because methods are highly contextual and dependent on the topic, situation, environment, and other factors, we must not go to extremes with one method. There must be combinations. Furthermore, it (the method) depends on us as the facilitators, where we can interfere with their discussion and let them do their work. We need to be very smart to allow them to intervene and intercept this with our teaching." (R1).

"The choice of a student-centric or teacher-centric method should be based on the level of the students' self-efficacy. Maybe for postgraduates, it is beneficial to be student-centric, even though the teachers have to design the task. If the students do not have self-regulated learning and do not have the will to study and do well, then things might go wrong. For undergraduates, you need constant monitoring to check on them, so the specific thing you need is teacher-centric, where the teacher gives information and gives activities for them to do." (R3).

Type of Technology and Purpose of Technology Usage

Lecturers use technology to meet their diverse courses' objectives and as complementary tools for their teaching and students' learning. This diversity is indicated in the assortment of different technologies used to engage and improve students' academic performance, such as the usage of Facebook, WhatsApp, Wiki, Forum, Spectrum, Blog, and Game. Lecturers are more attracted to using technologies that allow lecturers-students two-way interaction to inform them of students' involvement and responses.

Facebook

"I do not use Spectrum much because there is no two-way interaction; you will upload the documents, but you do not know if they use it. I am using the Facebook group for two reasons: it allows two ways of interaction, and Facebook features allow sending of notifications to students when I post something. Therefore, they cannot argue that they did not see it." (R6).

"I upload my slides in Spectrum, but all the other communication is through Facebook or Microsoft Teams. I posted the related video and documents on Facebook, and I asked students to comment, which created a discussion among all the students in the group. Even students who never talked in class commented on the post." (R7).

Wiki

"I use Wiki, which also has a forum at the end of their page; they can also ask questions and share things there. I used Schoology, and Edmodo at the school level to improve students learning." (R2).

WhatsApp

"I have this WhatsApp class group to share some questions with students. I posted some examples I did not have time to explain in class and sometimes exercises. Sometimes I post one small problem, and I ask them to respond, and they do, and I give feedback. It is a good way because we have time at home to detect the difficulties they have or their misunderstanding and then explain these in class. In this way, students get better results, and they improve continuously" (R3).

Module and PowerPoint

"I am using Module and PowerPoint. But sometimes, I'll ask students to use social media to search for information, and they will present it in the classroom. It improved their knowledge and quality of their work." (R9).

Blog

"I think it is a good idea. I try to form a blog site, but again it is Mathematics. The problem again is how to write mathematical symbols in a blog. That is the constraint. I had the same problem during an online class on how to write the formula, and in the end, I have to buy some IT gadgets to write it." (R1).

Game

"I am teaching a theoretical subject that is 3 hours long. It is difficult for most students to concentrate, but social media and gamification can attract them. I am using games such as Kahoot and Padlet to teach that. Kahoot is a web page that enables us to test the students' understanding. Usually, before the class, I'll usually design some questions according to the learning outcomes and then ask students to answer them. In the Kahoot game, we can include some music, pictures, or graphs. So it attracts students, and they do not feel so bored during these 3 hours. I use Padlet, I am present, and I see my students" (R2).

Lecturers use technology to increase student engagement and improve academic performance. They indicated that the usage of different types of technologies is for different purposes, and the main purpose is to provide information for students and facilitate their learning.

"I used different tools and platforms for different purposes. For example, I use Movenote and videos to give information for the interaction. I used online tools like the Discussion Forums. "Spectrum" for uploading lecture notes and videos so students can access them anytime and anywhere. I found that when you use social media, the student can fully concentrate and participate as compared to the others. So it would be best if you have a combination of many tools for different purposes" (R2).

Student's Performance

The usage of Information Technology in combinations of different tools and learning methods influenced students' performance. The use of a combination of both the traditional teaching method and blended learning (before Covid-19) indicated that these complementary tools improve students' performance. Students were more satisfied with such methods and performed better in class.

"I used both traditional and online methods, and the results of using combined (online and traditional) methods were more efficient for teaching. Students scored higher, and they were more satisfied with my class and teaching style" (R7). "However, my students' performance dropped during the pandemic when the class was entirely online, and I could not monitor the activities during class". (R7)

"Before COVID-19, using computers and online interaction helped students to focus, and they could analyze the information easier; I observed that when they were using the internet during class, they could analyze the results in SPSS better." It is not the same when the class is online; some students follow the class very well, and some are left behind (R8).

Limitation of Technology

Although using technology for teaching is attractive for the students and facilitates teaching and learning, for a subject such as mathematics, it is challenging to write mathematical formulas online, and it creates difficulty for the lecturer and students to communicate and discuss.

"You can only discuss when you talk about history and education. The usage of technologies in some disciplines is not easy. For example, it is impossible for Mathematics to write and sketch on WhatsApp, Blog, and Facebook group applications. Cause when you want to write some symbols, you cannot. I have to snap a picture of the symbols and send it, and they respond. We do not have platforms to entertain discussion that involves symbols" (R9).

Findings from interviews with lecturers indicated the benefits and limitations of technology usage. Interviews were conducted with students to identify the effects of technology usage and their perceptions of the effectiveness of technology in learning. Findings from interviews revealed that students were more satisfied with classes that used technology for teaching before COVID-19. The following section discusses themes that emerged from interviews with student participants.

4.2 Results from Students Participants

Improved Concentration and Learning

Student participants indicated that technology usage improved their concentration and learning as it enabled them to understand the subject better.

> "Using a computer helped me to focus and understand faster; having the flexibility to explore things online is fun." (R2).

> "I had a difficult time during the pandemic in the online class; even though I wanted to participate, the internet connection was terrible, and I had difficulty concentrating. The lecturer's quality of teaching was not good, and most of the time it was just video recording. We could not even ask questions. I could not perform well." (R2).

Availability of Complementary Information Online

They indicated that using the internet allows access to more information that enhances their learning. Access to information via the internet allowed students to see problems from different dimensions, and they could understand the concept easier.

> "Using the computer can get me more information, enhancing my sense of exploration. The internet provides a 3D perspective to help me explore all possible views on problems that may occur in my subject (blended learning)." (R3).

> "Online class was not effective for me. In the physical class, I discussed with the lecturer and other classmates, and we shared what we found and discussed, which was more interesting than working online alone" (R3).

Increased Cognitive Presence

Cognitive presence involves exploration, the search for information, and solutions. Students indicated that technology usage increased their cognitive presence as it stimulated their learning, and exploration and improved their level of thinking.

> "It stimulated me with more ideas and increased the level of my thinking; it also boosted my knowledge of things that I did not know" (R1).

> "The links that the lecturer shared via Facebook group during online class helped me to explore, and I have enough time to watch similar videos and learn deeply" (R1).

> "I like online classes; it was easy to ask questions and write my answer in the chat box" (R6).

Enjoyment

Technology usage was a pleasurable experience for the students. The enjoyment of technology usage in learning attracted the students to pay attention to lectures and the information shared by their lecturers. It also created opportunities for students to discuss and share their knowledge.

"Using a Facebook group is attractive and allows me to comment and share more" (R4).

"Using the Internet led me to understand the concepts taught, and I did not feel bored during the lesson" (R5).

"It was more fun to have an online class without any limitations or monitoring; I just relaxed while listening to the lecturer since we did not have to be on the camera". (R6).

Results from both lecturers (Table 3), and student participants indicated that technology usage facilitated teaching and increased students' understanding and academic performance when combined with physical and online methods. However, fully physical or online classes cause some problems for lecturers and students.

Table 3. Main Themes From Instructors and Students

Instructor	Student
Technology Usage Before and During COVID-19	Improved concentration and learning
Motivation to Use	Enjoyment
Teacher-Centric or Student-Centric	Availability of complementary information online
Type of Technology and Purpose of Technology Usage	Enhancing my sense of exploration
Student's Performance	Increased cognitive presence
Limitation of Technology	Not effective

5 Discussion

This study identified the usage and effectiveness of different types of technology on students' performance from lecturers' and students' perspectives. In this section, we connect the results and extant literature to provide insights on the influence of technological progress on the education system and recommend ways for technology to be used as complementary tools for teaching and learning.

Technology usage influences students' performance and improves student engagement [10, 12, 24, 33–36], as is evident in the technology usage literature. Using different tools and technologies in different contexts revealed that combining traditional methods and technology (blended learning) facilitates students understanding of the subject more efficiently and improves their performance [12]. This is supported by our findings, which indicated that using different types of technology, including social media

(Facebook, WhatsApp, and YouTube), games, wikis, blogs, PowerPoint, and modules, increased students' engagement and academic performance. Increasing student engagement is always a challenge for the lecturer, while the use of technology in the class can be a solution to the problem. As the results show, technology usage will influence shy students to provide comments and share their information, particularly if they recognize that they can be anonymous (an example is Kahoot, where they can use a nickname). Some students may feel insecure about asking questions or discussing topics in class, while the online platform provides a safer alternative for them to discuss the topic. Additionally, technology usage captures students' attention as it is deemed more attractive. More importantly, technology usage stimulates students' thinking and exploration and increases learning speed.

Findings also indicate that students' satisfaction with technology usage is dependent on their perception that "lecturers do all the work" in education. Suppose students expect to receive all information from the lecturer. In that case, they will not use the other complementary tools for learning as they are expecting the traditional teaching methods. Sometimes, they are unwilling to use new technology because it creates additional work or because they are unfamiliar with the specific technology. This is consistent with the Bamwesiga et al. [23] study.

Lecturer participants indicated that the usage of different technologies depends on the purpose of use. They use technology to share information (upload course materials), increase engagement through two ways of interaction and discussion, and increase students' exploration and improve their learning. Lecturers believed that combinations of different techniques were more practical to satisfy the different needs of the students. The finding is consistent with Moghavvemi et al. [12], who indicated that using different technologies may affect student performance and that combining traditional methods and technology will create better results. However, it was difficult for the lecturer to conduct the class entirely online or have online activities when they teach mathematics or other courses with some formula.

Decisions on the acceptance of student-centred learning or teacher-centred learning methods are inexplicit, as they depend on other factors such as the student's self-efficacy and their learning strategy. Findings suggest that combining both methods is more effective as it creates the flexibility to deliver information more effectively. The teacher-centred method is more effective for students with lower self-efficacy and learning strategies, as they require more attention and monitoring. In comparison, the student-centered method is more suitable for students with higher self-efficacy. These results differ from previous studies that suggested either teacher-centric or student-centric methods [19, 22] and highlighted the effectiveness of combinations of both.

Technology usage in teaching increases students' engagement and encourages participation, leading to a higher cognitive presence and improved critical thinking and academic performance. Our findings revealed that technology enables students to understand the subject faster and more efficiently. The use of online tools provided students with the opportunity to explore more and access information. This imparts confidence for students to discuss in class and in online groups. Findings also indicated that access to more information enhances students' sense of exploration, stimulates new ideas, and boosts their knowledge. This is supported by earlier research [24, 28, 29] that suggested that technology usage improves critical thinking, increases students' sense of exploration of new ideas, and influences their academic performance. These improvements are the result of the environment that lecturers create as well as the presence of other students in the group, which generates discussion and gives students the opportunity to comment and explore ideas. Using online technology to search for information, interacting with other students online, and sharing the information during class is attractive for the students. It creates more excitement for them in comparison to traditional methods. This finding is consistent with Moghavvemi et al. [12] study that reported on the influence of the hedonic dimension in technology usage on students' performance.

This study has some limitations, including a small sample size and potential concerns about the representativeness of the participants. This may restrict the generalizability of the findings. However, these results can serve as a foundation for future research to explore the effectiveness of technology in teaching and learning post-pandemic, especially considering the extensive knowledge students and lecturers now possess regarding technology utilization for educational purposes. Future research can use the findings of this study to develop quantitative tests to test the conceptual model and validate the model developed by this study.

Our findings will assist the Ministry of Education in revising and proposing appropriate methods that use technology as a complementary tool and building new and strengthening existing infrastructure to facilitate technology usage in academic institutions and amongst students.

6   Conclusion

The findings from the extensive review of technology usage literature reveal a clear and positive impact of technology on students' academic performance and engagement. The integration of various tools and technologies, particularly through blended learning approaches, has been shown to enhance students' understanding of subjects and improve their overall performance. Our own research further supports these conclusions. We observed that diverse technology types, including social media platforms, games, wikis, blogs, PowerPoint, and modules, significantly increase student engagement and academic achievement. Importantly, technology addresses the perennial challenge of fostering student engagement in the classroom and facilitates shy students' participation by offering anonymity. The online platform also provides a secure space for students to actively contribute to discussions, particularly for those who may feel uncomfortable doing so in traditional settings. Additionally, technology's attractiveness and capacity to capture students' attention stimulate critical thinking, exploration, and accelerate learning. However, it is essential to acknowledge that students' satisfaction with technology usage is closely linked to their perception of the lecturer's role in education. Educators should be attentive to students' expectations and concerns regarding technology integration to ensure a seamless and successful learning experience. Striking a balance between traditional teaching methods and technology incorporation and addressing any resistance or unfamiliarity with upcoming technologies will be crucial for optimizing technology benefits in education.

Acknowledgement. The University of Malaya Equitable Society Research Cluster provided financial support for research assistance and project team meetings under Project ED002C-17SBS.

References

1. Serbessa, D.D.: Tension between traditional and modern teaching-learning approaches in Ethiopian primary schools. J. Int. Coop. Educ. **9**(1), 123–140 (2006)
2. Erdamar, G., Demirel, M.: Effects of constructivist learning approach on affective and cognitive learning outcomes. Turk. Educ. Sci. **6**(4), 629–661 (2008)
3. Chatti, M.A., Agustiawan, M.R., Jarke, M., Specht, M.: Toward a personal learning environment framework. Int. J. Virtual Pers. Learn. Environ. **1**(4), 66–85 (2010)
4. Higgins, S., Xiao, Z., Katsipataki, M.: The Impact of Digital Technology on Learning: A Summary for the Education Endowment Foundation. http://educationendowmentfoundation.org.uk/uploads/pdf/The_Impact_of_Digital_Technologies_on_Learning(2012).pdf
5. Kirkwood, A., Price, L.: Technology-enhanced learning and teaching in higher education: what is 'enhanced' and how do we know? a critical literature review. Learn. Media Technol. **39**, 6–36 (2014)
6. .Boulton, H.: Exploring the effectiveness of new technologies: improving literacy and engaging learners at risk of social exclusion in the UK. Teach. Teach. Educ. **63**, 73–81 (2017)
7. Spector, M.J., SLFG (The Smart Learning Futures Group): Smart learning futures: a report from the 3rd US-China smart education conference. Smart Learn. Environ. **5**(5), 1–10 (2018). https://doi.org/10.1186/s40561-018-0054-1)
8. Menon, A.: Effectiveness of smart classroom teaching on the achievement in chemistry of secondary school students. Am. Int. J. Res. Humanit. Arts Soc. Sci. 15–132 (2015). http://www.iasir.net
9. Ganyaupfu, E.M.: Factors influencing academic achievement in quantitative courses among business students of private higher education institutions. J. Educ. Pract. **4**(15), 57–65 (2013)
10. Gupta, M., Singh, K.: Effect of smart classroom teaching on achievement of students: a closer focus on gender and intelligence. Imp. J. Interdiscip. Res. (IJIR) **3**(1), 1077–1086 (2017)
11. Moghavvemi, S., Sharabati, M., Klobas, J.E., Sulaiman, A.: Effect of trust and perceived reciprocal benefit on students' knowledge sharing via facebook and academic performance. Electron. J. Knowl. Manag. **16**(1), 23–35 (2018)
12. Moghavvemi, S., Sulaiman, A., Jaafar, N.I., Kasem, N.: Social media as a complementary learning tool for teaching and learning: the case of YouTube. Int. J. Manag. Educ. **16**(1), 37–42 (2018)
13. Moghavvemi, S., Paramanathan, T., Rahin, N., Sharabati, M.: Student's perceptions towards using e-learning via Facebook. Behav. Inf. Technol. **36**(10), 1081–1100 (2017)
14. Shafiq, M., Parveen, K.: Social media usage: analyzing its effect on academic performance and engagement of higher education students. Int. J. Educ. Dev. **98**, 102738 (2023)
15. Gopika, J.S., Rekha, R.V: Awareness and use of digital learning before and during COVID-19. Int. J. Educ. Reform 1–3 (2023). 10567879231173389
16. Yee, C.P.: COVID-19: impact on the tertiary education sector in Malaysia. Crisis Assessment, Penang Institute, Pulau Pinang, Malaysia, Technical report (2020). https://penanginstitute.org/publications/covid-19-crisis-assessments/covid-19-impact-on-the-tertiary-education-sector-in-malaysia/
17. Yusof, Y., Roddin, R., Awang, H.: What students need, and what teacher did: the impact of teacher's teaching approaches to the development of students' generic competences. Procedia Soc. Behav. Sci. **204**, 36–44 (2015)

18. Tan, Y.P., Arshad, M.Y.: Problem-based learning: implementation issues in Malaysia secondary school's science classroom. International Conference on Science & Mathematics Education (CoSMEd) (2011)
19. Nazzal, N.: Modern vs traditional teaching methods. Gulf News (2014). http://gulfnews.com/news/uae/education/modern-vs-traditional-teaching-methods-1.1418127
20. Spahiu, I., Spahiu, E.: Teacher's role in classroom management and traditional methods. Angl. J. **2**(3) (2015)
21. Cunningham, P.M.: Making seatwork work. Read. Horiz. **31**(4), 3 (1991)
22. Liu, C., Long, F.: The discussion of traditional teaching and multimedia teaching approach in college English teaching. In: International Conference on Management, Education and Social Science, pp. 31–33 (2014)
23. Bamwesiga, P.M., Dahlgren, L.O., Fejes, A.: Students as learners through the eyes of their teachers in Rwandan higher education. Int. J. Lifelong Educ. **31**(4), 503–521 (2012)
24. Zhu, Z., Yu, M., Riezebos, P.: A research framework of smart education. Smart Learn. Environ. **3**(4), 2–17 (2016)
25. Saba, A.: Benefits of technology integration in education (2009). http://edtech2.boisestate.edu/sabaa/502/Saba_Synthesis_Paper.pdf
26. Sharma, H.L.: Effectiveness of EDUCOMP smart classroom teaching on retention in mathematics at elementary level. Int. J. Multidiscip. Res. Dev. **3**(6), 160–164 (2016)
27. Taleb, Z., Hassanzadeh, F.: Toward smart school: a comparison between smart school and traditional school for mathematics learning. Procedia Soc. Behav. Sci. **171**, 90–95 (2015)
28. Emmanuel, C., Ekpo, A.: Facilitative learning and students engagement in electrical technology for developing critical reasoning and lifelong learning skills in the university of Uyo, Akwa Ibom State, Nigeria. J. Educ. Pract. **7**(22), 36–40 (2016). www.iiste.org
29. Middleton, A. (ed.): Smart Learning: Teaching and Learning with Smartphones and Tablets in Post-Compulsory Education. MELSIG & Sheffield Hallam University, Sheffield (2015)
30. Malik, N., Shanwal, V.K.: A comparative study of traditional and smart classrooms in relation to their creativity and academic achievement. Integr. J. Soc. Sci. **4**(1), 15–19 (2017)
31. Aksoy, G.: The effects of animation technique on the 7th grade science and technology course. Creat. Educ. **3**, 304–308 (2012). https://www.scirp.org/journal/paperinformation.aspx?paperid=19798%
32. Siddiqui, A.T., Masud, M.: An e-learning system for quality education. IJCSI Int. J. Comput. Sci. Issues **9**(4), 375–380 (2016)
33. Phoong, S.Y., Phoong, S.W., Moghavvemi, S., Sulaiman, A.: Effect of smart classroom on student achievement at higher education. J. Educ. Technol. Syst. **48**(2), 291–304 (2019)
34. Phoong, S.Y., Phoong, S.W., Moghavvemi, S., Sulaiman, A.: Measuring the influence of hedonic value, social presence and teaching presence on students' cognitive presence through the implementation of the smart classroom. Int. J. Learn. Technol. **15**(2), 130–149 (2020)
35. Sulaiman, A., Naqshbandi, M.M., Mogavvemi, S., Jaafar, N.I.: Facebook usage, socialization and academic performance. Comput. Educ. **83**, 64–73 (2015)
36. Klobas, J.E., McGill, T., Moghavvemi, S., Paramanathan, T.: Compulsive YouTube usage: a comparison of use motivation and personality effects. Comput. Hum. Behav.. **87**, 129–139 (2018)

Satisfaction and Acceptance of ICT in Learning Activities During Covid19: The Case of Moroccan Students

Abdelmounim Bouziane[1]([✉]) [iD], Wadi Tahri[1,2], and Karima Bouziane[2] [iD]

[1] Interdisciplinary Laboratory for Research On Organizations (LIRO), National School of Commerce and Management, Chouaib Doukkali University, El Jadida, Morocco
bouzianeabdelmounim@gmail.com

[2] Laboratory for Applied Language and Culture Studies (ALCS), Faculty of Letters and Humanities, Chouaib Doukkali University, El Jadida, Morocco

Abstract. The aim of this paper is to study students' acceptance and satisfaction with Information and Communication Technologies (ICT) in learning activities during the Covid-19 crisis. We used Technology Acceptance Model (TAM) to investigate the level of acceptability of technology-based teaching methods and satisfaction with various courses and trainings delivered in distance. Our sample is made up of students from different universities in Morocco. Data collection was accomplished through questionnaires and then analyzed via SPSS. The results of this study revealed that the level of acceptance is determined by the perceived utility and the perceived ease of use. Students' satisfaction with ICT is mainly impacted by the level of acceptance of these technologies and the teaching methods of professors and instructors.

Keywords: ICT · students' reaction · e-learning · Covid-19 · TAM

1 Introduction

Following the spread of Covid-19, a state of health emergency was established in Morocco in March 2020 followed by an unprecedented period of lockdown in order to deal with the spread of the virus. Academic institutions were among the first institutions affected by an immediate closure. The education professions appear to be the most subjected to the massive shift to teleworking. Indeed, the field of higher education has been particularly affected by these reorganizations since the supervisory authorities have decided to implement educational continuity. This continuity was "intended to ensure that students pursue school activities allowing them to progress in their learning to maintain the achievements already developed since the beginning of the year (consolidation, enrichments, exercises, etc.) and to acquire new skills when distance learning methods allow it".

Since Information and Communication Technologies (ICT) have been the only alternative to guarantee the continuity of learning in the Moroccan universities, they have

Ł. Tomczyk (Ed.): NMP 2022, CCIS 1916, pp. 254–265, 2023.
https://doi.org/10.1007/978-3-031-44581-1_18

acquired a crucial importance since the outbreak of Covid-19, especially in their relationship with the various stakeholders. Although many students have acknowledged the value of ICT, controversies still continue to exist, in many Moroccan universities, regarding the efficiency and desirability of these technologies. Hence, the focus of this study is to investigate students' perceptions of these technologies. More specifically, this survey attempts to answer two main questions: Are the new technology-based teaching methods accepted by the students? Has this experience satisfied students' learning needs?

2 Literature Review

2.1 Distance Learning During Covid-19

E-learning experiences can be analyzed and interpreted from several perspectives. The satisfaction of the main actors -teachers and the students- can be considered as the most important perspective.

Lassassi et al. (2020) conducted a study on the satisfaction of Algerian teachers in regard to e-learning experience during Covid-19 pandemic as, in that period, distance education was the only alternative to ensure pedagogical continuity. Their study concluded that the technical and environmental working conditions of teachers were generally acceptable. They were able to deliver their courses online although the majority of them had explored distance teaching for the first time. Thus, two main difficulties were noted, firstly the lack of contact with the students and secondly the quality of the internet connection.

In another study, Bączek et al. (2020) analyzed students' perception of online learning during the Covid19 pandemic. They conducted a survey based on questionnaires that they distributed to Polish medical students. According to respondents' answers (804 students), the main advantages of online learning is the ability to stay at home (69%), continuous access to online materials (69%), learning at your own pace (64%), and comfortable surroundings (54%). The authors confirmed that e-learning is a powerful tool for teaching medical students. However, the successful implementation of e-learning in the program requires a well-developed, long-term strategy and a more active approach.

Similarly, Moawad (2020) conducted a survey on Saudi educational institutions during Covid19. The author reported that the quick and sudden shift, that changed the mode of teaching from a conventional standard system to a virtual framework, might have caused intense stress on students. The analysis of his survey on students of King Saud University, College of Education, revealed that the issue with the highest percentage of stress among students was related to their uncertainty over the exams and assessments.

In the same logic, Anwar and Adnan (2020) conducted a study to examine the attitudes of Pakistani higher education students towards digital and distance learning during Coronavirus. The findings of their study stated that online learning could not produce desired results in Pakistani institutions. Many students were unable to access to a good quality internet and equipment due to technical and financial issues. The lack of face-to-face interaction with the instructor, response time, and absence of traditional classroom socialization were among the issues reported by higher education students.

Still, other researches such as Dineshkumar et al. (2020) found out that e-learning had a very beneficial role during the pandemic in spite of challenges encountered such as the lack of online teaching skills in educators, the massive time consummation of online preparation of classes, and the lack of an appropriate support from the technical team. The authors also stated that e-learning visualized inequalities faced by learners and educators in terms of quality or educational tools and equipment. The authors have thus, suggested solutions such as TV broadcast, online libraries and resources, guidelines, online channels, video lectures to have a real instructional strategy and improve student's engagement during e-learning. Several other studies have tried to understand and analyze the behavior of students in the face of distance learning in times of health crisis. Han and Sa (2021), conducted a study to examine Korean students' acceptance of online courses using the technology acceptance model. The results of their study emphasized three conclusions; First, the perceived ease of use of online courses has a positive effect on perceived usefulness. Second, the perceived ease of use and usefulness of online courses has a positive effect on educational satisfaction. Third, perceived usefulness and satisfaction showed a positive effect on intention to accept online education.

The previous studies carried out on distance learning during Covid19 pandemic have been very useful and motivating to conduct another survey to illicit students' perception of e-learning in the Moroccan universities. The results of the study of Han and Sa (2021) has motivated us to use the TAM theory of conduct a study on students' acceptability and satisfaction with technology- enhanced learning in Morocco.

2.2 Technology Acceptance Model (TAM)

Assessing the acceptance of the technology by different users is of crucial importance in evaluating its performance. It is a concept that requires the integration of several elements in order to appreciate the human/technology relationship. Research on technology is numerous, and concerns several phases: Acceptance of the technology, its implementation, its evaluation, its continuity… In all this researches, several authors have turned to the TAM theory in its various versions to conclude their findings (Jelassi and Herault 2015); (De Benedittis and Benhayoun-Sadafiyine 2018);….

Technology Acceptance Model (Davis 1989) is one of the most influential models of technology acceptance, with two primary factors influencing an individual's intention to use new technology: perceived ease of use and perceived usefulness. An older adult who perceives digital games as too difficult to play or a waste of time will be unlikely to want to adopt this technology, while an older adult who perceives digital games as providing needed mental stimulation and as easy to learn will be more likely to want to learn how to use digital games.

Although TAM has been criticized on a number of grounds, it serves as a useful general framework and it is consistent with a number of investigations into the factors that influence adults' intention to use new technology. Still, TAM theory is the most used theory to explain the link between the human being and technology (Brangier et al. 2009). It is used mainly to understand and evaluate the acceptance of the technology by users (Venkatesh and Davis 2000; Venkatesh et al.2003) in different domains (Roberts and Henderson 2000; Colvin and Goh 2005).

As stated previously, there are several versions of the TAM theory [TAM3 (Venkatesh el al. 2008)].…. However, we will use the original version of the TAM theory (Davis 1989) because we aim to test student acceptance and satisfaction with technology as set out by the study by Han and Sa (2021). The use of this version of the TAM theory can also be justified by the fact that we aim to analyze the satisfaction and acceptance of the technology by users who have been forced to use it and not by choice.

3   Methodology

Data collection was fulfilled through questionnaire (primary data). The questionnaire was sent to 732 students from different universities in Morocco. Six public universities out of 12 universities are represented in our sample, i.e. a percentage of 50%. For private institutes/universities, we have a representation of 18% of the total of private establishments in Morocco.

The level of acceptance was analyzed based on TAM theory. So, a large part of our questionnaire concerns perceived ease of use and perceived usefulness.

For the satisfaction, we analyzed it based on the level of achievement of training objectives and the nature of the relation and interactions between students and teachers/trainers.

The questionnaire is divided into three parts: A first one for general questions; a second one to investigate the acceptance in relation to ICT in learning; and a third part to investigate the satisfaction in relation to ICT in learning. Data analysis was done via SPSS software by a linear regression.

We sent our questionnaire to students from different faculties - private and public schools and institutes in Morocco. We have randomly chosen 5 public business schools, 5 public faculties and 5 private schools and universities from all over the country. This sample is made of institutes, schools and universities that have effectively adopted a distance learning policy. They are listed below:

- National School of Commerce and Management (ENCG) of El Jadida;
- National School of Commerce and Management (ENCG) of Settat;
- National School of Commerce and Management (ENCG) of Dakhla;
- National School of Commerce and Management (ENCG) of Tangier;
- National School of Commerce and Management (ENCG) of Casablanca;
- Higher School of Commerce and Business Administration (ESCA EM), Casablanca;
- Institute of Advanced Studies in Management (HEM), Casablanca;
- International University of Casablanca;
- Faculty of Science and Technology of Settat;
- Faculty of Economics of Settat;
- Faculty of Economics of Agadir;
- Faculty of Economics of Oujda;
- Faculty of Letters and Humanities of Rabat;
- International University of Rabat;
- Private University of Marrakech.

Our questionnaire contains several questions including personal information (gender and school), the perception of the level of usefulness of ICTs and their performance during distance learning courses, the number of distance sessions given during the health crisis, etc.

Two analyzes were made: the first one is related to student satisfaction and the second one is linked to their level of acceptance. We will use the same explanatory variables.

In this part we will analyze the satisfaction and acceptance of ICT separately compared to the following variables:

- Gender;
- School (private or public);
- The level of familiarity of Information and Communication technologies;
- Possession of computer equipment;
- Distance learning experience acquired before the health crisis;
- Distance courses provided during the health crisis;
- The perceived ease of use;
- The effectiveness of the courses in terms of achieving educational objectives and the development of students' knowledge.

For each analysis, we will present the summary of the models in order to visualize that the model is reliable and the table of correlations between the different variables.

4   Results

Tow statistical analyses were carried out. A first analysis for the study of students' acceptance of ICT in education and a second to study their satisfaction. To study the feasibility of the statistical method used (Linear Regression), several tests are extracted and interpreted, namely: The DW test, the R and R2, and the F statistic.

4.1   Satisfaction with ICTs in Students' Learning Activities During the Covid-19

The preliminary tests carried out to confirm the method used to analyze the data related to the students' satisfaction with ICT were as follows (Table 1).

Table 1. Linear regression model (1st test).

	Tests performed	Results
Linear regression	R	0.902
	R^2	0.813
	R^2 adjusted	0.805
	DW	1.160
	Probability of Fisher	0.000

The DW test is upper than 1, we can say that the model is relatively significant.

The correlation index $R = 0.9$ close to 1. So, we can conclude that there is a correlation between the level of employee satisfaction and the explanatory variables that we have included. The R2 = 0.81, and therefore we can say that the explanatory variables explain about 81% of our variable to be explained.

Through the statistical tests carried out, it was found that R2 is equal to 0.8, and therefore there is a correlation between the explanatory variables and the satisfaction of students. We can also say that the independent variables chosen in this model explain more than 80% of audit quality. Also, DW is close to 2 and F-statistic is lower than 5%, we can confirm that our statistical model is valid.

After the analysis of the feasibility of the statistical model, it seems necessary to present an extraction of the table of correlations in order to visualize the various existing relations between the satisfaction of the students compared to the ICT and the various explanatory variables incorporated in this model. The Table 2 gives an idea about the level of correlation existing between each of the explanatory variables and the acceptance of ICT.

Table 2. Correlations model (1st test).

	Code - Variables	ICT - Satisfaction
Pearson production	ICT – Satisfaction	1
	Gender	−0.1
	Knowledge – after – Learning	0.534
	Ease – ICT - Technology	0.534
	ICT Learning Objectives	0.534
	Distance Learning COVID19	0.534
	Exp – Distance – Learning	0.534
	Private – Public – Institute	0.899
	Equipment	0.534
	Familiarity - ICT	0.765

Student satisfaction with ICT in the training process depends on several elements. We find as variables with a strong influence:

- *The nature of the school (private or public):*

Most of students who are from faculties and private schools were satisfied with the experience of e-learning and distance learning provided during the lockdown.

The level of familiarity of Information and Communication Technologies:

This variable has a high correlation coefficient with the level of student satisfaction with ICT. The easier the technology is to handle and use, the more satisfied users will be with it. We find also as variables with an average influence:

- *Perceived ease of use:*

This variable has an average correlation coefficient (0.5) with the level of student satisfaction with ICT.

- *Possession of computer equipment:*

Having computer equipment (PC, tablet, etc.) is a crucial element in having experience in distance learning. This is why it still has a relationship with the level of student satisfaction with distance learning using ICT.

- *Distance education experience acquired before the health crisis:*

The more students are used to participate in distance training outside the context of a crisis, the better they are adapted to this new rhythm during the crisis. The experience gained before the crisis period will help teachers, faculties and students to be well adapted to this critical context and to succeed in this experience.

- *Distance learning courses provided during the health crisis:*

It can be said that it is logical that we find that the existence of training provided during the health crisis is correlated with the satisfaction of students about distance training techniques. If we did not participate in distance training during the health crisis, we would not judge if it is satisfying or not.

- *The effectiveness of training:*

Satisfaction also depends on the level of achievement of objectives perceived by beneficiaries. If, after a course, students feel that their knowledge has evolved well, and that the educational objectives assigned to the course have been achieved, they will directly show satisfaction.

However, the gender of students has little or no impact on the level of student satisfaction with ICT in the training process.

4.2 Acceptance of Use of ICT in Students' Learning Activities During the Covid-19

The preliminary tests carried out to confirm the method used to analyze the data related to the students' acceptance with ICT were as follows (Table 3).

Table 3. Linear regression model (2nd test).

	Tests performed	Results
Linear regression	R	0.902
	R^2	0.813
	R^2 adjusted	0.805
	DW	1.160
	Probability of Fisher	0.000

The DW test is upper than 1, we can say that the model is relatively significant.

The correlation index R = 0.979 close to 1. So we can conclude that there is a correlation between the level of employee satisfaction and the explanatory variables that we have included. The R2 = 0.958, and therefore we can say that the explanatory variables indicate about 96% of our variable to be explained.

Also, the level of correlation existing between each of the explanatory variables and the level of acceptance of ICT by students were as follows (Table 4).

Table 4. Correlations model (2nd test).

	Code - Variables	ICT - Satisfaction
Pearson production	Acceptance – Use - ICT	1
	Gender	−0.166
	Knowledge – after – Learning	0.647
	Ease – ICT - Technology	0.647
	ICT Learning Objectives	0.647
	Distance Learning COVID19	0.647
	Exp – Distance – Learning	0.647
	Private – Public – Institute	0.975
	Equipment	0.647
	Familiarity - ICT	0.852

The acceptance of ICT in the learning process depends on several elements. We find mainly and with a very strong correlation:

- The nature of the school (private or public).
- The degree of familiarity with ICT tools.

There are also other variables that show remarkable correlations, namely:

- The perceived ease of use;
- Possession of computer equipment;
- The experience in distance training acquired before the health crisis;
- Distance courses provided during the health crisis;
- The effectiveness of training.

5 Discussion

In accordance with several previous studies (Rizun and Strzelecki 2020); (Racero et al. 2020)…, the TAM theory was used in this study to explain and identify the elements influencing the acceptance and satisfaction of Moroccan students with respect to the use of ICT.

Through the various analyzes carried out, we notice that despite the differences in the correlation coefficients, the factors affecting the acceptance of ICT in learning during covid19 are the same as those influencing the satisfaction of students.

According to TAM's theory (David 1989), the acceptance of the use of technology depends on its usefulness and the perceived ease of use seen by the user. Our research confirmed this result; we find that its usefulness and the ease of use perceived by the user are among the variables strongly correlated with the acceptance.

Satisfaction also depends on factors influencing the acceptance of technologies defined by TAM theory along with other variables such as possession of computer equipment and experience in distance education. These results were confirmed by the study of Han and Sa (2021).

Our study joined an array of other studies that have asserted that the level of student satisfaction with the ICT and their acceptance is strongly correlated with the perceived usefulness and the perceived ease of the technology (Syahruddin et al. 2021); (Sakka 2022); (Drueke 2021); (Fauzi et al. 2021) and (Antón-Sancho et al. 2023…).

Another point to be interpreted and explained is the nature of the school or faculty that influences student acceptance and satisfaction of ICT. After analyzing the responses, we interviewed several students from the various private schools constituting our sample. These institutions used to offer seminars before the lockdown. Thus, their websites had online courses that students could consult at any time. Hence, we have found that the students who studied in these faculties/schools are more experienced and familiar with the concept of distance learning courses.

6   Recommendations

The study we have carried out aims at determining and defining the factors impacting the acceptance and satisfaction of learners with the use of ICT in the distance learning process during the health crisis and the lockdown. The study has, specifically, attempted to find out the factors impacting distance training in order to provide recommendations that can ameliorate distance training experiences within Moroccan universities. Our recommendations will therefore be oriented towards the practices to be set to improve the concept of distance training based on ICT.

Improving students' performance and knowledge are the main purposes of any university. Thus, the forms of training/teaching differ from one university to another, depending on the nature (private or public) of the fields of specialty of its faculties and/or schools (Human Sciences, Pure Sciences, Management) and many other elements. Based on the results of our study, we will present the main elements that Moroccan universities should improve in order to be efficient in distance education.

- *Improving ICT in the Moroccan universities:*

Moroccan universities suffer from several problems. The inability to meet educational needs appears to be a major shortcoming. This incapacity results from the limited number of places offered by schools and faculties and the low number of teachers recruited.

ICT can be used to remedy these weaknesses through two main actions: investing in communication technologies and introducing students and teachers to these technologies. To do this, Moroccan universities and the ministry of higher education must, first, generalize the IT courses in all faculties (where students do not receive IT courses). These courses must be more practical (or project-based) than theoretical. The content of these courses must also be updated to integrate the latest software designed (depending on the specialties).

Additionally, initiations and introductions to distance education platforms and applications should be available to all students. This can be solved by setting up tutorials for the different distance learning platforms on the university website and making them accessible to both professors and students.

The ministry of higher education is responsible for directing universities towards the acquisition of software, the design of educational platforms and the encouragement of students and teachers to use ICT in teaching and research. The integration of ICT in the teaching process will allow students a permanent learning and a better preparation for post-graduation life. The investment in digital infrastructure will help to improve scientific research and reinforce links between Moroccan researchers and researchers in neighboring countries.

- *Distance learning platforms:*

Universities must invest in interactive platforms (Zoom, Teams, etc.), to enable users (professors and students) to benefit from all the advantages of these platforms such as: "reliability, simultaneous screen share, virtual background, active speaker view, desktop and application sharing, private and group chat, the option "Raise hand", breakout rooms" (Nurieva and Garaeva 2020). Universities must conclude agreements with the various providers of these services to allow unlimited access to these various platforms.

- *Continuity of digital training:*

Distance education should be seen as a structural element but not a cyclical one. It continues to be a beneficial form of teaching to improve students' skills. This form can also help in providing/receiving academic or professional trainings/seminars to/from other universities abroad. This practical and continuous form of training can also help in the face-to-face form that exists within universities. Universities and the supervisory ministry are required to introduce this form of education after the period of Covid19. This practice may help the government to alleviate the overcrowded classrooms in the faculties and may give the possibility of creating virtual universities.

In brief, we can state that distance education must be institutionalized as a permanent form of education in Morocco. The Covid-19 crisis has pushed us to rethink already existing practices in all sectors of human life, including the education sector. However, institutionalization imposes new structures and new procedures including didactic and pedagogical approach of educational institutions. This new framework also requires new forms of public-private partnership with the integration of research centers. The foundation of a new model in the field of education requires the establishment of a national dialogue which allows all stakeholders (students, teachers, managers, researchers, associations, unions, etc.) to participate.

7 Conclusion

The use of Information and Communication Technologies is not new in universities. However, this new experience offers a new appropriation that could have a profound effect on the way education activities are organized and also on current teaching practices by redefining the roles of the different actors involved in the training process, requiring a prior analysis of training needs, explaining the objectives, supporting and investing in infrastructure and adapting the training method to different specialties and fields of expertise.

This study, which aimed at evaluating the experiences of integrating information and communication technologies into the training process of students in the Moroccan context, allowed us to clearly determine the factors influencing satisfaction and the level of acceptance of these ICTs by users in the process of university training. Our research can serve as a support for the various changes experienced by the Moroccan universities and the major changes undergone by educational actors whose experiences are increasingly publicized. However, the main limit of this work revolves around the weakness of our sample. The results, although interesting, cannot be generalized due to the non-representative nature of our sample. However, this limit can constitute a starting point for research aimed to analyze the acceptance of Moroccan students related to the use of ICT in learning activities by defining a larger sample and targeting more universities. This contribution conceives the integration of ICT in education and training not only as a cyclical means to respond to a crisis situation, but much more as a structural element aiming to bring profound changes to the conception of ICT as a real means of learning in Morocco.

The study we conducted was able to determine the factors with a significant correlation with satisfaction and acceptance of ICT in learning in order to draft recommendations aimed at improving the experience of distance learning in Morocco. We have proposed a set of lines in which public responsibles should be interested. These recommendations revolve around the design of training courses, the choice of interactive or non-interactive training courses, investment in technology and perpetuating the concept of distance learning as an effective means of teaching.

References

Antón-Sancho, A., Fernández-Arias, P., Vergara-Rodríguez, D.: Impact of the COVID-19 pandemic on the use of ICT tools in science and technology education. J. Technol. Sci. Educ. **13**(1), 130–158 (2023)

Bączek, M., Zagańczyk-Bączek, M., Szpringer, M., Jaroszyński, A., Wożakowska-Kapłon, B.: Students' perception of online learning during the Covid19 pandemic: a survey study of Polish medical students. Research Square (2020)

Brangier, E., Dufresne, A., Hammes-Adelé, S.: Approche symbiotique de la relation humain-technologie: perspectives pour l'ergonomie informatique, Le travail humain 2009/4, vol. 72, pp. 333–353 (2009)

Colvin, C.A., Goh, A.: Validation of the technology acceptance model for police. J. Crim. Just. **33**(1), 89–95 (2005)

David, F.D., Bagozzi, R.P., Warshaw, P.R.: User acceptance of computer technology: a comparison of two theoretical models. Manage. Sci. **35**, 982–1003 (1989). https://doi.org/10.1287/mnsc.35.8.982

De Benedittis, J., Benhayoun-Sadafiyine, L.: VI. Viswanath Venkatesh – Différentes perspectives sur l'implémentation des technologies. Dans : Isabelle Walsh éd., Les Grands Auteurs en Systèmes d'information, pp. 127–147 (2018). Caen: EMS Editions. https://doi.org/10.3917/ems.walsh.2018.01.0127

Dinesh Kumar, A., Karthika, R., Soman, K.P.: Stereo camera and LIDAR sensor fusion-based collision warning system for autonomous vehicles. In: Jain, S., Sood, M., Paul, S. (eds.) Advances in Computational Intelligence Techniques, pp. 239–252. Springer, Berlin (1989). https://doi.org/10.1007/978-981-15-2620-6_17

Drueke, B., Mainz, V., Lemos, M., Wirtz, M.A., Boecker, M.: An evaluation of forced distance learning and teaching under pandemic conditions using the technology acceptance model. Front. Psychol. **12** (2021)

Fauzi, A., Wandira, R., Sepri, D.: Exploring students' acceptance of Google classroom during the Covid-19 pandemic by using the technology acceptance model in west Sumatera universities. Electron. J. e-Learning **19**(4), 233–240 (2021)

Han, F., Ellis, R.A.: Predicting students' academic performance by their online learning patterns in a blended course: to what extent is a theory-driven approach and a data-driven approach consistent? Edu. Technol. Soc. **24**(1), 191–204 (2021)

Jelassi, K., Herault, S.: Continuité d'usage et appropriation de l'Internet mobile: un essai de modélisation. Manag. Avenir **78**, 59–77 (2015). https://doi.org/10.3917/mav.078.0059

Lassassi, M., Lounici, N., Sami, L., Benguerna, M., Tidjani, C.: Université et enseignants face au Covid19: L'épreuve de l'enseignement à distance en Algérie. Les Cahiers du Cread **36**(03) (2020)

Moawad, R.: Online Learning during the Covid-19 Pandemic and Academic Stress in University Students. Web of Science (WOS) (2020)

Nurieva, R., Garaeva, L.: Zoom-based distance learning of English as a foreign language. J. Res. Appl. Linguist. **11**, 439–448 (2020). https://doi.org/10.22055/rals.2020.16344. Proceedings of the 7th International Conference on Applied Linguistics Issues, Saint Petersburg, 13–14 June 2020

Racero, F., Avila, S., Gallego, M.: Predicting students' behavioral intention to use open source software: a combined view of the technology acceptance model and self-determination theory. Appl. Sci. **10**(8), 2711 (2020)

Roberts, P., Henderson, R.: Information technology acceptance in a sample of government employees, a test of the technology acceptance model. Interact. Comput. **12**, 427–443 (2000)

Rizun, M., Strzelecki, A.: Students' acceptance of the COVID-19 impact on shifting higher education to distance learning in Poland. Int. J. Environ. Res. Public Health **17**(18), 6468 (2020)

Sakka, Y.: Students' acceptance of distance learning as a result of COVID-19 impact on higher education in Jordan. Educ. Res. Int. **2022** (2022). Article ID 7697947

Syahruddin, S., et al.: Students' acceptance to distance learning during Covid-19: the role of geographical areas among Indonesian sports science students. Heliyon **7**(9) (2021)

Venkatesh, V., Davis, F.: A theoretical extension of the technology acceptance model: four longitudinal field studies. Manag. Sci. **46**(2), 186–204 (2000)

Venkatesh, V., Morris, M., Davis, G., Davis, D.: User acceptance of information technology: toward a unified view. MIS Q. **27**(3), 425–478 (2003)

Venkatesh, V., Bala, H.: Technology acceptance model 3 and a research agenda on interventions. Decis. Sci. **39**(2) (2008). https://doi.org/10.1111/j.1540-5915.2008.00192.x

Literacy and Professional Training - A Factor for Overcoming the Digital Divide: Experts' Opinion from Bulgaria

Plamena Zlatkova[(✉)] [iD] and Marchela Borisova[(✉)]

University of Library Studies and Information Technologies, 119 Tsarigradsko Shosse Blvd.,
Sofia, Bulgaria
{p.zlatkova,m.borisova}@unibit.bg

Abstract. The publication aims to present a current picture of the competence gaps in Bulgaria regarding literacy and the integration of innovations in business, education, and culture. We identify measures enshrined in several national documents related to reducing the consequences of inequality in access and skills in information society conditions.

The material also includes data from a sociological study using the in-depth interview method, which presents the vision of experts from the educational and cultural sectors about the spectrum of necessary competencies and the impact that technological innovations have on educational and cultural institutions (schools, universities, libraries).

Keywords: competencies · literacy · digital divide · survey · digital fluency · education and trainings · ICT

1 Introduction

In Bulgaria and on a global scale, the problem of literacy, in its broadest sense, is not only current but also unlikely to "subside" soon, regardless of the efforts and the policies assembled at the national and supranational levels. The issue becomes increasingly acute in the post-COVID conditions exacerbated by the military conflicts on the EU's borders. Apart from serious political, economic, social, etc. negatives, a significant increase in the spread of information with unreliable content and conspiracy theories has appeared. This "phenomenon" is inextricably relevant to the level of skills that people form throughout their life. As well as with the help of institutions covering formal and non-formal education.

PISA 2018 results reveal that 47% of 15-year-old Bulgarian students fail to develop a minimum level of reading literacy, 44% demonstrated a score below level 2 on the PISA scale of achievement in mathematics, and almost as many, 47%, have the same level of preparation in science. These results rank the country below the OECD average. The general conclusion is that "students have great difficulty in applying in practice the knowledge they have in different, close to real-life situations" [12]. In 2018, Bulgaria

Ł. Tomczyk (Ed.): NMP 2022, CCIS 1916, pp. 266–280, 2023.
https://doi.org/10.1007/978-3-031-44581-1_19

participated for the first time in the PISA assessment module dedicated to financial literacy, country score "statistically significantly lower than the Organization for Economic Co-operation and Development average" [11]. Its main findings relate to the extremely strong relationship "between students results in financial literacy and those in the main areas assessed in PISA – reading and mathematics…, with the correlation coefficient between financial literacy and mathematics results being 0.85, and between financial literacy and those in reading – 0.84" [11].

These data confirmed by the study carried out by the NGO Media Literacy Coalition, and the Center for Assessment in Preschool and School Education at the Ministry of Education and Science (MES). According to the study: "students in grade 10 have serious difficulties in retrieving and the interpretation of information from text, including media texts and data, and these difficulties are particularly visible when assessing their competencies and cognitive skills through open-ended questions and especially in tasks that require them to articulate reasoned reasoning, but they also have quite a few knowledge and skills gaps affecting safety both on the internet and on the devices used, data protection and privacy" [14].

The analysis of the Media Literacy Index 2022 (a study conducted by the Open Society Institute – Sofia, a non-governmental organization that works to support the country's EU integration processes) identifies Bulgaria, among the EU countries, as "potentially more vulnerable to fake news because several conditions are missing – the quality of education, media freedom, interpersonal trust or a combination of problems in these areas". According to the findings, attention needs to be paid not only to students and young people, but also to media and digital education of adults, including training of the trainers [15]. A significant part of the civil organizations in Bulgaria, which participated in a survey on the topic "What affects disinformation and fake news and how?", have a rather skeptical attitude towards the effectiveness of regulations and institutions in countering fake news and disinformation [13].

The need for serious rethinking is also evidenced by the results of the project "Ready for digital transformation through joint actions of social partners for the development of specific digital skills of the workforce in enterprises" as part of the activities within its framework. A study has been conducted on the needs of digital skills in 16 economic activities [7]. According to the authors of the study, "only 19% of the research participants cover the required level of digital competence for the key position they hold", and "significant differences (digital divide) in the level of digital competence between different economic sectors, as well as between individual enterprises within a sector. The levels of digital competence are in direct dependence, both on the differences in the degree of maturity of the technologies used, and on the policies of the enterprises in the development of human resources" [9], therefore, "significant deficits are emerging for a number of skills, generally in demand at a higher level than actually possessed, as well as a deficit of skills that will be needed in the next 5 years, in view of advancing digitalization and the introduction of new technologies. In this regard, lifelong learning has emerged as a key moment for all sectors, as technology is entering work processes extremely quickly." [8, 10].

Confirmation of all presented sociological studies and analyses is also found in the annual report of the European Commission (EC) on the progress regarding the introduction of digital technologies in the economy and society – DESI 2022. Among the main conclusions, the insufficient growth rate stands out of the implementation of technologies in the economy and society; the low share of individuals possessing digital skills above the basic ones (8%); the insufficient share of predominantly active citizens with basic digital skills, (31%); an insufficient degree of integration of digital technologies into business activity, with "adoption of advanced technologies such as AI and cloud computing services being even weaker"; the still intangible effect of several major digitalization initiatives in public services [2].

2 Context of the Study

Although the same research also found some positive aspects of both the studied populations and the general situation in terms of the development and use of the information infrastructure in Bulgaria, they bring to the fore valid competence deficits that seriously diverge from the requirements of the labor market. Therefore, as a logical consequence, there is a display of national development strategies and documents that target improving educational opportunities to enhance the skills of both – those who are not yet actively working and those who already have experience. Reaching out to the two groups of citizens is crucial to reduce the negative impact of the emerging digital divide related to the skills and characteristics between the generations. There is a clear shift in following the European policies and standards concerning the development of technologies and their integration into the economy and social life, the formation of highly qualified individuals competitive on the market, and overcoming the inequality between opportunities. The positive measures are incorporated in several national documents, such as the National Plan for Recovery and Sustainability, the National Reform Program for: Update 2022, the National Development Program Bulgaria 2030, the National Program Digital Bulgaria 2025, the National Operational Program Development of Human Resources 2021–2027, the Development Strategy of e-government in the Republic of Bulgaria 2019–2023, the National Strategy for Small and Medium Enterprises 2021–2027, etc. considering the transformative potential of technology to deliver the Fourth Industrial Revolution and the demands on human potential [16–18]. All the listed documents also propose policies/measures in two important directions: improving the existing infrastructure and expanding the opportunities for acquiring skills through the participation of all stakeholders. This also includes the network of informal and social partners, libraries and other cultural institutions, recognized by the EU and member states as a valuable and important partner for reducing differences in providing access and opportunities for personal and professional development.

All studies and documents (Media Literacy Index, PISA, DESI etc.) identify deficits in the complex of competencies and skills (different literacies: information, digital, media and information, etc.), including personal qualities and skills, applied complexly in certain life situations in the context of a large technological dynamics. These deficits require a reorganization of teaching approaches. The reorganization should be directed not only to the formation of a skill sets, but also to their meaning in a specific context and their integration into the complex of the learner's views. A similar philosophy of interaction and interdependence was proposed in the early twenty-first century and contained in the term "transliteracy" proposed by a team of researchers at the University of California, Santa Barbara. They believe that it is "the ability to read, write and interact across a range of platforms, tools and media from signing and orality through handwriting, print, TV, radio and film, to digital social networks" and "might provide a unifying perspective on what it means to be literate in the twenty–first century" [6] or the interaction of skills with different contexts. In 2016, Suzana Sukovic [5] further developed the idea, and defined it as ease and confidence in using a range of technologies, media and contexts ("fluidity of movement across a range of technologies, media and contexts") or skills, knowledge, thinking and acting, which enable a fluid 'movement across' in a way that is defined by the situational, social, cultural and technological context. The ease that Sukovich proposes can be seen as confidence in one's own skills, knowledge and experience adequate to the modern environment. Consequently in the process of lifelong learning (in formal and informal environments) we actually do well to strive not only to build skills but also to build confidence. Jennifer Sparrow [3] explains the difference, indeed the connection, between digital literacy and digital confidence as follows: in learning a foreign language, a literate person can read, speak, and listen to understand the new language. A confident (proficient) person can create something in the language: a story (narrative), a poem, a play or hold a conversation. Similarly, digital literacy is the understanding to use tools, while digital confidence is the ability to create something new with these tools. Or, to paraphrase Barbara Stripling [4], today's learners are not limited to the information from textbooks and books and the knowledge of their teachers. To grow in this environment, it is necessary for them to form their own research position, to be interested, to ask questions and seek answers, to become independent learners who build their worldview. When over time they develop the skills they need, they realize their responsibility and role in the lifelong learning process.

3 Methodology

It can be concluded from the exposition that the complex of competencies denoted by the term "transliteracy" is particularly important for the formation and construction of individuals who have knowledge, skills and confidence adequate to modern society and the changes in it. In the context of the European Year of Skills 2023, concerning reducing digital inequality and as a consequence of COVID19, the European Commission has made some proposals. The proposals aimed at supporting Member States and the education and training sector in providing high-quality inclusive and accessible digital education and training to develop digital skills. They relate to the two main common challenges identified jointly by the Commission and the EU Member States: 1) the lack of a comprehensive national approach to digital education and training and 2) difficulties in providing people with the necessary digital skills. The Commission has also expressed its support for digital education and skills through cooperation within the European Digital Education Center and through funding, including through the Erasmus + program [1].

Within the framework of the project TLIT4U Improving Transliteracy Skills through Serious Games 2021-1-BG01-KA220-HED-000027624, financed under the Erasmus + program, exploratory sociological research was conducted using the in-depth interview method. The sample includes an analysis of the opinions and attitudes of 18 responding participants (teachers, professors, experts from state institutions, library specialists, etc.) selected at random. A structured questionnaire with separate information blocks has been develop for them.

Individual in-depth interviews have been conducted with the invited experts, through which to study and present the level of familiarity and perception of the respondents to high-quality information in education, the complex of competences and skills integrated into education, the place of new generation technologies in the work of Bulgarian educational and cultural institutions, which are important from the point of view of the increasing connectivity between different spheres of activity.

4 Results

Asked about the **relationship between the concepts of information and digital literacy, education, and libraries**, the experts gave their definitions of the concepts, according to which digital literacy is *"the ability to use digital technologies, devices and social networks to find, organize, process, evaluate and communicate information appropriately"*, and information literacy is most commonly defined as *"a set of abilities that require people to recognize the need for information, find and evaluate information and use it effectively"*.

Three of the experts have analyzed the relationship between the two terms (information and digital literacy), concluding that they are interrelated concepts, with information literacy being *"the more general concept focused not only on the use of digital resources"* but often defined as the ability to discover, evaluate and effectively use the necessary information. In their opinion *"information literacy is a condition for the development of digital literacy"*. On the other hand, digital literacy as the understanding of how to use technology and different tools is a condition for developing information literacy. Without developed skills for working with technologies, the effective discovery, evaluation and use of the necessary information would not be possible.

We can conclude that by its core, information and digital literacy are interconnected with the creation, design, and information acknowledging, as well as the degree of acquired skills for research and proper usage by the assistance of technologies.

The interviewed experts are united in their beliefs about the direct and inseparable connection between education and libraries, with educational institutions being responsible for building a *"digitally and informationally literate person"*, through libraries, which are seen as *"the closest collaborator of educational organizations"*. *"They give the opportunity to consolidate the acquired skills, expand and upgrade learning"* because libraries as *"part of the main flow of information"* contain and unite information and digital literacy and education.

The respondents agree on the role of modern educational institutions and libraries – *"to assist in the construction and development of knowledge, skills, habits for effective discovery, evaluation and use of the necessary information (i.e. to support the construction of the information and digital human literacy in the twenty-first century)"*. According to them, *"the essence of education is expressed in the construction of a system of knowledge, skills, habits, as well as the level of the intellectual development of one or another person, of one or another set of people"*.

One of the experts also reflects on the readiness of libraries to transmit information through various media – paper, braille, CD, films, etc. The expert considers the digital age as a revolution in the way information is transmitted since *"the Middle Ages and as a result today of the ease of transmission, scanning, translation of information and online tools to analyze it"*. The expert concludes, *"that a synergy is reached that takes things to a higher level – interconnectedness, without barriers of language, race, document format, location of the recipient"*.

New educational tendencies and relevant to the economy skills are also included into survey. In the conducted in-depth interviews, a set of questions was prepared for the experts, referring to terms that have gained more and more popularity in recent years, such as digital fluency, media literacy, information literacy, ICT literacy, digital scholarship, learning skills, communications and collaboration, career management – career and identity management.

When asked about the role of libraries, schools and universities in the formation of Digital Confidence among users, all 18 experts are of the same opinion about its *"key"* role, considering that the improvement and high level of digital literacy is a condition for the development of digital confidence. Without the understanding how to use the technologies and the different tools, the creation of new information and/or a new product would not be possible. Respectively, digital confidence takes digital literacy to a higher level, requiring both the effective use of information and the ability to create a new product.

More than half of the interviewees agreed that being digitally literate means *"having the skills to create new content, knowing well how to select and use technologies to create it"*. According to them, digital confidence is built on the basis of the existing personal knowledge of learners.

Experts also agree on the institutions in which digital confidence should be formed. Universities and university libraries, schools and libraries are the institutions to build digital confidence. In all university majors and curricula, class time should be set to acquire these skills. According to the experts, this can and should happen with the help of libraries, because *"libraries have the necessary resources for users to use the acquired knowledge and realize production"* and they are the most suitable place where the user can *"exercise digital confidence"*.

The main problem, according to half of the interviewed experts, is the insufficient understanding of the importance of both information skills and competences, as well as skills related to digital confidence. They find the *"lack of trained personnel in the libraries to develop such curricula and courses"* as a drawback. According to the respondents, on one hand, training courses are needed for trainers. On the other hand, it is necessary to take actions related to ensuring good working conditions in university libraries, in which to attract motivated specialists, *"ready to upgrade continuously their skills and competences, so that they can adequately meet the expectations of them not only from the university, but also from society as a whole"*.

More than half of the experts shared that digital confidence, like any other, comes from knowledge and sufficient opportunity to use it into practice. If it is missing, *"confidence is replaced by timidity and indecision to even try"*. Therefore, the role of schools and libraries is important and decisive. We might suppose that if they provide substantial training in these areas and extensive opportunities to practice the knowledge of using the various tools, then the digital confidence of the learners will increase. According to the respondents, it is necessary for students to acquire *"serious digital literacy"* even in primary education; one of the experts also proposes an implementation: *"it would be good if tasks related to working in a team were set for students from different schools and the libraries (as a connecting link) in an online environment"*. The opinion of the interviewee is that most *"library specialists, especially in school libraries, do not have digital literacy and this makes the task even more difficult, but working on common projects (students, teachers and librarians) would be useful for each of them. Together, they could learn and gain digital confidence"*. By continuing their studies in higher education institutions, learners can have absolute confidence that they are capable of handling technological tools for the purposes and in accordance with the profile of their studies.

Of interest is the opinion of one of the experts, who compares digital confidence and digital literacy to riding a bicycle, whereas *"literacy is explaining how to sit, how to pedal, how to hold the handlebars, and confidence is after having learned everything to be able to carry on alone"*. Another expert likens confidence to *"... an artist who has outgrown the coloring book"* which he says suggests *"talent, freedom, high intelligence"*. It gives an idea of *"Montessori for librarians and students"* – with games, polls, tutorials, that is, not something mandatory and therefore boring", taking into account that *"people with talents should be left free to develop, not to make them perform some formal steps"*.

These are the theoretical and practical understanding and mastery of information and communication technologies in modern society is essential because of the need to manage an ample amount of information in various spheres of human activity – health care, libraries, schools, universities, radio, television, etc.

Asked about the role of libraries, schools and universities and librarians, teachers and educators in shaping each of the seven elements of digital literacy in users/learners, nearly a quarter of the experts responded: *"when we manage to master ICT literacy from the school or at a later stage – at the university, then we could realize and understand the seriousness of the other elements"*. The educators builds the skill for learning, communication, and cooperation. Three of the interviewed experts consider that *"information and digital literacy help to further develop and shape as individuals in the digital environment"*. The statements suppose that the digital collaboration: *"cloud technologies that enable users located at great distances from each other to work at the same time, on the same documents, help"*. In the last several years (with the start of the COVID pandemic), working online increasingly became a norm: working from home, leading workshops, online training for career and personal growth, webinars, seminars and, last but not least, school classes and university lectures. Enabling online work and study, requires information and digital literacy.

Experts are united around the thesis that good information and digital literacy, in the presence of such an immense quantity of data and sources, *presupposes the natural formation of critical thinking skills in the learner*. Fostering critical thinking requires special attention at school, at higher education. Each of the elements of digital literacy should be established and recognized at the very beginning of digital literacy. They are like *"pieces of a puzzle that will allow us to see the whole picture"*. The initial talk about "*socialization of children in schools and kindergartens, now we are talking about digital collaboration and communication skills*". That is, experts reflect on the ability to use technologies for teamwork (working on one project from different parts of the world) and career development in a much larger collective.

In a rapidly evolving digital world, librarians are even more determined to elevate the status of the library in society by "*improving every day to be as useful as possible to their users*". As a result of their initiative to update their professional practices, libraries fit into our world increasingly. According to the experts, media literacy is delicate, which necessitates the *need to distinguish between misinformation and reliable information*. To reach a comprehensive level of fluency in media literacy, it *is necessary to apply the lessons learned in school, university and seek advice from the libraries*. One expert elaborated on the role of the librarian "*to educate appropriately for different audiences*" and applied the seven elements of digital literacy to users. The following parallel is drawn: "*we divide people into analogue literate and illiterate without a chance to find a job and be fully present in society, so without ICT technologies there is neither present nor future for a student or teacher*". This also reflects on possible "roles" for the librarian: *multiplexer, rights activist, hacker, manager, self-esteem booster*. At universities and especially in the library, Media literacy suggests students search in recognized databases; Information literacy – expects an understanding of the library's electronic catalog and the specific functionalities of the full-text and abstract databases; ICT literacy – work in different formats; plagiarism software; Learning skills – students to search for information on their own; unified search in databases, where there helps and tutorials for the software they are interested in; Communications and collaboration – creating a community of library users; Career and Identity management.

One of the interviewed experts provides an in-depth analysis of each of the elements, correctly noting that all seven elements of digital literacy are key "*competencies of the modern person in the twenty-first century*". The development of media literacy could be achieved through "*the use of interactive teaching methods, experiential learning, problem-solving learning, group activities and projects*". Regarding the "*communication and cooperation*" element, the expert notes the key "*teamwork – part of the so-called soft skills*", such as teamwork, is "*a necessary condition for successful implementation in modern society*". The role of schools, universities and libraries is to create favorable conditions for the development of teamwork skills "*by involving pupils, students and users in group and partner tasks, simulations, educational games and joint projects*".

For effective career management development, experts believe that it is necessary to build "*skills to understand and critically evaluate one's own development needs in order to manage one's career and achieve professional success*". Schools, libraries and universities could support this process with the help of existing career centers, individual counseling and personal development programmes with closer connection to Ministry of education and science and administrated by it National portal for students' career orientation [18].

A significant opinion of the one of the experts is about the *necessity for educators and teachers to build and form all 7th elements of digital literacy*. And libraries are the institutions that *should support and assist both teachers in schools and university professors.* Some of these skills can be developed with the help of library specialists only. However, *Bulgaria has a long way to go before the actual entry into practice.*

A set of questions was also prepared for the conversations with the experts, referring to the importance of the elements of Digital Confidence for library users, learners and library specialists, teachers and lecturers. Interviewees were asked to rank the items in order of importance. Everyone agrees on the importance of the specified elements of Digital Confidence (Data fluency, Innovation fluency, Curiosity fluency, Creation fluency, Communication fluency), since technology and digitization, which are in all spheres of life, are a prerequisite for the need to the mastery of each of the elements. First and second most important are creative confidence (Creation fluency) and confidence in professional communication (Communication fluency), and the remaining three elements are interconnected and derive from each other: Curiosity fluency, Innovation fluency, Data fluency.

Conducted survey **sought to explore the intersection between the innovations, education and culture**. Regarding the relationship between Education 4.0, Industry 4.0, Internet of Things, Artificial Intelligence, Big Data and libraries, schools and universities, the interviewed experts pointed that *Education 4.0 is a comprehensive concept of modernization and digitalization of education, which is inspired by the fourth industrial revolution related to the promotion of high technologies in production (Industry 4.0).* In order for learners to be prepared for life and their profession, they must be trained using modern methods and training tools, including the use of Artificial Intelligence, Internet of Things and Big Data. The implementation of this modernization process requires a *complex approach and cooperation between libraries, schools and universities and the implementation of joint projects with the participation of a team of specialists.* Experts believe that libraries are "*base and play a nodal role; they can actively assist in the implementation, realization and realization of the above*".

One of the experts reflected on Industry 2.0 and the role of libraries – *they kept patents for machines, blueprints and much more.* Since then, there are also the first copyright protection laws. "*Industry and Education 3.0 introduced greater communication between the teacher (previously an unchallenged authority) and students, and ushered in the use of computers and other IT to make the creation and transmission of information incredibly easy*".

In Education 4.0, Industry 4.0, and IoT, where everything is interconnected and aided by artificial intelligence algorithms and the overall advancement of digital technologies, the library's role *is to be engaged with protecting their users from content that is not relevant, peer-reviewed, ethical, harmful content,* etc.

According to the expert, "*perhaps one day, just as we have the first humanoid robot with character and intelligence close to human – Sophia, we will also have our improved version – a librarian who we have trained to have our expertise, but who does not suffer from fatigue, health problems and pay problems to reduce his effectiveness*".

The rapid pace of technological advancement compels us to constantly update our skills. The ability to navigate different fields of these technologies in the educational process is fundamental and valuable for the development of Bulgarian society. It boosts scientific research because as technology advances, so does science.

In this context, a set of questions has been prepared, where the Bulgarian experts are asked to share a reasoned opinion about the significance of technology in the fields of education and scientific research.

Respondents were on the same opinion about technology's improvements as the driving force for society, and science: *"knowledge and the constant effort to increase human understanding through research. This effort 'gives birth' to technologies through which we more easily conduct research into unexplored human realms"*. One of the interviewed participants highlights the importance of technologies that *"give new horizons and opportunities for deeper studies and restorations of springs"*. The expert provides an example of archaeologists achievements with the most modern techniques. After the objects are photographed and reconstructed – *"unique opportunities for making new discoveries, and hence analyses"* are available.

Half of the interviewed experts see technology importance in most spheres of activity: medicine, transportation, the economy, etc. In scientific research, they see technology as a mechanism that drives progress, which can contribute to the whole society and literally change our lives, and they give an example with the *"hadron collider"*, *"transplants"*, *"space travel"*. According to the interviewed specialists, in the education sphere, technologies have more of a supporting and facilitating function since: *"a person can be taught to think with a sheet and a pencil"*, *"it facilitates the work of communication of discoveries, file sharing, information retrieval"* and as the CORONA-pandemic shows – *"the possibility of virtual classrooms, conferences and the 'going online' of all professional life"*.

Another significant topic associated with the subject concern to the **disinformation, digital safety and the role of teachers, university lecturers and library specialists**. The experts participating in the survey were asked to share their opinions and thoughts on the necessary skills in order to successfully distinguish between reliable and non-reliable information. All respondents agree that false information is exponentially increasing and it is important for consumers to be able to recognize and distinguish between reliable and non-reliable information. It is necessary to select and use authoritative sources – such sources can be both mainstream media and blogs, specialized publications, official institutions (e.g. ministries, universities, etc.), and/or *"the good old books in the library"*. This is one of the ways to successfully *"sift"* true from false information, emphasizing that it *"should not be forgotten that history is written by people and this is their reality, point of view and absolute objectivity does not exist. So it remains, the skill to find reliable information from different points of view about facts, events or definitions, which would help to look at our "assignment" as a 3D model from all sides and thus make an adequate decision for the implementation of the project"*. Disinformation is increasingly reaching people through a large selection of social networks. But, although increasingly used by politicians, and government organizations, they remain *"sitting and playing a game of broken phone"*.

One expert suggests building a *"network of people and sources you can trust"* such as sites, agencies, publishers, etc., that are secure and verify information. The interviewee gives an idea for courses involving new applications – reverse image search, videos, plagiarism detection software.

Regarding the current topic of digital safety and whether the librarian, teacher, lecturer have a role in forming such skills in users/learners, experts are of the opinion that librarians have a major role in building skills to safely search, find and evaluate the necessary information. The teacher's role in this process is fundamental for young students who have not yet developed the skills and habits to search for information safely, which is why. Experts believe that a meaningful librarian's role is building digital safety skills and they need to be *"resourced, knowledgeable, and willing to educate users"*. Experts also reflect on the various areas of application of digital skills that are becoming wider, giving the example of mobile phones, where digital skills are required to be used safely and without risks.

Most governments train teachers in digital skills. The purpose of this strategy is to implement the educational plans that have been developed in this matter. We can apply them to all those economic activities that require the use of computer systems and web surfing. On the other hand, they are also necessary in the process of teaching so many students through information seeking.

Digital entertainment also expects this type of skill, for example when we watch a movie on an audiovisual content platform or on social networks themselves. Digital skills are the knowledge and skills that enable us to navigate the web or use electronic devices safely and effectively.

The conveniences and facilities that the Internet does not bring solely positive outcomes. *"Every luxury has a price, and in this case, it is the "complete exposure of personal data"*. This digital *"undressing"* of our activities and preferences, on the one hand, makes it easier to offer information and interests, but on the other hand, exposes us to a risk that should not be underestimated. Cyberbullying and hacking attacks on personal data are risks to recognize and respond to, so they can be minimized. These are serious crimes that can have consequences, especially for teenagers. An expert gives an example: If at one time in an electrical engineering class we were introduced to a contact and how *"electricity works, it was MANDATORY to explain what we should not do to avoid being electrocuted and what to do if we are!"*. The respondent concluded that the topic of digital safety should not only be one of the first in digital literacy education, but should not stop being present as a core lesson from primary school *"and all the way to the completion of primary and secondary education"*. An increasing number of young children are dexterous with smart phones and other types of devices and we admire *"the technological gene of young children, not realizing that this goes hand in hand with risk and children should be aware of it, as they know how to play clips on YouTube!"*.

The COVID pandemic has categorically proven the importance of technology in all spheres of public life, including education and. Without technology, education would not fulfill its role, which is to prepare the younger generation for life and the future profession.

The final part of the interviews with the Bulgarian experts was focused on the **key skills of the twenty-first century**, namely: reading literacy, mathematical literacy, scientific literacy, emotional intelligence, personal development skills, creativity, innovation; finding and using relevant information, critical thinking skills, communication skills (written and verbal communication), teamwork skills, fake news recognition skills, safe behavior in the digital ecosystem, curiosity, persistence, creativity, financial literacy and digital literacy. To maintain and improve these skills, *"we must educate and develop throughout our lives; a desire to continuously learn and acquire the relevant knowledge, skills and competences to be better citizens and professionals"*.

Some of the experts (five) highlight adaptability and flexibility, as well as the skills to evaluate information and the ability to *"interact with people, the ability to be an intersection between industry, copyright, education, university projects, laboratories, creativity and leisure"*.

5 Discussion and Conclusion

The partnership between educational and cultural institutions is hindered by the lack of a comprehensive state approach to digital education and training, which affects learning in schools and universities. A comprehensive state approach is not extensive enough or fails to help gain digital confidence in using different tools to create a new product. Serious and thorough training in information and digital competences in the curricula at school and university level is needed, which will help *"with ease and confidence, people find a path to realization and improvement"*. The elements of digital confidence are important for all who would like to be adequate in the modern world, to have a successful professional realization and career development, and to move both themselves and society forward. All elements of Digital Confidence (Curiosity fluency, Communication fluency, Creation fluency, Data fluency, Innovation fluency) are in synergy and/or intersection. The ability to create a new product or new information could not be achieved without purposeful work to develop each of these elements. The foundations of digital confidence should be laid as early as primary school age. This requires both teachers and university lecturers and librarians to *"have, develop and improve their digital confidence by engaging in training, exchanging experiences and collaborating with other professionals"*. If digital confidence is not mandatory for library users and its lack is not fatal (after all, not every user is a learner or specialist in a certain field), then it is important for library professionals to have the confidence that they can meet the needs of everyone or almost every user. This is not an easy task, considering that some librarians and teachers still do not take advantage of the full range of technological tools to facilitate both their work and the tasks of learners. The *"OLD SCHOOL"* generation of teachers and librarians do not feel „in their own waters "in the digital environment, but although timid, if they themselves have a curiosity about the surrounding technology, they could gain the necessary confidence. Moreover, the *"discovery" of technologies together (learners, trainers and librarians) would bring special pride in what has been achieved"*.

Libraries, universities and schools are part of a rapidly changing digital world, and technologies, industries and societal patterns and processes are changing every day along with the digital and information society.

The common link between Education 4.0, Industry 4.0, Internet of Things, Artificial Intelligence, Big Data helps the faster development and improvement in each of the institutions, because without education, there will be no development, without development there will be no industry, without the industry, there will be no technology either – *"This is the chain of the successful person, business and profession"*.

The technological advancement is what drives the development of humanity and the economy these days. These processes will not slow down, but rather accelerate.

As the entire industry modernizes, formal education will also. Almost every profession today operates in a highly technological environment. New technologies are being implemented as quickly as possible for more production and profit, but in education, progress is much slower and relatively conservative and traditional. This means that we might thinking on an overall philosophy for the modernization and digitization of formal education, with the main goal being through technological tools and resources, to stimulate education in a non-traditional way. In Bulgaria, curricula in schools and universities must be updated. They should include all the key competences related to information, digital and media literacy, because school and university are the places where knowledge and skills on the use of digital technologies are formed and developed, and libraries contribute to this process.

In recent years, the topic of the place of libraries as centers for digital inclusion and improvement of citizens' digital competences has been increasingly discussed in Bulgarian society due to the libraries resources and means to provide an opportunity and continue the process of upgrading digital competences. Librarians possess the necessary skills to enable users to build, refine, and understand digital technologies, use them and solve complex problems.

They (libraries) follow the standards of digital, information and media literacy. As for media literacy, vigilance is needed to distinguish between reliable information and misinformation, and libraries, to a large extent, have licensed databases that contain a high percentage of reliable information. And the formation of media literacy, recognized as one of the key competences of the twenty-first century, should be a priority and be developed from primary school age. This can be achieved through joint programs between libraries, schools and universities.

Viewing libraries and universities as an environment for the development of digital literacy and digital confidence, institutions carry out research on the need for training for the development of digital literacy and digital confidence, and at the same time create individual curricula and programs tailored to the level of development of students' digital literacy.

In conclusion, the role of modern educational institutions and libraries is to assist in the construction and development of knowledge, skills and habits for effective discovery, evaluation and use of the necessary information (i.e. to support the construction of the information and human digital literacy in the twenty-first century). And the essence of education is expressed in *"building a system of knowledge, skills, habits, as well as the level of intellectual development of one or another person, of one or another group of people"*.

The conducted research presents the opinions of Bulgarian experts from the educational and cultural sector, who in a situation of catch-up development and as representatives of the formal and informal learning environment, find it necessary to re-examine the frameworks, forms and approaches of cooperation in order to expand the scope of access to education and technology to a wider range of citizens. Only the understanding of the important role of lifelong learning and the timely adaptation and participation of all stakeholders in sync with technological developments can be a prerequisite for reducing the existing digital inequalities.

References

1. European Commission: European Year of Skills 2023 (2022). https://commission.europa. eu/strategy-and-policy/priorities-2019-2024/europe-fit-digital-age/european-year-skills-202 3_en. Accessed 02 June 2023
2. European Commission: The Digital Economy and Society Index (DESI). Shaping Europe's Digital Future (2023). https://digital-strategy.ec.europa.eu/bg/policies/desi. Accessed 02 June 2023
3. Sparrow, J.: Digital fluency: preparing students to create big bold problems. EDUCAUSE Rev. **53**(2), 54 (2018)
4. Stripling, B.: Teaching deep reading skills during inquiry. Can. Sch. Libr. J. **5**(3), (2021). ISSN 2560-7227. https://journal.canadianschoollibraries.ca/teaching-deep-reading-skills-during-inquiry/. Accessed 24 Sept 2023
5. Sukovic, S.: What Exactly Is Transliteracy? Elsevier SciTech Connect (2016). https://scitec hconnect.elsevier.com/what-exactly-is-transliteracy/. Accessed 02 June 2023
6. Thomas, S., et al.: Transliteracy: crossing divides. First Monday **12**(12) (2007). https://doi. org/10.5210/fm.v12i12.2060
7. Българска Стопанска Камара: БСК стартира проект за повишаване на дигиталните компетенции на заетите в икономиката (2022). https://www.bia-bg.com/news/view/ 29580/. Accessed 02 June 2023
8. Българска Стопанска Камара: Проведоха се дискусии за резултатите от 16 секторни проучвания за потребностите от дигитални умения (2022). https://www. bia-bg.com/news/view/31491/. Accessed 02 June 2023
9. Българска Стопанска Камара: Нивото на дигитални умения изостава от изискванията на пазара на труда (2023). https://www.bia-bg.com/news/view/31555/. Accessed 02 June 2023
10. Българска Стопанска Камара: Преобладаващата част от предприятията са с ниско ниво на дигитализация (2023). https://www.bia-bg.com/news/view/31523/. Accessed 02 June 2023
11. Василева, Н.: Българските петнадесетгодишни ученици и парите: резултати от участието на България в модул финансова грамотност в PISA 2018 (2020). https://www.copuo.bg/sites/default/files/uploads/docs/2020-05/FinLit_PISA2018_ BGR.pdf. Accessed 02 June 2023
12. Василева, Н.: Резултати от участието на България в Програмата за международно оценяване на учениците PISA 2018 (2020). https://www.copuo.bg/sites/default/files/upl oads/docs/2020-07/Pisa_2018_full.pdf. Accessed 02 June 2023
13. Захариев, Б.: Какво и как влияе на дезинформацията и фалшивите новини?: представяне на данни от анкетно проучване сред граждански организации – бенефициенти по Фонд Активни граждани България (2022). https://osis.bg/wp-con tent/uploads/2023/01/Disinformation-v9.pdf. Accessed 02 June 2023
14. Коалиция за медийна грамотност: Национално изследване за оценяване на дигитално-медийните компетентности на гимназистите: аналитичен доклад (2022). http://short.bg/yLhSI. Accessed 02 June 2023
15. Лесенски, М.: Как започна всичко и как продължава?: Индекс на медийната грамотност 2022: доклад (2022). https://osis.bg/wp-content/uploads/2022/10/HowItStar ted_MediaLiteracyIndex2022_BG.pdf. Accessed 02 June 2023
16. Министерство на транспорта, информационните технологии и съобщенията: Национални стратегически документи [във връзка с цифровата трансформация] (2023). https://egov.government.bg/wps/portal/ministry-meu/strategies-policies/digital.tra nsformation/itis-national-strategic-documents. Accessed 27 July 2023

17. Министерство на транспорта, информационните технологии и съобщенията: Стратегически документи на ЕС касаещи цифровата трансформация и развитието на информационните технологии и обществото (2023). https://egov.government.bg/wps/portal/ministry-meu/strategies-policies/digital.transformation/itis-strategic-documents. Accessed 27 July 2023

18. Национален портал за кариерно ориентиране на учениците. https://orientirane.mon.bg/programa/. Accessed 07 July 2023

Digital Divide as a Challenge for Polish Social Gerontology

Łukasz Tomczyk[1]([envelope]) [iD], Joanna Wnęk-Gozdek[2] [iD], and Katarzyna Potyrała[3] [iD]

[1] Jagiellonian University, Stefana Batorego 12, 31-135 Kraków, Poland
lukasz.tomczyk@uj.edu.pl
[2] Pedagogical University, Romana Ingardena 4, 33-332 Kraków, Poland
[3] Cracow University of Technology, Warszawska 24, 31-155 Kraków, Poland

Abstract. Along with the intensive development of the information society, many beneficial phenomena improving the quality of life of Internet users have appeared. Unfortunately, there is still an unharmonic participation of all age groups in cyberspace. This phenomenon is described as digital exclusion. This digital divide has been studied in detail and described in the sociological, pedagogical and gerontological literature. Despite a solid theoretical basis and many activities aimed at digital inclusion, so far the digital divide has not been completely eliminated. More than two decades of research allow us to notice several important regularities about the phenomenon of lack of full participation of older people in cyberspace. This chapter is unique due to the first attempt to systematise the phenomenon of digital exclusion in Poland with the use of the popular J. V. Dijk concept. The article presents several perspectives: individual conditions, systemic solutions and gaps to be filled. Despite its theoretical nature, due to the methodology used, the text has a number of postulates useful in gerontological practice. The individual perspective refers to the needs of seniors, their physical conditions and cognitive characteristics. The community perspective, on the other hand, aims at presenting proven and useful practices for digital inclusion in various non-formal education institutions. Thus, the text intertwines the perspectives of individual and horizontal conditions. The study is the result of the international project "REMEDIS is supported in Poland by the National Science Centre - NCN [021/03/Y/HS6/00275]".

Keywords: Poland · Digital Divide · Digital Inclusion · Social Gerontology · Geragogy · Universities Of The Third Age · Volunteers

1 Introduction

It may seem that today's societies have the privilege to live in the times of great opportunities and unlimited possibilities. The previous time and space limits have been overcome thanks to the latest technologies and digital solutions are being introduced into every area of human life Unfortunately, progressing digitisation and computerisation are not followed by the development of digital literacy of individual citizens. The concepts of digital or information society [1] are not fully adequate if we consider the indicators of

Ł. Tomczyk (Ed.): NMP 2022, CCIS 1916, pp. 281–294, 2023.
https://doi.org/10.1007/978-3-031-44581-1_20

participation of certain individuals in using digital technologies and information processing. Some social groups, like seniors, the unemployed or people with disabilities remain less active and sometimes passive in these areas [2]. In addition, it should be mentioned that the way the information society is currently being defined is changing, which is sometimes referred to not only as an information or network society, but also as a platform society [58]. The accessibility to platforms, i.e. e-services, is an important determinant of belonging to the group of e-citizens or the digitally excluded.

This situation requires the implementation of wide-scale actions to minimise the digital divide in every aspect and area of human life. The goal of digitisation of the society is to increase the individual participation in the social life and the chances for self-development. However, we must remember that this process has various consequences. On the one hand, popularisation of the modern technologies helps to level social inequalities and fight exclusion [3]. On the other hand, it may lead to even greater divide [4–8]. According to research [9] digital gap is not only the result of the lack of access to modern technologies or insufficient digital literacy but depends on such subjective factors as distrust, ignorance, lack of faith in own abilities or interest [10, 11]. And while mass-scale computerisation really levels the access and enables participation in the social life, thus, reducing the risk of social exclusion [12] (p. 173), it is not capable of eliminating the subjective, psychological barriers mentioned above.

Since 2000 (Strategia Lizbońska), Poland has been taking different initiatives to develop the information society. All refer to the three strategic objectives adopted by the European Commission: access to cheaper and faster Internet, mobilisation of the citizens to use it and investing in people by increasing their competencies [3]. Digital inclusion is being implemented country-wide and locally. Some of the initiatives, especially these focusing on overcoming the motivational barriers, are implemented based on Reder's pathway to digital inclusion [13]. The interventions address elimination of barriers at the following stages: digital access, digital taste, digital readiness and digital literacy. The needs in this area are great as there is still a great percentage of Poles, especially the oldest citizens, who for different reasons remain offline [14].

In the age of general ageing of the human population, the issues of inclusion and participation of seniors in the social life have become particularly relevant. According to the UN estimates, by 2030 people aged 65 and more will constitute 23.8% of the global population. In Poland, senior citizens will be 1/4 of the population by that year [15]. For different reasons, some of them will remain at social margins. One of the key challenges of the humanity is to create the conditions which would facilitate inclusion of this population into all forms of activity, also the ones using new technologies. Active participation of seniors in the global network will allow us to benefit from their potential to even greater extent.

The problem of participation of the older people in the cyberspace presented herein is a valuable contribution to the global discourse about reduction of social inequalities and promotion of active ageing. Learning about the nature of digital inclusion of the oldest citizens in different European countries supports the effective continuation of the already implemented actions and the development of new, holistic solutions. The goal of this publication is the exchange of opinions and experiences related to digital inclusion. It is the contribution of Polish researchers to the development of an interdisciplinary space for collaboration to solve the problems of digital divide. It shows the characteristic features of digital divide and documents the selected good practices in the area of inclusion. The authors present the actual state of research into the activity of Poles in the cyberspace and attempt to implement the concept of J. V. Dijk to Polish conditions. The implications discussed in the paper are based on the experiences related to teaching seniors in U3As or the Lighthouse Keepers of Digital Poland project. They are a valuable source of practical knowledge and inspiration to continue the studies in the area of reducing the "digital gap". The final recommendations are universal and may be useful for all the international community.

2   Digital Divide – Theoretical Framework

Research on digital exclusion generally focuses on socioeconomic factors, although basic internet access is no longer a major obstacle to digital integration. Individual factors are considered less frequently, which causes some people to remain unadjusted to the surrounding world of new media. This is because in this case, you cannot generalize the results on the reasons for digital exclusion and you cannot predict changes in the population due to a lack of involvement in digital media. However, many negative attitudes towards the Internet are identified. They are related to a lack of confidence in digital technologies, perception of the age as exclusion factor or a lack of digital knowledge.

In the light of the analysis carried out by Jasiński and Bąkowska [16], the fact of being a senior does not increase the risk of social exclusion. Rather, exclusion is associated with specific traits and behaviors that may accompany old age, e.g. material poverty, negative stereotypes widespread in society, less physical fitness or disability.

Literature in the field of digital participation highlights both the material factors that lead to digital exclusion and the attitudes, skills and culture of using the Internet [17]. Exclusion patterns persist even when access is almost universal and many services are only available online [18].

Helsper, Reisdorf [18] cite studies that show that there is rarely a direct relationship in which one indicator pierces all others as an explanation of digital exclusion, while three indicators consistently appear as strong predictors of Internet access and use: age, education and disability. In 2010, Van Dijk and Van Deursen [19] noted that the level of education is a key explanatory variable in understanding differences in Internet literacy.

The concept of digital exclusion is generally associated with unequal access and the ability to use information and communication technologies that are perceived as necessary for full participation in social life [20]. Digital division is defined as inequality in access to information and communication technologies, and above all the internet [21]. In 2005, Van Dijk [22] identified a sequential relationship between social inequalities and unequal access to digital technologies.

In 2012, definitions based on the terms "user/non-user" and the internet ("have/do not have") were moved to the exploration of the gradation of Internet use and skills that are the cause of the "digital divide" between people [23]. In 2012, van Dijk cited the concept of "digital skills" as a series of several types of skills. The most basic are "instrumental skills" or "operational skills", the ability to work with hardware and software, however, he also drew attention to all types of skills related to content required for the effective use of computers and the Internet, distinguished "structural/information skills" from "strategic skills". Information skills are the skills to search, select, and process information in computer and network sources. Strategic skills can be defined as the ability to use computer and network sources as a means to achieve specific goals and the overall goal of improving position in society [24].

The digital division of society can also be understood as inequality in four further types of access: motivation, physical access, digital skills and various uses [24]. The current, mainly European situation of all four types of access is described in details. For example, the differences in digital engagement were identified from basic use involving individual communication, through indirect use involving individual networking to advanced use involving civic participation. Therefore, more recent literature focuses on areas related to skills and knowledge in understanding digital exclusion as much as Internet access.

Van Dijk and Van Deursen [25] tackled the digital divide in terms of differences in Internet skills. They include operational (basic skills), formal (navigation and orientation), information (information needs for users), strategic (ability to use the Internet as a means to achieve specific goals and improve position in society), as well as social skills, creative and mobile. Helsper and Van Deursen [18] add that communication and socio-emotional skills should be included in this framework, as these are important skills in the context of social media. It is emphasized that the development of digital skills is also influenced by social environments and learning patterns by family, friends, school and workplace [26].

Already in 2012, Scheerder, van Deursen and van Dijk [9] wrote that social conditions could, for example, be used for qualitative research, how individuals interact and negotiate with others in various contexts, such as home or work, but social and cultural conditions require additional information to interpret their meaning.

In digital exclusion studies, Śmiałowski [27] describes two approaches: lenticular and holistic. In the lenticular approach, the phenomenon of digital exclusion is analyzed independently for each of the dimensions (access, use, skills), which leads to difficulties in the overall assessment of the scale of digital exclusion. However, in a holistic approach, all dimensions are taken into account simultaneously. The most frequently studied dimensions in the holistic approach are: infrastructure, availability and application. For some indicators, the following conditions are also taken into account: political, economic and socio-demographic. The most popular holistic measures include: DIDIX (Digital Divide Index), NRI (Network Readiness Index), IDI (ICT Development Index) and DDI (Digital Divide Index). The CSO report from 2007–2011 contains information that shows that among people aged 65–74 in 2011, only 10.8% regularly used a computer, while among people aged 55–64 - as much as 31.6%. In response of the Undersecretary of State in the Ministry of Administration and Digitization to the interpellation on the digital exclusion of seniors in 2014, we read that only 12% of Polish people in the 55–64 age group and 19% in the 45–54 age group have an average level of computer skills, while the average level of internet skills is declared by 11% of Polish people in the 55–64 age group and 17% in the 45–54 age group. The above data indicate a significant barrier to professional exclusion of the 45+ age group, which is the lack of basic competences and digital skills. The report on the quality of life of the elderly, prepared by the Central

Statistical Office in 2015, shows that 13% of people 65+ use the Internet every day or almost every day. In turn, statistics obtained by Megapanel/PBI show that every fifth Polish 55+ used the network in 2016, when in 2005 it was only a percentage (3.4%) [27].

The conclusions of the Aasa Report - Digitally Excluded Polish Women 2017, largely focus on the fact that digital exclusion concerns almost every third Polish woman aged 45–70, as a result of which more than 2 million women are within the problem. As many as 38% of digitally excluded women do not have access to the Internet, and 39% do not use the network despite having access to it. Among the digitally excluded women, a large proportion are rural residents (43%) and people with secondary education (43%). The share of women in the digitally excluded group increases with age. For women aged 45–49, it is 8%, and for women aged 65–70 it is 35% [27].

Research carried out by Śmiałowski [27] indicates the existence of a large diversity in the access and use of ICT. In the period of his analysis (2003–2015), the phenomenon of digital exclusion is steadily decreasing, however, the problem of digital inequality is still significant in Polish society, despite the fact that almost 80% of households were equipped with a computer and Internet connection, the percentage of people digitally excluded in 2015 still accounted for over 50%, and the percentage of people fully using the latest ICT solutions was only 24.8%. The obtained results confirm that the scale of digital exclusion is increasingly influenced by the dimension of digital competences, and with a smaller impact of having ICT [27].

The digital exclusion of older people in the face of the growing number of seniors in the population may in the future be a serious social problem and also the loss of a large market for suppliers of goods and services. Social exclusion is a multidimensional phenomenon and means the inability to participate in economic, political and social life as a result of a lack of access to resources, goods and institutions, limitation of social rights and deprivation of needs.

Focus studies carried out by Huterska [28] pointed to the important role of so-called soft factors (i.e. not related to physical access to the Internet) in deciding to opt out of certain activities (online purchases) by people over the age of 65 [28].

This is confirmed by research on access to and use of the Internet by Polish society, conducted periodically by the Central Statistical Office. Walkowski [29] states that digitally excluded people are much more difficult to overcome psychological than technical barriers to Internet access and learning basic computer skills. This situation requires urgent improvement. People who do not use the Internet are socially and professionally limited or practically disabled, which causes measurable economic losses.

In Poland, according to Eurostat data, the group of people who have never used the Internet is 22%, while for the entire EU this percentage is only 14%. This share would certainly be much higher if people aged 75 and older participated in the study. Most people regularly use the Internet in Denmark, Luxembourg, Great Britain, Finland, the Netherlands and Sweden (over 90%). In these countries, the percentage of people who have never used the internet reaches a maximum of 5%, and the least people regularly use the internet in Bulgaria (59%), Romania (60%), Italy (69%), Greece (69%) and Portugal (70%). In these countries, the highest percentage of people who have never used the Internet was also identified (from 25% in Italy to 33% in Bulgaria). The level of all tested skills related to using the Internet was lower in Poland than the average for the European Union. For example, the average percentage of people using e-mail in the EU is 72%, and in Poland only 60%. The results of the analysis indicate that Poland is in a group of nine countries where the extent of the threat of digital exclusion is the largest [30].

Statistics in this respect are not satisfactory for Poland - the level of socially and digitally excluded people is higher than the European average [31]. In 2019, 86.7% of households had access to the Internet in Poland, which means an increase of 2.5 pp. compared to the previous year. Therefore, it seems that counteracting digital exclusion should focus mainly on overcoming psychological barriers and therefore it is important that the assistance program be adapted to the needs, possibilities and individual characteristics of the beneficiaries [31].

To the above data showing the level of digital exclusion in Poland, the most recent results of analyses conducted by Eurostat should be added, which show that 92% of households in Poland have access to the Internet. This result places Poland among the European Union average. However, the same report notes that the frequency of regular Internet use decreases with metric age. For example, in the 45–54 interval, 91.5% use the Internet, while in the 55–64 interval, this rate decreases to 75.5%, and in the 65–74 interval, only 51% of respondents use the Internet. Metric age is also a key factor not only for the regularity of Internet use, but also for the level of digital competence. For example, in the 65–74 age bracket, only 13.4% can copy files, 9.4% can install software and 7.0% can change the settings of any software. Based on the cited data, it is apparent that digital exclusion is a real challenge for the Polish information society [32].

3   Digital Inclusion - Polish Case Study

This chapter presents a review of the most popular educational solutions in Poland, related to digital inclusion of the senior citizens. It should be pointed out that in this aspect, Poland stands out compared to other countries in the region due to, among others, very active Universities of the Third Age or NGOs [33]. The uniqueness of the initiatives presented herein has been proved by the number of seniors engaged in the information society or the number of volunteers or organisations working with older people. What we present is only a brief description which does not fully cover all the methodological, administrative or conceptual solutions.

3.1   Lighthouse Keepers of Digital Poland

One of the interesting and innovative projects aimed at minimising digital divide in Poland is the project Lighthouse Keepers of Digital Poland. Given the high percentage of digitally excluded senior citizens who do not have the access to digital education offered by U3As, senior activity centres or commercial institutions, a non-standard initiative has been launched. In small towns and villages, which lack senior-oriented educational infrastructure, the concept of social forces has been implemented as volunteers educate seniors in the area of new media. In reference to the classic theory of social forces which very often become the grounds for many activities in local settings, every community, even a small one, has its own, internal resources which can be used to meet important social challenges. In this case it was the human capital, that is volunteers called the Lighthouse Keepers of Digital Poland, who became the agents of digital inclusion. The word lighthouse is not accidental here, as it represents the light (digital enlightenment, education). The Lighthouse Keepers - properly trained and prepared volunteers took on the role of educators of the seniors and so far have introduced almost 300,000 of them into the digital world. The Lighthouse Keepers worked thanks to the Cities on Internet Association from Tarnów, which provided methodological support. The volunteers did not collect any remuneration and they were mainly: librarians, IT and other teachers, local government administration staff, local activists, school and university students or simply, enthusiasts of the idea - in total, more than 2 thousand individuals. The majority of them did not have advanced knowledge of adult education methods. The Lighthouse Keepers of Digital Poland project has been recognised by many international organisations [34].

The vast majority of the volunteers declared they used classic social pedagogy methods and forms. Thus, the initial phase involved: environmental diagnosis (collecting information about the older citizens and their needs), selection of the operator (analysis of the map of resources: computer laboratories), attracting allies in the local communities (schools, libraries, NGOs, church organisations), development of action plans (What actions? When? How?), implementation of the plans using local resources and monitoring and promotion of the activities. When analysing the Lighthouse Keepers of Digital Poland project, we need to refer to several important aspects of social forces. Frist, motivation of the volunteers seems interesting. The most frequent reasons for engaging in education of older people were: the necessity to help others, creating new educational opportunities for seniors, opportunity to acquire new didactic and organisational competencies, strengthening self-esteem, sympathy for older people, desire to improve own well-being. The Lighthouse Keepers often emphasised that when they taught others, they gained many new competencies themselves and strengthened their own psychosocial functioning. Thus, as they worked for others, the volunteers have benefited from many new opportunities themselves [35].

The success of the social forces is not only the increase of the level of digital literacy among the senior citizens and digital inclusion (as a form of social inclusion). It also brought about other positive consequences. The volunteers mentioned the following personal achievements: change of attitudes of their students towards new technologies, changed view of themselves (by both seniors and educators), strengthening the idea of lifelong learning, assuming the role of public persons (especially in small communities), higher visibility of the role of education in active ageing, engaging in new activities beyond digital education, networking with many local stakeholders, new relationships. All these positive outcomes show the power of senior education. The project Lighthouse Keepers of Digital Poland revealed the needs of small local communities (mainly villages) which do not have U3As or senior activity centres. However, with proper support individuals with no previous experience of working with this target group were able to introduce seniors into the virtual world without large financial investments from the central budget. The Lighthouse Keepers of Digital Poland project may be an inspiration and a good practice example of universal solution for digital education - not only of people who lack digital literacy but also for those who want to expand their own skills in the area of transforming digital services [35, 36].

3.2 Universities of the Third Age

Education is one of the significant activities which improve the quality of life of the elderly [37]. In the light of the demographic changes, the concept of active ageing have become the key issue in the European policy. This assumption is exemplified by the growing number of institutions supporting the psychosocial functioning of seniors in Poland. As pointed out by Polish researchers into social gerontology, in the U3A movement has been developing very fast in the recent years both in Poland and abroad [38]. At present, only in Poland there are more than 600 institutions of this type. Despite the unquestioned positive influence on the quality of life of its students, the Universities of the Third Age are still not accessible for an average senior due to location, financial conditions and individual willingness to participate in such activities. Besides, most beneficiaries of these institutions are seniors who have some biographical experiences in improving their knowledge and skills in their middle adulthood. However, we must emphasise that, based on the qualitative analyses, participation in U3A classes has significantly changed the way older people see the process of ageing and functioning in the old age and has greatly improved the quality of their life [39, 40]. This relation is particularly noticeable among U3A students who are active in the sections dealing with different aspects of new technologies. Based on meta-analyses of Czech and Polish U3As, we have noticed that new technologies used by the senior students facilitate: social participation, maintaining proper intellectual ability, access to information, quick communication, shopping, paying and ordering services provided offline [41]. Thus, we can see that seniors use new technologies in similar way to other age groups. This is connected mainly with the communication, utility and entertaining nature of the Internet. What is different in many cases, is the level of digital literacy. This group is very heterogeneous in this area.

Digital education of seniors in the U3A is organised differently than in case of the previously presented voluntary project. U3As are based on the academic model. The classes are usually led by academic teachers who have professional experience in working with university students. The meetings are arranged as trainings with clear operational goals set depending on the level of digital literacy of the participants. The classes are scheduled in line with the traditional academic year. Depending on the methodology adopted by the teacher, the course objectives are sometimes negotiated (e.g. to include the needs declared by the participants) or follow arbitrarily adopted curricula. The U3A courses usually take place in academic facilities (universities, colleges), which symbolically lifts the status of the trainings. The only issue which still needs to be discussed is methodical preparation of teachers. Trainers hardly ever have sufficient knowledge of andragogy or gerontology [42, 43]. They use methods which have proven effective in other age groups and this may generate some dissonances between the desired and obtained outcomes. Many educators adapt their teaching forms, methods and tools in response to the didactic challenges they experience as they introduce seniors to the information society. However, we must clearly emphasise that despite the ongoing challenges related to the preparation of teachers, it is U3As where "mass" education of seniors in terms of new technologies has began in Poland. In addition, almost all Polish U3As have interest sections or courses on Internet, smartphones or computers, that is, widely understood digital technologies.

3.3 Senior Activity Centres

The two solutions mentioned above are complemented by the local senior activity centres which also teach seniors how to use computers and Internet. Usually, institutions of this type are treated as leisure activity centres. They are independent institutions or units within the the networks of community culture centres, religious organisations or informal groups. In 2019, the Ministry of Family, Labour and Social Affairs established more than 500 of such institutions in Poland. Of course, apart from the centrally supported activities, we have numerous self-financing senior activity centres or the centres financed from grants or local government resources. Senior activity centres also offer classes in using new digital technologies. However, these courses are less formal. The curricula are more freely compiled that in U3As. In many cases, the main goal of these meetings is more to socialise rather than complete certain educational programme [44]. However, we must remember that often (especially in small towns or villages) these places are the only ones to advance digital inclusion. They also play many other important roles in adult education.

4 Implications for Gerontological Practice

Nowadays, rapid changes affect every area of human life. The dynamic development of information technologies changes the way of functioning of people in every age and forces them to adapt to new conditions [45]. This need refers in particular to those individuals who, due to different circumstances (demographic, health, environmental) are at risk of exclusion. With all its benefits, computerisation of social life aggravates the already existing divisions. Thus, there is the necessity to introduce some wide-scale actions to include these groups and equip them in the necessary competencies. One of the crucial tools to do it is education. It enables (but also necessitates) building the community of people who, thanks to their competencies, will be able to adapt to any civilisational changes. Education should promote emancipation, which would serve the following goals: changes in mentality, revealing agency, strengthening independence and liberation from the existing objective and subjective limitations [46]. It should be formal and informal.

Educational efforts addressed to seniors should be based on a thorough diagnosis of all the aspects of their functioning: health, financial, environmental and psychological. The focus should be on developing sensitive measuring tools which would provide information about the needs, conditions and expectations of this age group. Formal and non-formal leaders emerging from this population will play a vital part, like in case of U3As or Digital Lighthouse Keepers 65+. The fact of being part of the certain community will help them to overcome the fear of reaching out, and it will allow them to asses the situation in a reasonable way, often with support of their own experience.

Successful actions require collaboration between different subjects and institutions. It is important to build networks (form local to international) and develop social capital. Exchange of ideas and experiences, in particular those resulting from the good practices, is one of the key determinants of the effectiveness of educational initiatives. Such collaboration should involve both people who manage the inclusion, education and adaptation processes professionally, as well as seniors themselves, especially the leaders. One of the elements of building this global capital is the exchange of knowledge. Leaders and seniors should have access to scientific publications and reports on digital divide and inclusion, according to the timeless principle: nihil novi sine communi consensu. Gerontology environments should ensure that there are different platforms of thought exchange developed and popularised, starting from the simplest ones such as online forums, through social media to education platforms.

The foundation of successful awareness raising and education is the proper motivation of the process participants. According to various scientific reports [41], the matters of motivating seniors to embrace changes and take learning initiatives still require systemic solutions. Senior educators need resources with practical guidelines. The most valuable are those developed during years of practice. It is also important to include the voice of the seniors. Very often, they are the best experts.

Another issue are mentality changes resulting from the stereotypisation of ageing and old age [41]. We need to emphasise the correlations between the change of the way seniors see their own abilities and the quality of their life. These activities should be implemented as campaigns reaching as many senior communities as possible. According to educators, motivating the elderly to take part in education initiatives is only half of the success. The biggest challenge is to sustain their engagement and faith that they have all they need to be active citizens of the information society. They need to be given as many opportunities as possible to recognise and experience the tangible benefits of learning in their private lives. The role of the gerontologists is to create opportunities to use the competencies acquired during different trainings and U3A classes in practice. As many initiatives to include seniors in the cyberspace as possible should be taken. Advisory roles played by people in their late adulthood are extremely valued in the societies in the countries with highly developed economy and humanistic culture [45].

Trainers interviewed in the SELI project pointed out that they lack practical methodology materials which would facilitate their teaching [47]. There are some publications available in the market [41] but the trainers need very specific guidelines how to deal with the barriers to digital inclusion or the challenges of keeping their students motivated throughout the training. Publications presenting good practices in different countries are also in demand. Some of the available digital inclusion trainings and activities are based on the inter-generational integration and creating and strengthening the solidarity between the generations. Despite many limitations, members of the oldest generation have a lot to offer to the younger ones. This potential includes: life wisdom, social (relational) potential, family life potential, psychological potential of culture transfer and mastery in various professions [45]. In addition, active integration of seniors into the public life, including life in the cyberspace, contributes to building the social capital [48]. Gerontologists study this capital in the three fundamental aspects: improvement of own existence through restoration of the relationships with the environment (for example, thanks to digital literacy); becoming a unique social force (involvement in different voluntary initiatives, also regarding digital inclusion) and fulfillment of the idea of self-education by being socially useful [49, 50].

The experiences of different countries show that the oldest citizens are very grateful new technology users and reliable testers. If only they are provided with safe conditions, they willingly explore the new areas and share their experiences with their peers. Senior-oriented portals are very popular, as well as various offline and online training offers. The wide choice of such offers is one; other issue is the feedback from the seniors about which areas in their lives require technological support. Sometimes seniors do not know that certain solution or support is available to them. The role of social gerontologies is to identify and describe these "blind spots", followed by the efforts to link the needs with the offers. This in turn requires detailed, often interdisciplinary research.

5 Conclusions

Digital divide is still a challenge, especially in the countries where information society have been developing heterogeneously. The process is observable globally both in Europe and in other continents [51]. However, not all digitally excluded individuals experience live a lower quality life. When analysing digital divide, we must be aware that some seniors meet all their daily needs using analogue solutions. Thus, despite this group being digitally excluded, the divide is only apparent. This phenomenon is connected with other important issue, namely those who experience the actual digital divide but due to, for example, lack of access to education institutions are not able to develop one of the key competencies - digital literacy [52, 53]. A solution in this case may be the activities offered by the Lighthouse Keepers of Digital Poland of Equal Opportunities or other voluntary-based initiatives [54]. Even though the problem of digital divide and digital inclusion has been discussed for many years, it is still relevant. The area of research are determined by the development of the information society [55–57], change of life style of older citizens and transformations of lifelong learning institutions.

This article was written as part of the REMEDIS project, which is supported in Poland by the National Science Centre - NCN [021/03/Y/HS6/00275] under the CHANSE ERA-NET Co-fund. The project has received funding from the European Union's Horizon 2020 Research and Innovation Programme [contract number 101004509].

References

1. Duff, A.S., Craig, D., McNeill, D.A.: A note on the origins of the "information society." J. Inf. Sci. **22**, 117–122 (1996). https://doi.org/10.1177/016555159602200204
2. Tomczyk, Ł., Mascia, M.L., Gierszewski, D., Walker, C.: Barriers to digital inclusion among older people: a intergenerational reflection on the need to develop digital competences for the group with the highest level of digital exclusion. InnoEduca **9**, 5–26 (2023). https://doi.org/10.24310/innoeduca.2023.v9i1.16433
3. Koćwin, L.: Digital society in Poland – strategies, plans, and reality. https://www.repozytorium.uni.wroc.pl/publication/95528
4. Batorski, D., Zając, J.: Między alienacją a adptacją – Polacy w wieku 50+ wobec internetu. Raport Otwarcia Koalicji "Dojrz@łość w sieci". http://dojrzaloscwsieci.pl/tl_files/pliki/Raport.pdf
5. Dominik Batorski, D.B.: The usage of new communication technology (Korzystanie z Technologii Informacyjno-komunikacyjnych). Contemp. Econ. **5**, 299 (2011). https://doi.org/10.5709/ce.1897-9254.o220

6. Huang, C.-Y., Chen, H.-N.: Global digital divide: a dynamic analysis based on the bass model. J. Public Policy Mark. **29**, 248–264 (2010). https://doi.org/10.1509/jppm.29.2.248

7. Szpunar, M.: W stronę nowych mediów. Wydawnictwo Adam Marszałek, Toruń (2010)

8. Tomczyk, Ł.: Seniorzy w świecie nowych mediów. E-mentor **4**, 52–61 (2010)

9. Scheerder, A., van Deursen, A., van Dijk, J.: Determinants of Internet skills, uses and outcomes. A systematic review of the second- and third-level digital divide. Telemat. Inform. **34**, 1607–1624 (2017). https://doi.org/10.1016/j.tele.2017.07.007

10. Molinari, A.: Let's Bridge the digital divide. http://www.ted.com/talks/aleph_molinari_let_s_bridge_the_digital_divide.html

11. Tomczyk, L.: Edukacja osob starszych. Difin, Warszawa (2015)

12. Statystyczny, G.U.: Wskaźniki zrównoważonego rozwoju Polski 2015. Urząd Statystyczny w Katowicach , Katowice (2015)

13. Reder, S., Soroui, J.: Digital Inclusion and Digital Literacy in the United States: A Portrait from PIAAC's Survey of Adult Skills (2015)

14. GUS: Społeczeństwo Informacyjne w Polsce. Wyniki badań statystycznych z lat 2013–2017. https://stat.gov.pl/obszary-tematyczne/nauka-i-technika-spoleczenstwo-informacyjne/spo leczenstwo-informacyjne/spoleczenstwo-informacyjne-w-polsce-wyniki-badan-statystyc znych-z-lat-2013-2017,1,11.html?contrast=default

15. Liu, J.X., Goryakin, Y., Maeda, A., Bruckner, T., Scheffler, R.: Global health workforce labor market projections for 2030. Hum. Resour. Health **15** (2017). https://doi.org/10.1186/s12960-017-0187-2

16. Jasiński, A.M., Bąkowska, A.: Are seniors digitally excluded? Analysis of the needs of older adults in terms of information support. Rozprawy Społeczne **15**, 48–59 (2021). https://doi.org/10.29316/rs/135468

17. Mihelj, S., Leguina, A., Downey, J.: Culture is digital: cultural participation, diversity and the digital divide. New Media Soc. **21**, 1465–1485 (2019). https://doi.org/10.1177/146144 4818822816

18. Helsper, E.J., Reisdorf, B.C.: The emergence of a "digital underclass" in Great Britain and Sweden: changing reasons for digital exclusion. New Media Soc. **19**, 1253–1270 (2016). https://doi.org/10.1177/1461444816634676

19. van Deursen, A., van Dijk, J.: Internet skills and the digital divide. New Media Soc. **13**, 893–911 (2010). https://doi.org/10.1177/1461444810386774

20. Schejter, A.M., Ben, R., Tirosh, N.: Re-theorizing the "digital divide": identifying dimensions of social exclusion in contemporary media technologies. In: Conference: European Media Policy 2015 (2015)

21. Castells, M.: The Internet Galaxy : Reflections on the Internet, Business, and Society. Oxford University Press, Oxford (2001)

22. Van Dijk, J.: The Deepening Divide. SAGE Publications, Thousand Oaks (2005)

23. Van Dijk, J.: The Network Society. Sage, London/Thousand Oaks (2012)

24. Bus, J., Crompton, M., Hildebrandt, M., Metakides, G.: Digital Enlightenment Yearbook 2012. IOS Press, Amsterdam (2012)

25. van Deursen, A.J., van Dijk, J.A.: The digital divide shifts to differences in usage. New Media Soc. **16**, 507–526 (2013). https://doi.org/10.1177/1461444813487959

26. Mervyn, K., Simon, A., Allen, D.K.: Digital inclusion and social inclusion: a tale of two cities. Inf. Commun. Soc. **17**, 1086–1104 (2014). https://doi.org/10.1080/1369118x.2013.877952

27. Śmiałowski, T.: Assessment of Digital Exclusion of Polish households. Metody Ilościowe w Badaniach Ekonomicznych **20**, 54–61 (2019). https://doi.org/10.22630/mibe.2019.20.1.6

28. Agnieszka, H.: Digital exclusion as a barrier to online shopping by older people in Poland. In: Proceedings of the International Scientific Conference of Business Economics, Management and Marketing 2018, pp. 108–114. Masarykova univerzita nakladatelství, Brno (2018)

29. Walkowski, M.: Digital exclusion as a hindrance to the emergence of the information society: the case of Poland. Przegląd Politologiczny **3**, 167–181 (2018). https://doi.org/10.14746/pp. 2018.23.3.13
30. Ćwiek, M.: Digital divide in Poland and in the European union. Ekonomiczne Problemy Usług **131**, 217–224 (2018). https://doi.org/10.18276/epu.2018.131/2-21
31. Jedlińska, R.: Digital exclusion in Poland compared to the European union countries. Ekonomiczne Problemy Usług **131**, 225–236 (2018). https://doi.org/10.18276/epu.2018.131/ 2-22
32. Główny Urząd Statystyczny: Społeczeństwo informacyjne w Polsce w 2022 roku. Statistical Office in Szczecin, Warszawa, Szczecin (2022)
33. Remigiusz J. Kijak, Zofia Szarota, Starość. Między diagnozą a działaniem, Centrum Rozwoju Zasobów Ludzkich, Warszawa 2013, ss. 122. Rocznik Andragogiczny **21**, 581 (2015). https:// doi.org/10.12775/ra.2014.042
34. Hofmann, D., Łukasz, T.: Działalność Latarników Polski Cyfrowej Równych Szans jako innowacyjna forma przeciwdziałania wykluczeniu cyfrowemu. Rocznik Andragogiczny **2012**, 372–382 (2012)
35. Tomczyk, Ł., Uniwersytet Pedagogiczny w Krakowie: Wolontariusze i seniorzy w programie Polski Cyfrowej Równych Szans. O siłach społecznych w procesie minimalizacji wykluczenia cyfrowego w Polsce. Uniwersytet Pedagogiczny w Krakowie (2018). https:// doi.org/10.24917/9788380842304
36. Ziemba, E.: The contribution of ICT adoption to the sustainable information society. J. Comput. Inf. Syst. **59**, 116–126 (2017). https://doi.org/10.1080/08874417.2017.1312635
37. Mackowicz, J., Wnęk-Gozdek, J.: Transformation of an older women under the influence of education at the university of the third age – a case study. E-mentor **2016**, 45–55 (2016). https://doi.org/10.15219/em64.1238
38. Mackowicz, J., Wnek Gozdek, J.: Informal learning in the experience of a polish centenarian— case study. In: EduLearn. EDULEARN 2018 (2018). https://doi.org/10.21125/edulearn.2018. 0889
39. Maćkowicz, J., Wnęk-Gozdek, J.: Late-life learning for social inclusion: universities of the third age in Poland. In: Formosa, M. (ed.) The University of the Third Age and Active Ageing. International Perspectives on Aging, vol. 23, pp. 95–105. Springer, Cham (2019). https://doi. org/10.1007/978-3-030-21515-6_8
40. Szarota, Z.: Starzenie się i starość w wymiarze instytucjonalnego wsparcia, pp. 129–132. Wydawnictwo Uniwersytetu Pedagogicznego, Kraków (2010)
41. Tomczyk, Ł.: Vzdělávání seniorů v oblasti nových médií. Asociace institucí vzdělávání dospělých ČR Praha (2015)
42. Veteška, J.: Kompetence ve vzdělávání dospělých. UJAK, Praha (2010)
43. Šerák, M.: Zájmové vzdělávání dospělých. Portal, Praha (2009)
44. Fabiś, A.: Ludzka starosc. Impuls, Kraków (2017)
45. Jakrzewska-Sawińska, A., Sawiński, K.: Wielkopolskie Stowarzyszenie Wolontariuszy Opieki Paliatywnej Hospicjum Domowe: Medyczne i społeczne potrzeby osób starszych (2017)
46. Freire, P.: Education: The Practice of Freedom. W.R.P.C (1976)
47. Tomczyk, L., et al.: Digital divide in Latin America and Europe: main characteristics in selected countries. In: 2019 14th Iberian Conference on Information Systems and Technologies (CISTI) (2019). https://doi.org/10.23919/cisti.2019.8760821
48. Marcinkiewicz-Wilk, A.: Drukarnia I Agencja Wydawnicza "Argi: key competence for lifelong learning. Agencja Wydawnicza". Argi, Wrocław (2016)
49. Gates, J.R., Wilson-Menzfeld, G.: What role does geragogy play in the delivery of digital skills programs for middle and older age adults? a systematic narrative review. J. Appl. Gerontol. **41**, 1971–1980 (2022). https://doi.org/10.1177/07334648221091236

50. Dubas, E.: Geragogy as a pedagogical subdyscipline. Studia z Teorii Wychowania **XI**, 143–167 (2020). https://doi.org/10.5604/01.3001.0014.3653

51. Tomczyk, Ł., Oyelere, S.S.: ICT for Learning and Inclusion in Latin America and Europe Case Study from Countries: Bolivia, Brazil, Cuba, Dominican Republic, Ecuador, Finland, Poland, Turkey, Uruguay. Pedagogical University, Cracow (2019). https://doi.org/10.24917/9788395373732

52. Stošić, L., Stošić, I.: Perceptions of teachers regarding the implementation of the internet in education. Comput. Hum. Behav. **53**, 462–468 (2015). https://doi.org/10.1016/j.chb.2015.07.027

53. Stosic, L.: Does the use of ICT enable easier, faster and better acquiring of knowledge? Int. J. Innov. Res. Educ. **4**, 179–185 (2017). https://doi.org/10.18844/ijire.v4i4.3256

54. Tomczyk, Ł., Mróz, A., Potyrała, K., Wnęk-Gozdek, J.: Digital inclusion from the perspective of teachers of older adults - expectations, experiences, challenges and supporting measures. Gerontol. Geriatr, Educ. 1–16 (2020). https://doi.org/10.1080/02701960.2020.1824913

55. Wątróbski, J., Ziemba, E., Karczmarczyk, A., Jankowski, J.: An index to measure the sustainable information society: the polish households case. Sustainability. **10**, 3223 (2018). https://doi.org/10.3390/su10093223

56. Lythreatis, S., El-Kassar, A.-N., Singh, S.K.: The digital divide: a review and future research agenda. Technol. Forecast. Soc. Chang. **175**, 121359 (2021). https://doi.org/10.1016/j.techfore.2021.121359.57

57. Acilar, A., Sæbø, Ø.: Towards understanding the gender digital divide: a systematic literature review. Global Knowl. Memory Commun. ahead-of-print (2021). https://doi.org/10.1108/gkmc-09-2021-0147

58. Van Dijck, J., Poell, T., De Waal, M.: The Platform Society. Public Values in a Connective World. Oxford University Press, Kettering (2018)

Author Index

Ł. Tomczyk (Ed.): NMP 2022, CCIS 1916, p. 295, 2023.
https://doi.org/10.1007/978-3-031-44581-1

Printed in the United States
by Baker & Taylor Publisher Services